Legal Codes and Talking Trees

Published in cooperation with the

William P. Clements Center for Southwest Studies
Southern Methodist University

Legal Codes and Talking Trees

Indigenous Women's Sovereignty in the
Sonoran and Puget Sound Borderlands, 1854–1946

Katrina Jagodinsky

Yale UNIVERSITY PRESS
NEW HAVEN & LONDON

Published with assistance from the Mary Cady Tew Memorial Fund.

Yale University Press books may be purchased in quantity for educational, business, or promotional use. For information, please e-mail sales.press@yale.edu (U.S. office) or sales@yaleup.co.uk (U.K. office).

Set in Ehrhardt type by Newgen North America.

Printed in the United States of America.

ISBN 978-0-300-21168-9 (cloth : alk. paper)

Library of Congress Control Number 2015946933

A catalogue record for this book is available from the British Library.

This paper meets the requirements of ANSI/NISO z39.48-1992 (Permanence of Paper).

10 9 8 7 6 5 4 3 2 1

For all those still returning from the enemy

Contents

Acknowledgments

I have looked forward to thanking the many supporters of this project since it began in 2008 at the University of Arizona. Karen Anderson, Martha Few, Tom Holm, Ben Irvin, Tsianina Lomawaima, Bob Martin, Katherine Morrissey, Roger Nichols, Nancy Parezo, Luci Tapahonso, and Rob Williams proved to be very influential faculty mentors and I am grateful for their collective insights. As my dissertation adviser, Roger Nichols deserves special credit for pushing me forward and onward. My peers at the University of Arizona likewise contributed to this undertaking, reading many incoherent drafts and offering moral support as well. Cody Aune and Megan Prins have remained steadfast readers and friends through every phase of this project, while Marcus Burtner, Vilja Hulden, and Neil Prendergast also gave helpful comments in its early stages.

The manuscript began its metamorphosis from dissertation to monograph through a generous fellowship year at the Clements Center for Southwest Studies at Southern Methodist University. Andrea Boardman, Ed Countryman, Crista DeLuzio, Ruth Ann Elmore, Andy Graybill, and Sherry Smith proved very helpful throughout that transitional period. James Brooks, Alexandra Harmon, and Jeff Shepherd gave incredible reads at the manuscript workshop, as did my fellow Clements Fellow Sascha Scott. With the book still in chrysalis form when I left the Clements Center for the University of Nebraska–Lincoln, new colleagues also proved generous with their time. Dawne Curry, James Garza, Margaret Jacobs,

Jeannette Jones, Laura Muñoz, and William Thomas have offered feedback on a number of the chapters included here and I am fortunate to have their encouragement and mentorship.

In addition to those who have worked with me on this project at the University of Arizona, Southern Methodist University, and the University of Nebraska–Lincoln, other colleagues and friends have offered invaluable feedback through conference discussions and informal swaps of drafts in the past few years. Those include Cathleen Cahill, Miroslava Chávez-García, Grace Peña Delgado, Susan Gray, Anne Hyde, Betsy Jameson, Susan Johnson, Mary Mendoza, Pablo Mitchell, Erika Pérez, Adele Perry, Lindsay Robertson, Virginia Scharff, Shannon Smith, Linda Waggoner, and Vicky Saker Woeste. For making this book so much better than I might have managed on my own, I thank editor Laura Davulis, her assistant Eva Skewes, and manuscript editor Deborah Bruce-Hostler along with the generous staff at Yale University Press, artist Bunky Echo-Hawk, and cartographer Ezra Zeitler. Of course, the anonymous readers of the manuscript have also been tremendously helpful and I thank them here as well. I look forward to returning the many favors I have incurred along the way for all of this help.

Without key funding support at each stage of this project, I would not have had so many drafts to share with colleagues. At the University of Arizona, the Faculty Women's Club, the Graduate College, the History Department, the Social and Behavioral Sciences Research Institute, and the Women's and Gender Studies Department provided financial support. The U.S. Consulate General in Calgary provided a Western Canadian Studies Research Grant as well. At the University of Nebraska–Lincoln, the History Department and the Office of Research and Development have continued to finance this project. The American Philosophical Society's Phillips Fund for Native American Research has proven helpful in completing the research necessary for this project. In addition to providing a fellowship year, the Clements Center for Southwest Studies provided a research stipend and a publication subvention. Thanks to Gina Wasson, Ruth Ann Elmore, and Sandra Pershing for their help in administering these funds.

Such support has allowed me to cull federal and state archival material in Arizona, British Columbia, California, and Washington over the past seven years. Staff at the National Archives and Records Administration regional branches in both Laguna Niguel (now Riverside), California, in Seattle, Washington, and at the BC Archive in Victoria, British Columbia, proved essential interpreters of their vast collections. In particular, Patty

McNamee, Charliann Becker, and Ken House at the Seattle NARA branch have been wonderful to work with. This project also benefited from state records at the Arizona State Library, Archives, and Public Records, the Arizona State Historical Society, Sharlot Hall Museum Library and Archives, and the Special Collections at both the University of Arizona and Arizona State University. The staffs at each of these repositories have made my work both pleasant and productive, but John Langelier and Fred and Sally Veil of Sharlot Hall Museum were especially supportive. In Washington, I relied on the assistance of staff at the Washington State Historical Society Research Center, the Washington State Archive Regional Branches in Olympia, Bellevue, and Bellingham, the Center for Pacific Northwest Studies at Western Washington University, the Puyallup Tribal Archive, and the University of Washington Special Collections. Midori Okazaki and Phil Stairs at the Puget Sound Regional Archives and Ruth Steele and Roz Koester at the Center for Pacific Northwest Studies provided outstanding assistance.

In addition to these archival repositories of knowledge, I have relied on community and tribal members as vital contributors to this project. As friendly readers and interested listeners who raised important questions and made thoughtful suggestions, I thank Mary Jack, Norma Joseph, Scott Kwiatkowski, Kathryn Marquez, Ronda Metcalf, Patricia Hackett Nicola, Linda Ogo, Astrida Blukis Onat, Viola Romero and Robert Marron Romero, and Guard and Connie Sundstrom.

Many friends hosted me as I carried out research: Allison Augustyn and Michael Kollins, Brandie Ishcomer Barrett, Ingrid and Brandon Beaver, Andrew Cecka and Mo McKenna, Andy Low and Megan Prins, Julie Lucht and Nik Siefter, Luis Rubschlager, Dylon Tubb, Dan and Charlotte Waugh, and Kristina Sunde Wood and Eric Wood. Other friends encouraged me when the project seemed too far from completion, most notably: Liberty Heidmann, Christy Kowalewski, Heidi and Matt Landis, Courtney Lind, John McClain, Adam Pelzer, and Monica and Neil Prendergast. There are many others who gave support along the way, too many to mention here, but I am grateful to have such a strong network both within and beyond the academy.

Last, I thank my family for their encouragement, particularly my husband, James Chamberlain. This book has occupied seven of our thirteen years together, and already he is encouraging me to take on the next one. It is because of his presence that I can spend so much time in the past and still look forward to our future.

Legal Codes and Talking Trees

CHAPTER 1

"Returning from the Enemy"
The Poetics and Politics of Indigenous Women's Legal History

Long ago, before the United States and before Mexico and be-fore Canada, but not before borderlands, a tree spoke to the people. Some say it was a palo verde tree that made strange, unintelligible noises; others call it an old mesquite, but all agree that the Surem wisemen could not make out the buzzing words repeated in the branches. A council of elders decided to seek out the aid of twin daughters who lived on Grandmother's Mountain. The girls (some call them women) agreed to help despite their father's doubts, but the family went first to the ocean—most likely the Gulf of California—rather than the desert grove and the talking tree. From a saltwater fish, the sisters learned a new language, unfamiliar to their Surem people, and the fish taught them how to inter-pret the strange message. The family returned to their concerned people, and the sisters stood on either side of the dry tree to translate an ominous prophecy. The tree told the Surem of the coming tide of conquest, coloniza-tion, and Christianity. Although the sisters repeated warnings of violence and devastation—even self-destruction—the Surem also listened to de-scriptions of creative inventions and renewal through baptism. When the girls finished their recitation, the Surem found themselves divided. Some people chose to face these strange events and enemies head-on, and today they call themselves the Yaqui, the Baptized Ones. Those who turned away from the prophecy went underground and are still known as the Surem, the Enchanted People.[1]

Perhaps around the same time that the sisters bent their heads to translate whispers in Sonoran branches, the people on the shores of the Salish Sea and throughout Puget Sound interpreted signs of change and transformation as well. In variations on a theme, Indigenous storytellers described the heroic interventions and intrusions of the changer. Twanas called him Dokibatt, while the Salish named him Dokwibalth. The Klallam called *her* Nukimatt, and some said there was not one, but rather four sibling transformers, three male and one female; or they were twins, one creative and the other destructive. Whether singular or plural, male or female, change and transformation were born of the interracial union between a mortal mother and a celestial father. Together these supernatural, shapeshifting, multiracial beings delivered the moral and practical lessons that made sense of the Salishan and Sound world, preparing the people to confront secular challenges with sacred knowledge. The changes and transformations wrought by these figures have been both creative and destructive, but collectively, like a natural law, their actions balance and order the world. Some might recognize the unions of familiar women and strange men as a sign of change on the horizon or perhaps as an abomination, but many are sure that the transformer "came once to create, a second [time] to change, and will come again to make the world over again when it becomes old."[2]

Through the efforts of girls and women able to import knowledge from other worlds and with the help of their daughters' mixed-race progeny, Indigenous North Americans have managed to survive centuries of change foretold by talking trees and wrought by unpredictable transformers. Tribal oral traditions explain communal strategies to comprehend and control ruptures in the social order, including those initiated under colonialism. Stories like the talking tree and transformer narratives describe the importance of Native women's roles in both encountering and engendering change and conflict. A central assumption of this book is that such stories, though they serve here only as a starting point, should prepare scholars to anticipate and indeed seek out evidence of Indigenous women's prominent roles in negotiating conquest and navigating change—whether in the past or the present—and that these and other stories constitute a form of "case law" that makes up the legal traditions of Indigenous people.[3] For historians of the North American West, evidence of Indian women's confrontations with colonizers who spoke foreign languages and fathered tumultuous children should be abundant, and signs that Indigenous women faced imperial legal regimes with their own legal philosophies in hand should be obvious—and yet, such histories remain to many as unintelligible as the sound of talking trees and the howling winds of change.

Although many historians have been reticent to link laws to legends, this work builds on generations of interdisciplinary scholarship that pays critical attention to the poetics and politics of Indigenous legal history, while setting its focus on the efforts of Indian women to achieve corporeal sovereignty— authority over their own bodies and progeny. An important argument underlying this book is that Indigenous women's efforts to claim and defend personal and embodied autonomy deserve the same sort of historical scrutiny that histories of treaty negotiation and federal Indian law have attracted in the years between Felix Cohen and Robert A. Williams. This introduction's title draws on Joy Harjo's poem "Returning from the Enemy," which shifts between mythic sagas, pointed critiques, and tragic memories to chronicle a woman's personal journey toward decolonization.[4] In linking the personal and political struggles of twenty-first-century Indigenous women to epic origins and violent pasts, the poet offers historians a useful model in conceptualizing Native women's encounters with colonialism and the law.

> *I have bowed my head to those who would disrespect me.* My neck appears
>   to be broken in half by shame. I have lost my country.
> *I have handed my power over to my enemies.* My shoulders bear each act
>   of forgetfulness.
> *I have abandoned my children to the laws of dictators who called*
>   *themselves priests, preachers, and the purveyors of law.* My feet are
>   scarred from the steps taken in the direction of freedom.
> *I have forgotten the reason, forgive me.* I have forgotten my name in the
>   language I was born to, forgive me.
> The enemy immigrated to a land he claimed for his God.
> He named himself as the arbitrator of deity in any form.
> He beat his Indian children.
> The law of the gods I claim state:
> *When entering another country do not claim ownership.*
> *It's important to address the souls there kindly, with respect.*
> *And ask permission.*
> I am asking you to leave the country of my body, my mind, if you have
>   anything other than honorable intentions.[5]

Harjo's verse suggests that modern-day Indian women can point to oral traditions as evidence of their creative and critical power, recite histories

of survivance—the combined acts of survival and resistance in the face of
colonial denigration and dispossession—and formulate sophisticated critiques of North American imperialism and occupation.[6] Taking its lead
from Harjo and a growing cadre of Indigenous women who are simultaneously academics, activists, and artists, this book takes seriously the claims of
those who call themselves Native feminists that their activism is the legacy
of deities and grandmothers who faced down the enemy in epic and historic
times.[7]

The pages that follow chronicle the remarkable efforts of six Indigenous women and their families to survive settler-colonialism—a unique
brand of colonialism in which colonizers took up permanent and intimate
residence among the Native people they exploited and resources they extracted rather than occupying temporary posts.[8] This book argues that, like
the protagonist in Harjo's poem, nineteenth- and early-twentieth-century
Indian women critiqued their economic and sexual vulnerability under the
legal regimes imposed on them by "enemy immigrants" and "purveyors of
the law" who sought to dispossess Native people of their country and culture.[9] Whenever possible, special attention is devoted to the tribal philosophies that such women drew from in order to make cultural and gendered
claims to protect their bodies, progeny, and lands threatened under imperial
legal regimes. Characterizing Native women's legal philosophies requires
the careful reading and application of oral tradition to Native women's legal
actions in territorial, state, and federal legal spaces—sometimes in courts,
sometimes in correspondence, and sometimes in conversation. At times,
the evidence is not strong enough to suggest a particularly Indigenous legal
philosophy, but these women each espoused a view of the law and justice
that was their own when challenging the American legal system that infil-
trated their world after 1854.

A second argument of this book is that the project of American conquest
and settler-colonialism depended upon newcomers' abilities to claim and
control Indigenous women's productive and reproductive labors and access
to land in addition to the use of legal and military violence to incarcerate
or incorporate Indigenous men that historians more frequently recognize.[10]
Western historians who include Native perspectives have typically concen-
trated on federal Indian policies, Indian wars, treaty-making and breaking,
or the heroics of particular Indian men. While such histories are important
and reveal the centrality of Indigenous people in the West, many tend to
marginalize Indian women, or blur their personal experiences under the

catchall category of "women and children." A closer and gendered reading of legal and personal sources from nineteenth- and early-twentieth-century westerners reveals the omnipresence of Indian women in territorial legislators' bedrooms, in pioneer women's kitchens and nurseries, and in frontier taverns and courtrooms alike. To explore patterns and trends in Indigenous women's relationships with western newcomers, this book makes Native women central actors in overlapping phases of western history: territorial development and settlement between 1854 and 1880, the transition from an Indigenous and transnational West to an American and Anglo West between 1865 and 1890, and the formation of a national West with secure racial and political borders between 1890 and 1946. These periods overlap with known epochs in federal Indian policy (the Indian Wars period, the assimilation period, and the Indian New Deal era) that influenced, but did not necessarily dominate the lives of the women in this book—all of whom lived outside of reservation, and thus federally managed, communities.

Comparing Indigenous women's experiences during these periods reveals that regardless of region or decade, they fought constantly to maintain what body theorists, gender historians, and political scientists call corporeal sovereignty. Although the term is used sparsely throughout the book, it is noted here to direct readers' attention to the particular importance of Indigenous women's bodies in debates over Indigenous and tribal political autonomy. Territorial senators and federal officials worked to grant themselves sexual and economic access to Indian women's bodies, custody of their progeny, and title to their land. As Native women articulated their critique of such prerogatives—many of which were codified in territorial and federal law—they also expressed a defense of their autonomy over their bodies, their children, and their lands. Referring to these attitudes and actions collectively as corporeal sovereignty helps to demonstrate the interrelatedness of Indian women's productive and reproductive labors and their sacred and secular relationships to homelands.

Another important argument made in this book is that not all settler-colonists claimed the privileges of whiteness and that some made efforts to recognize, if not always uphold, Indigenous women's corporeal sovereignty.[11] Each chapter includes the familiar acts of dispossession and exploitation that made the West a place of conquest for those struck down in the name of progress. It is difficult not to villainize the men who fathered and then abandoned Indian women's children or those who evicted and defrauded Native women from their lands, but as other historians have found, many of these men simultaneously befriended and relied upon Indigenous men and women in other aspects of their western lives, and for the most part, they acted within the bounds of the law. For this reason, this study turns its criticism upon the law, a hegemonic system that served elite interests, as often as on its practitioners and beneficiaries. While readers are no doubt familiar with the duplicitous acts of the citizen men and women who benefited from their legally sanctioned superiority, there were also those who questioned the legitimacy of laws that degraded Indian women's corporeal sovereignty. These citizens worked as lawyers to prosecute rapists and protect heiresses, served as agents to secure land and as administrators to secure custody of children. Some readers might find these lawyers compelling figures in Native women's legal history, but the focus of this narrative has required that they remain marginal characters in each chapter. As ambivalent as the legal practitioners who aided Indian women for financial and other reasons, local journalists celebrated the triumphs of white supremacy and the disappearance of the Indian as often as they critiqued the detrimental effects of federal and state Indian policies and the destruction of Native communities. Putting Indian women at the center of western history brings all of these voices to the fore and challenges the assumption of inevitable hostility between Natives and newcomers in the North American West.

The book is organized into three overlapping thematic and chronological sections: sex and servitude; gender and family property; and space, race, and gender. Each of these three subject categories is given two chapters, the first chronicling a woman in Arizona and the second focusing on a Washington woman's experiences. Women in both regions shared a marginalized status under legal regimes that reveal the stark tension between implementation and interpretation of the law when analyzed in comparative light. As becomes clear in the following chapters, Arizona's legal code more explicitly oppressed Indian members of the population than Washington's legal code did, and yet Native women in both regions faced remarkably similar challenges to their corporeal autonomy. This comparative view of the laws that supported settler-colonialism complicates the responses of "enemy immigrants" to racial and sexual tenets in the law that did not serve all white citizens' interests despite their service to patriarchy and white supremacy.[12] Readers will find that some of the citizens best positioned to benefit from laws granting them access to Indigenous women's bodies and lands in fact protested those legal inequalities in their service as allies, friends, lawyers, and witnesses working on behalf of the Indigenous women in the six cases profiled here.

Chapters 2 and 3 of the book consider how Indigenous women faced the laws that bound them to American masters and made them sexually vulnerable to male citizens' whims.[13] Yaqui woman Lucía Martínez survived the intertribal slave trade that crisscrossed the Arizona-Sonora border in the mid–nineteenth century and endured an adolescence of servitude under a territorial Arizona senator, King S. Woolsey. Woolsey fathered three of Lucía's children and indentured two of them. Lucía Martínez became the first Native woman to use Arizona's legal system when she sued Woolsey in 1871 for custody of her children. While Martínez challenged the putative father of her illegitimate children in civil court, a territorial Washington girl would sue the putative father of her unborn child in criminal court. Nora Jewell of San Juan Island—a territory claimed by both Americans and Britons when she was born around 1864—lost her Salish mother and Danish father to unknown circumstances and became a ward of Washington Territory at the age of twelve. In 1880 she sued her American guardian for rape, charging that the court-appointed master had impregnated her and claiming the rights of a citizen woman to state protection. Both of these cases are representative of Indian women's shared economic and sexual vulnerability under settler-colonial law and offer insights into the exploitative interracial intimacies so commonly associated with conquest and expansion in the North American West. That the challenges to these women's corporeal sovereignty were so similar under such different legal regimes bears an important lesson in the flexibility of the law to serve the racial and sexual interests of those who hold power.

Chapters 4 and 5 focus on the efforts of the children of Native women like Lucía and Nora to claim and retain family ties and land rights. These cases reflect the challenges unique to the descendants of Indian-white households as they came of age in the second wave of settler-colonial conquest, when interracial intimacies became less acceptable and more regulated. Juana Walker sued her American uncles in 1893 for the estate of her deceased father, who had accumulated his substantial wealth because his Akimel O'odham wife—Juana's mother—had granted him access to tribal mineral deposits and manual labor. Juana's mixed-race status made her an illegitimate heir under territorial Arizona law, though many of her father's citizen peers supported her familial and legal claims. Comparing

Juana Walker's Arizona case to Rebecca Lena Graham's trial in Washington demonstrates the wide range in western elites' attitudes toward the mixed-race daughters of their colleagues. In 1894, Rebecca Lena Graham sued for her rights as the only daughter of a prominent territorial settler who was fondly remembered by Seattle's founding fathers, but who died intestate and unmarried. Graham would win her case and be acknowledged in a federal court as the rightful mixed-race heir to a white man's estate for two reasons: first, Washington's convoluted miscegenation laws had protected the inheritance rights of mixed-race and illegitimate children, and Graham constructed an argument about the relationships between Duwamish and settler-colonists that held particular resonance for District Judge Cornelius Hanford, who ruled on the case. Juana Walker, on the other hand, whose case highlighted the dependence of American men on Indigenous women to accumulate wealth in the early West, failed to secure federal review and met the condemnation of Arizona judges anxious to forget their colleagues' indebtedness to Indian women in the earlier years of territorial settlement.

While women like Lucía and Nora challenged their sexual subservience in non-Indian households early in the settler-colonial period, and women like Juana and Rebecca struggled to link their Indigenous identities to inheritance rights, some Native women practiced survivance in more subtle ways. In 1913, Yavapai woman Dinah Foote Hood and her grandmother Tcha-ah-wooeha tested American officials' authority to subpoena American Indian witnesses, indicating that not all Indian women wanted a presence in courts that served the mission of imperialism. Although Dinah Hood and her female relatives sought the right to remain silent, they also squatted on lands sacred to their people until the tribe achieved federal recognition of their right to occupy tribal homelands in 1935. Louisa Enick raised a family with her husband on Sauk-Suiattle lands in northwestern Washington in the last decade of the nineteenth century, but in 1897 her lands became incorporated as part of the Washington Forest Reserve, today part of the Mount Baker–Snoqualmie National Forest. Enick's daughters would spend the first half of the twentieth century petitioning federal officials to keep their lands in family and then tribal hands, but became caught up in the web of allotment law and bureaucratic incompetence and prejudice. The tribe would achieve federal recognition in the 1970s, but the early efforts of women like Louisa Enick to hold their off-reservation lands would make tribal recognition possible generations later. Together, these cases emphasize Indigenous women's vital role in maintaining land-based corporeal sovereignty—a concept with cultural and personal as well as political implications—under "the law of dictators."[14]

Organized thematically and chronologically, each of these women's personal histories illuminates previously neglected patterns of Indigenous women's critiques of their gendered vulnerability in the face of legal conquest.[15] In neglecting individual Indian women, historians of the North American West have not recorded the tenacity of their claims to corporeal sovereignty in the shifting legal regimes that characterized the tumultuous region between 1854 and 1946. To make more sense of the laws defining American Indian women's ambiguous legal status as noncitizen wards—what historians of racial-ethnic women's experience have described as a "kaleidoscopic morass" and "a morass of conflicting jurisdictions and statutes"—these comparative microhistories are based in the distinctive yet interrelated settler-colonial regions of the Sonoran Southwest on the Arizona-Sonora border and the Pacific Northwest on the Washington–British Columbia border.[16] Readers should note the importance of borders in this study, both because Indigenous women came to understand the implications of American, Canadian, and Mexican Indian policies in relation to their ability to maintain corporeal sovereignty, and because the six women in this book learned firsthand the frustrating complexities of navigating the jurisdictional borders between tribal, territorial, state, and national legal regimes that emerged upon their homelands.

These seemingly disparate borderlands shared a number of basic similarities in the second half of the nineteenth century that are important here. First, tribes in both regions practiced extensive intermarriage and intertribal slavery that transgressed international borders established by nineteenth-century Americans, Britons, Canadians, and Mexicans. These bonds of exploitative and intimate cross-border kinship among Indigenous people and newcomers produced multivalent identities—*mestizaje* in the South and *métissage* in the North—and sophisticated understandings of conquest by the early twentieth century. Most notably chronicled in James Brooks's study *Captives and Cousins,* the intertribal slave trade in the southwestern borderlands linked families through intimate violence throughout the colonial period; so too, did Native people on Puget Sound and the coastal islands trade slaves and wives through raids and rituals that bound bands intimately together.[17] Transnational and intertribal relations were also consensual and ceremonial. Intermarriage linked bands and tribes as allies and traders so that in the Sonoran Southwest generations could continue to

survive on scarce, seasonal resources, and in the Pacific Northwest generations could leverage and share resources that varied widely throughout the
Salishan Sea, Puget Sound, and the Cascadian Divide.

Slavery and intermarriage are important to this study because these
systems placed high value on women's productive and reproductive labors
as the bearers of children, distributors of food, and transmitters of gendered
knowledge—making them central contributors to their communities even
if they were not always equal members of their households. During settler-
colonial conquest, characterized in the North American West by gendered
demographic imbalance in its early phases, citizen men depended heavily
on Indigenous women as objects of desire and productive subjects. Familiar
with the traffic in women and children that crossed colonizers' cultural and
political borders, Native women in Arizona and Washington understood
that they were simultaneously valuable and vulnerable in the negotiation
of Native-newcomer relations that took place between 1854 and 1946. This
understanding made them especially vocal critics of their codified inferior-
ity in the American legal system.

Indian women in the Puget Sound and Sonoran Desert regions also
shared the experience of encounters with remarkably similar settler-
colonists in the second half of the nineteenth century. Acquired as portions
of New Mexico Territory in 1846 and as Oregon Territory in 1848 during
the expansionist presidency of James K. Polk, Arizona and Washington attracted many of the same people for a variety of reasons. Serving the expansion of American jurisdiction and territory through war with Mexico
and the threat of war with Britain, many of the same soldiers who served
in the U.S.-Mexican War between 1845 and 1846 also fought Indians on
Puget Sound during the 1850s, were stationed during the Pig War with
Britain between 1859 and 1874, and then returned to fight Apaches in the
Sonoran Desert during the 1860s and 1870s.[18] Some of the white male intimates of women in this book fought Indian people both in Washington's
Puget Sound and along Arizona's Mogollon Rim. With international and
territorial boundaries established and enforced by the U.S. military, mineral booms and railroad ventures attracted many investors and itinerants to
Arizona and Washington once the California gold rush went bust.[19] Some of
the men who sat as jurors in Arizona Indian women's trials had come to the
southwestern territory from failed farming and mining expeditions in the
Pacific Northwest. These men lived and worked intimately with racially ambiguous immigrants and Indians whose place within settler-colonial racial

and sexual hierarchies was not always certain or conceded. Together, these settler-colonists erected a legal regime that limited Indian women's ability to claim and retain corporeal sovereignty. Although statutes regarding women and noncitizens differed in Arizona and Washington, the people who shared courtrooms and kitchens with Indian women had much in common: most were multilingual, few were unambiguously American—especially after the Civil War—and many counted on favors more often than they collected on debts.[20] Of course there are many distinctions to divide them, but here the histories of the Pacific Northwest and Sonoran Southwest are presented in tandem to more effectively depict Indian women's legal encounters with American settler-colonialism.

Scholars seeking Indigenous women's legal history have made other borderlands in the North American West—California, the Great Lakes, or the Southern Plains, for instance—the focus of their study.[21] This book makes Arizona and Washington its focus because both regions came under American jurisdiction in the same period, as noted above, but also because each territory framed its legal relationship to Indigenous residents differently. As discussed in the chapters that follow, Arizona's earliest legal codes made very clear that Native people were the targets of subjugation, while Washington's early drafts entertained interracial marriages and even granted voting rights to the children of white fathers and Indian mothers. Despite these varying approaches to Indian people's legal status, Native women in both regions experienced remarkably similar demands from citizen men and women on their bodies, progeny, and lands. Considering how and why that happened offers a unique opportunity to highlight the malleable nature of the law to serve elite interests and to chronicle the way settler-colonists revised legal codes to ensure dominance over Indian neighbors and relatives.

This study also constitutes a careful and transparent effort to retrieve evidence of Indian women's formulation of a legal culture and practice to challenge their dispossession. Although this study has uncovered substantial documentary evidence of Native women's legal efforts, such narratives were generated in the course of conquest, making it difficult to amplify and interpret the voices and perspectives of Indian women. In addition to a reliance on both cultural and legal narratives, employing historical imagination makes it possible to reconstruct the cultural, social, and political contexts in which these women lived, even when their actions and choices failed to attract chroniclers' consistent or diligent attention.[22]

The six women featured in this book are those whose "return from the enemy" generated sufficient documentary evidence to present a well-rounded view of their participation in western legal history.[23] Some, like Lucía Martínez, Juana Walker, and Rebecca Lena Graham, have attracted other historians' attention, while the others have been left out of memory or print for nearly a century and are known only to their relatives, fellow tribal members, or local history enthusiasts—many of whom have contributed their critiques and insights to this project. Exceptional because so much of their history can be reconstructed from textual records, these women represent hundreds of others who engaged the legal system as defendants, heirs, plaintiffs, victims, and witnesses, though they were not recognized as citizens.[24]

Three questions led me into academic repositories, federal archives, historical societies, local libraries, state archives, and tribal offices: How did federal and territorial law influence Native-newcomer relations? How did Indian women respond to the social and political upheaval wrought by the imposition of an American legal regime? What do these responses reveal about Native women's legal strategies and the hegemonic nature of American law? The answers to these guiding concerns emerged from court transcripts and census schedules, ethnographic reports and ethnohistories, manuscript collections, newspaper accounts, probate records, and pioneer journals. Initial reviews of legal records included all civil and criminal cases with female Indigenous participants, but the study quickly came to center on those legal actions or complaints initiated by Indian women and their children (some of whom are mixed-race) or which centered on the question of Native and mixed-race women's status as rights-bearing individuals. Although scantily documented, these other cases, some of which I have discussed in other publications, allowed me to make stronger arguments about the engagement of Native women and their daughters with settler-colonial legal regimes.[25]

Because this study aims to chronicle women living outside of reservation communities, the research did not include the federal archives housed in Washington, D.C., that so many other western historians have relied upon to chronicle Indian-white relations. Native women's reservation histories have been and continue to be well told by other historians, allowing for this focus on Indian women who lived much of their lives outside of the purview of federal Indian agents and their institutions and within the realm of local, municipal, state, and territorial authority. In fact, this study's reliance on state archives to tell Indigenous women's histories is one of its innovations in the field of western legal history.

Of course, many of these women maintained vital ties to their reservation kin, and as chapters 6 and 7 argue, their off-reservation settlements extended tribal sovereignty beyond federally recognized boundaries. It is ultimately Indian women's implicit boundary-crossing that makes them borderland dwellers even if they are removed from international boundaries. This study's approach to characterizing borderlands histories draws from three specific historiographies that are discussed below: the study of Indigenous borderlands, legal borderlands, and political borderlands.

For Indian women living outside of reservation boundaries, where the political and racial categories of Indianness become blurred, and beyond the special relationship between tribal members and the federal government outlined in federal Indian law, vulnerability under the "laws of dictators" did not always take explicit form. Because legislators—and subsequent historians—often assumed Indians fell under federal laws, Native women repeatedly found themselves tangled in legislative webs of racial and gendered inequity that were not specific to their Indianness. These webs constitute legal borderlands: ambiguities in the law that result in inconsistent, irregular, and inexplicable applications and interpretations of statutes in western courtrooms. Guardianship laws in Washington that bound Nora Jewell to an abusive master, for instance, made no reference to race or ethnicity. Arizona laws restricting Indian women from testimony likewise applied to other nonwhite women as well. Few scholars have considered the engagement of Indigenous actors with legal regimes not particular to Indians in the American West, choosing instead to focus on more explicit patterns of subjugation with federal Indian law.[26] Historical imagination allows historians to fill in gaps or creatively interpret ambiguous actions in the legal record, but a combination of creative and critical inquiry is essential for uncovering Native resistance where no exploitation seems apparent.

Drawing new focus on these subtle layers of exploitation in territorial and state legal regimes requires an intellectual balance that scholars concerned with the intersections of race and gender within the law have mastered, and this book relies on a number of their insights. First, readers should remind themselves that the concepts of race and gender are socially constructed categories that change over time. The women featured in this book observed radically shifting notions of indigeneity and whiteness during the settler-colonial period between 1854 and 1946 and did not share a fixed sense of their own or others' racial-ethnic identity. American, Indian, and white (in addition to other categories) were all identities in flux during this period that were especially complicated in both Puget Sound and Sonoran borderlands. Second, readers should consider the law as a system designed to serve elite (often white and patriarchal) interests, but one that makes occasional concessions to those judged inferior for their economic, gender, or racial status.[27] Each of the women chronicled here managed to make at least some headway in staking legal claims within a hegemonic system, or one that absorbed critique by incorporating critics, and some of them even managed to recruit unlikely allies along the way—including American citizens who entertained racial and sexual hierarchies in conflict with elite juridical authorities.

These two critical assumptions about the interrelated workings of racial categories and legal exclusion and inclusion are teamed with feminist ethnohistorians' assertion that Indian women's access to and leverage of power relations have changed over time. Related to the concept that women faced "double colonization," these scholars' interest in Indigenous women's manipulation of power is perfectly suited to a study of Indian women's engagement with the American legal system in the settler-colonial West.[28] The women featured here encountered legal regimes that simultaneously excluded and incorporated them, and their interactions with newcomers reveal an ambiguity and fluidity of gender and race characteristic to the North American West.[29]

Indigenous studies scholar Devon Mihesuah has argued that Native women share a "commonality of difference," both historically and today.[30] Writing an Indian women's legal history requires specificity that accounts for individual, regional, and tribal differences. For this reason, the microhistories presented here use methodological and theoretical approaches differently across each chapter. For instance, Lucía Martínez and Nora Jewell both lived in worlds recognized by most readers as borderlands: Lucía's Yaqui kin fought against genocidal campaigns in Sonora while she struggled to survive her masters' abuses in Arizona; Nora's Indigenous kin defended their Coast Salish domain in British Columbia and Washington while her father balanced a Danish immigrant identity on an island claimed by Britons and Americans. Their chapters are presented in a context that accounts for a claim by scholars of borderlands that border-dwellers like Lucía and Nora "adapted the knowledge gained in one borderlands to the challenges posed by its northern or southern counterpart."[31] Lucía's understanding of Mexican and American practices regarding Sonoran tribes and Nora's familiarity with Canadian and American treatment of métis (mixed-race) women likely informed the choices they made in engaging the territorial legal system in Arizona and Washington.[32]

The notion of borderland worlds as zones where multiple cultural, legal, and social frameworks coexist, however, holds true for the women in chapters 4–7 of this book as well. Scholars have identified legal borderlands not only as places where international boundaries transect communities, but also as ambiguous jurisdictional spaces—such as those between reservation and municipal lands—and as murky points of law—such as the regulation of property rights distributed among mixed-race heirs.[33] As the products of interracial unions, Juana Walker and Rebecca Lena Graham crossed borders within their own households, regardless of the fact that both women lived their entire lives within U.S. boundaries. As women who claimed federal lands as their own, and in so doing ensured that their tribes could reclaim those lands through the federal recognition process, Dinah Foote Hood and Louisa Enick created jurisdictional and personal borderlands when they staked their claims. Readers will note, then, that this book relies upon a concept of borderland as a zone where one nation's political dominance is not tacitly established for all residents and where multilingual and multi-racial communities persist. It is in such zones that Native women managed to manipulate legal ambiguities and stake vital claims, even if they did not always convince jurists or officials of their rights to corporeal sovereignty.

More historians are acknowledging as Indigenous borderlands what previous scholars have called middle grounds and Native empires.[34] All of the women in this book, whether they crossed international boundaries or reservation boundaries, recognized and remembered Indigenous border-lands that crisscrossed Puget Sound and the Sonoran Desert and remained visible to those who understood Indigenous peoples' land claims in Arizona and Washington. This study repeatedly employs the term "borderlands" to remind readers that the women in this book marked borders between Indig-enous and American communities in their very bodies and on the lands and homes that they claimed as their own. Furthermore, like the borderlands ideology first described by Gloria Anzaldúa, these women and their mixed-race progeny embodied intimate border-crossings as well as the geographic and legal borders their lives transected.[35] Readers will note various concepts of borders throughout the book that are employed in tandem, whether legal and intimate, Indigenous and national, sexual and geographic, depending on the claims made by the women in each chapter. These references to borderlands are not meant to confuse, they are meant instead to mark persistent boundaries between family members, households, and nations, throughout Puget Sound and the Sonoran Desert.

Other frameworks that readers will recognize in the following chapters include gender historians' insights that the family is a site of conflict as well as cooperation and that laws regulating family interactions reflect the relationship of the individual to the state. Lucía's children were borne of an exploitative sexual union, though they managed to retain close lateral ties among themselves and their own children. Nora's family failed to achieve state sanction and as a result she suffered abuse at the hands of a court-appointed family. Juana and Rebecca lodged their inheritance claims both as the dependent daughters of propertied men and the dependent wards of a sovereign state, though their choice to file lawsuits in contradiction to antimiscegenation statutes and in contrast to assumptions about male-headed and monogamous households documents these women's critiques of their status as dependents—whether rooted in their intersecting femaleness or Indianness. Local jurors and federal and state jurists heard these women's family disputes and handed down supreme decisions that upheld patriarchal and white authority when Indian women's claims threatened to overtake white men's interests. These racially charged inheritance cases—both of which took place at the same time that white women were working hard to dismantle the veil of coverture that had historically made them simultaneous dependents of fathers, husbands, and the state—raise important questions regarding Americans' formulation of Indian and female in their concepts of citizenship and land ownership.[36]

Chapters 6 and 7 continue to emphasize an interrogation of the relationship between citizenship status and land ownership, but use a spatial and environmental analytic to examine Dinah Foote Hood's and Louisa Enick's efforts to protect their claims to lands held by the Yavapai and Sauk-Suiattle—both tribes who had to overcome histories of genocide and removal to achieve federal recognition. Cultural geographers have noted that claiming space is claiming power—an apt observation useful in describing Indigenous women's ability to inherit, own, and transfer land under settler-colonial regimes. Often silenced within American legal regimes, Indian women articulated a spatial sovereignty to claim legal rights to identity and land when depositions and testimony failed or frustrated them. Both women also espoused a gendered use of the land in contrast to the claims of farmers, miners, surveyors, soldiers, conservationists, and congressmen that are familiar to environmental historians. As squatters and allottees on "public lands," Dinah's and Louisa's families challenged many Americans' views of proper use of the land at the turn of the twentieth century. Dinah Foote Hood's squatter practices and Louisa Enick's allotment petitions held spaces open for Yavapai and Sauk-Suiattle families until their tribal leadership garnered enough power to claim those lands under federal recognition. Particularly for these women, whose tribes had survived genocide, relocation, and ethnic erasure, claiming space allowed them to negotiate shifts in settler-colonial attitudes toward Indian land ownership and tribal status when avoidance and adaptability paved the way for direct confrontation in later generations.[37]

This book offers extraordinary examples of ordinary women to argue that Indigenous women acted as more than occasional bearers of culture or as intermediaries and depicts Indian women as principal actors in the history of the North American West. Putting Native women at the center of western history—as participants in territorial settlement and the expansion of law and order, as critics and transgressors of racial and national borders, as tenants of the land—remains important work. In particular, this project focuses on Indian women's encounters with the law, an aspect of western history that scholars have been particularly reticent to people with Indigenous female protagonists; much more remains to be done.[38] As implied in the title of this introductory chapter, Indian women's legal history entails a certain set of poetics and politics. The poetics of oral tradition, which constitutes "the law of the Gods [some Native women] claim" and the politics of legal status, or the condition that makes it (im)possible for Native women to defend "the country of [their] mind, [their] body," are integrated in the creative and critical analysis offered here.[39] Marginalized within the legal regimes imposed under settler-colonialism and institutionalized during state formation, Indigenous women's legal philosophies and strategies did not always take documented form, requiring creative interpretations and critical acts of retrieval on the part of descendants and historians alike.[40] In some instances, Indigenous women's knowledge can be clearly traced to a broader tribal tradition, as in Lucía and Nora's histories, whereas other sources of such knowledge seem based more explicitly on personal experiences, as in Juana Walker's and Dinah Foote Hood's histories. Whether reflective of their tribal backgrounds or indicative of individual choices, the Indigenous knowledge that the women in this book espoused certainly countered the implicitly white male supremacist assumptions embedded in Arizona and Washington's legal regimes. Applying Joy Harjo's creative and critical "effort of retrieval" makes the connections between the legal and legendary, the poetic and political, perfectly clear and helps historians and readers to perceive Indian women as acting both individually and communally in their legal challenges.

My primary goal in researching and writing this book is to depict Indigenous women's participation in the struggle for cultural and political sovereignty during the peak of American settler-colonialism in the North American West. Like other anticolonial histories, this work is driven by "the desire . . . to retrieve a subaltern history that rewrites the received account both of the colonizing academics and of the native ruling elite, a history of the excluded, the voiceless."[41] Rather than merely arguing that Native women exercised agency, this book strives to normalize Indigenous women's subtle and overt critiques of their dispossession. Instead of being surprised to learn of Indian women's agency, readers might more readily recognize evidence of Indian women's participation in American legal history elsewhere, whether in their own communities or in their own pasts.[42]

Indebted to Joy Harjo's cautionary tale and to many others who have taught me the poetics and politics of Indian women's legal history, I do not claim ownership of these women or their histories, which likely mean something very different to the people who knew and loved them. In archives, on back porches, and in tribal offices, the souls and histories in this book have been addressed kindly and with respect. I have asked permission of descendants when possible, but have not always been granted audience with tribes whose members are still busy "returning from the enemy." The concluding chapter of this book chronicles the interpersonal and archival work that underlies this study, and as a result of those connections, each of these chapters is written with honorable intentions: to historicize Native women's efforts to protect their country, their bodies, and their minds from "the purveyors of law." At times personal and political, at other times creative and critical, this narrative is for all readers of western history whose shoulders "bear the acts of forgetfulness."[43]

CHAPTER 2

Lucía Martínez and the "Putative Father"

Arizona, 1854–1900

In the very hot month of June 1880, Lucía Martínez opened her door to Yuma County sheriff Andrew Tyner, then acting as census enumerator for the federal government and Arizona Territory. The Yaqui mother of four illegitimate, mixed-race children may have been nervous. Her Indigenous status made her children subject to the minor Indian indenture law that allowed Arizona citizens to put Native girls to work as domestics until they reached eighteen and contract boys' labor until they turned twenty-one. Without a profession or visible means of support, Lucía might also have been concerned that Tyner could accuse her of prostitution in the home she made in Yuma's Main Street district of Indians and Mexicans. Whether her voice shook when she responded to Sheriff Tyner's questions, and whether she spoke broken English or he spoke broken Spanish, or both, historians will never know. Tyner recorded Lucía's lies about her past and creative construction of a false identity granting citizenship and legitimacy to herself and her children in his own handwriting as he marked her down as a "white" widow born in Sonora with four "white" children born in Arizona, whose deceased father shared her Sonoran birthplace.[1]

For a woman who had been abducted from her Sonoran Rio Yaqui home during an Apache slave raid in her early girlhood, Yuma would have offered an opportunity to live among fellow refugees of the Sonoran genocide campaign against Yaquis. A truly transnational territorial settlement, Yuma bustled as a port town that linked the borderlands of the American Southwest to Hermosillo, San Francisco, and even New York by ferry and

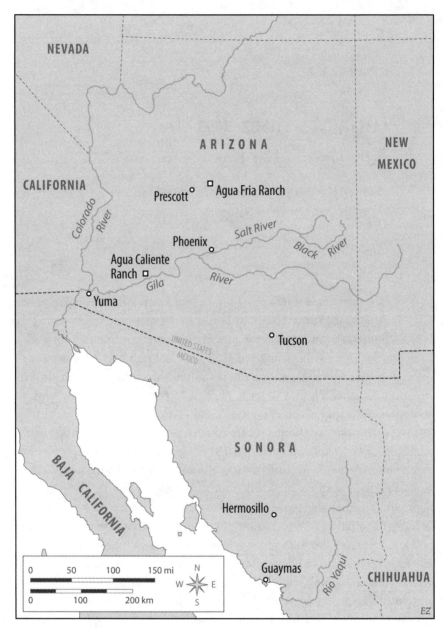

Lucía Martínez's Sonoran borderlands (Map by Ezra Zeitler)

then ship via the Colorado River and the Sea of Cortez. In the second half of the nineteenth century, Chilean laborers and Chinese gardeners, surveyors from Ireland and tailors from Prussia, filled Yuma's streets; passersby spoke English and Spanish with Cockney and Quechan accents and the chief of the Yumas lived two doors down from a Massachusetts-born wheelwright on Maiden Lane. Lucía Martínez and her children lived just a block or so from their priest, and prayed with him at the Immaculate Conception Church where they and other racially ambiguous Catholics found solace in a border town that some described as "hotter than hell."[2]

By 1880, Lucía's faith had certainly been tested by fire. In truth, Sheriff Tyner probably did not intimidate the woman who had escaped her Apache slavers at the age of ten and sued her master's wife for her children's inheritance in a court that did not grant testimony to Indians. To appreciate more greatly the significance—historical, legal, and personal—of Lucía's transformation in that year's census from slave to citizen, we must go back to 1854: the year Lucía was born, and the year that the Gadsden Purchase, or as she might have known it—the Treaty of La Mesilla—drew the northern portion of the Sonoran Desert and its inhabitants under American authority.

Lucía's story as told in this chapter marks her reenactment of the legendary Yaqui girls' translation of the Sonoran talking tree's message of conquest and survivance that opened this book. Just as her predecessors borrowed knowledge brought from other worlds to lead their people in the struggle against colonization, Lucía Martínez translated the buzzing noises of habeas corpus and census and baptism in her fight to keep her children and her dignity within territorial Arizona's legal regime. An unsung heroine in Native women's fight for corporeal sovereignty, the Yaqui woman navigated the racial and sexual hierarchies that Americans scratched onto her Sonoran Desert home with remarkable tenacity.

Although little is known about Martínez before she encountered her literate master in 1864, she claimed to have been born in Sonora in 1854 and was consistently identified by others as Yaqui.[3] Her parents might have been farmers in the Rio Yaqui *hiakim* (tribal homelands), or a mining family that traveled throughout southwestern mining camps and returned to the hiakim for important ceremonials.[4] Certainly the girl would have known the names Seahamut (Flower Girl), Yueta (Unusual Sound in the Air), and Yomumulia (Enchanted Bee) that were used to variously describe the child who translated the stark prophecies of the Talking Tree before the Spanish *conquistadores*, the Mexican *generales*, and the American soldiers came. In songs sung informally by men, women, and children in her family, Lucía might also have learned about the Catholic-Yoeme figure of Christ as a human manifestation of the deer dancer she knew from the ritual *pahkom* (deer dances) performed near her home. These and other stories about the *huya ania* (wilderness world), *tuka ania* (night world), *tenku ania* (dream world), *yo ania* (enchanted world), and the *sea ania* (flower world) taught the girl that the Yoemem, as the Yaquis called themselves, had chosen to face their Yori (Mexican) and Riingom (American) challengers head-on and drew strength from the natural and spiritual worlds of the Sonoran Desert.[5]

When she was born in the mid–nineteenth century, the girl's family lived in relatively peaceful relations with the Sonoran government. Survivors of and perhaps participants in Mexico's war for independence from Spain, Lucía's community had taken up settlement farming and gained a reputation as ideal mining laborers throughout the Southwest. Centuries of Spanish-Catholic rule had not diminished distinctively Yaqui cultural practices such as the pahkom deer dance, but had introduced innovations including the adoption of the Roman Catholic calendar of ceremonials and saint's days. June 24, San Juan's day, marked the commencement of summer planting; corn, beans, and squash would be harvested in late October or early November — just in time to prepare offerings for *el Día de los Muertos*, or Day of the Dead. Christmas in December ended the summer–autumn season of the Yaqui's dual year, a transition into the winter–spring season marked by Ash Wednesday and in early May the Finding of the Holy Cross. Before the infant Lucía had lived through a full calendar year of peaceful ceremonies that recognized significant natural and spiritual events, a new force rose to power in the Sonoran government and initiated a campaign of violent expulsion to drive the Yaqui from their fertile lands.[6]

Once General Ignacio Pesqueira gained the governorship, Sonoran Yaquis suffered over forty years of state-sanctioned genocide that would not end until 1910. Violence and exploitation ranged from extreme atrocities such as the Bacum Massacre of 1868 and enslavement on Yucatan henequen plantations, to daily insults and abuses from Mexican civilians.[7] Yaquis responded to those assaults in a variety of ways. Some joined guerrilla armies of resistance; some sought the dubious protection of Mexican ranchers who may have mistreated them, but at least did not kill them; still others fled the hiakim and adopted Mexican or American Indian identities on *el otro lado* — the other side — of the Sonoran-Arizona border.[8] Whether by choice or by force, "the Yaqui experience [of the mid–nineteenth through the early twentieth centuries] was characterized by long-distance movement. Removal from their land, life in exile, and the struggle to return [are] central themes of Yaqui historical narrative."[9] As we shall see, these were also the major motifs of Martínez's life among Mexicans and Americans.[10]

While fending off the incursions of Sonorans, the young girl's tribe also negotiated the pressures of an intertribal slave network that linked Catholics to Comanches and Seris to soldiers throughout New Spain, Mexico, and the southwestern United States. As an equal opportunity marketplace, the borderlands slave trade made everyone vulnerable. Yaquis captured Mexicans and sold them to Apaches; Apaches ambushed Sonorans in return and sold captives to Americans. As Mexicans and Americans alternately trusted and turned on each other, whites too became slaves of Yavapais and captives of Cocopahs. Nineteenth-century animosities and contestations of power skewed descriptions of this slave trade, making it difficult to chronicle the market, but within the Sonoran traffic in captives Yaquis found themselves subject to the whims of masters far more often than not.[11]

Tribal songs and dances describe a flower world of talking animals and women's art depicts colorful blossoms, hummingbirds, and deer, but nineteenth-century Yaquis lived in a genocidal world.[12] The sequence of events that forced Lucía out of the hiakim is unclear, but the power dynamics that led to her removal and enslavement are unambiguous. She was female and Indigenous in the southwestern borderlands, making her both valuable and vulnerable. Born in 1854 during peace but weaned during wartime, by 1864 the Yaqui girl had been carried off to el otro lado, the American side of the border, in the hands of Apaches raiding for captives and livestock.[13] Although she might have comprehended the future in store for her as a captive of Apaches or as a *criada* (servant) among Mexicans, she did not likely foresee her part in overtly challenging the laws that made her subject to the whims of men like King S. Woolsey, father of her illegitimate children and one of the first American citizens to claim Indian lands under a U.S. flag in the new Territory of Arizona.

Born to Michael Woolsey in 1832 in the slaveholding state of Alabama, young King proved himself capable of the gun-toting, lash-cracking work that westering required. Little is known of his antebellum upbringing in Limestone County. His family eventually relocated to Arkansas, where his siblings Michael M., Cassandra, and Daniel remained through adulthood. Perhaps intrigued by stories of fur-trade families who had spawned westering sons, the young upstart sought to manifest his own destiny, though he charted a peculiar route to California.[14]

In the aftermath of the U.S.-Mexican War and amid the growing debates over slavery and expansion at the end of the 1840s, Woolsey joined the filibuster movement growing throughout the South and reportedly participated in the attempted 1848–1849 invasion of Cuba to overthrow the Spanish. Although many of the men in Narciso López's campaign died, some found their own escape routes and Woolsey claimed he made it to California through the aid of a British consulate.[15] Despite his arrival "into one of the nation's hubs of filibustering intrigue," he did not become a career transnational marauder. The renegade's attitudes toward Indigenous westerners, however, echoed those of his compatriots, "who displaced Latin American peoples in the cause of progress much as settlers dispossessed Indian tribes," and coincided with the views of notorious filibuster William Walker, who claimed that he had only invaded Mexico in 1853–1854 "to provide the defenseless people of Sonora with protection against Indian attacks."[16]

During the 1850s Woolsey tried his hand at mining in Calaveras County, California, but there is no sign that he made any significant strikes and he eventually gave up on the Golden State to seek a new destiny in the Arizona portion of New Mexico Territory.[17] The fortune-seeker arrived in Yuma (then known as Arizona City and Colorado City) in 1860 or 1861, as the outbreak of the Civil War drew near. His contemporaries and chroniclers disagreed whether the southerner's loyalties were on the Confederate or Union side, but Woolsey began his Arizona career as a mule driver hauling wheat between the Salt River valley Pima villages and Fort Yuma. His Southern ties might have generated Confederate sympathies, but as he entered his thirties and the war between brothers began, the muleskinner found Union supply contracts a strong enticement and he did not formally enlist on either side. As he would soon prove, a distaste for blood did not engender the westering man's wartime neutrality. Perhaps his experiences filibustering and mining among myriad ethnic and racial groups in the transnational southwest dissuaded him from taking up arms against his white brethren.

Whatever the reason for his nonparticipation, Woolsey used the Civil War period to buy unceded land and haul Pima wheat. When Arizona became a territory separate from New Mexico in 1863, he was ready to greet eastern politicians and launch anti-Indian expeditions from his Agua Caliente ranch near the Gila River between Phoenix and Yuma, as well as from his Agua Fria ranch near Prescott. Early in 1864, politicians made their way west to take up their territorial appointments. To administer a violent solution to the "Indian problem" they feared, Arizona's first officials relied less on Union soldiers still needed in the war between North and South and more on unenlisted men like King S. Woolsey, whose ability to lead civilians against Arizona Indians had been well proven.[18]

The former muleskinner first demonstrated his macabre talent in January of 1864 when he led twenty-eight men to pursue Apaches accused of stealing livestock. Joined by forty-five Maricopa and O'odham men who also considered the Apaches their enemies, the party found themselves trapped in a canyon and surrounded by four hundred Apache warriors. The unflinching captain reported that he outsmarted the foes who outnumbered him by pretending to be a treaty party, not a war party, and through his Yavapai and Pee Posh interpreters, he negotiated a parlay that was in fact an ambush. Woolsey's men killed twenty-four Apaches, giving themselves time to escape under cover of fire, losing only one citizen and one Yavapai ally. This episode, later called the Pinole Treaty because the contentious hero had offered to negotiate over a shared meal of roughly ground corn called pinole, sealed the wily man's reputation as one of Arizona's frontier heroes.[19]

The January campaign lasted twenty-seven days and had been informal in nature—made up of friends organized to avenge a neighbor's loss—like many of the early skirmishes led by settler-colonists in unceded Indian lands. In March, the newly appointed territorial governor John Noble Goodwin made King S. Woolsey lieutenant colonel of the Arizona Volunteers; the one-time filibuster would now enjoy official approval of his savage exploits for the remainder of his career. In April his second campaign against the Apaches was an even greater success than the earlier unsanctioned one. This time he led ninety-three civilians and six soldiers armed and supplied with Fort Whipple munitions and killed thirty Apaches, also destroying their village and food stashes, with only two injuries among his command.[20]

As the Indigenous body count in Woolsey's wake continued to grow, some implied that the food he left for Indians might have been poisoned; some complained that he showed no restraint toward women and children. In response to such "psalm singing fanatics," Woolsey made it clear to those who commissioned him and the men who followed him that he advocated equal opportunity violence with no remorse.[21] He reported to his superiors that during his April 1864 campaign eight of the thirty Apaches killed were women and children. Instead of apologizing for his actions, he explained why there were not more female casualties: "We would have killed more women but owing to having attacked in the daytime when the women were at work gathering mescal. It sir, is next thing to impossible to prevent killing squaws in jumping a ranchero even were we disposed to save them. For my part I am frank to say that I fight on the *broad platform* of *extermination*."[22] Woolsey made it clear that he was not disposed to save Native women, whom he saw as equal opportunity targets for extermination. His choice of words also reverberated in popular calls for the extermination of Indians in similarly contested zones of western expansion — including Washington Territory.[23] In upholding Woolsey's position within the territorial militia, politicians like Governor Goodwin rewarded him for such sentiments and actions.

A son of the slaveholding South and the fur-trade Middle West, King S. Woolsey may have been accustomed to viewing nonwhite women and children as expendable commodities and appropriate targets of violence. For this conviction, Arizona's first territorial legislature commended his "great perseverance and personal sacrifice . . . against the Apaches," in the fall of 1864.[24] Arizona's territorial delegate Charles D. Poston remembered thirty years after meeting him that Woolsey was "a very intelligent man, and he saw at once that either the Americans or the Indians were to be slaughtered."[25] Woolsey proved to be very successful in a region that measured intelligence by a man's willingness to kill Indians.

While Woolsey polished his martial reputation, the Yoeme slave girl plotted her escape from the Apaches who had raided her Sonoran family and forced her north to the Mogollon Rim. Sometime in late June 1864, Lucía began the first phase of an epic journey that would require her to travel over two hundred miles through the Sonoran Desert. The Yaqui girl faced both environmental and human obstacles. The oncoming monsoon season offered cooling rains against the harsh desert heat, but also launched flash floods through the Sonoran arroyo system of washes that would have guided the girl to her Rio Yaqui homelands. Following the swollen arroyos would prove difficult as the Mogollon Rim crumbled into the Salt and Gila River valley, exposing sheer canyon walls and rocky mountain ranges. The strong-willed captive would not only have to navigate such treacherous terrain without supplies, she had to avoid Apache rancherias, O'odham villages, Mexican and American settlements — all dangerous sites for an un-claimed Yaqui girl. Born to people who fought desperately to remain within their hiakim, though, the child began the journey south and navigated the intersections of beauty and brutality that defined the huya ania, the wilderness world of her girlhood.

On June 1, 1864, Woolsey began his third and largest anti-Apache expedition from his Agua Fria ranch. He led ninety-three men on a journey lasting eighty-seven days. Afterward, he filed an extensive report describing the campaign as successful, "[n]otwithstanding the failure to . . . kill Indians."[26] After six weeks' traversing the watersheds of central Arizona, the bloodthirsty adventurer reconnoitered at Fort Goodwin, resupplied his men, and continued the expedition along the Gila River and its tributaries. Although Woolsey described at great length and with painstaking attention to cartographic detail the abundance of water and fertile land, the signs of "color" in the hills and Apaches in the valleys, of the girl he found at the edge of the Black River valley, he had few words. He noted only that "a Jaqui [sic] squaw about ten years of age came into our camp. She had been a captive among the Apaches, and had just made her escape. She came in with us, and is now at my Agua Fria ranch."[27] Other men who traveled under Woolsey's command also described their unexpected discovery of a young captive girl, and their myriad romanticized accounts describe the ways in which Americans benefited from the still active intertribal slave trade.[28] It is impossible to know whether the ten-year-old girl joined Woolsey's camp with trepidation or appreciation, but it may be that a well-supplied group proved a welcome sight to her as she faced a daunting journey through the Sonoran Desert in the sweltering heat that would bring on the monsoon season.

The girl who "came in" with Woolsey and his men in the middle of July 1864 was, of course, Lucía Martínez. She had escaped the Apaches only to be taken in by the territory's leading Indian killer. Woolsey would prove a far more difficult master to free herself from, and it took the girl seven years—almost to the day—to regain her independence. The frontiersman's anti-Apache expedition lasted another six weeks before he brought Lucía back to his ranch fourteen miles east of Prescott at the end of August.

On July 18, 1864—possibly the very day the American took the slave into his custody—territorial citizens nominated Woolsey to represent them in Arizona's first legislative session. Meeting in Prescott between September 26 and November 10, 1864, the new senator and his peers drafted into law the Howell Code, a nearly five-hundred-page codex that ensured the supremacy of white men over Indian women for nearly fifty years.[29] The girl settled into her new life of servitude on the Agua Fria ranch, though it is hard to believe that she had given up on a return to her Sonoran hiakim.

When King S. Woolsey joined his fellow senators at the first territorial legislative session on September 26, 1864, he had already put ten-year-old Lucía to work on his rancheria just a day's ride away. Listed as the delegate from "Aqua Fria Ranch," the man helped to put into place a penal code that regulated his and his neighbors' intimate and public lives and upheld the prerogatives of his fellow white male citizens to the detriment of Indigenous and other nonwhite and non-English-speaking Arizonans. The men acted in accordance with Governor Goodwin's exhortations, delivered in his first speech to the legislature. Echoing President Polk's inaugural address at the onset of the U.S.-Mexican War that had made Arizona and New Mexico Territory part of the United States, Goodwin linked settler-colonial households to the extinguishment of Indians and their title to land and depicted conditions in territorial Arizona:

> In the fierce conflicts for life waged by the people of this territory with the hostile Apaches, some young persons have been captured, and there being no provision made by the government for their custody or support, have been placed in families as servants or laborers. These captives, so far as I have information, have been kindly treated, and in some instances have become partly civilized, and would not now voluntarily leave the persons with whom they are living. But though no wrong or oppression may have resulted from this relation between the parties, it is certainly liable to abuse, and if permitted to continue should be regulated by law . . . where persons have become accustomed to civilized life, and are unwilling to return to the savage state [on reservations], there seems to be no good reason for compelling them to do so. I can suggest no better enactment in such cases than a system of apprenticeship similar to that existing in most of the states.[30]

In his address, Goodwin identified two major problems facing Arizona lawmakers: peonage and Indians. Calling peonage a "relic of barbarous law" that "debases the laboring man," the governor simultaneously promoted free labor among citizens and acknowledged the extralegal enslavement of Native Americans in the same breath. In proposing an apprenticeship system to regulate the already common practice of forced Indian labor, Goodwin described this and other territorial incursions on federal jurisdiction over Indigenous Arizonans as a justified response to "our isolated and remote situation, the large number of Indians in our midst that might be combined against us, [and] the long hostility and brutal ferocity of some tribes, [which] compel us to avail ourselves of all means for self-defense and protection."[31] Rather than using his first address to the territory as an opportunity to recognize the multivalent legal cultures in place in Arizona—Indian, Hispanic, and Anglo-American—Goodwin gestured toward specific mechanisms that the legislature could use to diminish those notions of justice that contradicted white citizens' claims to manifest destiny and describe anti-Indian violence as self-defense.

Arizona's territorial senators did not create a coercive Indian labor market; rather, they formalized what had been an extralegal trade that preceded American jurisdiction and featured interracial intimacies. With an American legal system in place, these politicians ensured that white men would become the sole beneficiaries of human commodification. The southwestern slave market connected Comanches and Seris, Utes and Pueblos, Mormons and Catholics; it predated the Arizona legislature, included residents from Texas to California and from Arizona to Colorado, and continued nearly into the twentieth century. Americans, Indians, and Mexicans who participated in this market targeted women and children for their reproductive labors and capacities as intermediaries, even as they murdered captives' male relatives in the struggle for frontier dominance. Slavers on both sides of the U.S.-Mexico border took advantage of racial ambiguity and sold Mexicans as Indians, redeemed Indians as white Mexicans, and, as in the renowned case of Olive Oatman, tattooed Indianness onto white slaves.[32] Although tribes often enslaved enemy tribal members, they sometimes incorporated them into their own families, linking exploitative labor and fictive kinship. Hispanos did the same, drawing Indigenous slaves into a complex caste system where they intermarried with free laborers and served elites as *criados*, or servants. As long as this system remained extralegal, American officials struggled to deter intercultural bonds that often formed as a result of the slave trade. Such widespread mestizaje, or interracial intimacy and reproduction, made it difficult to distinguish citizen from subject, patriarch from peon, respectable from rogue. In an unregulated market, territorial Arizonans bought laborers for companionship as well as for apprenticeship. Settler-colonists bought children to replace those who had died, mastering their way into an intercultural network that blurred the bonds of affection and indenture.[33]

Senator Woolsey and his friends, then, did what they could to produce a legal code that would protect the "laboring man," i.e., white male citizens, and divided the "large number of Indians" in their midst as either captive ranch hands or "savage" reservation prisoners. On November 10, 1864, King Woolsey and his fellow senators approved the lengthy code that determined the civil and criminal conduct of all men and women, minors and adults, citizens and subjects. The Howell Code they enacted defined deviant and acceptable behaviors and put into place the rules that made public the private details of territorial Arizonans' lives. The federal government withheld citizenship status from Native Americans, but Woolsey and his peers constructed a broad range of laws to circumscribe the daily interactions between Indigenous and newcomer westerners. The men elected to represent their citizen neighbors codified racial and gender hierarchies that were still being contested throughout the ethnically diverse and demographically imbalanced territory, so that Arizona might become recognizable as a modern state ruled by respectable white men—the project of territorial officials preparing for transition to statehood. When Woolsey signed the Howell Code, he affirmed the claims to young Lucía Martínez's body and labors that were a fundamental component of his civic and martial manhood.[34]

William T. Howell, appointed territorial Arizona justice, had drafted a set of laws in anticipation of the 1863 Organic Act making the region a U.S. territory. Howell found the laws of California suitable to the social customs and racial hierarchies endorsed by Arizona's Anglo elites, most of whom were Southern Democrats, so he adopted most of the neighboring state's legal code.[35] Its peonage and indenture laws offered little protection to non-Anglos, but favored white women's property and marital rights. The justice continued the national trend away from coverture, but offered women few political rights, and overall, upheld white male supremacy in the application of criminal and civil law, particularly where women's bodies were concerned. Fathers still determined sexual and marital consent for daughters between the age of ten and eighteen, female plaintiffs had to show proof of force in sexual assault cases, and women who did not carry pregnancies to term faced criminal charges if they could not prove miscarriage.[36]

The Howell Code privileged white patriarchs, though not all Arizona heads of household claimed their racial and sexual privileges equally.[37] Home to Confederates and other Anglo-Americans, European immigrants, free black Americans, Indians, Mexicans, and Chinese, the territory fostered racial ambiguities that senators sought to clarify in the Howell Code.[38] Citizens' dependence on nonwhite labor in a region defined by blurred color lines complicated official efforts to discourage intercultural intima-

cies. Working together often meant living together, which usually led people to share stories and secrets, germs and jokes. Goodwin, Howell, and
Woolsey knew that where there was exploitation, there was also affection—
sometimes mutual, sometimes not—and that the indenture of minor Indians was merely one phase in a long history of sex and servitude in the
Southwest.[39]

The captive Indian laborers and servants that Governor Goodwin had
"information" about were subject to a series of Howell Code provisions
that made them economically valuable as laborers and sexually vulnerable
as noncitizens in the eyes of Woolsey and other enterprising westerners.
Legislators fixed the age of sexual consent for females at ten years, defining
premenstrual adolescents as sexually available, but set girls' marriageable
age at sixteen.[40] Females over ten years old who withheld consent had to
prove sexual assault through evidence of physical injury, wives could not
deny their husbands sexual access, and women faced a minimum five-year
prison term if they terminated a pregnancy. Between 1864 and 1871, the
span of years Lucía spent under Woolsey's custody, nonwhite Arizonans
could not testify in criminal cases against white men, rendering nonwhite
sexual assault victims silent if their attackers were white. After 1871, legislators granted all residents the right to testify in criminal trials, though no
Indigenous woman testified against a white defendant until 1913 and nonwhites remained barred from testimony in civil trials until Arizona reached
statehood in 1912, suggesting that the restrictive power of the law outlasted
its penal authority.[41]

Arizona's pioneer fathers continued to have sex on their mind when
they passed a provision banning mixed-race marriages in the first draft of
the Howell Code.[42] Although Mexicans, Indians, and Anglos lived in close
proximity, legislators ensured that sexual relations among these groups
would remain illicit. Indigenous women could not use the courts to uphold
spousal rights to individual property rights and alimony in cases of divorce
that female American citizens enjoyed, and Mexican women depended
upon judges' discretion to enjoy white marital privileges since they might
easily be seen as Indian.[43] Importantly, the miscegenation law did not make
interracial intercourse criminal—the code simply put the burden of illegitimate progeny on the mother, deviating from the common-law presumption
of patrilineality and echoing a national trend to recognize bastard and illegitimate children as maternal, rather than paternal, property in order to
reduce dependence on the state.[44] This seemingly race-neutral move, very

familiar to legislators from slaveholding families, kept property in the hands of white fathers who practiced procreative sex with racially ambiguous and socially vulnerable women and maintained the patriarchal authority of the state to determine women's domestic rights.[45]

Legislators' particular concerns regarding miscegenation in the territory stemmed from their exposure to mestizaje in the southwestern borderlands.[46] Historians of borderlands who are interested in families, intimacy, and sexuality have found interracial unions to be a common characteristic of the North American West prior to the twentieth century. The first territorial governor recognized that citizens' dependence upon Indian labor could foster interracial sex when he proposed an apprenticeship system, and Anglo-American Arizonans could not help but notice their Mexican neighbors' mestizo past—a legacy celebrated in the rhetoric of the Mexican revolution of the 1820s, but subdued after the racial emphasis on whiteness imposed in the Treaty of Guadalupe Hidalgo in 1848. The territorial indenture system, then, constituted a pivotal shift from an extralegal slave trade to institutionalized unfree labor while also serving to discourage, if not actually prevent, interracial bonds of affection. As the Martínez-Woolsey family tree indicates, however, not all Arizonans used indenture to distance themselves from minor Indians or to discontinue pre-American labor systems.

Elected officials wrote a provision titled "Of the Support of Minor Indians" in response to Governor Goodwin's concern for young Apaches. The law declared that "[a]ny person into whose care or custody shall come any captive Indian child of a hostile tribe, or any minor Indian child of other than hostile tribes, shall, within twenty days thereafter, produce such child before the judge of probate or a justice of the peace . . . and may apply to . . . have such Indian child bound to him until he shall arrive at the age of twenty-one years; and if a female, at the age of eighteen years."[47] Contrary to other western laws regulating minors, indenture, and guardianship, the minor Indian indenture law did little to protect the welfare of indigent children.[48] Just a year after the Emancipation Proclamation had freed some black slaves and the California legislature had dismantled its own Native indenture system, Arizona lawmakers formalized and rationalized the region's tribal slave trade by legalizing the abduction and forced labor of minor American Indians like Lucía Martínez. This move allowed Anglo Arizonans to critique intertribal slave practices dominant in the first half of the nineteenth century, while granting legal and social mechanisms to claim Indigenous labor for themselves.

Between 1864 and 1873, legislators barred citizens from adopting Indian children and required that heads of households with Indigenous minors in their homes apply for a bond of indenture within twenty days of taking custody. When they wrote an adoption law in 1873, the legislature failed to mention Indigenous children at all and upheld the minor Indian indenture law for fourteen more years, which suggests that they believed white minors should be adopted while Native wards should be indentured. The law granted local justices of the peace the authority to place Indian children in non-Indian households until the age of majority in exchange for good treatment, food, and clothing. Despite the governor's suggestion to borrow apprenticeship models from other states, the code did not make basic education or occupational training a component of indenture, leaving it to household heads to determine the most suitable work for young Indigenous wards. As will be seen in the next chapter, stricter provisions regarding the treatment of wards in Washington Territory still did not protect Indigenous children from abuse, but Arizona's code made exploitation likely and not just possible.[49]

That Arizona citizens were at war with the Indigenous population during the indenture period of 1864 to 1887 explains why Indian children could simply be "found" in the hills and shows that the minor Indian indenture law was part of a complex extermination campaign against Native families. Woolsey captured Lucía while hunting Native Americans, making the girl a suitable subject for servitude and linking indenture to anti-Indian sentiments. Reservation internment proved difficult to enforce in nineteenth-century Arizona and killing adults while making servants of their children proved an effective way to legitimate extermination and domesticate assimilation. Geronimo's surrender in 1886 marked an official end to the Indian Wars in the territory and when the Allotment Act of 1887 held out the promise of citizenship to Native people, the legislature repealed the indenture clause. Other historians have shown, however, that citizen families continued to capture Indigenous children after 1887 without formally adopting them—indicating a continued interest in nonwhite child labor after the legislative assembly proscribed the practice.[50]

Arizonans could also use the minor Indian indenture law to exploit Native women's reproductive and productive labor and continue an antebellum legacy of white men's sexual access to laboring women.[51] Reproductive labor included management of the household: food preparation, child care, material maintenance, and emotional support.[52] Some masters, like King S. Woolsey, also demanded sexual services. Having silenced Indigenous voices through the witness exclusion provision and having legally defined Indian girls over ten as sexually available, Woolsey and his colleagues ensured that household heads enjoyed relatively free access to their servants' bodies with no concern for the support of illegitimate and mixed-race descendants. That male servants bore no children as a result of sexual assault and were also barred from testifying against their masters makes it virtually impossible to determine the frequency of sexual exploitation of Indian boys indentured under the Howell Code, though in theory the sodomy law, outlined in the same article as the rape statute, would have applied to them. The law upheld white men's economic and intimate demands on subordinates' bodies and then—through a criminal ban on abortive practices—required women to bear children that would likely become servants rather than heirs.[53]

These were the laws that Woolsey brought back to the Agua Fria Ranch where Lucía set the table, cleaned the floors, and made his bed. These Howell Code statutes collectively made the girl economically, racially, and sexually subservient to her legislator master. Lucía served Woolsey's workers and guests so that he could build a reputation for Southern hospitality and gentlemanly manners.[54] A visitor to the ranch described the "outpost settlement" as one where "castes and distinctions of social rank had quite as full play out here in the wilderness, as in the statelier mansions of Beacon Street or the 5th Avenue." District Judge Joseph Pratt Allyn outlined the racial and gender hierarchy that ordered the ranch staff, as related by the proprietor's own cook: "First, there's the black men, i.e., Mexicans, the herders; then there's the white men, i.e., the carpenters, masons, etc.; then there's Mr. King, i.e., Woolsey and his friends; and last . . . me [the cook], the Indian girl, an Apache captive, who is the personal attendant of Mrs. W., and the dogs."[55] If such racial and sexual divisions were apparent to a visitor, they were undoubtedly clear to Woolsey's "Indian girl." If she understood English in addition to Spanish and Yaqui, then Lucía also might have learned about the penal code that determined her subjectivity through the conversations her master shared with friends and partners at his table and with other servants on the ranch.

The cook described a spatial hierarchy that reflected Woolsey's habit of racial and sexual subordination. "Mr. King"—as his servants called him—

segregated his ranch by gender and ethnicity in a manner similar to the plantations of his Alabama childhood and employed workers as diverse as those found in the Arkansas River valley. Mexicans, categorized by Arizona southerners as "black men," worked farthest from the inner spaces of Woolsey's home, performing manual and field labor. The American "white men" performed skilled labor within the immediate vicinity of the ranch. Bound by no spatial or occupational limits, "Mr. King" and "his friends" roamed freely about the property and occupied themselves as they pleased. Grouped with the dogs and tied to the most intimate corners of the ranch, the cook and the "Indian girl" provided the domestic labor that satisfied the appetites of Woolsey and his men.[56]

Expected to provide both culinary and carnal labors under her master's watch, the servant found herself in a position similar to that of her Yaqui sisters in Sonora. Like Yaqui women working under *dueños*—Mexican masters—on Sonoran rancheros, Lucía was vulnerable to her master's sexual demands.[57] Her world thus continued to be marked by beauty and brutality. At the age of thirteen, the servant bore Woolsey's first child, a healthy daughter named Clara, on February 4, 1867.[58] During her pregnancy, Lucía survived an Apache raid on the Agua Fria ranch while Woolsey was away on an anti-Indian campaign. Although the Apache men merely rustled some of the southerner's livestock, the expectant servant may have been reminded of the traumatic assault that tore her from the hiakim just a few years earlier. Her pregnant state during the attack might have made clear to the girl that she was equally susceptible to Apache and American masters and discouraged her from escaping the Agua Fria ranch when Woolsey was away.[59]

In addition to bearing the tumult of a raid during her pregnancy, Lucía also endured her master's 1866 financial fallout. Woolsey had turned his efforts toward mining, an enterprise that made few rich and many poor. A Prescott newspaper described him as "the busiest man in the country." He oversaw operations at the Agua Caliente and Agua Fria settlements, built two stamp mills, and was looking to expand his mining interests throughout the central Arizona highlands.[60] By 1867, the year of Clara's birth, his investments in local mines collapsed; he declared bankruptcy and surrendered all of his properties except the Agua Caliente ranch to creditors. The financial failure convinced his neighbors only that their hero was ambitious and had no negative effect on his political or social status among territorial elites.[61] Indeed, some Prescott residents proposed naming the Agua Fria area "Woolsey Valley" after the insolvent rancher left it, though the name did not stick. When her daughter was only five months old, Lucía and Woolsey moved closer to her Rio Yaqui valley home and to the anti-Yaqui hostilities in Sonora that mirrored the anti-Apache sentiments held by Woolsey and his friends in Arizona.[62]

With the majority of his assets dissolved but his social capital undiminished, Woolsey removed his household to the ranch named for nearby hot springs between Phoenix and Yuma along the northern banks of the Gila River. Although now on the northern border of the Sonoran Desert that divided her from the Yaqui hiakim, little changed for Lucía with the move from Agua Fria to Agua Caliente—that is, her life continued to be fraught with attacks from within and without. In January 1868, unidentified Indians raided Woolsey's livestock, but by February he had 140 acres of barley in and was clearing 200 more acres of arable land.[63] He continued his demands on his servant's body, and in 1868 she was pregnant again.[64] She bore her second daughter, Johanna, in 1869 and continued to work at the ranch where Woolsey employed Mexican "black men," "white" Americans, Pee Posh, and O'odham. Now with two infant children, Lucía was even less likely to break loose of her master's grasp.

In October of 1870, though Lucía was heavy with her third child, the demanding Woolsey put his Yaqui girl to the task of guiding an exploratory mining mission through central Arizona. He hoped she had gained some knowledge of the region while under Apache captivity. He packed enough supplies to last at least three months for the fifty men who accompanied him and his captive consort.[65] A month later, a participant reported that "[e]verything was ready for a movement, when the woman who was to guide the party (an Apache captive) was delivered of a child, and was consequently prevented from accompanying the expedition at the promised time, although she was willing to go as soon as she should recover sufficiently."[66] It is difficult to imagine that Lucía agreed to lead a mining expedition expected to last three months when she herself was eight months pregnant and would have had to leave her daughters—Clara, five, and Johanna, three—behind. Her third child, a boy named Robert, was born with a lame foot. Woolsey's contemporaries charged that Robert's handicap might have been reversed under proper medical care that the father neglected to provide. Certainly Woolsey's willingness to push an expectant mother through uncharted territory for three months suggests his disregard for her or the infant's health. Perhaps the opportunity to reenact a Lewis and Clark expedition complete with his own Sacagawea and nursing babe proved too irresistible for him to give up easily.[67]

As Woolsey's mistress, Lucía most likely had the lamentable status of a favored captive among his laborers—all of whom would have been familiar with the gendered and racialized contours of human trafficking in the southwestern borderlands. Woolsey's mastery over Lucía enhanced his reputation for martial manhood among his white peers and marked him as an elite among the Gila River Indians who likewise kept and traded female captives.[68] Lucía's pregnancies, spaced at roughly eighteen-month intervals, were as much proof of the Indian killer's virility as his anti–Apache campaigns. Not one of his contemporaries ever praised him as a father, however, making it difficult to know what sort of status his illegitimate children held on the ranch. Rather than focusing on his paternal qualities, his peers emphasized his manly attributes.

Some Arizonans explicitly admired him: "He is an active man in all positions and places. . . . Col. Woolsey has worked shoulder to shoulder with the miners, farmers, teamsters, and business men. He has worn moccasins and fine boots, overalls and broadcloth, is a man among men."[69] Still others found him downright attractive: "His looks are in his favor—with the ladies, several of whom have adored him for his eyes, nose, or something."[70] Such unabashed affection from his peers might explain why in May 1871, when Woolsey decided to marry Mary H. Taylor, a newcomer to the territory, many of his friends quietly helped him to rid the ranch of his Indian intimates.

The newly arrived Mrs. Woolsey would make her attitudes toward Lucía and her husband's children clear after the patriarch died, but as a new bride she kept her feelings from public record. That she was known as an "unreconstructed rebel" whose family members had been on the Confederate side of the Civil War in Georgia indicates that Woolsey's new wife was no stranger to the antebellum phenomenon of illegitimate children who resembled their masters. Within a month of his marriage, and perhaps at his bride's insistence, the pioneering father sent his dark-skinned daughters to a neighboring ranch and evicted their mother.[71] Seventeen years old and still nursing an illegitimate child when Woolsey and Taylor married, Lucía Martínez remained both vulnerable and valuable when she left the Agua Caliente ranch without her toddler daughters.

By 1871, the Yaqui Wars in Sonora were in full swing, and returning to the hiakim south of the border would have been reckless when so many other of her people were fleeing north. The resourceful mother settled with her infant son in Yuma, a hub that was home to a diverse Indigenous population from Arizona, California, and Sonora, and where she could turn to

two Catholic churches for support to regain custody of and raise her illegitimate family.[72] Young, healthy, and by now well trained to cater to the needs
of the territorial elite, the determined woman had skills that made her an
ideal servant for any respectable Yuma household.

Whether she had chosen the Colorado River town over others in the
Sonoran Desert region is unknown, but in relocating to Yuma, Lucía settled in a town that was attracting other Indigenous refugees as well. Yuma
had, since the Quechan dynasty of the seventeenth and eighteenth centuries, served as a river crossing that connected tribes who traded goods that
came from the Sonoran coastline, California forests, the Great Basin plains,
and the Pueblo villages. The settlement continued to be a major gateway for
Indigenous border crossers seeking work in mines and on railroads or seeking refuge from Mexican and American assaults.

Once they built Fort Yuma, Americans used the town as a major southwestern portal, hauling goods into Arizona Territory on steamboats and fer-
rying goods across the Colorado River for those traveling the Gila Trail that
connected Los Angeles to Tucson. By 1870, the Southern Pacific Railroad
bridged the Colorado, making Yuma Arizona's most significant frontier
crossing. Refugees of the anti-Yaqui campaigns in Sonora built settlements
on Yuma's outskirts that became known as Hollywood, Siva Kova, and
Somerton.[73] Here were survivors who valued Indigenous women's participation in the transmission of culture and independence to their children,
and would come to celebrate heroines like Ricarda Leon Flores, a "principal
defender of Yaqui traditions," who "breastfed dignity to her babies so they
would defend their inherited territory with their blood."[74] Roughly one
hundred miles from the Agua Caliente ranch and nearly six hundred miles
from the redeemed woman's childhood home, Lucía rebuilt a community
for herself within the Yaqui diaspora.[75]

Meanwhile, back at the ranch, the Woolseys might have hoped to begin
their honeymoon without the specter of sex and servitude by ridding themselves of Lucía and her children, but miscegenation and indenture remained
an integral part of their union for the remainder of the decade.[76] Woolsey's
former servant was building a case against her children's father from Yuma.
Although Arizona's territorial code offered little or no way for disfranchised
Indian women like Lucía to protest their treatment at the hands of white
male citizens, Martínez nonetheless managed to find attorneys and friends
willing to pull the threads of sex and servitude that ran through the Howell
Code. Her ability to find legal representation is surprising not only because

she was not a citizen, but also because territorial Arizona jurists worked within a small legal community and knew the men they argued against personally and professionally. Practitioners of law were few in number, and appointed judges often heard federal, county, and appellate cases, representing both local and federal interests even where they conflicted.[77] Despite these factors, Lucía mustered the courage and counsel to face her captor and his friend Judge John T. Alsap in the Maricopa County courthouse and ask that her daughters be returned to her.

On July 29, 1871, just a few months after Mary Taylor and King Woolsey's marriage and almost seven years after Woolsey had abducted Lucía and prevented her from returning home, Martínez's lawyer filed a petition of habeas corpus on her children's behalf. Marcus D. Dobbins, a man who must have been well acquainted with Woolsey since they served as territorial legislators together, represented the distressed mother's claim. The jurist's motives in taking her case are difficult to determine and his compensation for doing so is impossible to ascertain. Perhaps Dobbins and Woolsey had not made friends while working together in the heated halls of Arizona's legislature.

Marcus Dobbins's personal history of Indian relations reveals the distinctions settler-colonists made among Arizona's Indigenous residents as enemies and allies, savage and pacified. In February 1871 he helped compile a report to the federal government on Apache "outrages" against Arizona citizens that was later used to justify the O'odham, Mexican, and American attack on Apaches known as the Camp Grant Massacre in April of that year. Focusing his anti-Indian views on Apaches while supporting O'odham and, through Lucía, Yaqui interests, Dobbins made distinctions among tribes that mirrored those made by other Anglo elites like Woolsey, who fought Apaches, hired O'odham, and fathered Yaquis. That Dobbins chose to represent Lucía's interest against "Mr. King" also indicates that not all white men agreed that their legal and sexual privileges trumped those of Indigenous women—a dispute that recurred in the lives of others chronicled in this book.[78]

Difficult as his motives are to determine, Dobbins stood next to his client in what must have been a very intimidating courtroom. Territorial probate judge John T. Alsap, who owned land near Woolsey's and shared membership with him in the Fraternal Order of Masons, heard the wronged woman's complaints. Lucía's habeas corpus petition charged that her two daughters "were wrongfully in the possession of" their "putative father" and she "pray[ed] that they be restored to her." Marcus Dobbins and his client's choice to use habeas corpus against King S. Woolsey in the summer of 1871 reveals much about the context of Woolsey and Martínez's relationship that contemporary jurists and subsequent biographers chose to ignore. Reading any of the hobbyist histories cited in this chapter will make immediately apparent the romanticization of Woolsey's relationship with Martínez, whom many pioneer historians have strained to depict as the senator's common-law wife by completely disregarding the evidence that suggests otherwise—namely the lawsuits she filed after leaving his ranch, his indenture of her children, and his unwillingness to assist her or the children economically.

The habeas corpus petition indicates that Lucía and her counsel saw her case both as an issue of detainment or imprisonment and as a parental custody issue. Jurists primarily used the writ during this time period on behalf of detained prisoners, but were beginning to view the legal mechanism as a custody tool.[79] Their move also suggests that Dobbins and Martínez sought the intervention of federal jurisdiction into territorial laws that they felt deserved review—such as the minor Indian indenture clause and the nonwhite witness exclusion statute. Their use of the measure also shows that some Arizonans were willing to invite federal scrutiny into the intimate and domestic affairs of territorial families and to challenge the assumption of white patriarchy over Indian women's interests.[80] The lawyer and petitioner may also have been trying to invoke federal guardianship over Indigenous wards, thus hoping to achieve a more beneficent form of paternalism than the one Woolsey practiced. The lack of records describing this case is particularly frustrating, but territorial jurists frequently cited Indians' status as federal rather than territorial subjects in their arguments in cases featuring Indigenous plaintiffs and defendants. This was also a concern for Indian agents unsure of their jurisdiction over off-reservation Indians.

Among other things, the Northwest Ordinance of 1787 promised territorial residents access to habeas corpus and the Howell Code had eliminated peonage, giving Lucía the appropriate legal context to file the petition.[81] In so doing, she challenged her captor's authority to detain her children as his servants and as his progeny. This confrontational action flies in the face of historians' depiction of the Yaqui servant as "Lucy Woolsey," the common-law (and deracialized) wife who conveniently faded into anonymity along with her children once the rancher legitimately and officially married Mary H. Taylor. Had her former master not withheld her daughters from her, Martínez might have gone more quietly to Yuma, but he did and she did not.

In filing a habeas corpus petition, the young mother not only articulated a direct challenge to Woolsey's authority to detain her daughters, she invited federal scrutiny into territorial domestic matters. The Habeas Corpus Act of 1867 "enabled the federal courts to assert their primacy in deciding questions affecting personal liberty."[82] Martínez had at least two reasons to seek federal jurisdiction. First, she might have been anticipating that Woolsey would indenture her children and wanted to challenge the constitutionality of the minor Indian indenture law. Second, Lucía and her children's Indianness not only excluded them from territorial civil courts (which means that Alsap broke federal and territorial protocol when he heard the case), but it made them subject to federal and not local authority. She was also appealing to a federal government that might still be willing to recognize Indian legal rights when the territorial Arizona government was obviously not.[83] In choosing federal over territorial jurisdiction, Lucía sought to overcome mechanisms in the Howell Code that simultaneously obscured and promoted the linkages between sex and servitude. Lucía's habeas corpus petition, then, disputed Woolsey's access to her daughters even though she had been unable to deny him access to her body.

The former captive appeared in the Maricopa County courtroom and the judge arranged for a two-day visit between the young mother and her daughters, who were present under the custody of Maricopa County sheriff, Thomas Barnum—a business partner of Alsap's. When all parties returned to court on July 31, Sheriff Barnum confirmed that the girls had been returned to his custody and that they had previously been living with their father's codefendants, Mr. and Mrs. John Ammerman, who owned 225 acres in the recently formed Phoenix Settlement. The girls' "putative father" requested a postponement of the hearing so he might gather "material witnesses, some of which were in [Maricopa] county and some in Yuma county."[84] The judge granted his fellow Mason's motion, ordering that the children remain in Sheriff Barnum's custody until a hearing on August 30, keeping the distraught mother from her daughters for another month.[85]

Perhaps recognizing that Judge Alsap showed no indication of honoring her habeas corpus petition as an opportunity to critique the minor Indian indenture law or to challenge Woolsey's paternal authority, Martínez and Dobbins changed tactics.[86] She withdrew her request for custody on August 1, 1871, and then signed a contract with her mark that indentured both girls to their father until they reached the age of eighteen, which would be in 1884 for Clara and 1886 for Johanna. "Lucía Martínez of the County of Yuma," gave "King S. Woolsey of the County of Maricopa" "complete and absolute" control over Clara and Johanna Martínez. "The putative father of said children" agreed to provide them with clothing, food, and sustenance, as well as "a good and substantive English education," even though the indenture clause did not require him to do so. Perhaps Dobbins's challenge to Woolsey's paternal authority or Woolsey's desire to demonstrate chivalric paternity to his new bride prompted him to provide his illegitimate daughters with some benefits. Those benefits would not extend to Lucía, however, since the girls' father agreed that their mother could have temporary possession of the children, provided that she pay "all their expenses and out lays" until he resumed custody. Martínez would maintain physical custody of her children for the meantime, though she remained subject to the whims of their elite father and he remained free of any financial or paternal obligations even though he held legal authority over both of his daughters.[87] It seems likely that Woolsey submitted to an informal surrender of custody because of the children's age, young enough to be categorized as dependent upon their mother, and because his recent marriage complicated his ability to maintain interracial intimacies within his household.[88] Allowing Lucía to retain conditional custody enabled Woolsey to uphold his patriarchal authority without contributing to tensions within his state-sanctioned marriage.

The justice system failed Martínez on a variety of counts. Although it is tempting to suggest that Maricopa County jurists conspired against Woolsey's former servant in the interests of white male supremacy alone, it seems more likely that they misunderstood the complex legal issues at hand or were not willing to put jurisprudence before their alliance with Woolsey. In short, Lucía's attorney should not have allowed her to file a petition of habeas corpus in Alsap's probate court and Judge Alsap should have acknowledged that he lacked the authority to hear the motion. The territory's probate courts mediated estate disputes and financial claims, not petitions for federal review of unjust detainment.[89] Hearing Lucía's petition in the Maricopa County probate court indicated either that Woolsey's friends preferred to keep her complaint among themselves and dodge federal intervention, or that they viewed Martínez's children as chattel and interpreted her claim as a property dispute rather than a matter of personal liberty or maternal custody. The former captive and her attorney applied the "great writ" in a way that showed an innovative use of jurisprudence that other women's stories in this book reveal was characteristic of Indigenous women navigating territorial, state, and federal legal regimes; her petition, however, was heard in the wrong venue, and was ultimately quashed. In hearing a motion outside of the proper venue, by failing to acknowledge in writing the racial-ethnic identities visible in court, and in mediating family disputes without acknowledging paternity or sex, Maricopa County jurists obscured the interracial intimacies within their jurisdiction Martínez's petition failed because territorial jurists buried the motion in a legal culture of collusion; historians need not continue that pattern by denying the significance of Indigenous women's challenges to exploitative legal regimes in the North American West.

Occasionally as difficult to interpret as the buzzing of Sonoran trees, the legal records do reveal that the case generated considerable agitation for Woolsey and his friends. Although Alsap denied the Yaqui petitioner access to federal jurisdiction in order to grant Woolsey the favor of his territorial authority, the indenture agreement the three parties signed proves the marker of Indianness that the records fail to disclose in otherwise explicit terms. Racialized language is remarkably absent from the transcripts, but the legal mechanisms at play would not have made sense in regard to a family dispute among white parents over white children. It is through such neutered language that the territorial justice system in Arizona cloaked the linkages between sex and servitude embedded within the Howell Code.[90] Because of the miscegenation laws that barred Lucía from making spousal or paternal claims against him, Woolsey could use his surname to claim his children as chattel without being pressured to claim them as his progeny or heirs. How the new—and state-sanctioned—Mrs. Woolsey felt about sharing her name with her spouse's illegitimate children was not to be disclosed until 1880, just after her husband's death.

Before dismissing Martínez's case as a failure to overturn white supremacist and patriarchal authority in the Sonoran Southwest or as an aberration in territorial Arizona legal history, it is important to note that Lucía succeeded in redeeming her children from indentured servitude on Maricopa County ranches by managing—amazingly—to retain physical, if not legal, custody of them. Lucía continued to exercise maternal authority over her children despite lacking legal authority when the family returned to Yuma. The single mother turned to the Immaculate Conception Church for support and in 1877 she baptized both Clara and Concepción (Johanna)

Clara and Concepción Martínez's baptismal entry (MS 296 Catholic Church, Diocese of Tucson Records, vol. 12: Yuma—Church of the Immaculate Conception, 1866–1880, p. 75, no. 768, September 10, 1877, and no. 769, September 11, 1877; reproduced with permission from University of Arizona Special Collections)

there with Dolores Naldonado and Eulalia Casares serving as witnesses and perhaps comadres (godmothers or co-mothers).[91] Martínez did not name her daughters' father and gave them her maiden name, though the priest listed both of them as legitimate, suggesting that Lucía may have been presenting herself as a widow prior to her encounter with Sheriff Tyner in 1880, or that the priest knew exactly who the children's father was and wanted to provide support without raising questions—a distinct possibility since the editor of the *Arizona Sentinel* would claim just a year later that Yuma residents had been caring for Woolsey's illegitimate family despite his blatant disregard for their welfare.[92]

From the southern to northern boundaries of the Sonoran Desert, the indomitable woman had lived a life of exile characterized by long-distance movements prompted by outsiders. Her life consisted of struggles to protect her body and progeny once she was forcibly removed from her people's lands. She would find in Yuma, however, that she shared many experiences with Yaquis living in an age of Sonoran genocide and Arizona refuge. Sharing many of the struggles that Indigenous mothers faced in diasporic settlements like Yuma, Lucía bore a fourth child (with undocumented paternity) and she remained the head of her own household. As a single, unmarried mother she was similar to other Yaqui women who bore children of multiple fathers, left husbands because of abuse or dissatisfaction, cohabited without marrying, and had multiple partners throughout adulthood. Lucía and her children also used multiple names during their lifetime, a common practice of Indigenous and mestizo Catholics in the southwest. The former slave chose "Lucía Martínez" as her legal identity in documents that survived her, though others referred to her as Lucille and Lucy. All of her children alternated between the surnames Woolsey and Martínez, though in legal documents their mother witnessed they were named Martínez, an indication of her matrilineal concerns. Other than Clara, the mestizo children's given names changed repeatedly. Second-born Johanna was baptized as Concepción, a name she continued to use as an adult, but her mother also referred to her as Joseta. Robert seems to have become Joseph and then José.[93] Like other displaced Yaquis, the family continued to take multiple given names and surnames into the twentieth century, for both personal and political reasons, making it difficult for modern descendants to trace their histories to the age of Yaqui diaspora in the U.S.-Mexico borderlands.[94]

Between 1871 and 1878, the resourceful woman managed to keep herself and her children out of the public eye, though Woolsey's political cachet continued to grow in territorial Arizona. With Lucía on his ranch, he had served in the legislature for Yavapai County in the first and second sessions. His 1867 relocation from Agua Fria to Agua Caliente distracted him from politics but after he reestablished himself as a savvy rancher and entrepreneur with a respectable wife, he served as Maricopa County representative in the seventh, eighth, and ninth sessions—as council president in the last two—between 1872 and 1878.[95]

While he represented his neighbors' interests in the territorial council, the legislator also saw to his own concerns, increasing agricultural output at his Agua Caliente ranch and expanding operations to Stanwix Station, established in the 1850s as a stop on the Butterfield Overland Trail about eighty miles east of Yuma along the Gila River.[96] Just as Lucía's labors aided Woolsey's financial and political interests by allowing him to host elite guests and provide for a troop of laborers, Mrs. Woolsey served her husband's goals by working the Stanwix operation mostly without her husband. While Woolsey attended to his political affairs, he also oversaw his crops and occasionally chased down Indians. Without children to take up her time, Mary Taylor Woolsey ran the general merchandising store her husband had built at Stanwix and "supplied foodstuffs to practically all travelers."[97] The Southern belle turned settler-colonist sold eggs, butter, grains, and produce

from her own and neighboring farms. Chroniclers credited her with importing "the first bees ever brought into Arizona," and she sold honey to
Gila River residents and passers through.[98]

As Mary Woolsey offered sweets and supplies, she often found herself the sole proprietor at Stanwix Station and she earned a reputation as
a woman who could hold her own. Twice she defended her station at gunpoint, likely well trained by her Confederate brothers and filibustering husband. In the first incident, she reportedly outdrew a Mexican intending to
rob her store, admitting later that she "was afraid the gun would discharge."
When another "hard case" tried to pilfer goods in her store, she came out
of the back room with her .45 revolver drawn and made him empty his
pockets before leaving. Her peers remembered Woolsey's wife as a woman
who worked hard and expected the same of those around her, much like
her husband. "Many a time she has gotten up at midnight and cooked us
something to eat when we have come in after chasing Indians. Woolsey was
pretty sharp, but she was sharper."[99] Mary Woolsey proved well equipped
to manage a household built on the social, economic, and political privileges
gained through Indian killing.

Mrs. Woolsey's unflinching nerve and keen intuition undoubtedly affected her husband's behavior toward the Martínez family. Certainly Lucía
and her son Robert's departure from Agua Caliente within a month of
Mary's arrival and King Woolsey's decision to put his daughters into service at the nearby Ammerman ranch around the same time show signs of
her influence. The indenture document that quashed Lucía's habeas corpus
petition referred to the westering man as Clara and Johanna's "putative
father" and failed to mention Robert at all; further signs that the Southern woman would not tolerate ambiguous paternity where her husband was
concerned.

Perhaps it was out of respect for Woolsey's wife that territorial newspapers observed silence regarding his Yaqui family throughout the 1870s.
The Woolseys appeared often in regional papers as they made a name for
themselves as one of territorial Arizona's most respected families. The frontier southerners enjoyed prosperous ranching and retail profits and joined a
number of partnerships in development ventures.[100] In 1874, Woolsey and
his laborers arrested and killed a Mexican suspected of murder on their
Agua Caliente ranch, earning accolades from concerned citizens.[101] The
couple attended an 1875 camp meeting where he delivered an address entitled "No Man Knoweth When the Son of Man Cometh," though there is

no other indication of his spiritual pursuits.[102] Once the senator announced his bid to become territorial delegate to Congress in the spring of 1878, however, the media broke their courteous silence and forced Mrs. Woolsey to reexamine her husband's premarital intimacies.

Although newspapers in Florence, Phoenix, and Prescott endorsed Woolsey's campaign for congressional delegate, the *Arizona Sentinel* in Yuma opposed him vehemently. Woolsey had opposed politicians from Yuma in the past, characterizing their representatives as Catholic Hispanics not qualified for membership among Arizona's Anglo political elite.[103] Under the headline, "Bound to Destroy Himself," the weekly publication first denounced Woolsey in an article on May 25, 1878, just after he had announced his candidacy. Among other things, the editor tarnished the rancher's reputation as "the Slayer-of-Indians (of assorted ages and sexes)" and questioned Woolsey's standing as a "good Democrat" by alleging that he "could betray the South for money."[104] Throughout the summer months of 1878, the Yuma paper released a series of articles accusing the dubious hero of incompetence, duplicity, and selfishness while other papers—most notably the *Weekly Arizona Miner* in Prescott—defended and championed the rancher as one of Arizona's most notable and respected pioneers. The *Sentinel*'s critique of Woolsey's personal and political, racial and gendered violence coincided with increasing tensions among Hispanic and Anglo elites that marked particular cities like Yuma and Tucson as marginally white, while cities like Prescott and Phoenix touted a form of Yankee whiteness that would become more important in the campaign for Arizona statehood, which required achieving a satisfactorily "American" and "white" population.[105]

As the election drew closer, the *Sentinel*'s attacks centered on the politician's illegitimate daughters. The editor suggested that the candidate's concern for his children's welfare was motivated by his interest in office: "Woolsey's children have derived some benefit from that gentleman's candidacy for Congress. For the past six or seven years they and their mother have lived here, assisted by friends and strangers. Since Col. Woolsey became a candidate for Congress he has allowed them a monthly stipend." The Yuma paper expressed concern for Lucía's children should Woolsey's campaign fail: "If Col. Woolsey is not a popular candidate in Yuma, it is partly so because people here think that a man who 'throws off' on his children may also neglect his constituents. Let us hope their stipend will not be cut off after the election."[106] Legal claims filed after Woolsey's death in

1880 show that the "stipend" he provided did not subsidize Lucía's upkeep of their children, but removed his daughters from their maternal home and placed them in a Catholic boarding school.

The *Sentinel* editorial of October 5, 1878, outed the patriarch for abandoning his children and their mother, but stopped short of revealing the interracial nature of his indiscretions and allowed the Martínez family to remain somewhat anonymous—and racially ambiguous—by not including names. The specter of interracial intimacy behind such silences would have been apparent to local readers familiar with Woolsey's frontier indiscretions. The indenture record King S. and Lucía had signed in 1871 made Martínez responsible for the children's support while they remained in her custody, and this 1878 article confirmed that the single mother depended on others for assistance in Yuma after she left Agua Caliente. Although the report did not explain who befriended the refugee family or how they had survived for seven years, the piece suggested that they had been known in Yuma as Woolsey's dependents and that local residents expected the notorious candidate to uphold his paternal obligations long after the campaign. Beyond its political critique of Woolsey's candidacy, the editorial also suggests that not all Arizonans agreed that Native mothers' rights should be so easily diminished.

Although other papers had not found it an appropriate item to include in their commendations, Woolsey had in fact begun paying for Clara and Johanna's care in July of 1878 just as the *Sentinel* reported—though Lucía paid the price of separation from her daughters in return. The superior of the Convent of Sisters of St. Joseph, who knew the girls as Clara and Concepción Woolsey, testified that their father had placed them under her care in Yuma. The candidate reportedly authorized the nuns to tutor and care for his daughters at his expense, though no arrangements were made for Robert and his mother, who had renamed her oldest son Joseph and had borne her second son, Louis, to an unnamed father in 1873.[107] Lucía's resistance to her daughters' removal to the Catholic boarding school is evidenced in the case that she would file against their father's estate after his death.

Throughout the 1870s, Woolsey's former servant had quietly managed her difficulties in Yuma. She revealed nothing about her youngest child's paternity and did not respond publicly to the editorial that exposed her dependent condition—even if she was not literate, her implied linkage to the territorial politician in the local paper could not have escaped her knowledge. Perhaps Lucía believed that openly voicing her tribulations would jeopardize her tenuous custody of the children since their father held legal custody. Martínez's silence did not indicate that she had yielded to patriarchal or white supremacist authority, however. Her reliance on the charity of Yuma residents had not reduced her ability to protect the children she had borne under duress and hardship. Although she had lost her daughters in July 1878, Lucía regained custody within a year and firmly established their paternity, if not their legitimacy, for anyone who cared to notice.

After losing his bid to be territorial delegate to Congress in November 1878, the girls' father returned to business as usual at his Agua Caliente ranch. Woolsey and his laborers put in the winter wheat crop, and in the spring of 1879 he purchased seventy-five head of cattle.[108] He did not live to reap the fruits of his laborers' labors, however. On June 29, 1879, he died unexpectedly at his Lyle ranch property near Phoenix.[109] Apparently unconcerned with his own mortality, Woolsey died intestate, leaving his friends in the Maricopa County probate court to interpret his intentions and obligations toward Lucía and her children, and to protect the interests of his bereaved widow.

When her husband died, Mrs. Woolsey acquired the rights to administer his estate and set to work having his properties appraised and his debts reconciled. Laborers and merchants came forth immediately, claiming payment owed for services rendered and showing itemized bills for materials sold on credit. Among those who submitted claims on the rancher's estate were Mother Superior Marguerit Croisat and Sister Mary Monica of St. Joseph's in Yuma, who showed an itemized bill for $183.17 to cover the care of Clara and Concepción Woolsey from April to June 1879. Their claim, entered on July 21, 1879, opened the door for the determined mother to introduce the interests of her children in Woolsey's estate, and she again recruited a neighbor from Yuma.

Lucía lived just a few blocks from Henry S. Fitzgerald. Congress appointed the immigrant from England postmaster at Yuma in 1874 and he used the appointment to draw business to his already successful general store. Fitzgerald was a popular sort of man whose general merchandise store offered Yumans regular mail service and quality whiskey—frontier essentials indeed.[110] The 1880 census shows the Fitzgerald and Martínez families living near each other on Yuma's Main Street, a vital thoroughfare only seven blocks long near the railroad depot. The Fitzgerald home sat "in the swankiest neighborhood in Yuma" among other local elites; the census record notes a preponderance of Indians in the surrounding blocks, suggesting that domestic and manual laborers like Lucía would not have been hard to come by for Yuma's notable families.[111] Although records are silent on the exact relationship Fitzgerald and Martínez shared, the skills she developed on Woolsey's ranches would have made her an ideal servant in his household.

Like Martínez's attorney in the 1871 habeas corpus petition, Fitzgerald shared connections with King S. Woolsey. Judge Alsap, who had dismissed Lucía's habeas corpus petition and shared a close friendship with Woolsey, had presided over the postmaster's 1874 wedding.[112] Throughout the 1870s, the Yuma merchant cosigned a number of bonds and served as witness to oaths of office with David Neahr, one of Woolsey's business partners.[113] On December 13, 1879, Fitzgerald filed a petition before the Maricopa County probate court as the children's guardian ad litem and asked that Clara, Johanna, and Robert be recognized as heirs of the deceased and provided a monthly allowance of seventy-five dollars from their father's estate, as well as a homestead chosen from Woolsey's vast real estate holdings.

Woolsey's "sharp" widow denied vehemently that the children were her husband's heirs.[114] She claimed that, in spite of the indenture contract, Woolsey had never acknowledged or adopted the children and she argued that his inaction made them illegitimate heirs. Such a tactic did not allow the respectable woman to avoid discussions of her husband's premarital indiscretions; she soon had to face his improprieties head-on.

While the 1871 habeas corpus petition indicated that Lucía had no desire to make spousal claims against her former master, her suit eight years later suggested that she had reconsidered her legal strategy. Previously Martínez had been as reticent as Woolsey to acknowledge his paternity of her children, but when she sought an inheritance for Clara, Johanna (Concepción)—and, this time, Robert as well—Lucía inverted the logic Maricopa County jurists had used to deny her habeas corpus petition (that it was an issue of chattel or kinship and under the purview of the probate court) and attempted to use it against the Woolsey estate. Perhaps when the father of her children visited Yuma in July 1878 and put Clara and Concepción in the care of the nuns at St. Joseph's Indian School and orphanage, he gave his former servant no more reason to obscure the ties of sex and servitude that had bound her to him.[115] Whatever her reasons, she put everything on the table when he died less than a year after taking her daughters from her and left no will to definitively acknowledge or deny his status as "the putative father of said children." Lucía's attorney asked the probate court to make Woolsey financially accountable for the legal authority his paternity had granted him in the 1871 indenture bond. Would judges agree that Woolsey had to pay for his patriarchal privileges?

The short answer is no. The long answer is that territorial jurists defined sex with Indigenous servants as a form of extralegal cohabitation unworthy of inheritance and defined monoracial marriage as a state-sanctioned contract or economic transaction worthy of financial settlement. The woman who had twice wielded a gun to defend her property eventually admitted that her deceased husband had cohabited with Lucía Martínez prior to their marriage and that the unsanctioned union had produced the children Fitzgerald represented. Stressing not only that territorial miscegenation laws invalidated Woolsey and his consort's cohabitation, the determined widow argued that the captive's Yaqui identity made the children illegitimate because Arizona's inheritance laws classified mestizo children as illegitimate.[116] The language used by the widow's attorney is clear, if repetitive:

> About the latter part of the year 1865 or the beginning of the year 1866 King S Woolsey now deceased without being lawfully married and without any marriage contract began to live in unlawful and illegal cohabitation with a Jaqui Indian woman commonly called "Lucy," that he continued to so live or cohabit with her until about the summer of the year 1869 when the said illegal relationship between them ceased and was never thereafter resumed. That the said Woolsey was never at any time married to said woman Lucy and all of his transactions with her were unauthorized and unsanctioned by the bonds of wedlock or marriage; that the said minors were as the administratrix is informed born of said woman Lucy during such unlawful cohabitation and are therefore illegitimate children; that King S Woolsey after their birth nor at any time [illegible word] never did intermarry with their mother Lucy.[117]

Using a timeline that ensured no suspicion of overlap between Woolsey's sexual relationships with Martínez and Taylor, the attorney went on to stress with continued redundancy that Woolsey at no point acknowledged his illegitimate children "with intent and for the purpose of making them or either of them his heir or heirs at law."[118] Woolsey's actions suggested that indeed he had never intended to acknowledge Clara or Johanna as his legitimate children and so the widow's attorney made a sound argument. The court endorsed the territory's amalgamation laws banning miscegenation and in 1881, the bereaved and childless widow won full inheritance rights against her husband's children. The court's ruling against Lucía in this suit was very straightforward in following the Howell Code's antimiscegenation provisions and statutes barring illegitimate progeny from heirship, but Woolsey's extralegal family did not give up.

Likely expecting Martínez would be barred from making a civil claim because of her Indianness, Fitzgerald stood in as her children's legal guardian and asked $75 a month from Woolsey's estate for their support. The court rejected their request and upheld the widow Woolsey's claim as his only legitimate heir. Still convinced that her family deserved some form of legal acknowledgment, however, the single mother directed Fitzgerald toward the indenture bond that she, Woolsey, and Judge Alsap had signed in the very same court nine years earlier. Fitzgerald countered the loss of their inheritance claim with a new claim on the 1871 indenture bond against Woolsey's estate, filed in DeForest Porter's second judicial district court rather than the Maricopa County probate court, thus appealing to a higher jurisdictional authority than the one occupied by Woolsey's circle of friends.

And so it turned out that the indenture record that Lucía and Woolsey had signed almost a decade earlier would benefit Clara and Johanna. In binding his daughters, Woolsey had made himself responsible for their educational and material support until they each reached age eighteen; he put up a thousand-dollar bond to cover the costs. In fact, Woolsey had acted exceptionally when he filed one thousand dollars in support of his bond indenturing his daughters. Other indentures of minor Indians were filed with no financial backing or as little as forty dollars.[119] These varying and often negligible amounts seem to have been at the discretion of the judge, though they might also have been a reflection of the indenture holders' financial worth. As such, securing one thousand dollars for his daughters' indenture may have allowed Woolsey to advertise his fiscal solvency just four years after he had declared bankruptcy.[120] The financial commitment may also have helped Woolsey to resolve any personal concerns regarding his paternal commitment to the daughters—a difficult explanation to accept given an unwillingness to establish support for his son. Regardless of the motives and factors shaping the decision he made in 1871, once deceased, Woolsey forfeited the bond and gave Martínez an opportunity to make good on the indenture she had granted under pressure from Maricopa County jurists. Through indenture rather than inheritance, attorneys managed to extract a settlement of one thousand dollars for the mixed-race girls.[121]

Just as Alsap's counterstrategy to Lucía's habeas corpus petition in 1871 had been a sophisticated misapplication of jurisprudence, when he faced Fitzgerald's charge on the indenture bond he signed, Alsap feigned ignorance. The man who had once manufactured a ruling in his friend's favor and had served as a fellow Mason with the deceased patriarch stood again in opposition to Woolsey's captive mistress. Now litigating his friend's estate, Alsap and his colleague M. W. Kales filed to dismiss the daughters' claim on the grounds that the plaintiffs lacked a crucial piece of evidence—the original 1871 bond that Alsap administered had been lost and the former judge now claimed that it had never existed at all.[122]

In no uncertain terms, Clara and Johanna's attorneys argued that to rule against them would be a miscarriage of justice. They came very close to suggesting that Justice Hancock, who had initially denied the girls' inheritance claim against the widow Woolsey, had acted as incompetently as Alsap: "Wm A Hancock, the Hon Probate Judge of said Maricopa County in the successor of the said John T Alsap, in office, and trustee in said Bond [of indenture] refuses and declines, to initiate proceedings therein, for the benefit of plaintiffs [Clara and Johanna], . . . by their . . . guardian ad litum [Fitzgerald] [who demands] judgment against defendant."[123] Such collusion among Maricopa County probate judges justified the appeal to Judge Porter's district court jurisdiction.

In what must have been a heated moment in the Phoenix courtroom, Clara and Johanna's legal team produced a copy of the 1871 indenture bond in time to circumvent Alsap and his team's motion to dismiss the claim. In light of such indisputable evidence, the judge ruled in favor of the Woolsey girls after eighteen months of hearings.[124] According to local newspaper editors, "[t]he little Woolsey children, after a hard fight at Phoenix, have at last recovered the small allowance of $400."[125] The sympathetic report reveals that lawyer fees took up more than half of the one thousand dollar judgment in the girls' favor. Judge DeForest Porter gave the Sisters of St. Joseph legal custody of Woolsey's daughters, though their mother again managed to retain physical custody of the children with the Sisters' permission. As in her encounter with the law in 1871, the determined mother achieved a truncated victory in 1881: she had physical custody, but not control.

That the judge denied Martínez legal custody of her children indicates that Arizona's territorial justice system continued to devalue maternal authority and Indigenous family structures. Members of the legal community likewise continued to use coded language that obscured the racial and sexual aspects of Lucía's persistent efforts to assert punitive claims against her former master. At no point did jurists mention the children's mixed-race status, though it was exactly their Indigenous identity that made them subject to the indenture bond and ineligible as heirs in the first place. Although lawyers referred to the daughters as "the natural children of the defendant intestate" and once again called King S. Woolsey "the putative father of said children," jurists remained silent regarding the obvious connections between Lucía's servitude, the sexual relationship she had with Woolsey, and the progeny that he indentured. It is such silences that make the critical legal scholar's work more difficult; these silences make up the "acts of forgetfulness" that haunt Indigenous women and their descendants by obscuring their struggles in the historical record.

With her difficult past revealed, it might be easier to understand the lies Lucía told Sheriff Tyner when he came to her door in 1880 to ask personal questions about a household being disputed in Maricopa County court. Knowing what we do about her struggles to maintain custody of her children, it is perhaps no surprise that Martínez described herself as a Mexican widow with legitimate children, even if she had no legal claims to such status. Lucía's transformation from Yaqui to Mexican, a relatively common transition for Indigenous women living in Yuma, made her children white, rather than Indian or mestizo, and therefore liberated them from the state-sanctioned Indian labor market even if not ensuring their equality among Anglo whites. This practice was not uncommon for Indigenous refugees in the late nineteenth century, since legal whiteness had significant benefits and did not have to entail a suppression of cultural Indianness, particularly for Catholic Yaquis who had successfully integrated Catholic and tribal identities for centuries. Although American Anglos hardly recognized Mexican American equality, in spite of the Treaty of Guadalupe Hidalgo's granting of both citizenship and whiteness to Mexican Americans in 1848, Martínez found it beneficial to don Mexican whiteness because it meant protecting herself and her children from continued exploitation as Indians in a territory that continued to claim Indigenous women and children's productive and reproductive labors. Arizona's Indian Wars were still in full swing in

1880, and achieving any semblance of non-Indianness likely promised the Martínez family a cloak of security in that tumultuous world.

In lieu of legal legitimacy for her children, Martínez had sought spiritual legitimacy and on September 10, 1877, she had her daughters baptized as Clara and Concepción Martínez at the Immaculate Conception Church in Yuma.[126] On March 18, 1882, Lucía baptized a third daughter, two day-old Maria, and Clara Woolsey stood as her sister's godmother. Their mother's passing is not recorded in Arizona's historic or vital records, but Lucía's children recorded their ties to the Catholic Church even as they moved to the Phoenix area in adulthood. By the end of the nineteenth century, each of them dropped the Martínez surname and took on their father's name in defiance of the judicial ruling that they were not King S. Woolsey's heirs.

On April 8, 1885, Father Bloise of St. Mary's in Phoenix joined Clara Woolsey and Julio Marron in marriage. By 1901, King S. Woolsey's eldest daughter had lost five children in infancy, but had managed to keep four alive. Her younger siblings followed Clara to the Phoenix area, and Mrs. Marron served as the informant on both of her brothers' death certificates in 1907 and 1913. Concepción died in Phoenix in 1912, widowing her husband Juan M. Vega with seven children. When Clara died in 1947, she had lost her husband and two sons, but was survived by three daughters and seven grandchildren—one of whom has a daughter practicing law today in Tucson, Arizona. In their various birth and death certificates, King Woolsey's children appeared as both "white" and "Mexican," but never "Indian," demonstrating the social frailty of the court decision that classified them as illegitimate Yaqui descendants of the famous Indian killer. These vital records likewise show that the borderlands family celebrated marriages and births, mourned stillbirths and the loss of loved ones, balancing the fine lines between blessing and tragedy that characterized the Yaqui world at the turn of the twentieth century.[127]

Lucía's children's transformation from Martínez to Woolsey within a lifetime echoed a shift in Yaqui claims to whiteness and citizenship in territorial Arizona. Their story, perfectly compelling as the narrative of a pioneer family in America's borderlands, can only be pieced together using faith in marginalized women's presence in archival records, imagination to bridge the gaps between documentary silences, and skepticism toward simplistic historical narratives that obscure Indigenous women's struggles. The evidence that can be found using these affective methodologies constitutes the

Clara Woolsey Marron and grandson Robert Marron Romero, 1937 (Romero family private collection; reproduced with permission from Robert and Viola Romero)

logic that drives the poetics and politics of Indigenous women's legal histories. Despite the prolific biographies of great men and their wives compiled in Arizona's historical institutions, Lucía Martínez's legacy as one willing to challenge the white supremacist and patriarchal presumptions of men like Woolsey and his westering friends has been buried in the annals of frontier boosterism and Indian fighting. As recently as 2013, popular historian Al Bates briefly chronicled her tale, under the headline "Lucy Martinez's Love Story," and concluded that of the lessons drawn from her experiences we can only say, "¿quién sabe?"—who knows?[128] More than a good story, however, her ability to challenge the laws that ensconced patriarchy and white supremacy in the territory deserve our attention. "¿Quién sabe?" Well, historians can know much if they are able to recover marginalized women's voices in repositories of the state and comprehend the intricacies of the legal strategies practiced by Indigenous women who translate both talking trees and legal codes.

CHAPTER 3

Nora Jewell "In Family Way"
Washington, 1854–1910

On February 24, 1880, the fourteen-year-old orphan daughter of a British Columbian Native mother and Danish immigrant father stood before her court-appointed guardian and accused him of repeatedly raping her in the marshy fields of central San Juan Island. A grand jury of twelve men, directed by Judge Roger S. Greene, District Attorney Irving Ballard, and defense attorneys Jacobs and Bradshaw, heard Nora Jewell's tragic story corroborated and contested by witnesses for and against her guardian for the next two days.[1]

The testimony revealed a constrained social world for the mixed-race girl who had grown up amid intercultural and transnational families like her own in the San Juan Island border region. A local newspaper reported that "the Territory prosecuted Jas. Smith, of San Juan Co., on an indictment for an alleged rape upon the person of Norah Jewett [*sic*], a half-breed girl. The jury acquitted Mr. Smith. The case excited considerable interest . . . Another heavy bill of costs for San Juan county."[2] Readers in eastern Washington opened pages to another casting of the trial in the *Spokane Times*, which reported on the "case of rape in San Juan county where the lawful guardian of a 'half-breed' girl aged thirteen or fourteen years, accomplished her ruin. Probably the worst feature in the case is the fact that the brute is still allowed his liberty."[3] Although period observers noted sardonically and skeptically the trial's outcome in 1880, subsequent chroniclers of the region have been as apt to overlook Nora Jewell and her encounter with Washington Territory's legal and social hierarchies as Arizona historians have been

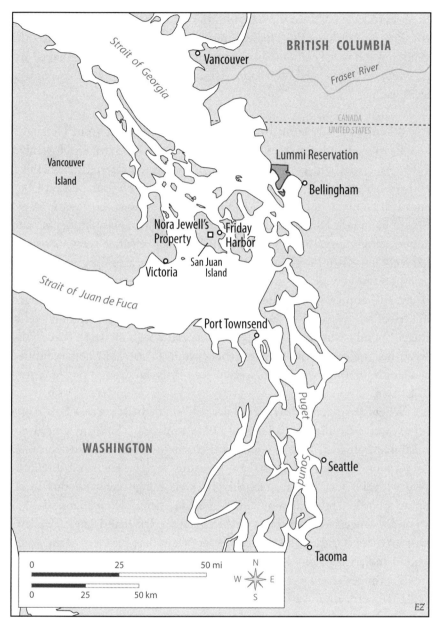

Nora Jewell's Salishan borderlands (Map by Ezra Zeitler)

to obscure Lucía Martínez's struggles to protect her body and progeny in the Sonoran borderlands. This chapter focuses on Nora's story to chart the gendered and racial contours of change and transformation that shaped Indigenous women's legal philosophies and their encounters with territorial legal regimes.[4]

When Nora was born to Peter Jewell, an immigrant from Denmark, and Fanny, an Indigenous woman from British Columbia, in November 1866, American and British troops occupied the southern and northern ends of her island, defending their settler-colonial interests in Salish territory.[5] The Oregon Treaty of 1846 had left ambiguous the aquatic Puget Sound boundaries dividing the San Juan Island chain between British and American territory. Coast Salish people had long relied on seasonal fishing harvests along San Juan Island's southwest point, an area Americans would call the Salmon Bank and use alongside their Salish neighbors into the early twentieth century, when industrial techniques and imperial attitudes edged out tribal fishery practices. Because Coast Salish peoples still dominated the Puget Sound island chain in 1845, the international boundary proved relatively insignificant to the earliest settler-colonists, many of whom identified as Danish, German, Irish, Norwegian, and Prussian rather than American or British.[6]

When Washington Territory was established in 1853, Coast Salish and other Native families and a handful of Hudson's Bay Company employees inhabited San Juan Island, which was closer to the British settlement of Victoria on Vancouver Island than it was to the U.S. mainland. Preoccupied with the business of establishing a territorial government and developing a borderlands economy, few American settler-colonial families — or troops — concerned themselves with regulating San Juan Island. The laws written to limit Indian and white interactions in the aftermath of the Puget Sound Indian Wars of 1855–1856, however, would affect interracial families like the Jewells, who lived extralegal lives on San Juan Island.[7]

Five years after Washington Territory was carved out from the northern portions of Oregon Territory in 1853, about two dozen Americans lived on San Juan Island as farmers and fishermen, joining British subjects who worked a sheep farm and maintained Hudson's Bay Company interests on the island, still claimed by Salishan peoples living and harvesting there seasonally. In June of 1858, an American killed a British-owned pig, unleashing the "Pig War" on San Juan Island. American and British politicians used the incident to justify military occupation of the island, which both nations claimed as their own in light of the vague boundaries established in the Oregon Treaty. Soldiers remained in British Camp on the northwestern end of the island until 1873, though no troops fired shots during the fifteen-year standoff and American legislators carried on as if San Juan Island belonged indisputably to Washington Territory and not British Columbia.[8]

Aged fifteen at the outbreak of the Pig War, Fanny must have held her own opinions about newcomers' legal title to the island, but since Pig War events did not threaten her own occupancy, she had no reason—and as a noncitizen, no venue—to air those beliefs. Whether Fanny was born on the island or not is impossible to determine, since records describe her only as an Indian born in British Columbia around 1843—when Indian, British, and American empires still shared the Pacific Northwest and boundaries proved liminal.[9] Other Indigenous women on San Juan Island had come from as far as Alaska through an expansive network of slavery and kinship similar to the intertribal and international web of economic and emotional ties that Lucía Martínez navigated in the Sonoran Southwest. Fanny's younger sister Ellen also lived on the island with her, suggesting that the siblings had local family ties and were not transported to the island through coercive means like other Indigenous women they knew.

Still, were Fanny and Ellen from elsewhere in the vast Coast Salish region, they could easily have maintained kinship networks throughout the island chain and coast on both sides of the international border, since important tribal and settler-colonial settlements were within rowing distance of San Juan Island and marine traffic accelerated throughout their adult lives. Twentieth-century Lummi elders described their childhood in the island chain, when they called newcomer Americans Xwenitem, and continued to maintain traditional subsistence and spiritual practices despite interference from settler-colonial residents who demanded food, labor, and land. Some Lummi remembered that Xwenitem also demanded Salishan women, explaining that "[the] white men never brought their womens along when they came to this country. The white men comes by themselves. They look for Indian womens. That's why there were so many Indian womens married to white men." Many described international and interracial family trees that crossed the Canadian and American borders on the mainland and throughout the island chain. Clearly, Fanny and her sister's families typified the Salishan experience in the second half of the nineteenth century. It would be Nora Jewell who would have to navigate those racial and political crossings into the twentieth century.[10]

In addition to being home to interrelated Salishan band members who trafficked the island chain for seasonal harvests and ceremonial gatherings, the late 1850s brought travelers from all over the world through her people's waters and to their shores. The island community maintained regular travel to British settlements at Victoria and Vancouver, as well as American port towns like Bellingham, Anacortes, and Port Townsend, in vessels ranging from hand-hewn canoes and rowboats to sloops, schooners, and ferries. The 1849 gold rush in California had lured many fortune seekers to the Pacific Coast, and for those who had failed to capitalize on the quick flash in the California pan, the Fraser River gold rush of 1858 offered a second chance. Many of the men drawn to mineral wealth north of the U.S.-Canadian border would find no gold, of course, and a handful of those disappointed panners sought land titles through donation lands and homestead claims offered in Washington Territory.[11]

Although British and American soldiers stood guard on opposite ends of the island throughout the 1860s, transnational residents traded with and toasted one another in promiscuous disregard of national and racial identity. Elite colonial observers attributed intimate interracial encounters to a proclivity for drunken rowdiness among Indians and immigrants alike, while others suggested that islanders enjoyed raucous celebrations of their hard work and that bachelor citizens naturally sought the company of Native women while white women remained rare. Conservative and Victorian descriptions of racial and sexual dynamics on San Juan Island may not accurately express the attitudes and expectations of men who had traveled the world and seen interracial and intercultural intimacies throughout the British and American empires, or of women accustomed to intermarrying among bands throughout the vast Coast and Inland Salish territories prior to European and American interventions.[12]

For those wayward travelers who settled on San Juan Island in the 1850s and 1860s, Indigenous women like Fanny and Ellen proved ideal domestic partners and their unions should not be so easily dismissed as the remnants of fur trade and gold rush moral laxity. Newcomer men who married Native women benefited from their access to local economic and political networks, extensive knowledge of natural and seasonal resources throughout the maritime region, and gendered work ethic that valued women's productive and reproductive labors in household economies. Despite the laws that invalidated Indian and white marriages, thus making Native women vulnerable to abuse and abandonment, and laws subsidizing white male ownership of territorial lands to the detriment of female Indians, newcomer husbands like Nora's father might have recognized their utter dependence on women like Fanny. After all, immigrant men on the island defied antimiscegenation statutes, bequeathed property to mixed-race progeny, and encouraged métis (Indian-white) families to intermarry with those who continued to make fresh arrivals on San Juan Island shores throughout the 1870s and 1880s.[13]

Perhaps then when seventeen-year-old Ellen took up housekeeping with Frederick Jones (who had come from Holstein, now northern Germany) as late as 1862 and nineteen-year-old Fanny coupled with Peter Jewell of Denmark as late as 1865, these sisters were simply expanding their own intimate access to the transnational Puget Sound economy and anchoring their claims to land and kin on San Juan Island. Certainly they were choosing to follow the course of many Indigenous women in the region when they made their homes with emigrant farmers. Although the Jones and Jewell families are not widely known among current San Juan Islanders and historical accounts seem to have missed them, a number of interracial, or métis, families rose to prominence in local history. For instance, when Anna Pike's Tsimshian family arrived for the annual salmon harvest in 1861, she married German immigrant Christopher Rosler, who had just been discharged from service at the American Camp. The Roslers developed a productive homestead remembered for Anna's flowers, and their métis children married into other pioneering San Juan Island families into the twentieth century. Patrick Beigin of Ireland married Haida woman Lucy Morris around the same time and the family became known for hosting large parties for friends and family as late as World War I. In 1870, when Nora's family first appeared in the U.S. census, enumerator Edward Eldridge also recorded nine other Indigenous women married to white men, one Native woman married to a black man from Canada, and six families headed by Kanaka (Hawaiian) men and Indian women, most of whom probably lived in the area called Kanaka Bay on the southern end of the island. These sixteen métis families constituted a significant proportion of the civilian population—just under three hundred people—and Nora would have grown up among cousins and friends whose households were much like her own.[14]

Although born under the shadow of an international boundary dispute, Nora seems to have enjoyed a rather ordinary homesteading childhood. Her mother, Fanny, bore two other daughters in the 1860s: Roma in 1868 and Eliza in 1869. Less than four miles from the Jewell farm, Nora's aunt Ellen had a daughter Jennie in 1862 and a son George in 1867. Prior to 1873, when the island dispute ended through German mediation, San Juan Island families enjoyed limited interventions from territorial or federal governments, though without bureaucratic practices such as elections, probates, or taxation, fewer records were kept and the early years in Nora Jewell's life are difficult to describe. Before the establishment of San Juan County on October 31, 1873, residents fell under the jurisdictions of Island County, Jefferson County, or Whatcom County, depending on the year and type of legal or personal business. Once the island became its own county, residents could begin the business of collecting taxes and building infrastructure that would benefit the economic interests of families like Fanny and Ellen's. During summer months as they grew older, Nora and her cousins might have attended school a little more than three miles away on Portland Fair Hill. Certainly during other parts of the year she helped her mother and father on their 160-acre farm in the central portion of the island, valued in 1870 at six hundred dollars. Perhaps Nora and her mother Fanny visited Salish kin throughout Puget Sound between fall harvests and spring planting.[15]

San Juan Island men demonstrated their esteem for Peter Jewell when they elected him road supervisor for San Juan County road district no. 2 sometime between 1873 and 1874. Nora's father monitored and maintained road conditions throughout the district, a job that would have made him well known among neighboring families. His duties also included assessing and overseeing labor dues from able-bodied men over the age of twenty-one, expected to work two days a year on public roads or pay a road tax in their stead. In November 1874, Peter Jewell was working to collect road labor from neighboring men late into the fall. When he approached the property of John Keddy, a farmer from Canada, Jewell found the well-to-do man away for business in Victoria on nearby Vancouver Island. In anticipation of the road supervisor's visit, Keddy had informed his farmhands Joe Bull, John Ritchinman, and C. Nisson to serve as his agents and perform his road labors for him. According to Keddy and his employees, Jewell refused to accept Keddy's arrangement, and the road supervisor seized one of Keddy's cows and sold it for eight dollars to Robert Douglas in order to cover Keddy's 1874 road tax.[16]

John Keddy filed a civil suit against Peter Jewell in March of 1875 that seems to have sparked the Jewell family's ruin. With witnesses overwhelmingly in the plaintiff's favor, which is not surprising since most of them were Keddy's employees, justice of the peace D. W. Oakes—a man married to a First Nations woman from British Columbia—ordered Jewell to pay Keddy $60.00 for damages and court costs of $46.90 on March 29, 1875. Nora's father managed to obtain the assistance of friends Carl Ostergard and J. C. Archambault, a Canadian farmer active in San Juan County's business and legal community who had also married an Indigenous woman, as sureties on his bond to pay the fines, but the three worked for the next several months to overturn the initial ruling. Jewell requested a new trial on a variety of procedural grounds, a process that even involved Nora, who was sent to report to Archambault at one point that her father was injured and could not appear on his own behalf. This encounter with the territorial legal system at such an early age no doubt fostered in the métis girl a view of the courts as a venue for grievance that did not necessarily ensure justice.[17]

By November 1875, Peter Jewell had still not paid his fines, and the district judge ordered that his property be seized in order to recover the damages owed—a judgment that imperiled the assets of Archambault and Ostergard as well. Luckily for Jewell's friends, the road supervisor paid his debts to H. W. Whitener, the San Juan County sheriff, on January 27, 1876.[18] Whitener would become very familiar with Nora's continued ordeals as she grew older. To pay for the court-ordered judgment, Peter Jewell mortgaged his unplanted crops to local merchant and lawyer Israel Katz. He borrowed $145.00 from Katz on December 6, 1875, and put the case behind him. On March 22, 1876, Jewell borrowed $36.75 from Katz, putting up fifty head of sheep as collateral, and probably prayed for a successful year on his humble homestead.[19] Although the first decade of Nora Jewell's life seemed relatively ordinary among the métis families who similarly depended on good crops and healthy sheep, 1876 would prove to be a turning point. Through a sequence of undocumented events taking place between March and November, the mixed-race girl lost her father and became the only named heir to Peter Jewell's estate.

Two days after the Danish immigrant's death, Israel Katz filed papers with the local probate court to be the administrator of the Jewell estate. He wrote to Judge John H. Bowman: "Whereas Peter Jewell . . . leaves behind him considerable real and personal property in San Juan County [and] seems to have no particular relations here, excepting a young child of about twelve years of age which is not able to take care of anything—as the deceased is largely indebted to the undersigned I. Katz . . . he hereby prays to be appointed as administrator . . . and have his indebtedness settled and what there will be left pay'd over to the lawful heirs."[20] Judge Bowman appointed respected members of the community Christopher Rosler (Anna Rosler's husband), Robert Firth, and Charles McKay to assess the estate and appointed Katz its administrator. The court records from Peter Jewell's probate include much financial and accounting detail that illustrates his full integration into San Juan Island's economy—he owed for services rendered and goods bought on credit that included chickens, calico, and candy, tea, tobacco, and a toy set. As evidenced by the inventories filed in his estate case, Nora's father had provided his métis family with the humble indulgences of a middling homesteader.[21]

Katz's acknowledgment of Nora as her father's heir was no small issue, and stands as evidence that not all settler-colonists took advantage of a legal system that could easily be used to defraud Indigenous and mixed-race women and children. The witnesses, bondsmen, and creditors who appeared in the Jewell estate case and decided Nora's fate knew the family intimately—as attested to in a brief statement signed by neighbors Peter Nelson and T. W. Boggess: "we know Peter Juell deceased, when alive for 6 year that he acknowledge himself to be the father of Nora Juell a minor child . . . for 6 year . . . treated her in every respect as were it his legitimate child. And further that he acknowledge to us that it always has been his will that said child Nora Juell be his acknowledge heir."[22]

Fanny and Peter's eldest daughter was born legitimate in the eyes of the law in 1866, but her parents' marriage remained clouded under the antimiscegenation statute. Washington's territorial legislators had agreed since 1854 to invalidate mixed-race unions, but in their thirteenth session, between 1865 and 1866, they chose to recognize mixed-race progeny born out of wedlock.[23] Their position reflects the abundance of métis households in the territory, headed by men interested in bequeathing property and surnames to their children, and offered legislators an opportunity to uphold white patriarchy—making whiteness and property inheritable by citizen men's children—without acknowledging Indian wives' rights to fair treatment, inheritance, or maternal custody. Although territorial politicians would go back and forth on miscegenation law—recognizing Indian-white marriages in some years and restricting them in others—some residents of territorial Washington viewed the revised marriage statute as legitimating marriages between whites and mixed-race Indians rather than Indian women like Fanny.[24] Racial exclusions to marriage were removed from marital statutes after 1868, but the law had not actively granted Nora's mother spousal inheritance rights to Peter Jewell's estate and probate judge Henry Tenschau recognized ten-year-old Nora Jewell as her father's only heir. With Fanny's help, Peter had built an estate sufficient to pay its debts and still provide their daughter Nora with a modest inheritance that he no doubt hoped would give her some security in the transnational borderlands world in which he had lived.[25]

Although no doubt tragic and felt deeply by many, the circumstances surrounding the death of Peter Jewell on November 8, 1876, and the disappearance of his wife Fanny and two youngest daughters remain unknown to historians. Like the evidentiary trail that chronicles each of the women in this book, the documentary record's silence regarding Nora Jewell's mother and sisters speaks to the simultaneous omnipresence and anonymity of borderlands métis families in the late nineteenth century. Before continuing this chronicle of Nora Jewell's legal encounters with San Juan County and Washington Territory jurists, it is worth noting the overall silence in the record regarding the circumstances of Peter's death and the disappearance of Fanny, Roma, and Eliza. Although newspaper notices, census schedules, and county offices announced other deaths, the Jewell family's passing went unrecorded. For Peter Jewell, a newspaper notice to creditors of his estate served as an obituary, but the nonwhite members of his family earned no notice.[26]

Probaters were quick to identify Nora as a legitimate and sole heir to the Jewell estate, but none mentioned Nora's mother and sisters. The statement signed by Peter Jewell's neighbors to affirm Nora as his "legitimate child" indicates that her legitimacy was not presumed under the law, raising some doubt as to the stability and legal standing of Peter and Fanny's marriage. As in Arizona, territorial Washington legislators banned Indian women like Fanny from testifying in cases involving white interests, so even if she survived her husband, the law ensured her silence. Not until 1880 would Nora describe herself as an orphan, both mother and father dead, which raises a question impossible for historians to answer, but essential to ask. Did Fanny choose to return to her birthplace in British Columbia rather than remain on San Juan Island as the widow of a husband she could not claim by law and in a territory that recognized the legal rights of her children, but not her own? In other words, if Fanny and her other children survived Peter just as Nora did, what choices did Fanny have when Peter died?

In 1867, Great Britain acknowledged the semi-independence of colonies north of the 49th parallel and the Canadian government took over management of First Nations affairs. Canadian officials proceeded to negotiate a series of land cessions with Native people, including Fanny's Coast Salish relatives in British Columbia. While these agreements set aside reserves for First Nations communities, the arrangements drew dissatisfaction from Indigenous Canadians much as treaties between the United States and Washington tribes caused animosity. In addition to isolating Indigenous people on reserves much smaller than their claimed territories, the Canadian government passed its first Indian Act in 1876, which denied First Nations status to Indigenous women who married white men and granted Indian status to white women who married Indigenous men. For Coast Salish women who had long practiced interracial marriage, this law denied them access to land and status rights guaranteed them as First Nations people, and forced them to choose between a non-Indian spouse and state and their Indigenous family and nation.[27]

If she returned to British Columbia after Peter's death in 1876, Fanny would have faced a legal regime that recognized and sanctioned her interracial marriage to Peter Jewell—if they knew about it—but that would have classified her as "white" and not "Indian" by virtue of that union. While this would have barred her in 1876 from claiming treaty status, the distinction would not have prevented her from returning to a Coast Salish family still living on Vancouver Island or the British Columbia mainland. Such a move would have allowed her to benefit from the support of relatives in raising her mixed-race and legally white children and might have appealed to her since Salish villages still surrounded urban settlements like Victoria and Vancouver and Indigenous residents traveled frequently across the U.S.-Canadian border in the last quarter of the nineteenth century.[28] Unable to inherit her husband's estate and with no legal standing before a territorial court, Fanny would have depended on the probate judge's willingness to let her keep her children and the Jewell farm she had helped to build. Unlike her female Salish relatives in British Columbia, Fanny had resigned her claims to tribal land by settling on San Juan Island prior to 1876, and so she might have viewed her (lack of Indian) status under Canada's Indian Act as an ideal alternative to her utter lack of rights under territorial Washington's system.[29]

Like Lucía Martínez in Arizona, Fanny Jewell faced a daunting challenge to her maternal authority and personal sovereignty. Forced to remain within the territorial Arizona legal system because of the Sonoran government's active campaign of genocide against her people south of the U.S. border, Martínez won physical custody of her daughters in 1871 because they were only three and five years old; the probate judge in territorial Arizona cited their young age as his reasoning, but still granted legal custody to their white father via a minor Indian indenture bond. Jewell's daughters were beyond "tender age" by 1876: ten-year-old Nora, eight-year-old Roma, and seven-year-old Eliza would have been viewed in territorial Washington's probate law as minors in need of a guardian once their father passed away, and the law did not recognize Indigenous maternal custody. The guardianship statute required probate judges to assign guardians capable of managing a household and their wards' estates when children under fourteen came before the court—children over fourteen could request a guardian, but even in those cases, the judge had the authority to assess the guardian's qualifications. As a nonliterate noncitizen Native woman, Fanny Jewell would not have been able to meet the law's qualifications to claim her children.[30]

Faced with the very real possibility of losing all three of her children to court-appointed guardians and being evicted from her home, Nora's mother may have assessed her vulnerable situation on the American side of Coast Salish territory and chosen to take her youngest daughters to the Canadian side on nearby Vancouver Island or even the mainland in order to preserve some semblance of family cohesion. Indigenous women had long intermarried with newcomer men on Vancouver Island, and by the late nineteenth century many Native families remained in established villages on the periphery of white settlements.[31] Fanny might have hoped that her eldest daughter Nora could inherit the estate under the law legitimating the children of Indian-white unions, and come of age as the ward of her sister Ellen and brother-in-law Frederick Jones. Twentieth-century accounts of nineteenth-century life on San Juan Island indicate that many Indigenous women made heart-wrenching choices about which side of the border they and their children might fare better in the midst of territorial state formation and widespread Native dispossession. A man with Semiahmoo and Lummi parents was born on San Juan Island, but then lived with older half-brothers and grandparents on Vancouver Island. As an adult he moved to the mainland and alternated between residency on the Canadian and American sides of the border in Lummi and Cowichan communities.[32] A Lummi woman described first cousins born of aunts who had married white men in the island chain: "I don't know where they are. You become lost. I don't know one of them now. Knowed them when they was small . . . Don't know where they are now."[33] While some Coast Salish recall the myriad border crossings of their family members with great detail, some families were lost in the Salish Sea currents. Historian Paige Raibmon describes the consequences of these intimate historical losses within the framework of settler-colonialism as "the microtechniques of dispossession," and it is clear that after 1876, Fanny and her daughters faced great difficulties in maintaining the networks they sustained while Peter was alive.[34]

An overview of guardianship cases in Washington's territorial courts reveals that judges often placed white children in the homes of relatives or family friends, even if they tasked financial matters to professional administrators (men like Israel Katz).[35] In this way, American legal practice conformed to Indigenous local practices emphasizing bilateral kinship ties among siblings where the informal adoption of children was concerned.[36] With Nora's maternal aunt so near, Fanny could confidently hope that the local probate judge would grant Frederick and Ellen Jones custody of her daughter, particularly since Nora had an inheritance to sustain her and would not be a burden on Jones family finances. In what must have been an unexpected judgment, however, probate judge Henry Tenschau put ten-year-old Nora under the guardianship of T. W. Boggess, a widowed homesteader who had affirmed Nora's paternity during probate proceedings.[37]

Judge Tenschau's decision to separate Nora from her métis family reflected a shifting attitude among Puget Sound residents toward interracial unions and mixed-race families in the late 1870s. The antimiscegenation statute remained in effect in territorial Washington until 1868, when territorial legislators removed racial restrictions on marriage—though they did not speak to the question of common-law unions initiated prior to 1868. Such relationships would remain unsanctioned without a marriage license issued after 1868. Local jurists had been lax in prosecuting such offenders under cohabitation or fornication laws, which were more often reserved for married violators charged with adultery by spouses filing for divorce. The Indian-white marriage ban effectively served to ensure that white men's property would only pass into the hands of state-recognized progeny or white heirs and was beyond the reach of Native domestic partners, not granted the privileges of spouses. The material effects of the law made policing unnecessary until social concerns about métis families and their political influence drew a rash of cohabitation charges toward the end of the territorial period against prominent American men whose unions with Indigenous women failed the test of state scrutiny.[38] Although a member of the community that legalized such unions, Judge Tenschau's disdain for

Nora Jewell's guardianship record, January 27, 1877 (*Territory of Washington v. James Smith*, 1880, Case No. 1055; reproduced with permission from Washington State Archives, Northwest Regional Branch, Bellingham, Washington)

interracial families found much support in territorial Washington's legal and borderland communities in the mid-1870s.

In the years following the Indian Wars early in the territorial period, the Office of Indian Affairs had been working steadily to isolate Native people in reservation communities on the Washington mainland, though there is much evidence to suggest the futility of their efforts. Indian agents' goals were twofold: first, to achieve the separation of Indian people from the influence of unsavory whites—like those left over from the fur trade and gold rush eras of interracial interdependence—and second, to assimilate Native Americans as subservient members of mainstream society.[39] Intermarriage of Indian women and white men, then, complicated this notion of controlled assimilation, while mixed-race children in particular threatened notions of racial separation and aggravated those territorial elites sensitive to increasing rhetoric in favor of racial purity and eugenic superiority.[40] Newspapers and pioneer journals from the period include frequent references to the doomed fate of mixed-race children and the degraded condition of métis families—typecast as homes occupied by abusive white fathers prone to abandonment and alcoholic Indian mothers prone to prostitution.[41] Fanny might have chosen to avoid a direct confrontation with these stereotypes in Tenschau's court, but Nora was forced to live with them when the judge placed her in the home of T. W. Boggess, a crippled man born around 1815 in Tennessee.[42]

Although his participation in the U.S.-Mexican War, the Civil War, and the Puget Sound Indian Wars is not documented, the man shared a profile similar to these who did serve in such conflicts and his interests as a homesteading American male were certainly well served in territorial Washington—a region that was home to both Confederate and Union veterans.[43] Given settler-colonists' reliance on Indigenous and mixed-race women's labors in the North American West, Tenschau might have viewed Nora an ideal helpmeet for the aging and disabled farmer and hoped that Boggess would be able to instill in the mixed-race girl an appropriate understanding of racial and sexual hierarchies in the island chain still too métis for some. Tenschau may not have been in favor of interracial intimacy, but he proved himself in favor of métis assimilation when he placed Nora in Boggess's care. Boggess must have proven either too feeble or too fierce to be a suitable guardian, however, and by the end of January 1877 Tenschau revoked the widower's guardianship papers without explanation and assigned Fanny's daughter to the household of James F. Smith, another homesteading farmer who lived with his wife within a quarter mile of the Jewell property. In April, Israel Katz, the administrator of Peter Jewell's estate, turned Nora's inheritance—which included the Jewell homestead—over to James F. Smith, who accepted the responsibility of furnishing his ward with clothes and an education. For the first two years he seems to have upheld Tenschau's expectations.[44]

For his part, Nora's uncle Frederick Jones signed as a witness to Smith's guardianship bond and seemed to find ways to support his niece though they lived apart. Testimony would later reveal that Judge Tenschau had advised Smith to keep a strict eye on the girl and to not let her associate with the Jones family. Accounts of Nora's experience in the Smith household between 1877 and 1879 varied widely, some describing the man as a rough taskmaster who overworked his ward at home and abused her in public and others claiming he treated her like a daughter and offered recreational rewards as often as he assigned domestic duties. What all witnesses described, however, was a social environment in which Smith was master and both his wife and ward were subservient, and where Nora's mixed-race status—especially once she reached the age of sexual consent at twelve years old in 1878—made her vulnerable to both sexual advances and sexual suspicion.[45]

When Nora came forward in February 1880 to report that she was pregnant as a result of James F. Smith's repeated sexual assaults upon her, she revealed the vulnerable status of mixed-race women within the San Juan Island community. By the time she told her heart-wrenching story before the audience of white men assembled in the Third Judicial District Court in Port Townsend, Fanny and Peter's daughter had already sought help and counsel from friends and relatives on the island. These witnesses' testimony suggest that San Juan Island residents held a range of opinions regarding the girl's circumstance and "condition," many of which depended on their views toward Indigenous and mixed-race women's sexual proclivities.

That Nora's case was granted legal venue suggests the importance of her mixed-race, "not Indian" status, and that judges had come a long way during her lifetime in considering the importance of protecting marginalized women's bodies. In 1861, a *Puget Sound Herald* piece reported the murder of an Indian woman in Steilacoom (just south of Tacoma) and noted that "Every member of the jury was conscious that it was an idle mockery to hold an inquest upon a murdered squaw, for there is no law punishing such an offence when committed on an Indian." Taking the same tone of the Port Townsend reporter who complained that Nora's case cost taxpayer dollars, this journalist asserted that "at present the whole thing is a humbug, from the Coroner's inquisition to the trial by jury. A lawyer can find, any day, twelve men who will say under oath that killing an Indian is not murder, because the dust of the earth of which a white man is made is of a little better quality than that of which an Indian or negro is made."[46] This editorial openly acknowledged Indigenous people's lack of protections under the law, contradicting the sentiments of the Spokane coverage of Nora's trial that opened this chapter and indicating that newspaper readers in territorial Washington shared differing opinions regarding justice for nonwhite residents. By 1880, Nora Jewell still faced an all-white and all-male jury unconvinced of the quality of the dust that made her different from them.

Nora, fourteen when she became pregnant, described her wardship under Smith as one of domestic, field, and sexual servitude—not unlike the conditions Lucía Martínez endured on King Woolsey's ranch in territorial Arizona.[47] Nora told jurors that Smith had kept her at home—violating his obligation to school and socialize her—rarely letting her out of his sight. In order to maintain constant watch over the child, Smith put her to work in the fields with him while he was on the farm and gave his wife instructions to keep her in the house when he was away on other business—which included mining and prospecting, harvesting with other neighbors, and occasionally performing in a brass band throughout Puget Sound. In April 1879, Nora's guardian required that she help him build a fence row on the perimeter of his property, which stood within sight of her own family home just a quarter mile away. It was at this time, Nora testified, that the man began a regular practice of forcing her to have sex with him in the fields. Although she resisted her guardian, he threatened her with death if she betrayed him, so she suffered his abuse for the next nine months.[48]

While preparing for the Christmas holiday, Mrs. Smith—whose given name does not appear in the record, and who did not testify in the trial—confronted Nora about her increasingly obvious signs of pregnancy, which included frequent illness and a growing abdomen. Nora recalled to the jury that she did not reveal her guardian's complicity to his wife, but that she had no other explanation to offer, and that the Smith couple fought violently over her condition for the remainder of the month. Unable to obtain aid or sympathy from her guardian's wife, Nora turned to Sarah King, the Ohio-born wife of Francis King, who had been born in Canada during American and British joint-occupation of the Pacific Northwest. Their San Juan Island family enjoyed the respectability of whiteness that came from their combined descent from colonial and immigrant claims to the region. They had daughters about Nora's age, which might explain why the desperate girl hoped Mrs. King would empathize with her, but Mr. King and his eldest son, John, a young and popular bachelor in 1880, doubted the métis girl's capacity for virtue. Although Mrs. King might have offered a kind ear and sympathy, the King family gave Nora no guidance, so Fanny's daughter turned to her aunt and uncle.[49]

That Nora turned last to her mixed-race family—one not yet legitimated under territorial law—suggests that she understood the pressures of shifting racial and sexual hierarchies on islanders' attitudes toward her virtue and Smith's guilt. She may have hoped a respectable white ally untouched by interracial intimacies could aid her cause. With nowhere else to turn, however, Fanny and Peter's daughter sought advice and assistance from her métis kin. Nora's aunt Ellen Jones assessed her niece's prenatal condition and guessed that she should be due for a June delivery and together they estimated the unborn child had been conceived in October. Her uncle Fred advised her to report the assaults to the local judge and insisted that once told, her story could not change—likely aware that his niece would endure aggressive questioning and character slander should the case go to trial. Nora Jewell gave a sworn statement before justice of the peace William H. Higgins on February 10, 1880, and his indictment of Smith brought the parties before a district court holding jurisdiction over major crimes in the territory's third judicial district.[50]

Nora's mixed-race status might have made her vulnerable to stereotypes and advances based on settler men's assumptions about the sexual availability and promiscuity of Indigenous women, but being half-white also made her eligible to file charges and testify against white men under territorial law. Since her mixed-race cousins were minors—like her—they were not called to testify, and neither was her Indian aunt, barred from testifying on racial grounds. James Smith's wife was not asked to testify because spouses did not have to testify against one another in civil or criminal actions. Married women testified with the consent of their husbands, but were not often compelled to appear in court, so Mrs. King—whom Nora first confided in—did not testify, though her son James represented the family in the trial and testified against Nora, presumably on behalf of his mother. Once the sheriff subpoenaed witnesses and lawyers selected the jury, the trial began and Nora repeated a version of her story almost identical to the one she had given Justice Higgins just weeks earlier. When she finished, the prosecuting district attorney, Irving Ballard, called his only other witness: Fred Jones.[51]

Fred Jones testified that his wife was Nora's maternal aunt and that he and his family lived just outside of Friday Harbor, about four miles from the Smith property. Within the previous year, Jones had been to Smith's house to see the girl five or six times. Fanny's brother-in-law reported that Mr. Smith did not allow his niece to "go anywhere for the last two or three years, she was never allowed to go anywhere, nor speak to anyone unless the [Smith] family were with her." He told the judge that he had not known that Judge Tenschau "didn't want her to associate with my family," but that if Nora "was in trouble I would have helped her . . . I didn't tell her what she ought to do . . . I told her that what she'd said once if truth she should stick to." Jones countered some of the statements that others would make on Smith's behalf, denying that he had counseled his niece to charge Smith with her pregnancy and had promised her a home with his family if she did so. Although Smith and his allies would make this allegation, they made no effort to explain what Jones's motivations might have been for turning his niece against Smith—perhaps they hoped it would be obvious to the court that the actions of a white man married to an Indian were always questionable.[52]

When Jones finished answering attorneys' questions, the court adjourned for the day. It opened with James F. Smith's testimony the following morning. Smith told the courtroom audience that he was thirty-nine years old and that he had been married for thirteen years, though he and his wife had no children. Smith said he had "been living with [his] wife during all last thirteen years except three or four months when I started out west." He claimed that he and his wife had treated Nora well in the three years she had lived with them, sending her to school and even taking her along to community balls and parties. The guardian admitted he had used the girl for field work, explaining that not only did his own wife assist him with farm work, but Nora "never made objection to working on farm . . . She worked with me making fence row . . . chopping brush and making space for fence." Smith swore that he never "made an assault upon her." In fact, he claimed his "instruction of her has been good. [I] have prevented her from running around as I was ordered by Probate Court. I was summoned before Probate Court and told she was suffered to run around with a cousin of hers and with Siwashes and that I must keep her more strict—I did after that."[53]

Although no record exists of the probate proceeding, Smith used the supposed episode to cast doubt upon Nora's behavior and to make the only racialized reference to appear in the trial transcripts. By associating Nora and her métis Jones cousins with "Siwashes," a derogatory term that included all Puget Sound Indians regardless of tribe, Smith implied that his ward had loose moral values and invited jurors to imagine her deviant behavior as a by-product of Indian association. Immoral and criminal behaviors jurors might have associated with Nora and Indianness—which were frequently reported in local newspapers and prosecuted by territorial lawyers—included alcohol consumption, gambling, prostitution, and smuggling, if not more violent acts. Fred Jones, the only witness who had testified on Nora's behalf, would also have been discredited by Smith's derogatory comments, since he had married an Indian woman and joined her "Siwash" family.

Once Smith had effectively undermined Nora and her uncle's credibility by marking them as racially ambiguous at best and racially deficient at worst, he proceeded to deny the charges that had been made of him. He admitted that he had threatened his ward with violence: "If she would not do so and so, as in driving cattle . . . I would tell her that I would so and so . . . [but I] never told her if she didn't do so and so she'd be hung." Smith said he did not remember having called her "a bitch for not driving [cattle] as I wanted." He said that he "did not horsewhip [Nora] for speaking to [James] King at party . . . I did not strike her when she came home from party in eye, so as to make it black and blue."[54]

Because the trial records are incomplete, historians cannot know what context drew these defensive claims from Smith. What is remarkable about these denials is not that Smith made them, but that the incidents he denied did not appear in Nora's sworn statement, suggesting that other witnesses reported them in their descriptions of Smith's treatment of his ward. Smith did not claim to know who else might have fathered Nora's unborn child—he left that to his corroborating witnesses—but he did say that he did not know of her being with other men unsupervised and that he only found out she was pregnant because his wife told him and Nora refused to reveal the father. Although he denied a sexual relationship with Nora, Smith's testimony implies that he had worked to impose his authority in private and in public, using threats of violence if not actually delivering blows against the twelve-year-old girl.

Twenty-year-old James King, the son of Francis and Sarah, followed Smith on the witness stand. The confident bachelor—who would enjoy a lifetime of prominence on San Juan Island—reported to the court that he interrupted Nora's conversation with his mother and did not know its substance. He said that he and the métis girl spoke later, however, and that "I asked her what was wrong and who was the party—she said Mr. Bogus [*sic*] was the father—I said he wasn't allowed about [the] house—She said he came around anyway." Nora denied that she had ever named Boggess, her first court-appointed guardian, as the father, but others would repeat King's story, which gives some disturbing indication as to why Nora might have been removed from his home so quickly and then placed under Smith's care, where she apparently faced the same sexual advances. T. W. Boggess would not be called to answer the accusations made against him, however. King went on to say that Smith's treatment of the girl was good and that he thought she did go to school the previous summer and that he had seen her at a few dances with the Smith's, but that he had "never paid special attention to Nora—danced with her at San Juan—don't remember doing it at Lopez."[55]

James King deftly distanced himself from Nora's behavior by diminishing the importance of his social encounters with the métis girl, though he gave no explanation for his intimate and confessional encounter with Nora in his parents' home. King's testimony did the important work of questioning Smith's paternity by raising the specter of another—albeit elderly and crippled—father. King's reference to Boggess as a man not "allowed about the house" raises unanswered questions about the aged man's respectability in the community. The young man also damned Nora's reputation by implying he chose not to dance with her very often and by reporting to the court that "the reputation of Nora in [the] neighborhood is bad—they say her reputation for truth is bad—[I] heard . . . others speak of it."[56]

James King included Antone Gesselman among the "others" who had told him about Nora's "bad" reputation. Next on the stand, Gesselman struggled to distance himself from the case. Although Gesselman lived about a quarter mile from Smith's farm and had prospected with him in 1879, he was also the local constable, and had served the subpoenas on the Smith and Jones families. He testified that Smith "has been working hard in farms last season" and that he had "frequently seen Smith away from here at other times," affirming the notion that Smith was a typical male westerner—at work on farms and in mines simultaneously. The constable also claimed, however, that he did not "know Nora's reputation for truth and veracity" and that he had not overheard Fred Jones pressuring his niece to charge Smith with the assault. Gesselman proved unwilling to uphold the solidarity of white male privilege by slandering Nora's reputation when he refused to choose sides between Jones and Smith. John Dougherty, who followed Gesselman's testimony and was also called by the defense, testified in similarly noncommittal ways. He only acknowledged that he was Smith's neighbor, that he saw the man work hard on his farm, and that of Nora he knew "nothing about her general reputation for truth and veracity."[57] Probably both men were annoyed that they had to travel from San Juan Island to Port Townsend to give testimony, or perhaps, like those men who had helped Lucía Martínez, they disagreed that Indigenous and mixed-race women's bodies were freely available to white men in North American borderlands.

Before the case closed, prosecuting attorneys called Fred Jones one more time to put on record that "Nora's reputation for truth and veracity is good." District Attorney Irving Ballard, likely in an effort to bolster Gesselman's lukewarm testimony, called H. W. Whitener, San Juan Island sheriff, to the stand as well. Sheriff Whitener testified that he was "acquainted with Nora's general reputation for truth and veracity—It is good. [I] have heard a number talking about it—even [the] probate judge—never heard any one say anything against her." Whitener had known Nora for much—if not all—of her life, since he had served as sheriff during John Keddy's case against Nora's father in 1875 and would record major changes in Nora's life as one of the census enumerators for San Juan Island in the 1870s and 1880s. Perhaps less concerned with métissage and miscegenation than others in the Puget Sound region, Sheriff Whitener swore his oath to Nora's moral character and made it clear that not all San Juan Island residents associated her Indianness with sexual immorality.[58]

That jurors and jurists, witnesses, and chroniclers would have made these racialized connections to sexual deviance is indicated not only in the unsympathetic local press coverage of the "half-breed" girl's ordeal quoted at the beginning of this chapter, but also in the legal culture in which they lived. Although Indian and white marriages had been decriminalized since 1868, Puget Sound residents became increasingly concerned about the economic, political, and social status of interracial families, who in some communities leveraged considerable influence. Whatcom County, San Juan County, Jefferson County (which included Port Townsend), and Island County made up the territory's third judicial district, and Indian-white households remained prevalent there, despite federal and territorial officials' hopes that Indian-white social promiscuity would wane and the Pacific Northwest could move forward with Indians on reservations and citizens in factories and on farms.

These concerns came to a head in a series of cohabitation and fornication charges against nine métis families in Whatcom County. Described by historians as "the Whatcom County Nine," the eight men and one woman singled out in this campaign held significant sway on local politics and were identified as notorious examples of immorality by political opponents who used antimiscegenation rhetoric to launch their attacks. These debates were heard in June and July 1879 before Judge Roger S. Greene—the same judge and same jury pool that heard Nora Jewell's case against James F. Smith. Although cloaked in deceivingly objective legal arguments that pointed to jurisprudence and the rule of law, both trials centered on the status of mixed-race progeny of Indian-white unions and the stain of sexual immorality that marked Indian and mixed-race women as the drudge wives of "squaw-men."[59]

Without explaining their opinion or the particular evidence it was based upon, the jurors in Judge Greene's district court acquitted James F. Smith of rape.[60] That jurists brought no charges against T. W. Boggess, and that he was not subpoenaed to testify regarding his involvement in Nora's pregnancy, indicate that the practitioners of territorial law were unconcerned with paternal guilt and that they doubted the métis girl's testimony about sexual consent. When the daughter of a Coast Salish mother and a Danish immigrant father told jurists that "the first time was against my will and consent," but that she had given up resistance when her guardian said he would hang her, the mixed-race girl articulated her understanding of American and Indigenous concepts of consent and the law.

Although often overlooked by historians, the legal mechanism of consent is an important and complex provision that is central to North American colonization. Without going too far afield, it is worthwhile to link the importance of treaty diplomacy and interracial marriages (a connection illustrated in widely circulated reproductions of Alfred Jacob Miller's 1850 painting *The Trapper's Bride,* for instance) as fundamental tools in the consensual transmission of land and power from Indigenous to Euro-American hands throughout the continent. Because Europeans and Americans depended heavily on Indigenous cooperation in the earliest states of colonization, interracial marriages proved to be a social lubricant easing the rough edges of treaty negotiation. Both consensual and forced intercourse between Euro-American men and Indigenous women became a fundamental component of settler-colonialism, since the first waves of settlers were men who used sexual acts to claim Indian women's bodies, progeny, and lands in one fell swoop. The mixed-race or métis generation did the cultural and physical work that made frontier and border zones more tolerable for Euro-American women, whose intercourse with settler-colonial men was also important, since they bore the third generation of Euro-Americans who would orchestrate the pioneer myths of the North American West.[61]

Once land and power had been exchanged through sex and treaty, both often engaged with the looming threat or aftermath of violence, Euro-Americans convinced themselves of their own rights by elevating the rhetorical importance of Indigenous consent. Pointing to treaty signatures, which tribes often protested, and weaving legends of princess brides disenfranchised under miscegenation laws, British-Canadian and American Anglos cited treaties and agreements with Indigenous people as evidence of their superiority to one another.[62] This posturing stance is particularly true in the British-American disputes over the Pacific Northwest borderlands, and of the San Juan Island chain especially. Newcomer arrivals to the Pacific Northwest accelerated between 1778 and 1805 with James Cook's survey for the British and Lewis and Clark's survey for the Americans. The British dominated the early years of settlement, primarily through the Hudson's Bay Company fur trading networks. After the successful establishment of a few forts, however, the British sought to establish more permanent settlements and in 1839 organized the Puget Sound Agricultural Company. Historians have already shown the importance of intimate unions with Indigenous women for early British settlers in the borderlands. Because British colonial fur trade success depended on tribal favor, scholars have depicted these sexual unions as consensual, demonstrated by their long-term and reproductive nature. That would soon change, however.[63]

Americans joined British agriculturalists and traders in small numbers in the 1830s, but they soon trampled down the Oregon Trail in the thousands. These Americans wrote about themselves as pioneering, heteronormative families—like the Whitmans and Spauldings of the Willamette Valley. Other signs, including census records and tribal oral history collections, suggest however that the first and largest wave of settlers came as single men, among them immigrants who could hardly be classified as American: disappointed miners crisscrossing the Pacific Northwest from boom to bust and colonial officials whose duties distributed them throughout the Pacific West over the course of a career. Records also show that in addition to one another, these men sought Indian women as sexual partners, both for long-term and reproductive unions as well as for short-term and violent gratification. Tribal oral histories of the American contact period describe newcomers as heavily dependent on Indigenous people for emotional support and physical sustenance, and Native women could meet these essential needs.[64]

By 1855, Washington and Oregon Territory represented American jurisdiction in the region, and British authority needed to be squelched through American treaties with Pacific Northwest tribes. Negotiated in a flurry, these treaties infuriated Puget Sound tribes sufficiently enough to spark the Puget Sound Indian Wars of 1855–1856—a sure sign of nonconsent if ever there was one. American soldiers and local militias overpowered the tribes, who were unable to leverage support from relatives north of the Canadian border and east of the Cascade Mountains, though tribes in those regions skirmished with Euro-Americans as well. It was at this point, just as Peter and Fanny Jewell were building their interracial borderlands home, that Washington territorial legislators legislated consent as a positive assumption, and Indigenous people—women particularly—found themselves unable to any longer withhold consent through law, power, or suasion.[65]

In these first waves of settler-colonialism, Indigenous women frequently found their autonomy over their own bodies in question. Some women like Fanny Jewell and Ellen Jones shared lifelong, procreative relationships with newcomer men, though Fanny's daughter would not share the same fate in their changing world. As in the Sonoran borderlands, a traffic in captive women's bodies escalated during the mid–nineteenth century, in response to tribal competition for limited resources in the age of conquest and to meet newcomer appetites for sexual partners. Although many scholars argue that rape emerged as a concept among Indigenous peoples only after colonial conquest, scholars also know that tribal oral traditions reflect the lived experiences of each generation, that stories with long-standing symbols shift in meaning and relevance over time, and that Indigenous forms of justice coexisted with imperial legal systems well into the twentieth century.[66]

Ethnohistorians in the twentieth century collected many gendered and sexual stories among Salishan storytellers, some of which describe nonconsensual sex between transformative trickster figures and young women.[67] A number of Salish groups blamed a trickster being or "Coyote" for these episodes of sexual abuse, and the Thompson River Salish composed songs linking European men to Coyote behavior.[68] A Lushootseed woman described nineteenth-century white men as "despairing, destitute, and desperate," postures that typically led to Coyote's egregious behavior.[69] Settler-colonial men often behaved like Coyote: they violated social norms and taboos, they made foolish mistakes with dire consequences for themselves and others, they made demands that put others in danger. And in this case, they took advantage of Salish women's vulnerability for their sexual gratification. In stories, Coyote not only forced himself on young women, but these women reported his crimes and their communities punished Coyote for his sexual violations.

Generally, the stories outline episodes of nonconsensual sex and explain the possible outcomes for such transgressive sexual interactions. Specifically, they describe young women engaged in work away from home who are "tricked" into having sex and then impregnated. When the trickster violator is discovered, tribal members punish him with physical violence and expulsion. His victims undergo spiritual cleansing ceremonies for healing; sometimes they bear children and sometimes they do not. Like the talking tree story that illuminates Lucía Martínez's worldview, these stories are tied to Nora Jewell's experience because she, her mother, and her maternal aunt likely understood their symbolism and might have understood James Smith's assaults as parallel to those in the trickster stories.

Twentieth-century Salish reported that women on San Juan Island continued to practice healing ceremonies throughout newcomer settlement in the nineteenth century, suggesting that Nora and her female relatives would have understood the girl's assault in a spiritual and legal context. Nora may even have taken personal measures in response to her pregnancy that paralleled these stories. Her child never appears in the documentary record. A Salish woman in her place and time would sometimes terminate a problematic pregnancy by bumping "her belly on a rock . . . or she took strong medicine."[70] If Nora underwent a sweat lodge ceremony like the women in these stories, the extreme heat may have proven an abortifacient as well as a spiritual cleansing. Nora's contemporaries understood such painful ordeals as a source of strength or power, and might have perceived Nora's suffering as a sign of her growing authority.[71]

In his work on Indigenous legal systems, a field he describes as "ethnojurisprudence," James W. Zion argues that "stories are case law . . . These stories can be in the form of what appears to be fiction, such as the Coyote stories common to most North American tribes. They are told for the purpose of teaching legal principles."[72] Understanding Nora's sexual assault in these contexts helps to explain why she felt empowered to report Smith's crime in an imperial court when so few women achieved justice in similar instances. Like the women in Salish stories about sexual assault, Nora and her Salish aunt applied their own understanding of legal principles and reported Smith's misbehaviors, no doubt expecting their community to punish him. What they might not have expected is that territorial jurists had built a system that assumed female consent, while the Salish system had assumed Coyote guilt. Indigenous views regarding sexual consent espoused in Salishan oral tradition demonstrate that violations of women's bodies resulted in severe and corporal punishments, while Washington territorial law only protected girls under the age of twelve from sexual transgression. Females twelve and over, like Nora Jewell, had to prove their assaults in a court of law where they had to negotiate the intricacies of age of consent and rape law.

Age of consent laws were standard content in state and territorial legal codes throughout the nineteenth-century United States, though few historians have paid these important provisions much attention.[73] They may sound innocuous enough, but age of consent laws define the age at which sexual contact is considered rape, and are incredibly complex pieces of legislation. As in Arizona, territorial Washington's age of consent laws worked in tandem with other legal provisions to determine Indigenous women's ability to achieve corporeal sovereignty.

In 1854, when they ratified their first legal code, Washington territorial legislators passed "An Act Relative to Crimes and Punishments, and Proceedings in Criminal Cases." In "Chapter II: Of Offenses Against the Lives and Persons of Individuals," they agreed that "Every person who shall unlawfully have carnal knowledge of a woman against her will, or of a female child under twelve years of age, shall be deemed guilty of a rape, and upon conviction thereof, shall be imprisoned in the penitentiary not more than thirty years, nor less than one year, and in prosecutions for such offence, proof of penetration shall be sufficient evidence of the commission thereof."[74] It is worth noting straightaway that this is a gendered law in that the language of the provision presumes female victimhood; sodomy laws protected male victims, although territorial legislators did not legislate that "infamous crime" until 1873. When they did criminalize the act it was not age restricted and consent was unfathomable to jurists.[75]

For residents of Washington Territory, then, females aged twelve and over were sexually viable. Jurists assumed that they could consent to sex, and required them to prove they had not consented in order to claim that a rape had occurred. "Proof of penetration" consisted of signs of violent and forced intercourse, *or* of pregnancy after the crime was committed. Transcripts from rape trials in the period show that even girls and women who exhibited signs of violence had difficulty proving intercourse had occurred unless there was a subsequent pregnancy; jurists often dropped these cases from sexual to physical assault charges. Women who waited until they showed signs of pregnancy could obviously prove that penetration had occurred, but then—after the signs of violence had faded, if they were ever visible—they faced the burden of proving nonconsent and that violent force had been used. Thus, any female over twelve faced a tremendous burden of proof in cases of rape, despite the seemingly straightforward language of the age of consent provision.

Between 1855 and 1889, the span of Washington's territorial period, there were sixty-nine trials involving rape, attempted rape, or assault with intent to rape. These cases are archived under the male defendants' names; the plaintiff's name is always listed as "The Territory of Washington," making it somewhat difficult to pinpoint female victims' identities. Even when victims' names are apparent, their racial identity is often obscured in the record and is only made obvious when it is included in transcribed testimony. Despite these evidentiary hurdles, cross-referencing the names of rape trial plaintiffs with census records revealed two cases involving Indian victims in the Puget Sound region; one is Nora Jewell's. Remember that in her case, her mixed-race background was not directly identified in the case and only her association with "Siwashes" was cited as evidence of her sexual deviance. In reading these case files in search of Indian women, it quickly became clear that white women accusing white men of rape also rarely achieved convictions. Although the injustice of all of these women's experiences is obvious, the additional legal barriers that Indigenous and mixed-race victims faced in making their cases heard—beyond proof of penetration or use of violent force—deserve consideration.[76]

In addition to outlining penalties for rape and other crimes, the territorial legal code established a protocol for the territorial judicial system. Among these provisions was a list of those excluded from serving as witnesses.[77] Indians appeared as the only racial-ethnic group of people barred from testimony in civil or criminal cases involving non-Indian defendants. Other groups dismissed from testifying included children under the age of ten who appeared incapable of interpreting the facts, those of unsound mind, or those in an intoxicated state. The latter three categories fell under the discretion of the judge to determine whether they could testify, leaving Indians as the only category of witnesses permanently barred from testifying against those who exercised the most power over them in a settler-colonial context. This witness exclusion provision perhaps explains why so few Native women pressed charges against settler-colonial attackers—they had been silenced under the law, making it impossible for them to prove they withheld consent at all. The two Puget Sound cases involving Indigenous plaintiffs include Nora Jewell's, whose mixed-race status gave her the privilege of testifying, and an Indian girl whose white guardian actually pressed charges on her behalf—the girl never testified and that trial also resulted in an acquittal.[78]

Because the witness exclusion laws applied to civil cases as well as criminal cases, Indigenous Puget Sounders could not testify against citizens who defrauded them in economic transactions, could not file claims of their own for custody of children or minor relatives, and could not protest land fraud, all common practices in territorial Washington. As was the case for Nora's mother Fanny, the witness exclusion statute made it particularly difficult for Indigenous women to retain custody of their children, and in the case discussed in Louisa Enick's chapter, the provision also made it difficult for Indian women to protect their donation lands, homestead lands, and allotments from citizen incursions. That these women did not become American citizens until 1924 further exacerbated their vulnerability under the law.

Still "in family way," as she put it at the time of her February 1880 trial, Nora's premarital pregnancy seemed to concern San Juan Island residents more than her inability to withhold consent.[79] A single mother with a bastard child could put a lot of pressure on a small island community.[80] On March 15, just sixteen days after a jury of his peers acquitted Smith, fourteen-year-old Nora Jewell married E. Hitchens, a forty-one-year-old farmer from England. There is no indication in the island's census or vital records that Fanny's daughter knew her husband prior to the trial, nor was Hitchens involved in the case. H. W. Whitener, who knew Nora well, recorded Mr. and Mrs. Hitchens living on Orcas Island in the 1880 census he took in June of that year. Although Nora's baby was not enumerated, she may not yet have given birth, since her aunt Ellen had only estimated that the young mother would deliver in June. Or the fetus may have been lost as a result of the girl's intense duress, or the pregnancy may have been intentionally terminated, as discussed above. That Nora's marriage seems to have been one of convenience for the island community concerned with Nora's condition is suggested by the events that took place less than three years later. In 1883 E. Hitchens appeared in the San Juan County territorial census without Nora. The enumerator failed to indicate the noncitizen farmer as either "married" or "single," suggesting that the local census taker was too empathetic to ask a painful question with an obvious answer—Nora had left the middle-aged farmer and returned to her home island. In 1885, enumerator John Kelly listed E. Hitchens as a "single" farmer, erasing the immigrant's marriage in census records entirely.[81]

Nora's father had not been able to make his métis daughter's life easy, but he did manage to help her escape an unwanted marriage. Once Nora

Garry oak on Nora Jewell's property, 2014. This tree stood during Nora's lifetime and remains a witness to the family's legacy on the island. (Photograph by Guard Sundstrom, reproduced with permission)

reached the age of majority in 1882, she inherited unimpinged rights to the estate her father had left behind in 1876, which might explain why she waited two years to leave Hitchens. Aged twenty-two in 1886, Nora Jewell (not Hitchens) sold her father's property to Peter Gorman for a thousand dollars. Gorman paid Jewell two hundred and fifty dollars and mortgaged a second property to secure the remaining payment. No doubt the girl made powerful through suffering was motivated to sell the plot that had once been her childhood home but was also just a quarter mile from the scene of her repeated assaults. The funds granted her the autonomy to live independently and records show that she worked carefully to reconstruct her Puget Sound kinship and economic network.[82]

Twenty-six-year-old Nora Jewell appeared in the Ole Wold household in the 1887 territorial census, along with her twenty-five-year-old cousin Jennie Jones. The two women likely provided domestic service in exchange for their board in the household that included Danish patriarch Ole, his wife, also from Denmark, their five Texas-born children, and a daughter-in-law, Addie Boyce Wold. Addie's parents, Lucinda and Stephen Boyce, would have known Nora's father Peter Jewell prior to his death because Jewell had served as San Juan County's first road supervisor in 1873 and Stephen Boyce was the county's first assessor. Lucinda Boyce reportedly offered midwifery services to island women—Indigenous and newcomer—and would likely have known of Nora's troubled pregnancy in 1879–1880, given the notoriety of her trial. With these connections to Addie Boyce Wold, and perhaps also because of shared Danish immigrant heritage, Nora might have been very glad to find employment and shelter in the Wold household with her maternal cousin.[83]

Absent from the documentary record after 1887, Nora Jewell reappeared in Tacoma in the 1910 U.S. census. Between those years, Washington had matured into statehood and settler-colonists from Europe and Canada had by and large become American citizens, assured of their membership in the national body politic even if equally convinced of their regional and transnational exceptionalism. Although prior to 1887 they had lived in diversity in the island chain, citizens and subjects lived in 1910 divided by cultural and physical boundaries that made it difficult for mixed-race women like Nora Jewell to leverage métis authority that had once been widely acknowledged throughout the region. Her métis and Indigenous neighbors, however, overcame the sometimes subtle and often overt racism directed at mixed-race Puget Sounders by choosing between Indianness and whiteness to secure legal and social privileges.[84] The increasing ability of the state to enforce racial segregation through the twinning of state and federal laws that separated Indians from whites prompted Nora Jewell and others like her to make creative, but also probably painful, choices. This important shift in western legal regimes around the turn of the twentieth century affected all of the women in this book.

Nora's relative anonymity after the 1880 rape trial suggests that she chose—and maybe had learned from her mother—to avoid the bureaucratic interventions of the territorial legal system when legal whiteness and the notoriety of making private charges public failed her and her family. It is possible that the Jones and Jewell families had resolved not to let courts separate their kin again, even if they would have to struggle to maintain a cohesive network on San Juan Island. As with Nora's child, there is no evidence to demonstrate that Nora's mother and sisters—if their disappearance from records after 1876 does not indicate their death—reunited with her after she married, though these Puget Sound Indigenous and métis women had clearly learned the value of hidden transcripts as an important tool in subverting territorial interventions into their intimate family lives.[85] Historians may find it frustrating to tell the histories of women like Nora Jewell so incompletely, but perhaps such gaps reveal a more accurate depiction of their place within Puget Sound communities as defined by territorial law. The problem of sources and interpretation is one that historians of colonialism and Native race and sexuality face as a matter of course.[86]

To know any more about Nora Jewell, we must consider the choices available to Indigenous and métis women in the borderlands world in which she lived at the turn of the twentieth century. International, municipal, and reservation boundaries separated subjects (Canadians) from citizens (Americans), but also wards (Indians and First Nations) from the enfranchised (Canadians and Americans), so that property and residency became linked to legal and political status, a process more fully explored in the last two chapters of this book. Despite these developments, Coast Salish families and individuals long accustomed to traveling extensively throughout their territory continued to seek community, natural resources, and wage work across borders. As settler-colonial courts transitioned to provincial and national arbiters of justice and racial-sexual hierarchies solidified to diminish métis influence and segregate subjects from citizens, Coast Salish people like Nora Jewell adapted their transborder strategies.

Being American Indian in 1910 gave individuals access to extended kinship networks, educational and medical services delivered at Indian agencies, and eligibility for valuable tribal allotments. Being First Nations in 1910 likewise granted individuals access to extended kinship networks, but intertribal marriages limited Native women's ability to claim status under the Canadian Indian Acts, which in turn curtailed their access to tribal land holdings and services. Given the shockingly low quality of educational and medical services provided to tribal members on both sides of the U.S.-Canadian border and the difficulty in maintaining allotments or achieving self-sufficiency on reserved lands, such "benefits" of indigeneity did not always appeal to métis people like Nora Jewell. Claiming whiteness did not necessarily grant individuals greater access to education, land title, or medical care, but claiming whiteness did expand mixed-race peoples' access to portions of the Puget Sound world increasingly reserved for citizens and not subjects.

In the late nineteenth century, Seattle and Victoria had both passed codes denying residency to Indigenous wards and relegating Indians beyond municipal boundaries. Such statutes, though not enacted in every Puget Sound city or always effectively maintained (hop workers' camps are an example of lax enforcement), did work to discourage Indianness within urban spaces.[87] Nora Jewell, for instance, reported in April 1910 to the census enumerator in Tacoma, Washington, that she was a white widow and had borne no children. As in Lucía Martínez's case in 1880s Yuma, widowed status would have given the forty-five-year-old woman the respectability that her failed marriage and illegitimate child otherwise placed out of reach. She claimed her father had been born in Denmark and her mother in California—a fiction that would allow her to disguise any possible Indigenous racial phenotypes in a southwestern and possibly Hispanic origin. Nora rented a room in a home occupied by two other families and worked as a dressmaker, though she likely supplemented her income with proceeds from the sale of her father's San Juan Island farm in the late 1890s. Her move from the close-knit island community to the bustling port city may have helped her to shed markers of Indianness and memories of abuse— which happened to have taken place in a field within sight of the family home she had sold.[88]

Whether she knew it or not, Nora Jewell's move coincided with the U.S. government's effort to achieve an accurate count of Puget Sound Indians who had notoriously avoided Indian Office and territorial officials' efforts to enumerate and intern them on reserves since the close of the Indian Wars of the 1850s. Cloaked in a campaign to ensure delivery of treaty annuities and benefits to "undocumented" Indians living off reserves, the program for the "Enrollment and Allotment of Washington Indians" took place between 1911 and 1919 and was orchestrated by Special Agent Charles E. Roblin. The "Roblin Rolls" indicate that Nora Jewell's maternal aunt Ellen still lived on San Juan Island in 1919, while many of her children and grandchildren lived in Puyallup, a municipality bordering the Puyallup Reserve and Tacoma that had attracted Salish hop harvesters since the 1880s. Although Nora's cousins and aunt reported themselves on the Roblin Rolls so they could apply for allotments, Nora did not reclaim her Indianness through enrollment.[89]

The relocations of members of the Jones family throughout the San Juan Island chain and along the Puget Sound mainland reflect the geopolitical boundaries that shaped racial-ethnic and national identities for métis descendants like Nora in the twentieth century. Nora chose to claim whiteness and likewise resided in spaces designated for citizens, while her Jones cousins claimed Indianness and resided in spaces designated for subjects, each making choices about the privileges and risks these racial-ethnic categories offered. With her family living so near, Nora's declaration of whiteness did not necessarily sever her relations with métis kin from San Juan Island or in other parts of Coast Salish territory. In fact, it is possible that her status as a renter in Tacoma, and her mobile profession as a dressmaker—particularly well suited to urban settings—allowed her to travel along routes that Coast Salish kin had used throughout her lifetime, but which were increasingly closed off to Indians under pressure to enroll and take up permanent settlement on reserves. Nora's residence in Tacoma might have benefited her Indian kin in nearby Puyallup and throughout the island chain.

The relationships between Indigenous and métis families on San Juan and Vancouver Islands and along the mainland on both sides of the U.S.-Canadian border remained strong even into the twentieth century when individuals were making difficult choices between Indianness and whiteness and calculating which sides of provincial and national borders gave them better odds as citizens and subjects. Indigenous and mixed-race people remained highly mobile throughout the Puget Sound borderlands, but they likely shifted their declared racial, national, and gendered identities as they crossed the boundaries that divided subjects from citizens.[90]

When Nora was born in 1865, San Juan Island—literally on the border of U.S.-Canadian and Indigenous-immigrant political and cultural geographies—offered Native, newcomer, and mixed-race residents a wide range of opportunities to define their racial, ethnic, and national identities and to define their own gendered and sexual norms. It is in this context that the Jewell and Jones households formed and thrived. British Columbia fell under the British Colonial Office and remained largely under the control of the Hudson's Bay Company, while Washington Territory remained under the influence of métis and Indigenous families as Anglo immigrants struggled to escape their dependence on Native labor and knowledge. Over the course of Nora Jewell's lifetime, however, San Juan Islanders found their racial and sexual options severely curtailed and proscribed by their location within the island chain and mainland territories. Politicians in British Columbia and Washington state had instituted a segregationist legal and geopolitical regime by 1910 that obscured the interracial interdependence and flexible gender hierarchy that had characterized Nora Jewell's childhood in the border islands of the North American West.[91]

Described in this narrative as "mixed-race" and "métis," Nora Jewell was categorized in nineteenth-century records as a "half-breed" and as half-Indian. It is these halves of her life that were beyond the realm of imperial recorders and compilers. Nora Jewell managed to inherit her father's estate, because he was white, but Nora lost her mother because she was Indian. Fanny and Peter's daughter employed the privilege of whiteness to charge her guardian with rape, but it was her Indianness that made her, rather than James F. Smith, sexually deviant. Nora's half-whiteness made her a suitable bride for a man who was white, but not yet American, though it was her Indianness that ensured she could leave her husband and return to a community of mixed-race and Indian San Juan Islanders who would reclaim her as kin.

Nora Jewell's story, though at times ephemeral, demonstrates that the legal rights granted métis women in territorial Washington did not constitute the "privileges" of whiteness that could protect them from sexual and economic vulnerability. Although territorial Arizona's legal system included more explicitly exploitative statutes against Native women, Nora Jewell's experience in the Puget Sound region was not so different from that of Lucía Martínez in the Sonoran Southwest. Both women suffered legally sanctioned sexual exploitation and forced servitude at the hands of white men. Both women sought protections under the law and were denied on the grounds of race, though each pursued a less visible form of justice via Indigenous and mixed-race kinship networks not recognized by territorial law. Although James F. Smith and King S. Woolsey seemed to enjoy unchecked access to Indigenous women's productive and reproductive labors, their abuses did not go unchallenged because the law affirmed their white male superiority. Nora's and Lucía's cases demonstrate that male citizens' access to Indigenous women's bodies and progeny was based in a fantasy of patriarchy and supremacy upheld by an exploitative legal regime. Because Lucía's male allies and Nora's father and uncle repeatedly challenged the laws that barred them from having lifelong Indigenous intimates and sought to provide for their mixed-race children, we know that those fantasies were not shared by all settler-colonial men. Jewell and Martínez lodged savvy critiques of their guardians' presumed privileges, and both women wielded territorial law more creatively than contemporary jurists must have anticipated. Accustomed as they were to talking tree prophecies and the duplicity of coyotes who stole sex, Martínez and Jewell faced imperial legal regimes with legendary strength.

CHAPTER 4

Juana Walker's
"Legal Right as a Half-Breed"
Arizona, 1864–1916

> There appears to be no doubt of the parentage or moral rights of the newly
> discovered party to this remarkable and romantic case. Her legal right as a
> halfbreed remains to be established and nice points of law are involved in the
> establishment of it.
> —*Arizona Republican*, October 1, 1902

Juana Walker was born on September 17, 1873, in the "dry grass
month," a time usually spent working and celebrating the wheat
harvest with distant friends and relatives. A growing water crisis and small-
pox epidemic might have suspended festivities and feasting that year, however. Churga delivered Juana with the aid and support of female relatives living in the small village of Shuckma hudag (Blackwater), an Akimel O'odham
settlement in the eastern portion of the present-day Gila River Indian reservation. Juana's Miligahn (American) father, Captain John D. Walker, was
busy assisting Antonio Azul, a prominent O'odham leader, in the midst
of water and land rights negotiations in Indian Territory, and missed his
daughter's birth in southern Arizona. The relationship Juana shared with
her father has been clouded by time and disinterest, but the dramatic history of this mixed-race family reveals the intimate and controversial nature
of O'odham-Anglo relations in the second half of the nineteenth century
and Native women's efforts to define and determine their economic and
intimate ties to settler-colonists. The Walker family story—revealed only
through the remarkable testimony proffered during the lengthy trials over
John D. Walker's estate after his death in 1891—is one of shifting identities and loyalties, illustrating that where land and love were concerned, the

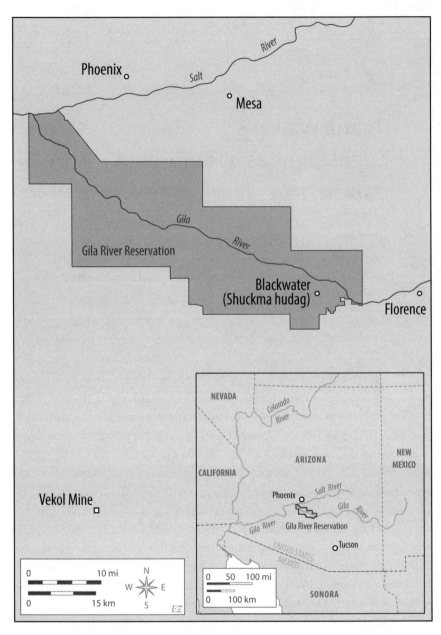

Juana Walker's Gila River borderlands (Map by Ezra Zeitler)

struggle to define whiteness and Indianness could drive a wealthy man insane and render his only daughter destitute.[1]

In 1892, about to turn nineteen, Juana Walker filed an inheritance claim against her deceased father's estate, challenging the rights of her American uncles and asserting her rights in the face of the territory's miscegenation statute. The case began in Pinal County's probate court, which ruled in Juana's favor, but moved on to district court and the Arizona Supreme Court, both of which overturned the lower court's decision. This chapter chronicles the trials and tribulations that shaped Walker family history, placing their experiences into the broader context of O'odham struggles for land, the complex debates over race and sexuality, and the place of mixed-race women in Arizona at the turn of the twentieth century. Although not always accurate portrayals of courtroom proceedings or trial outcomes, territorial Arizona newspaper reports regarding the Walker family trial like the one quoted above consistently identified the central issues their legal disputes raised for readers. Jurists nearly bent over backward to avoid such questions, but Pinal County jurors ultimately ruled on questions of Indigenous rights, interracial marriage, and the role of mixed-race persons in their communities when they upheld Juana Walker's inheritance rights in defiance of territorial antimiscegenation statutes.

Juana's legal challenge unpacks the significance of juridical silences and citizen sanctions that belie the seemingly rigid racial barriers prescribed in Arizona's penal code. The debate raised in Juana's estate case reveals that not all Arizonans supported the dispossession of their Indigenous friends, neighbors, relatives, and wives. In seeking to establish her "legal right as a half-breed," Juana's claims cut straight to the core of interracial sexual liaisons and property transmission that made up the "nice points" of miscegenation law in the second half of the nineteenth century.[2] Juana's family history includes the land and water disputes that might have prompted Akimel O'odham leaders like Antonio Azul and Juan José Gradello to turn to Juana's Miligahn father as a go-between in the 1870s and 1880s. John D. Walker's intimate access to O'odham women likely stemmed from tribal dependence upon his economic and political favor during a time of traumatic transition. Tribal and American views toward interracial sex and the mixed-race progeny such unions produced shifted during this period, as did assumptions regarding Indigenous peoples' capacities for citizenship. The disagreement between Pinal County jurors and territorial Arizona jurists regarding Juana's role in their community illustrates their fluctuating attitudes regarding sex and property, whiteness and Indianness. The distinction between "juror" and "jurist" is important since jurors are lay citizens obligated to pass judgment on their peers and jurists are the legal professionals—judges, lawyers, legislators—who interpret and make the laws that govern their fellow citizens. A significant class difference lies between these two groups in Juana's case, and jurors may not have always approved of the appointments or elections that determined jurists' elite positions in their communities.

Before Juana's birth in the fall of 1873, her father had lived among the O'odham for seven years and he likely knew those who attended his wife's labor while he was absent on tribal business. His military service introduced him to the O'odham and southern Arizona, though he had not sought an appointment in Indian Country. Walker accompanied his father from their Illinois home to California at the age of twenty. Like other young men, John D. chafed under his father's stern authority and joined the Union army on November 22, 1861, about a year into the Civil War. He later remembered, "My father let me go from home without a cent. I went into the army, not expecting to be thrown into a wild country, but it was so and I never saw my father again."[3] The rebellious son served as wagon master for the Fifth Regiment California Infantry, which drew him to the Pima villages near the Gila River where the O'odham supplied army troops with wheat because American farmers had not yet mastered Sonoran agriculture. Civil War service in Arizona (still New Mexico Territory at the time) introduced the young soldier to men like King S. Woolsey, who traded and transported wheat for the military as a private citizen. Although they did not appear to share social circles, the two frontiersmen would later fight Apaches along with O'odham and Pee Posh (Maricopa) warriors.

On November 30, 1864, just a few months after the adjournment of Arizona's first territorial legislative session, Corporal Walker received his discharge and settled in Ge e Ke (Sacaton), the main settlement and Indian Agency headquarters for the Gila River O'odham. While there, he struck up a close friendship with Antonio Azul, a tribal leader who would become the primary Gila River dignitary in federal negotiations and in such famous joint anti-Apache expeditions as the Camp Grant massacre in 1871.[4] After trading with the O'odham for three years, Walker had become fluent in their language. While living with Azul over the winter of 1864–1865, John D. learned much of the River People's history and traditions from elders. The soldier's ethnographic knowledge was even deemed newsworthy in Florence, where the *Arizona Weekly Enterprise* reported, "There is probably no living person among the English speaking people who can talk the Pima language more fluently than . . . Walker. His knowledge of Indian lore would make a very interesting volume."[5] Sadly, his familiar knowledge of tribal members and practices only made him more susceptible to later charges of insanity and incompetence.

In the 1860s, when John D. Walker entered O'odham territory in the Gila River valley, Antonio Azul's tribe had only recently transitioned from being citizens of Mexico to subjects of the United States under the stipulations of the Gadsden Purchase in 1854 and the Treaty of Guadalupe Hidalgo in 1848. The federal government's establishment of the Gila River reservation in 1859 without treaty negotiations perfectly reflected the tribe's status as a "domestic dependent nation," as the U.S. boundary commission recognized tribal land rights by setting aside O'odham lands.[6] But the United States did not acknowledge O'odham sovereign claims to the entire region from modern-day Gila Bend to the Pinal Mountains east of Florence.[7] Almost from the beginning of U.S.-O'odham relations, actors on both sides recognized the tribe's vulnerability to incursions from Americans and Mexicans attracted to the Gila River's fertile bottomlands and ready to benefit from the absence of Apaches that the O'odham and Pee Posh had fought so long to secure.[8] Nevertheless, policymakers did not grant American Indians the rights to protect their property—whether by title or force—from the farmers and miners who began to surround the reservation immediately following the conclusion of the Civil War.

Without the legal right to contract that came along with citizenship, Arizona's Indigenous occupants struggled to slow the dispossession and water theft that followed federal recognition of the territory. One way to assuage the effects of settler-colonialism was to secure white allies who could represent tribal interests, and serve as a buffer against anti-Indian sentiments among neighboring Americans and Mexicans as willing to fight O'odham as Apaches for their own piece of manifest destiny.[9] John D. Walker first came to the tribe as an agent of the U.S. military, then used his influence to remain within the Gila River valley as a helpmeet to tribal leader Antonio Azul. The go-between's exact status on the reservation remains unclear, as some sources refer to him as agency farmer, others as an agency interpreter, but Juana's father clearly proved himself valuable to the O'odham regardless of his official capacity in the postwar years.[10]

It might have been during this time that Walker met an adolescent Churga, but it was after he led Antonio Azul's warrior scouts alongside King S. Woolsey that the Anglo ally most likely impressed Juana's mother.[11] In June 1865, the territorial governor organized the Arizona Volunteers to protect citizens from Apache raids. Mexican American troops made up two companies, Pee Posh (Maricopas) comprised a third, and the Civil War wagon master became captain of the Pima Company with Antonio Azul serving as his first lieutenant. As Walker led O'odham warriors against Apaches as part of Company C of the Arizona Volunteers, he somehow managed to endear himself to other male members of the tribe. It is during this time that he probably earned his nickname, *Has Viakam*—large penis. In a tribe that frequently enjoyed sexual humor, the provocative moniker demonstrates that Juana's father had been informally, but intimately, inducted into tribal ranks.[12] Twenty-five-year-old Walker reported success against the Apaches, but also complained about lacking supplies. Territorial legislators sought federal support for their borderlands militia, but failed to retain the Arizona Volunteers for anti-Apache service. After July 1, 1866, Americans could no longer rely on commissioned Indians and Mexicans to protect them from Apaches, though these groups would reunite informally against the Apaches in the 1871 Camp Grant massacre because they shared a disapproval of the federal military's handling of Apaches in the region.[13]

Once again discharged from military service, the man from Illinois continued to make his home with Azul at Ge e Ke. Without a commission, the veteran sought other employment on the O'odham reserve. He showed interest in a teaching position, and Indian agent C. H. Lord reported to the commissioner of Indian Affairs in 1866 that the O'odham "desire to have a school. Lieutenant Walker, who lives with the Pimas and understands their language most perfectly, is competent to teach them. For a reasonable compensation he would take charge of a school."[14] Perhaps the salary was too low, or never offered. In any case, in 1868 Walker turned toward personal agricultural pursuits and, with help from others living near the Gila River settlements, he dug the Walker Ditch that put four hundred acres into irrigation nearly twelve miles west of Florence.[15]

The late 1860s proved a difficult period in U.S.-O'odham relations along the Gila and Salt Rivers; John D. Walker served as a critical ally to Antonio Azul in the struggle to find common ground with federal agents and officials as Miligahn demands for O'odham resources grew. Indian agents Ammi White and Levi Ruggles, charged with defending O'odham

lands against unscrupulous whites, actually founded Florence and Adamsville on lands just north of the reservation and helped Americans claim
uncultivated O'odham lands to the west.[16] Anglo citizens viewed unim-
proved lands as public domain and registered their plots despite protests
from tribal leaders.[17] While Walker and other Americans built homes and
irrigated fields in the midst of O'odham territory, some diverted water that
had fed O'odham crops and then made claims to the military for Indian
depredations that stemmed from tribal crop failures. In 1869, Azul's friend
interpreted Indian agent F. E. Grossman's speech to prominent Gila River
tribesmen regarding their "hostile" actions toward citizen property within
and bordering Indian Country.

When the Gila River began to fail in 1870 due to drought and upstream
water demands from white farmers, O'odham families found the lands they
had used for seasonal harvests and hunting occupied by settler-colonists,
so they began to move north toward the Salt River—an area that had not
attracted citizens because of its proximity to Apaches, who were feared
by many and misunderstood by all. In his role as intermediary between
O'odham and Americans, which he would fulfill for another twenty years,
Walker knew intimately the frustrations of his Indigenous friends and the
ambitions of his citizen neighbors. By 1870, Juana's father established his
ranch on O'odham land and married his O'odham wife in tribal tradition,
demonstrating that his service to Azul profited him personally and politically. With little access to capital or contracts, the O'odham used sex
and property to reward the citizens who befriended them. Contemporary
observers noted that while the tribe struggled to reestablish self-reliance
through agriculture on Salt River lands they claimed without federal sanction, some turned to "stealing, begging, and prostituting their women in
efforts to survive" the devastation wrought by starvation and sickness.[18]
Although outsiders viewed some O'odham practices as prostitution, it is
only because the federal and territorial governments barred the O'odham
from citizenship, thus waiving Churga's right to the marriage contract, that
her commitment to Walker lacked legal and moral sanctity. Were she and
her parents American citizens, Churga might have commanded more respect from Walker's Miligahn friends and relatives, and the tribal land that
Walker farmed might have been held in her name.

As noted in chapter 2, King Woolsey and his fellow legislators ratified the territory's antimiscegenation clause late in 1864: "All marriages of
white persons with negroes or mulattoes are declared to be illegal and void."

Agents who contracted such marriages faced a fine between one hundred dollars and ten thousand dollars and imprisonment from three months to ten years.[19] In the next legislative session, Woolsey's friends expanded these racial restrictions on marriage to include "All marriages of white persons with negroes, mulattoes, Indians, or Mongolians," likely because a year in the region in Arizona's early territorial period had given them time to realize that white men and women were far outnumbered and that intermarriage contradicted their efforts to maintain economic, legal, and social supremacy for Anglos.[20] Arizona lawmakers upheld these antimiscegenation statutes when they made the transition into statehood in 1912 and did not revise them until 1942, when legislators agreed to allow marriages between Native and white Arizonans—finally legitimating Arizona's substantial *mestizo* population.[21] Not only were Indigenous men and women barred from contracting interracial marriages during this period, but between 1864 and 1912 they could not testify in civil cases, making it impossible for Akimel O'odham witnesses to give evidence in estate disputes such as the Walker family trial.

On the surface, federal laws regulating financial transactions between individual citizens and Indians seemed to deter fraudulent dealings by barring unscrupulous whites from reservation economies. Similarly, antimiscegenation statutes seemed to restrict sexual exploitation of nonwhite women by denying white men access to their fidelity. Of no surprise to those who study federal Indian policy and the history of racial-ethnic women, however, the exact opposite has been the result in both cases. Deeper investigation reveals that federal oversight of land and trade contracts in the second half of the nineteenth century defrauded tribes of millions of acres to the benefit of citizens who profited from the Indian trade in myriad ways. Likewise, a closer examination of Indian-white antimiscegenation statutes demonstrates that such provisions ensured white men's sexual access to Indigenous women, but exempted men like Juana's father from the financial and paternal obligations that comprise the marital contract. Of course, as discussed in chapter 2, Arizona's territorial politicians were willing to grant Indigenous residents the right to sign indenture contracts—although they did not acknowledge American Indians' right to refuse indenture contracts.

Federal laws established in the early republic of the late eighteenth century and still applicable during westward expansion in the late nineteenth century required American Indians to trade and negotiate exclusively with

appointed government officials and prevented individual citizens from negotiating leases, sale of land, or trade contracts with tribal members.[22] Although part of this policy has allowed contemporary tribes to insist upon
their sovereign status as entities on par with federal and state governments,
such regulations also made tribes vulnerable to federal prerogatives in the
nineteenth century.[23] When U.S. boundary commissioner Sylvester Mowry
surveyed and established the Gila River reservation in 1859, Azul and other
O'odham disputed the boundary because it did not include their uncultivated lands beyond the Gila River alluvial area. As noted earlier, Indian
agents Ammi White and then Levi Ruggles used their position to speculate
on lands beyond the reservation boundary and established Florence and
Adamsville upstream from their O'odham wards. Drought exacerbated by
upstream water diversion produced starvation conditions on the reservation and families soon became susceptible to epidemic diseases like small-
pox. Although Juana's father lobbied in the tribe's favor and Indian department officials would revise reservation boundaries several times into the
twentieth century, the O'odham lost much of their land, mineral deposits,
and water rights in the Gila River valley to American and Mexican settler-
colonists.[24] In limiting O'odham individuals' abilities to choose buyers and
leasers for their land, federal law ensured that they could not reject lease or
purchase offers either.

It is in this tumultuous and sometimes desperate context that Juana's
father befriended and interpreted for Antonio Azul, claimed and fenced his
own Gila River ranch, fought Apaches with American, Mexican, O'odham,
and Pee Posh men, learned O'odham oratories and songs, and married
Juana's mother. Between 1870 and 1877, Juana's parents lived and procre-
ated on the Walker Ranch near Adamsville in violation of intercourse and
miscegenation laws. Regardless of his intentions, these legal provisions
ensured that Has Viakam was under no obligation to honor the trust his
O'odham family and friends had invested in him. Had they wanted to, Azul
and his friends could not forcibly remove the captain from the Gila River
valley, Churga could not reject his sexual advances, and Juan José Gradello
could not sue him for mineral rights to the Vekol Mine. Denied the right to
choose their economic and sexual partners, Gila River O'odham negotiated
with Walker over those things he could easily have taken—their land, their
bodies, and their resources. In essence, they offered what they could—sex
and property—to gain traction during a period of devastation and suffering.

In exchange, Walker translated for Azul when he could, made credit available to Churga during her lifetime, and employed O'odham laborers at the silver mine that made him, but no one's grandmother, wealthy.

How the captain and Churga viewed their relationship is difficult to determine from the available records, but their contemporaries disclosed their attitudes regarding tribal and interracial unions. In 1873 former Indian agent F. E. Grossman claimed that "many of the [O'odham] women are public prostitutes," and that "[m]arriages among the Pimas are entered into without ceremony, and are never considered as binding. . . . Wives frequently leave their husbands and husbands their wives. This act of leaving is all that is necessary to separate them forever."[25] He went on to say that "[o]nly the worst of the women of the tribe cohabit with the whites, but it is undeniable that the number of such women is increasing from year to year."[26] The agent occasionally relied on Walker's interpreting skills, making it likely that he knew of the go-between's marriage to Churga, but still maintained such prejudice.

Grossman's attitudes reflected a growing tide of Victorian antagonism toward interracial unions and mixed-race progeny, but it is difficult to determine whether Churga's O'odham relatives viewed her and the other O'odham women who would later live with her husband among the "worst" of her tribe.[27] Antonio Azul's likely involvement in the match—as Walker's friend and a respected tribal leader—would suggest that Churga held some status if she was viewed as an ideal match for the man that had lived with and assisted the tribe since 1864. By 1870, however, increasingly unstable living conditions may have prompted O'odham women to seek sexual liaisons with citizen men to gain leverage as they lost land and water, and so Churga may have been motivated by dependency. Her tribe told stories of women who had extraordinary sexual relationships with clouds, rain, or animals, and more ordinary liaisons with men from distant villages and foreign tribes. At times, these women were depicted as prostitutes, or "loose women," who suffered shame and sometimes worse. In other instances, however—such as the story of Corn Woman, who mourned her dead children and became promiscuous in her grief-stricken state, then returned to her husband with a collection of powerful songs—libidinous women brought valuable alliances or insights to their people.[28] These narratives, perhaps making up the "case law" of O'odham oral tradition that regulated extramarital and exogamous sex, suggest that Churga and her family upheld a cultural framework that anticipated interracial unions even if her tribe did not normalize such relationships. These factors, in addition to Churga's return to the reservation when she left her husband in 1877, indicate that her O'odham kin did not judge Juana's mother as the "worst" of her kind at all.

Indeed, from the O'odham perspective, perhaps it was Has Viakam who lived a "loose" life. His nickname, "large penis," certainly evokes virility if not promiscuity; the man would insist to his doctors and friends in the 1880s that he had contracted syphilis from sex with O'odham women. His friends and neighbors testified that he lived with multiple female tribal members throughout his lifetime. In September 1873, Churga bore her daughter at home in Shuckma hudag and returned to the Walker Ranch with a female companion to help her with the infant and household duties.[29] Churga's family may have expected her husband to share his wealth by taking in another dependent to ease their own dire straits on the reservation. Prominent O'odham men who could support large families occasionally practiced polygamy and if Walker chose to enjoy a sexual relationship with his wife's kin, he would have been acting within tribal protocol and according to his fellow citizens' presumption of sexual access to Indigenous women.[30] John D. was appointed Pinal County probate judge and surveyor shortly after Juana's birth and he may have used these positions of authority to claim male economic and sexual privileges deriving from O'odham and American cultural traditions. Perhaps Churga returned to Sacaton with her daughter in 1877 because it had become unbearable to live with the man who was simultaneously referred to as Has Viakam and Judge Walker.

Regardless of her reasons, Churga's return to the reservation signified her rejection of the marriage in accordance with tribal custom and indicates that she expected her family to support her decision. O'odham oral tradition describes interracial sex as a response to social ruptures, whether it be a death in the family or the arrival of strangers, and the desperate conditions wrought by territorial expansion and settler incursions in the 1870s and 1880s were not only disruptive, but traumatic. Such an understanding would explain why "not one of the chiefs or old men of the nation . . . thought it necessary to raise a warning voice [against interracial liaisons] . . . and prostitutes . . . are by no means treated with contempt or scorn."[31] Although it was Indian agent Grossman who first characterized women engaged in interracial relationships as prostitutes in the 1870s and not the O'odham, the tribe seemingly began to adopt similar attitudes by the end of the nineteenth century. As territorial legal structures disabled Indian women from negotiating the terms of their sexuality, and social structures barred them from gaining cultural, economic, or social benefits through intermarriage, O'odham attitudes toward interracial sex began to change. Instead of returning to their tribe with oratories and songs, O'odham women brought dependence and disease when their relationships with white men ended. When she returned to her O'odham family, Juana's mother brought a mixed-race daughter who others described as the spitting image of her father, as well as a line of credit at the Sacaton trading post funded by John D.

Although they likely knew they were taking a risk sending their daughter into a Miligahn man's home, Churga's family must have been convinced that the soldier from Illinois would provide for her even if they were uneasy about the encroachment of Mexicans and Americans onto their lands. It is unclear how Churga and Walker met, but if she had grown up in Shuckma hudag, where she gave birth to Juana, she and the captain most certainly crossed paths as she grew from adolescence to womanhood in the 1860s. When riding with Azul and the O'odham scouts, Walker reportedly "dressed like them, with nothing on but a breechclout, and whooped and yelled like his Indian comrades."[32] Perhaps Has Viakam courted like his O'odham friends as well, soliciting Azul's services as a proxy to carry his proposal to Churga's family. Describing his youthful years among the O'odham, John D. wrote in 1890: "I would have to be pretty strong nerved to resist the temptations that have been thrown before me. Take a young man and especially among the natives; youth and beauty are irresistible."[33] Walker's attraction to O'odham women may have encouraged Azul to identify an appropriate partner for his Miligahn friend.

Walker certainly had material comforts to offer Juana's mother. Pima-Maricopa agent Grossman submitted a survey of Mexican and American settlements north of the reservation being considered for an expansion of O'odham lands. The federal government had issued warnings advising non-Indians not to settle there, but Juana's father claimed two plots in the contested zone: one became the 266-acre Walker Ranch and the other stood as an eighty-acre farm. Enclosed by a mesquite brush fence, the ranch bordered the Gila River to the north. The purportedly well-endowed man had built a four-room adobe home and a granary to store wheat (the crop that he had once purchased and hauled for the army). He maintained 3,000 grapevines, 250 quince bushes, 200 fig trees, and 200 pomegranates. Grossman called it "the most improved of all those included by the extension," and noted that "Walker located and improved the land . . . after [former] Superintendent [of Indian Affairs George] Leihy issued his notice forbidding improvements."[34] For his part, Juana's father bragged that he had become an adopted member of the tribe by this time, and he likely viewed uncultivated Gila River bottomlands as acreage available for use and development, just as O'odham families did.[35]

Fluent in O'odham language and tradition, proven in battle against Apaches, accumulating wealth only five miles from Churga's home village, John D. must have been an ideal suitor. The young woman agreed to marry the captain in the O'odham way—in moving from Shuckma hudag to the Walker Ranch she followed the patrilocal tradition of her tribe. Although the union violated Arizona's miscegenation law banning Indian-white marriages, close friends recognized Churga and John D.'s marriage—reportedly performed on the Gila River reservation—as one that conformed to tribal practices, whereby a woman accepted a proposal by moving to her spouse's home in a settlement near her own.[36]

It is not known exactly when Churga moved to her husband's home. Assistant Marshal Charles A. Shibbell included the Walker Ranch in his 1870 census of the Adamsville district; perhaps Shibbell counted the household that was actually within the borders of the reservation so he could visit his old Civil War comrade—he and John D. had served together in the California Volunteers assigned to expel Confederates from Arizona. In recording Walker's property as a territorial, rather than a tribal household, the census agent validated his friend's tenuous claim to the land. Although they were likely "notorious in the neighborhood" because they were living in flagrant violation of the miscegenation law, Shibbell helped the Walkers obscure their interracial intimacy in the 1870 census.[37] The enumerator listed Churga as "Juana"—a common name among O'odham women—and scrawled a "W" for white over the Indian "I" he had originally marked. They reported the Native woman as twenty-one years old, though other friends described her as being closer to thirteen. The assistant marshal claimed that Mrs. Walker was "Keeping House," a common profession or occupation used to denote legitimate wives in Arizona households. Instructions to 1870 census enumerators stated that "women keeping house for their own families or for themselves, without any other gainful occupation, will be entered as 'keeping house,'" indicating that Shibbell categorized the O'odham woman as Walker's wife by labeling her thus.[38] Because the census schedule for 1870 did not demarcate household relationships or question respondents' marital status, Shibbell did not actually have to acknowledge

19	17	17	Ducivichan Demetri	24	M	W	Labrw			Sonora Mex	1
20			Grijalba Reyes	21	M	W	"			" "	1
21	18	18	Walker John D	30	M	W	Farmer	3500	2,000	Illinois	
22			—— Juana	21	F	W	Keeping House			Arizona	
23			Ellis Joseph	18	M	W	Farm Laborw			Jerusalem	1
24	19	19	Valenzuela Incarnacio	20	M	W	Farm Laborn			Sonora Mex	1
25	20	20	Garcia Demetrio	37	M	W	Brick Mason			Sonora Mex	1
26			—— Incarnacion	16	F	W	Keeping House			" "	1

Churga (listed as Juana) and John D. Walker household, 1870 U.S. Census, Arizona Territory, Pima County, Adamsville Precinct

an interracial, and thereby illegitimate, union while carrying out his official duties.[39]

Whether Walker proposed to his wife in O'odham or English, and whether he presented his household as normative or deviant, the young man offered his bride a married life that seemed to replicate her tribal pattern. Friends described the couple as living together and working apart in distinctly gendered ways. The rancher traveled among his properties to oversee crops and in the 1870s began to prospect in the Sonoran Desert. Although he had been decommissioned, Walker continued to fight Apaches with his O'odham friends and on August 20, 1872, he reported to the *Arizona Citizen* that "a few young Pimas" killed ten Apaches north of Florence. With his wife near the end of her pregnancy in the fall of 1873, Juana's father accompanied Azul and others to negotiate with federal officials in Indian Territory, now Oklahoma.[40]

Churga, too, left her home at the Walker Ranch on occasion. Although neighbors neglected to describe her excursions in detail, they noted Mrs. Walker's absences from the ranch even before she went home to deliver her daughter. She may have left Walker in the spring to harvest *ciolim*, cholla cactus buds that resemble asparagus tips, or just before the monsoons to harvest *baidac* (saguaro fruit) with female relatives. Perhaps she visited her village during the wheat harvest—a semiannual gathering that brought Tohono O'odham and Pee Posh friends to northeastern Akimel O'odham settlements. When the young mother returned to the Walker Ranch with the infant Juana in the fall of 1873, she also brought another O'odham woman—likely a younger female relative—to assist her in the domestic management of her husband's sizable estate.[41]

Walker's appointment as county surveyor and probate judge of Pinal County shortly after his daughter's birth required him to be in Florence for court sessions and in the field surveying roads and boundary lines—some of which divided Native and newcomer lands. While surveying the county, Walker worked with O'odham and Miligahn men to investigate mining prospects in O'odham territory. Perhaps unwilling to be left behind so often, or disturbed by her husband's willingness to work for the Americans who encroached upon her lands, Churga left the Walker Ranch for good in 1877 and returned home to the reservation, taking four-year-old Juana with her. John D. would later describe this as a painful parting, but never fully explained its cause.[42]

Much had changed on the reservation since Churga had left her childhood home to marry Walker at least seven years earlier. Reverend Charles H. Cook—who learned the O'odham language from Churga's husband—had established a day school for Indian children and a Presbyterian church for their families at the agency headquarters in Ge e Ke (Sacaton). Walker's younger half-brother, Lucien, and friend Isaac D. Smith, an occasional guest at the ranch, operated a store in Ge e Ke as well. Through these men, Walker maintained ties with his O'odham family and made a line of credit available for his wife and daughter at Smith's store.[43]

Although Churga and Juana likely benefited from the credit Walker extended them at Isaac D. Smith's store in Ge e Ke, by the late 1870s and early 1880s they and their family members faced increasing famine and disease. Despite officials' and O'odham leaders' complaints that Miligahn and Jujkum (Mexican) water use had disrupted the Salt and Gila River systems feeding O'odham crops, the tribal aquifer continued to sink as Arizona's farming reputation grew. In hopes of discouraging citizen encroachment and protecting O'odham access to the Salt River water table, between 1879 and 1883 Congress more than doubled the Pima-Maricopa reservation. Throughout the 1880s and 1890s these goals remained unmet, however, and widespread malnutrition and social duress made many O'odham vulnerable to disease during the subsequent famine. Churga died in the early 1880s of unknown causes. The Blackwater calendar stick annals for 1882– 1883 recorded a measles epidemic within the village, suggesting that Juana's mother may have been afflicted with the disease.[44]

While reservation-bound O'odham suffered the effects of their water sinking underground, Juana's father found buried treasure at the Vekol (Grandmother) Mine on unceded lands south of Casa Grande. His role as Pinal County surveyor would have made him privy to the mineral wealth his fellow settler-colonists were claiming throughout the Gila River valley and he likely desired some of his own. Juan José Gradello reportedly offered to show the silver mine to Walker because of his great respect for the former captain. Walker immediately staked a claim to the silver deposit. Gradello and other O'odham may have been seeking a means to cement their relationship to Walker after Churga had left him. Along with his friend Peter Brady, Walker set to work in 1880 and the mine became one of the most productive silver ventures Arizonans had ever known.[45] Except for an episode of illness that sent him seeking recuperation in California in 1886, Juana's father spent the 1880s primarily at the remote Vekol Mine, maintaining important friendships in Casa Grande and Florence, as well as lucrative financial relationships with California banks. Juana's Anglo grandfather had remarried in John D.'s youth and John's half-siblings helped him to oversee his financial interests in the Los Angeles area. Lucien Walker, younger by twelve years, joined his half-brother at Vekol Mine in 1882, when John D. and Peter Brady agreed to share a third interest with the young man. Lucien brought his wife to Vekol from California when he and his brother bought Brady's share in 1884 and established the J. D. Walker and Bros. Mining Company.[46]

Juana's father set up a small settlement at the Vekol Mine, roughly thirty miles south of Casa Grande on today's Tohono O'odham reservation. The Anglo Walkers shared the Vekol Mine camp with "Indian, Chinaman, Mexican [and] American" laborers, where they established a school for miners' children, a company store for provisions, and banned alcohol to keep order in the camp. Territorial newspapers described the "marvelous" Vekol Mine as a philanthropic enterprise. "Although [the Walker brothers] enjoy a monopoly of the merchandising of the camp, they do not compel their employees to purchase of them, and neither do they charge monopoly prices. . . . They never turn a stranger away hungry or weary."[47] Although his Indian family remained on the reservation, Has Viakam continued to live among O'odham friends and employees in the diverse industrial outpost he had established with their help.

As the water situation on the reservation continued to worsen, O'odham families relocated closer to the agency headquarters to collect rations or moved to citizen settlements to work for wages. Practically orphaned when her mother died sometime in the early 1880s, Juana's position in her community proved tenuous. Churga had likely shared her access to trading post credit with her family, but once she died, her family might have struggled to support Juana. When the Mormon Pomeroy family arrived looking for an Indian ward, Juana found herself put forward, perhaps much as her mother had been offered to her father, or perhaps to divert the Mormons' attention from the children of mothers still alive.

Gertrude Pomeroy took Juana from the Sacaton Indian Agency to live with her parents and ten siblings in Mesa City—a town cofounded by the Pomeroy patriarch about thirty miles northwest of Ge e Ke. The mixed-race girl's role among the Pomeroys is difficult to determine. She may have been put to work as a servant who could help Mrs. Pomeroy clean and feed ten children; she might have been a conversion project for the Mormon family living so close to the Indian Agency; or perhaps Juana entertained the Pomeroy children as a novel pet, wild and yet domesticated. Whatever her role, Churga's daughter lived with the prestigious Mormon family for the remainder of her childhood.[48]

Although no evidence has surfaced that Rosetta Pomeroy and Walker discussed the legal structures that made Rosetta guardian of Churga's daughter rather than Juana's O'odham relatives, in the late 1880s Rosetta corresponded with Juana's father regarding the girl's welfare. The eldest of the Pomeroy children, Rosetta had apparently taken over Juana's care from her own mother, Gertrude Pomeroy. Perhaps they had shared a special bond together in the Mormon household. Rosetta enrolled at Tempe Normal School while raising Juana and tried to give the child an education at the primary school in Mesa, but Churga's daughter suffered from seizures and rarely attended. Based on Rosetta's description of Juana's episodes, Juana's father diagnosed his child with epilepsy and sent her guardian medical advice and money for the girl's doctors. John D. remembered his daughter's birthdays with cash gifts, too, but it seems he never found time to visit Juana once she and Churga had left his ranch.[49] On November 8, 1889, John D. sent a belated birthday note to Rosetta, explaining that he had been "confirmed invalid" and had missed Juana's sixteenth birthday. Both formally and poignantly, he wrote, "Please give [Little Juana] my kindest regards; although it has been eleven years since I have seen her I shall never forget how she cried and begged not to be taken away."[50]

Less than ten days after writing these heartfelt words, Juana's father suffered from what doctors diagnosed as "softening of the brain" or "general paresis." John D. was examined by multiple doctors and it was reported that he had suffered a paralytic stroke at the Vekol Mine and felt "confusion in [his] mind."[51] Two O'odham women were the first to attend to him during his violent seizure, showing their intimate access to Juana's father, and they summoned Vekol Mine foreman William T. Day to restrain and aid the patient, who did not recover his ability to speak for more than a month.

Newspapers carried vague reports on Walker's health following the episode. On November 23, 1889, Florence's weekly paper wrote, "It is with

```
No 101.
G.W.Woodley,Cash.
signed to identify only.
                                        Casa Grande,Arizona,Nov.8th. 1889.

Miss Rosetta pomeroy
            Zance,Maricopa Co.A.T.

My Dear Miss
            I received your letter last year written but I was a confirmed invalid
aparently at that time a** neglected to write,expecting you would drop me a line at
some time,and I spent the summer and have no        here much improved in health
and hopes of enjoying life for some time yet. Please write me how the little girl,
she must be a big girl,is getting. I should have sent her a birthday present on
her last birthday,the 16th. of September,when she was sixteen. Please give her my
kindest regards; although it has been eleven years since I have seen her I shall
never forget how she cried and begged not to be taken away.
                              Very truly your friend,
                                                 J.D.Walker.


Plaintiff
        Exhibit D.
        ----------------------------------------------------

Lucien or Smith
            Let the bearer have 10 yards of calico for Juana, if Churya wants
a little provision at any time give it to her and charge my account.
                                        J.D.Walker.

Florence
        Oct. 9 1879.


Plaintiff
        Exhibit "E"
```

Letter from John D. Walker submitted as evidence in estate of John Walker, 1891, Case No. 128 (RG 111, Pinal County, SG 8, Superior Court Records, Civil and Probate, p. 655; reproduced with permission from Arizona State Library, Archives and Public Records)

exceeding regret that *The Enterprise* announces the serious illness of Judge J. D. Walker, at the Vekol, who is suffering with paralysis of the throat and is reported quite low." A Casa Grande report read, "[Judge J. D. Walker] contracted a severe cold and is laid up. A report has just reached this place that he has suffered a stroke of paralysis, but the severity of his affliction is not known."[52] Little Juana was on Walker's mind; as soon as he recovered his ability to communicate, Juana's father directed his friend William Day to send money to Rosetta Pomeroy. On December 10, 1889, Day wrote her on J. D. Walker & Bros. Vekol Mine letterhead. "Mr. Walker is quite sick and unable to write. . . . The Judge wishes you to write to him. The Doctor does

not allow him to see people or to talk to them. Yours truly, J. D. Walker &
bro—Day."[53]

Juana's father never fully recovered from his stroke. In May of 1890, his
older brother William applied for and was awarded guardianship of his estate and person when the former soldier was declared incompetent. Friends
and family claimed that the westering man was often confused and incoherent, and seemed crippled and frail. Many could not diagnose the illness, but
described him as "wildly insane." The invalid found respite in an asylum
near his brother William's home in California, but he constantly expressed a
desire to return to Arizona and his Vekol Mine. In July the *Arizona Weekly
Enterprise* in Florence reported that Walker's health "is constantly improving. . . . The many friends of Judge Walker hope to meet him again in Arizona, fully restored to health."[54]

While Juana's father underwent treatment in California and lost control of his personal and financial affairs, he renewed a correspondence with
Eleanor Rice, a childhood sweetheart he had left behind in Illinois. The
two had not written one another since 1867. Because he initiated their romantic relationship after he had been deemed legally incompetent, Walker's
American family members questioned his sincerity and prudence, particularly when he began to plan a reunion with the woman. In his letters to
"Nellie," as he affectionately called her, John D. complained bitterly of his
brothers' guardianship over him as he promised to regain control over his
own financial affairs.[55] Between October 1890 and February 1891, John D.
Walker wrote to friends and business partners seeking financial and medical
assistance so that he could resettle in Arizona's Salt River valley and begin
a married life with Eleanor Rice.[56]

Walker convinced his brothers to let him return to the Vekol with their
youngest sibling, Lucien, in November 1890. Once in the territory, Juana's
father traveled repeatedly to Florence, his former jurisdiction, to meet with
those who might help him regain his independence.[57] In December 1890,
Eleanor moved from Quincy, Illinois, to Los Angeles, California, and began her own campaign for her sweetheart's release from his brothers' legal
guardianship.[58] Ironically, the man who had benefited sexually and economically from the Akimel O'odham's wardship status now found himself
a dependent ward against his will. Walker's siblings later claimed they supported his affection for Eleanor, but were concerned that his mental state
made him vulnerable in love and—more important—marriage. Although

his non-state-sanctioned union with an Indian woman had made them all wealthy, his legal marriage to a white woman could as quickly destroy their fortune. Still, the brothers could not stop the star-crossed lovers from meeting in Tucson at the end of February 1891, thirty years after their separation in Illinois.

The *Arizona Weekly Enterprise* posted a terse notice six weeks after their reunion: "Judge John D. Walker and Miss Eleanor D. Rice, of Quincy, Ill., were married in Tucson, on April 18th, Rev. David Alva officiating. Although this announcement may surprise a vast circle of friends and acquaintances of Judge Walker, for the event was quite unexpected, they will all join *The Enterprise* in extending hearty and sincere congratulations."[59] Walker's brothers protested the arrangement with a writ of habeas corpus against Eleanor Rice for the custody of their beloved invalid. Under the headline "Vekol Walker's Marriage," the *Phoenix Herald* reported that "[t]he wedding . . . does not seem to have given complete family satisfaction as . . . Lucien Walker, brother to the groom, endeavored to separate him from his newly married bride . . . by virtue of a writ of habeas corpus."[60] The *Arizona Daily Star* of Tucson condemned William and Lucien's efforts to separate John D. and Eleanor: "If the Walker brothers desire their brother John's best interest to be subserved, they will simply let him alone. [T]he very best nurse and guardian he can possibly have is his wife. [H]e is just as sane as either of his brothers. This insanity dodge won't work in Arizona, especially in Tucson, where our people don't allow that kind of dust to [be] thrown in their eyes."[61]

Early in May 1891, Pima County probate judge Woods heard extensive testimony regarding John D. Walker's state of mind. While Anglo family and friends testified for and against his sanity, most observed that John D. "had many lucid intervals but was at all times liable to become violent."[62] Judge Woods, based primarily on physicians' testimony, concluded that Juana's forty-nine-year-old father was incompetent, thus upholding William's guardianship over his younger brother. Woods and Walker's doctors recommended that John D. be committed to a California asylum where he could escape the Arizona heat—a factor they believed aggravated his condition.[63]

William T. Day, who had been with Walker during his first seizure and had sent money to Juana's Mormon guardian in Mesa City on his behalf, served as John D.'s chaperone as he traveled from Tucson to Florence, then Casa Grande, and finally Los Angeles. Day reported that his friend was frequently upset and required restraint; that he destroyed furniture and broke windows in the hotel rooms they reserved. Shortly after arriving in Los Angeles near the end of May, Juana's father was arrested for "wildness" when he ran in the streets without pants. Doctor James J. Choate, who had treated Walker in 1889 and 1890, quieted John D. by telling him that the padded "crazy cell" was his office and that they had put him there so he could work undisturbed. Dr. Choate and William Walker soon committed their ward to the sanatorium in Napa, in northern California, where he continued to deteriorate.[64]

On September 2, 1891, two weeks before she turned eighteen and fourteen years since she had last seen him, Juana Walker's father died. An obituary in Florence remembered that he had "cherished plans for the advancement of civilization among the Pima Indians, and he expressed firm faith in the bright possibilities of their future under the methods he was arranging for their benefit." The editor supposed "not the least among the tears of sincere sorrow that now fall are those of his faithful friends of copper hue, who revere him with a grand and heroic devotion."[65] The town of Solomonville remembered that "for twenty years [Walker] lived with the Pima Indians. . . . For the past few years his mind has wandered at times, one of his imaginations being he was Chief of the Pimas. The Judge was married in Tucson . . . his brothers claiming that the woman he married was an adventuress." A Los Angeles paper eulogized the judge less sentimentally: "After John went insane he was bothered by a woman who came from the east, captured him . . . and married him. . . . This marriage will probably now be grounds for law suits." Each of these obituaries pointed to Walker's intimate relationships as they marked his accumulation of wealth and significance in Arizona's mining history and foreshadowed the legal disputes that his considerable wealth and elite status—imagined or real—in O'odham and Miligahn society would raise.[66]

As predicted by California journalists, the surviving Walker brothers took their claims on his estate and affection to the Pinal County courthouse in Florence within days of John D.'s passing. Eleanor claimed that she was the rightful inheritor of her husband's estate and produced her marriage certificate and his passionate letters as evidence in her case. William and Lucien subpoenaed American friends and associates who testified that their brother's mind had "wandered" from his seizure in November 1889 to his death in September 1891, and argued that Eleanor had manipulated their poor, confused invalid into a marriage contract he did not fully understand.

Juana—who avoided the fray until 1893—argued that she was the deceased's only daughter and that he had acknowledged her as such prior to his mental deterioration, making her the only legitimate heir to the vast income he had accumulated on O'odham lands. The testimony offered before Florence jurors, most of whom had known him in some capacity or another, both revealed and obscured Walker's penchant for forging extralegal intimacies. The jurors' sympathy for Juana's case indicated that it was John D. Walker's interracial intimacies that made the most sense to the Anglo men who made their livings alongside Mexican and O'odham friends and neighbors in Pinal County.

The legal contest between Eleanor and Juana's uncles proved compelling to Arizona's journalists, but their importance here is in regard to testimony that alluded to the relationships Juana's father forged with O'odham men and women. The testimony offered before the jury "covered nearly every day of the life of the deceased since he left his home in Illinois thirty years before, until the day of this death in the insane asylum."[67] Newspapers covered the case with prejudice, the Tucson-based *Arizona Daily Star* defending the widow's claims and Florence's *Arizona Weekly Enterprise* supporting the Walker brothers. After hearing testimony describing Walker's nonsensical schemes and incoherent ramblings, the jury found against the widow and ruled to allow A. J. Doran, an old family friend, to distribute the estate among Walker's siblings. The witnesses that recounted her father's delusions ultimately strengthened Juana Walker's claims against her Anglo uncles and aunts, since she and Churga were the focus of the frontiersman's fantasies.

In the Florence courtroom, friends and strangers alike recounted Walker's obsession with the Akimel O'odham following his November 1889 seizure. The doctor who attended John D. at the Vekol Mine reported that Walker's room was in complete disarray except for the photos of "half-nude squaws" that decorated his walls. Dr. Sabin told the court that his patient "would take up one of those photographs and say, 'this is one of my old girls, and this is another'—would refer to them in that way." The doctor reported that Juana's father suffered from hallucinations. "He told me that he had seen his girl from Mesa City and talked with her . . . there had been two squaws there to see him and talk with him and told him about the girl, and what the Mormons were trying to do with her, and he wanted to send over there and get her away from the Mormons."[68] Perhaps Dr. Sabin was unaware of Walker's O'odham family, and failed to consider that the two O'odham women attending to John D. could have communicated with him regarding Juana's welfare among the Mormon Pomeroy family in Mesa City.

Dr. Choate, who treated John D. in California between 1890 and 1891, related similar delusions that very clearly described his patient's heartbreak over the loss of Churga and Juana: "I think he told me that story that the Mormons had kidnapped an Indian maiden with whom he was desperately in love, and he was going to annihilate the Mormons and get his girl and bring her down. He told me that—some Indian name, I don't know what—had given him the Indian girl for his wife." Choate related Walker's plans for his daughter as a symptom of insanity: "at other times he was going to make the girl a teacher in the institution of learning that he was going to establish for the Indians." The doctor admitted he had difficulty identifying O'odham names and probably confused Walker's distinctions between Churga and Juana, interchangeably referred to as "his girl," and dismissed the heart-wrenching tale as a madman's obsession. The expert witness reported that Juana's father spoke in O'odham, Spanish, and English as he struggled to make himself understood, making it even more likely that the doctor confused Walker's distinctions between his O'odham daughter and the O'odham women he had claimed as his own.[69]

Walker's friends also described his references to the O'odham as the ravings of a lunatic, though they knew his intimate connections to the tribe and Dr. Choate might not have. William T. Day, who had written to Juana's guardian on his friend's behalf, testified that as soon as John D. regained his ability to talk, he "never seemed to lose the idea that he was Chief of all the Indian tribes . . . he would break off and talk Indian a great deal, and . . . he was speaking of some great meeting that all the Indian tribes were going to have in Southern Arizona and he expected to be their Chief." Such "rants" seem to describe Walker's role as interpreter and counselor during O'odham treaty and water rights negotiations in years prior to his illness. Day reported that after the mine owner fell ill, "[we] didn't permit the Indians to remain around there," though an O'odham attendant would undoubtedly have been helpful in translating Walker's multilingual rants.

When lawyers asked about John D.'s marital plans, Day related a conversation he had with Juana's father around 1885 or 1886, just a few years after Churga's death and Juana's removal into the Pomeroy family: "Upon my urging him to . . . get married he told me that he never intended to. . . . He said he had lived with the Indians too long. [He said], 'I have cohabited with the Indians till I am a physical wreck and there is no use talking to me about getting married.'"[70] Walker had a similar discussion with his friend A. J. Doran, who claimed he noticed something "unusual" in the man around 1888. Doran thought that married life might improve Walker's health. John D. told Doran about Eleanor, his lost love from Illinois. The witness recounted the conversation: "I said, 'Why not go back and marry her and build yourself a home?' He said he could not do it, that he never would marry or have anything to do with a white woman, he said his life he had led with the Indians precluded him from marrying a white woman or having anything to do with them."[71] Despite the implications of these recounted conversations, no witness in the dispute between Eleanor and Juana's uncles directly mentioned Churga or Juana.

Although the court showed no interest in delving into the Civil War veteran's life among the O'odham, it seems John D. was likely referring to the unfortunate result of his sexual liaisons with O'odham women when he spoke to his friends Day and Doran. Walker's doctors, when pressed, reported that their patient claimed he had contracted syphilis some years prior to his November seizure—indeed, in 1886 Churga's husband sought medical treatment for an undisclosed illness. Dr. Choate testified that he doubted whether Juana's father had ever had syphilis, but admitted that he had applied an antisyphilitic treatment regimen nonetheless. The antisyphilitic failed to show effect, but Sabin and Choate both acknowledged that if he suffered from syphilitic insanity, John D.'s case would have been too far advanced to respond to iodide treatments by the time he displayed seizures. They also explained that Walker's condition—which could have been caused by syphilis—was degenerative and fatal, but that the invalid could maintain moments of lucidity, so that anyone who conversed with him briefly might not think him insane.[72]

Territorial law prohibited O'odham friends of the deceased from testifying in the trial. The only witnesses who found Juana's father to be sane and coherent were those who had aided his efforts to marry Eleanor Rice in Tucson. Louis Cameron Hughes, who would be appointed territorial governor in 1893, and Colonel James A. Zabriskie, former attorney for Arizona Territory, both testified and served on the widow's counsel and acknowledged that John D. suffered from fatigue and anxiety, but neither thought him to be incompetent. According to Hughes, his friend Walker was very knowledgeable regarding Pima ethnohistory, mining, and geologic sciences, and even discussed the fine legal points of his brothers' habeas corpus writ against Eleanor. Hughes claimed that after Lucien and William tried to abduct their brother in the streets of Tucson, John D. began to have fits and locked himself up in Hughes's home. Seeing that his friend needed medical attention, Hughes arranged for a probate hearing in hopes that the afflicted man would be granted treatment under terms amenable to him—likely under Eleanor's guardianship and within Arizona Territory. After Judge Woods affirmed William's custody of John D., Juana's father could reportedly be heard shouting for Eleanor from a block away. Hughes took all of this to mean that it was the Walker brothers' rough treatment that caused John D.'s descent into a quite justifiable madness.[73]

Other friends also testified to the credibility of Juana's father. W. J. Osborn had served with Walker as a wagon master during the Civil War and later helped to manage his properties in Tucson. Osborn explained that he and Walker visited often throughout the 1870s and 1880s, and Osborn considered himself an intimate friend of Juana's father. Osborn testified that in 1891, his comrade seemed "perfectly coherent, though feeble."[74] If Osborn visited the Walker Ranch, he likely knew Churga and Juana, and John D.'s plans to return to the O'odham and finance a tribal school for his daughter may not have seemed so far-fetched. Another friend from Pinal County said he and Walker had been "intimate together in former years" and that he had seen the miner in May 1891, a month after his marriage to Eleanor. John C. Harris said he saw no indication of insanity during his conversation with John D.[75] Perhaps Harris's own intercultural marriage to a Mexican woman made him less concerned with Walker's interracial intimacies and less inclined to see them as signs of madness.[76]

After three weeks of contradictory and scandalous testimony, the combined reports of experts and intimates made it difficult to believe that Eleanor did not push a disturbed and feeble man to marry her, even if he did profess to love her.[77] Although friends disagreed whether Walker had lost his mind or had simply lost his vigor, doctors and family members convinced the jury that he had never recovered from his November 1889 stroke and that brother William had taken the necessary precautions to care for John D.'s estate and person. Juana's father had clearly degenerated since his violent seizure and when he died, Dr. Choate reasoned that his illness had been caused by "a combination of causes: exposure and excesses and irregularities." The doctor went on to describe a series of conditions that would have characterized the life of a man working and living in Arizona Territory's Indian Country, an American who fought Apache men and loved O'odham women, a person who mined for silver and administered law: ". . . excessive physical work, excessive mental work . . . Excessive indulgence with women: the irregularities of sleeping one night in a warm bed and tomorrow night on the ground: working hard two or three months in some big enterprise where the nervous system is tense and evidently under high nerve pressure, and the next day nothing."[78] It would seem that eking out a living among the Gila River O'odham as a man fondly known as both Has Viakam and as "the Judge" drove the Miligahn crazy and then killed him.

The cause of Walker's decline may never be known, but what the above testimony shows is that the symptoms of Walker's illness depended on one's attitudes toward interracial intimacies, and on one's claims to the wealth such intimacies generated. The jury that denied Eleanor Walker's claim to John D.'s estate heard cloaked references to his O'odham family and deemed him the insane ward of his older brother. Less than twelve months later, another Florence jury would hear explicit testimony regarding Walker's O'odham family and would deem him a frontier patriarch who had simply died without writing a will to recognize his paternal obligations to a mixed-race daughter. The jurors' finding in Juana's case, especially when considered in tandem with the testimony offered in Rebecca Lena Graham's inheritance claim discussed in the next chapter, indicates that Anglo westerners disagreed whether interracial intimacies were a product of borderlands settlement or a criminal indiscretion; they also disagreed whether mixed-race progeny deserved to inherit the wealth that white fathers amassed as a result of racial and sexual transgressions.

On September 30, 1892, after mourning her father's passing for just over a year, the mixed-race girl filed her claim on the Walker estate in Pinal County probate court. The *Arizona Republican* of Phoenix announced Juana's case with this headline: "Another Page in the Famous John D. Walker Case—A Daughter of the Chief of the Pima's Found, the Sole Surviving Heir of that Remarkable Man. The First Legal Steps for Her Restoration to Her Birthright Taken Yesterday."[79] The article observed that in Eleanor Rice Walker's case, testimony regarding Walker's connection to the Pimas was offered as evidence of the deceased's insanity, but that there were two "interested spectators" in that case who "saw more than a hallucination in the story of the Indian maiden." The two jurists "believed [Walker] would hardly have led the life of a celibate among the Indians and . . . [a]cting on this belief they . . . discovered . . . Juana Walker . . . The girl's facial resemblance to Walker is sufficiently strong to preclude all doubt that she is his child." No doubt attracted to the potential for a healthy commission as much as the potential to achieve justice for a vulnerable member of Arizona's borderlands community, H. N. Alexander (who had served Indigenous Arizona clients before) and G. C. Israel (who would be investigated in 1895 for defrauding his clients) offered to represent Juana Walker and, with her guardian Rosetta Pomeroy, challenged John D.'s brothers' claim to the $1,500,000 estate.[80] As the *Republican* noted, Juana's parentage was visibly apparent to many—the legal challenge for Alexander and Israel was not just to prove Walker's paternity, but to assert Juana's "legal right as a half-breed," which would involve "nice points of law . . . in the establishment of it."[81]

Juana's lawyers would need to take a different approach than the one Walker's Illinois widow had taken. Eleanor Rice Walker's claim to the Walker estate centered on John D.'s ability to enter the marriage contract competently. Before examining witnesses, Rice's attorneys established points of consensus and dispute before the court, but the widow's counsel refused to concede that the deceased had died childless. Because neither party claimed to represent Walker's extralegal child, however, all witnesses were barred from testifying explicitly regarding his progeny, making Juana the proverbial elephant in the Pinal County courtroom. The testimony and legal arguments offered in the first estate case often skirted around the "nice points" of law that regulated interracial sexuality even though friends and doctors openly discussed Walker's interest in half-nude O'odham women and his self-diagnosis of syphilis.

The jurors who heard nineteen-year-old Juana's case, on the other hand, would be asked to consider explicitly the question of whether Arizona's mixed-race progeny could make claims on their white fathers. Because the acknowledgment of interracial sex and cohabitation became the core issue in Juana's estate dispute, the testimony in the second case centered on the very questions that attorneys had previously avoided. The trial, which confounded territorial courts for four years before being thwarted on its way to the U.S. Supreme Court for lack of funds, was "watched with great interest by the legal profession and public at large, as the question as to whether a half-blood Indian can legally inherit from a white man is of great importance throughout the west."[82] Sarcasm in the press, both subtle and overt, indicated Arizonans' ambivalence toward households like the one at the Walker Ranch. Like the witnesses who would testify in Rebecca Lena Graham's case, happening simultaneously in Seattle, some of Juana's contemporaries saw interracial families as a frontier by-product, while others saw them as a modern liability.

Just as in the previous dispute over Walker's estate, friends and family offered contradictory testimony regarding John D.'s behavior. Isaac D. Smith, who had lived on the Walker Ranch from 1873 to 1883, owned the trading post in Ge e Ke, and spoke fluent O'odham, reported that Churga and John D. lived as man and wife. He described Juana's mother as fourteen years old before 1870 when she was preparing to move to the ranch with her husband. When Smith met her again in June of 1873, she was "quite far advanced" in her pregnancy. Smith spent the summer helping his friend to irrigate Miligahn and Jujkum (Mexican) farms in the area and in September, the month of Juana's birth, he moved in with the Walkers. The expectant mother left for Shuckma hudag two days after Smith arrived and returned with Juana and a female O'odham helpmeet three weeks later.

Smith testified that the Walkers spoke O'odham primarily and that he heard John D. refer to Juana in O'odham as "my child." Smith's own proficiency in the language allowed him to recognize that Walker's use of the phrase was not merely a term of endearment, but an acknowledgment of his own paternity, since O'odham kinship terms contain paternal and maternal indicators to clarify biological and social relationships.[83] Smith also explained to the court that the couple were married according to tribal custom as soon as they began residing together—that, in effect, the woman's very cohabitation with Walker was proof of the marriage ceremony. Attorneys pressed Smith to describe the living quarters and sleeping arrangements at the Walker Ranch. "There were two rooms, one front room and one back room. John D. Walker occupied the back room as his bed-room. The front room was occupied as an office and a sleeping room." Smith slept in the front room, while the interracial family slept in the back bedroom. When asked—and it is worth noting that he was asked directly—Smith reported that he had not at any time seen the couple in bed together. Smith did not explain the mother and child's departure in 1877, but acknowledged that Walker had instructed him in writing to extend Mrs. Walker credit at his store near Ge e Ke. Smith said he had last seen Churga in 1879, but admitted that he continued to see Juana Walker in Florence and Mesa through 1883.[84]

Lucien Walker, who had grown increasingly ill since 1892, submitted a deposition in Juana's case from his home in California. The girl's uncle reported that he had been his brother's business partner since 1877 and that he had come to know the O'odham living near Shuckma hudag "quite extensive[ly]" between 1877 and 1883. Although he claimed to know reservation residents well, name confusion quickly became a key component of Lucien's deposition. He denied knowing any O'odham woman named "Churga," a name that the court had asked Isaac D. Smith to spell out, but admitted knowing a woman named "Chu-hua" and another named "Juana"—a designation Churga had claimed in the 1870 federal census. He not only reported that he did not know Churga, but also that he did not know a "Chujia," though he later spelled Chujia's name as Chu-hua. He claimed that the adult "Juana" (who must have been Churga) had told him that the child "Juana" had an O'odham mother named "Jack" and an American father, possibly a John Brenner.[85]

Under cross-interrogation, John D.'s younger sibling explained that he had arrived at the Walker Ranch in the fall of 1876 and that John D. moved to a house in Florence shortly thereafter to take up his position as Pinal County probate judge and surveyor—this move from farm to office may explain Churga and Juana's 1877 return to the reservation. Lucien occupied himself in the Salt River valley until 1880, when he set out to aid his brother at the Vekol Mine. When not prospecting, the young man clerked on the Pima-Maricopa reservation between 1877 and 1879 and became fluent in O'odham while working alongside Isaac Smith. Juana's uncle reported that it was Chu-hua who had lived off and on at the Walker Ranch, but when he saw her in 1876 she had no child with her and he was "morally satisfied that at that time she had no children." He testified that he had "never heard it alleged that Juana is the child of Chu-hua," and indeed, no one did, since the girl's attorneys made claims only about Churga. Juana's uncle said he had first seen the girl when she was three or five, but that he did not know "just when or where [he] first saw her . . . or how [he] learned her name . . . and [he did not know] what became of her."[86] Rather than clarifying his older brother's ties to O'odham women, Lucien had confused them—an effective strategy for dissolving his niece's claim to the Walker estate. Lucien's testimony that he knew no woman associated with his brother by the name of Churga is severely undercut by a brief note that John D. wrote from Florence to the Sacaton trading post on October 9, 1879: "Lucien or Smith, Let the bearer have 10 yards of calico for Juana, if Churga wants a little provision at any time give it to her and charge it to my account. J. D. Walker."[87] The note was included in the evidence submitted in the Walker brothers' 1891 claim on the estate, though transcripts from Juana's 1893 suit show no indication that her lawyers challenged Lucien directly on the point even though Smith acknowledged the arrangement in his testimony.

Isabel Cosgrove also swore to a deposition she gave from California. Sometime neighbor and seamstress to John D. Walker, she considered herself "intimately acquainted with him since 1864." Cosgrove told the court that she was fluent in O'odham and knew the Indians living near Shuckma hudag and near the Walker Ranch. The witness declared that the Chujia and Chu-hua Lucien described were the same person and that the O'odham woman had lived with Juana's father near Adamsville. Cosgrove reported that Chujia and John D. had told her on separate occasions that they had no children—though Cosgrove did not say anything about whether the two shared a bed—and explained that Chujia was the adult Juana's niece (recall that Churga had taken the name Juana in the 1880 census and might have used the name in her association with nearby Anglos). She said that she did not know a "Churja," a "Chuga," a "Churga," or any O'odham woman called "Jack."[88] When cross-examined, Cosgrove said that in 1871 Chujia "was about nine years old. In 1876 she lived with Mr. Walker in Florence and brought with her a little Indian girl about seven years old by the name of Louisa. The child Louisa, Chujia said was her niece." Although the neighbor reported that she and Chujia saw and spoke to each other nearly every day in Florence, no one asked and she did not offer to explain why Juana's father was cohabiting with fourteen- and seven-year-old O'odham girls of no relation to him.[89]

No O'odham witnesses were called to offer explanations of relationship, identity, or chronology in John D. Walker's relations with O'odham women or men because Indians remained barred from presenting testimony in cases involving American claimants. It was John D.'s American neighbors and relatives who testified that their friend and brother cohabited with many O'odham women. Although they disagreed whether Juana's father had acknowledged his paternity, they unanimously stated that the mentally ill man's estate ought to rest in the hands of his siblings. Judge John Miller instructed the jury of twelve men to answer three questions: Were John D. Walker and Churga married according to "Pima tribal customs" prior to Juana's birth? Was John D. Walker Juana's father? And did "John D. Walker . . . acknowledge by acts, conduct, or declarations, Juana Walker as his daughter?"[90] Jurors answered yes to all three points. When pressed by Lucien's counsel, they acknowledged that Churga was Indian, but did not conclude that Juana was illegitimate. On July 28, 1893, the court turned John D.'s estate over to his mixed-race daughter.[91]

The borderland jurors' verdict indicates that they viewed marital choice as a white male privilege inviolable by territorial laws, if not a right that Indian women shared as well.[92] They also rejected the subjugation of Indigenous women in marriages to white men when they agreed that Churga was O'odham and that her mixed-race daughter deserved to inherit Churga's husband's property despite her Indian status.[93] The Howell Code required that all jurors be white citizens, but whiteness and citizenship did not ensure that borderland juries shared territorial legislators' concerns about interracial marriages or that they agreed with senators' efforts to disinherit mixed-race progeny like Juana Walker.

The jurors in Juana's case gave no explanations for their ruling in her favor, but a brief look at their backgrounds and social conditions offers clues regarding their permissive views toward interracial sex and property transmission. Everett E. Putnam may have brought relaxed views toward Indian-white unions with him when he arrived from Canada in 1888.[94] Freeman A. Chamberlin likely saw a number of similarly mixed households before moving from Oregon, where settler-colonists violated antimiscegenation statutes just as in Arizona Territory.[95] Rufus E. Kohler, raised by his stepfather in Pennsylvania, might have been empathetic to nontraditional family models and so ruled in Juana's favor.[96] Lucius Swingle, a farmer from Wisconsin, relied on O'odham and Mexican laborers and might have been comfortable with interracial intimacy.[97] Willis Black and his wife lived primarily among Mexican families and may have viewed Indian-white unions as a common, if not ideal, phenomenon in the Sonoran Southwest.[98] A miner from Wisconsin, Edward A. Clark, had been in the territory as early as 1870 and had more than likely seen a handful of marriages like the one John D. and Churga shared if he had not experienced his own share of interracial liaisons—Clark did not marry until 1898 at age forty-nine.[99] Another longtime miner on the jury, Herbert Pinching, married a racially ambiguous Mexican woman a few years after his service in the estate trial and might have felt that antimiscegenation statutes restricted his marriage choices.[100] Isaac Parkey, a single man from Tennessee, may have empathized with Walker's limited choice in marriage partners and agreed that Indian women ought to be legitimate wives.[101] Charles "Al" French, a stonemason from Indiana, would work on the Colorado River Indian reservation after his 1893 jury service in Pinal County, suggesting that he was not inclined to view relationships with Indians as illegal or insane.[102] All men who had crossed international, social, and racial borders in their pursuit of a manifest destiny, these jurors refused to uphold the antimiscegenation and property statutes that systematically benefited elite men like Lucien and William Walker but limited the marital rights of common men like themselves.

The day after Judge Miller delivered the jury's verdict in Juana's favor and against John D. Walker's brothers, they filed a motion requesting a new trial on the grounds that Miller had erred in allowing his jury to submit a ruling that violated territorial law. Justice Kibbey, who had ruled in favor of Lucien and William Walker in their 1892 case against Eleanor Rice, now served as their attorney, but Judge Miller denied his colleague's motion for appeal.[103] The next few stages in the Walker estate dispute show that John D.'s siblings depended very much upon their brother's wealth, since they scrambled for more than six months to gather sufficient funds for an appeal bond. A. J. Doran attempted to secure surety, but failed before the Vekol miner's old partner stepped in. Peter R. Brady gained the appointment as estate administrator and convinced Judge Miller to agree to an appeal trial in district court set for February 13, 1894, which ruled against the mixed-race heiress little more than a month later.[104] The determined daughter would fight her privileged uncles once more, and the Walker family settled with her because none of them could afford to continue to pay their attorneys. The men who backed Juana's 1895 appeal charged her the share of the Vekol Mine that she had briefly gained for their services and when Lucien Walker died in 1895, his widow sold his share of the estate to A. J. Doran.[105] The contradictory rulings had weakened both sides of the family even further, and none of Walker's relatives would keep the wealth John D. had earned through his alliances with the Akimel O'odham.

Likely fueled by the support of her Mormon guardians and Pinal County jurors, Juana pursued the case once more in the territorial supreme court, where she was stopped in her tracks. The high court of elite men ruled that the antimiscegenation statute voided her parent's marriage, that federal jurisdiction invested in the territorial government superseded tribal authority to sanction marriages on reservations, and that children of white men and Indian women were Indian and therefore illegitimate heirs. Although Arizona jurists invoked federal authority to disinherit and disenfranchise Juana Walker, the federal government had passed an act in 1888 that stood in direct contradiction to these territorial judges' presumption

---

JUANA'S SECOND ATTEMPT

To Get the Estate Left By Her Father.

From the Los Angeles Express.

Juana Walker, the Apache warden, who claims to be the only daughter and sole heir of John D. Walker, deceased, who died in September of 1891, leaving an estate valued at about $70,000, has again instituted proceedings to obtain possession of the property. The plaintiff alleges that the court which ordered a distribution of the property was misled by false representations and was thereby deceived and imposed upon.

Miss Walker prays that the decree be

"Juana's Second Attempt," *Arizona Republican* (Phoenix), May 17, 1895, p. 4 (Reproduced with permission from University of Arizona Library Microfilm and Newspaper Collections)

of patriarchal authority. The 1888 act made citizens of Indian women like Churga who married white men, but the act provided that tribal lands claimed by Indian women could not be inherited by their white husbands.[106] Local regulation of marriage, however, would ensure that regional racialism trumped national or federal trends in Indian and miscegenation law and Juana's residency outside of reservation boundaries made it difficult for her attorneys to invoke federal Indian law on her side. Of the four territorial supreme court judges who heard the arguments, J. D. Bethune recused himself because he had served as counsel for the petitioner in Judge Miller's probate court, A. C. Baker dissented, and O. T. Rouse concurred with J. J. Hawkins's opinion. Although the territorial supreme court established that white men could have sex with Indian women but could not share property with them, the justices' decision that Walker's daughter was a "Pima Indian" failed to acknowledge her biracial status and settle the dispute over her "legal rights as a half-breed."[107]

Juana's new legal status as an O'odham ward apparently did not encourage her to return to the Gila River reservation in 1896, where her family continued to struggle with the effects of land loss and water deprivation and sought ways to counter the assimilation pressures applied by Indian agents, missionaries, politicians, and reformers. To her relatives, Juana might have represented territorial officials' ability to impose racial hierarchies where cooperative interdependence had been, making her presence unwanted. Like her contemporaries Clara, Concepción, José, and Luis Martínez—the Yaqui and American children of Lucía Martínez and King S. Woolsey— Juana lived a largely undocumented life for the next twenty years. Each of these progeny of white fathers and Indigenous mothers kept their father's surnames, but were denied their father's wealth and status when territorial judges declared them Indian—even though civic officials would thereafter define them as white Mexicans in vital records. Their histories have been told as romantic frontier sagas with vague—and sometimes unfortunate— endings that coincide with a disappearance of Indian Arizonans from territorial history more generally (a trend this book aims to redirect).

In the aftermath of her legal battles, not all Arizonans were privy to the legal niceties and settlement details that left Juana Walker recognized as her father's daughter, but penniless as his illegitimate heir. When the *Globe Times* falsely announced Juana's engagement in 1901, they reported, "Juana is half Pima, but that matters not when she has a half million behind her. Most any white man would be willing to chew her biscuits the rest of his life." No other records confirm the *Globe*'s marriage announcement, though it was reprinted in the *Prescott Courier*, which also described John D. Walker's daughter as "an industrious young woman." The *Courier* stated that the girl had been working in hotels and private family homes in the small town roughly one hundred miles from her former home with the Pomeroys in Mesa.[108] Perhaps living with the Mormon family for so many years had well prepared Juana for service as a domestic, since like many Indigenous and mixed-race women in Arizona, she continued to make such labor her life's work.[109]

Churga's daughter relocated to Tucson in 1902 and though she lived a largely unobserved life, she caught journalists' attention in 1907 when she decided to fight for her father's wealth one last time. The *Tucson Citizen* described the mixed-race heir as "living in abject poverty" and revisited the courtroom drama that had followed Walker's death in 1891.[110] A sale of the Vekol Mine was being negotiated for a reported $250,000 and Juana's sense of injustice was renewed.[111] Juana's statement to the press on August 30, 1907, is a rare example of a mixed-race woman's challenge to legal and personal dispossession:

I, myself, am in very straitened circumstances, but have friends in this city who will advance me the money to make the legal fight for what is rightfully mine. . . . It is my candid opinion, which I do not hesitate in expressing publicly, that an uncle of mine, who was present at father's deathbed, destroyed the will, and set in a claim . . . for my father's estate. I had no money at that time to contest their claim, and although there was some trouble over the settlement of the estate, I never received a cent. My uncle [Lucien], whom I believe destroyed the will . . . [was] willing to make a . . . settlement with me. The effort . . . to make the reparation due me, however, was soon put an end to by the members of the family. . . . There still remains the Vekol mine, however, which is rightfully mine, and . . . I intend to take the matter to court.[112]

After just two weeks of investigation, however, Miss Walker's "friends" in Tucson failed to find legal merit in her case and advised her to abandon the claim. The *Arizona Daily Star* editorialized the situation by writing that "however much [Juana Walker] might be entitled to share in her father's estate by reason of her being in reality his child, the law is plainly against her inheritance and therefore she is barred as effectually as if she were the child of an absolute stranger."[113] Even Lucien had not described his niece as a stranger, but Arizona's territorial laws, reported here as being in defiance of reason, made her so.

Juana's claim that her father had acknowledged her as his progeny and heir in a destroyed will cannot be proven, but should be considered for a number of reasons. First, Juana's father served as Pinal County probate judge in the 1870s and it would have been logical for him to prepare his own estate as he divided others' in his Florence courtroom. Second, John D. made measures to provide for Juana in his lifetime through the extension of credit at Sacaton and through funds mailed to her guardian in Mesa and it would be reasonable to assume he intended to share his wealth with "Little Juana" after his death as well. Third, the frustration John D. exhibited in the throes of his illness might have come from his sense that Juana's uncles would deny his wishes and bar his daughter from a rightful inheritance. While these are speculative considerations, Juana's charges should not be quickly dismissed even if they were never proven.

The destitute heir apparently died in Tucson nine years later. A 1916 death certificate described her as a single woman in her late forties who had worked as a washwoman and died of acute endocarditis.[114] The document noted her previous address in Mesa and recorded her Tucson residence on the northern fringes of Barrio El Libre, a community of working-class Mexicans, Indians, and mixed-race people.[115] The undertaker, Arturo Carrillo, an ethnic Mexican who lived near Juana's neighborhood, reported that she had lived in Barrio El Libre for ten years and marked her race as "White," perhaps because he mistook the mixed-race woman as Hispanic.[116] The woman who was born in the "dry grass month" of dancing and harvesting was buried in the Evergreen Cemetery on July 8, 1916, with little fanfare.

Juana's only obituary was published more than two weeks later in *The Messenger*, a Phoenix-based newspaper that had previously been a Spanish-language journal. The two-column eulogy recounted Juana's bittersweet victory in the Florence courtroom without acknowledging her defeat in Arizona's district and supreme courts, suggesting that they endorsed her claim. The obituary, fairly lengthy for a mixed-race woman who died penniless, touched on all of the issues important to readers then and now.

Juana Walker Dead Daughter of Miner

Some twenty-three years ago the Juana Walker case was tried at Florence. Kibbey and Israel were her attorneys and after a hard fought battle they won the case, proving she was the rightful heir. Report comes of the death of Juana Walker, at Tucson. This event recalls the fact that Juana Walker was formerly of Mesa, and from babyhood to early womanhood was cared for by members of the Pomeroy Family.

Mrs. Ed. W. Jones, then Miss Pomeroy, cared for the infant Juana, after the death of the mother, and gave her the same care she would have given a child of her own. Juana was the daughter of John D. Walker and a Pima woman whom he married in Arizona. The history of Walker and that of Juana is connected with the discovery of the celebrated Vicol [sic] silver mine, one of the great producers of its day, and owned by Walker. . . . Walker became very wealthy, and on the death of his Pima wife, left the child Juana in care of the Pomeroys at Mesa. On Walker's death, there was a prolonged legal contest to secure for Juana a just proportion of her father's property. He had invested in a ranch or two, owned a block and good buildings in Florence and some property in Mesa. Juana finally won in the courts, but the attorneys and the court costs absorbed practically all that was set aside as her proportion of the Walker wealth.[117]

As the *Messenger* contributor hinted, and the retelling in this chapter has shown, the Walker family trial exposed debates over miscegenation, the appropriation of tribal lands, and the status of mixed-race women in Arizona communities and courts. In its recounting of Juana's struggle for legitimacy, the notice of her death made it clear that these issues remained unsettled for those who survived her. Juana's inheritance case illustrates that Arizona's legal regime systematically placed Indigenous women and their mixed-race progeny's bodies at the forefront of tribal efforts to retain lands and sovereignty, thus linking miscegenation codes to property rights and Indigenous women's bodies to their community's survival. And yet, when exempted from state jurisdiction because of their perceived status as federal subjects, Native women relied on the legal interventions of white men to protect them from other white men in cases of abandonment, adultery, or assault. State and territorial courts heard female Indians' cases at their pleasure or turned them away with federal corroboration.[118]

Juana and Churga's obscured place in Arizona's legal and social history affirms racial-ethnic women's historians' assertion that Americans have "suppressed the historical reality that a significant proportion of its citizenry has multigenerational multiracial roots," and that such "historical amnesia" has "fueled the oppression of . . . multiracial people in our country."[119] Although miscegenation scholars and historians of racial-ethnic women's experiences in the American West likely agree that interracial unions abounded during the nineteenth century, we share the frustration of documenting such relationships and the children they produced. Some historians suggest the challenge is structural, and that the "U.S. system has depended on very clear racial categories for its political, social, economic, and psychological organization. In an attempt to keep the categories well defined, two strategies have been employed: the creation of a negative mythology about people of mixed race and their families . . . and the denial of the existence of people of mixed race and their families."[120] In nineteenth-century Arizona, census enumerators wrote down "W" when they saw Indian because Mexican ethnicity served as a conveniently malleable category for mixed-race children whose parents violated Arizona's antimiscegenation statutes.[121] Rather than report respected patriarchs Woolsey and Walker as sexual deviants, their neighbors looked away—as long as property only passed from Indian women to white men (in contradiction to federal law), sex could be exchanged without disrupting racial hierarchies embedded in territorial laws.

Depicting Juana's case merely as a juridical debate over tribal and territorial marriage laws or an ugly family dispute makes sense only if historians dismiss those who argued on Juana's side of the issue and shared her critique of antimiscegenation statutes that disinherited mixed-race Arizonans. To conclude that the estate trial was an unfortunate by-product of the law, we must also forget that John D. Walker was a tribal adviser, county surveyor, and probate judge, and knew very well the laws that equated whiteness with privilege and that would deny his daughter's claims to those privileges. Such roles make Juana's claim that he had indeed provided for her in a will all the more plausible. Finally, historians can only imply that Juana's loss in court was inevitable if they ignore the charged testimony offered by friends and neighbors and the impressive arguments presented by her legal counsel.

This chapter argues against passive interpretations of the relatively unimpinged access to sex and property that Arizona's territorial laws granted men like John D. Walker. In the Walker family trial, Churga's daughter sought to establish her "legal rights as a half-breed," arguing against laws that exempted her white family from financial obligations to their Indian kin, that promoted unstable sexual relationships between citizen men and Indian women, and that relegated her to a lower racial and class status than her white father. Juana Walker died before the American Indian Citizenship Act of 1924 granted Indigenous women the limited economic and sexual privileges white women held, but she claimed those rights as early as 1893, leaving an indelible if somewhat obscured mark on Arizona's legal and social history.

CHAPTER 5

Rebecca Lena Graham and "The Old Question of Common Law Marriage Raised by a Half-Breed"
Washington, 1859–1946

The Mathias Heirs. Close of Argument on an Indian Marriage Case. A $50,000 Estate Involved. The Old Question of Common Law Marriage Raised by a Half-Breed Claimant.
—*Seattle Post Intelligencer*, headline, July 24, 1894

While Arizona residents and jurists debated Juana Walker's 1893 inheritance case in courtrooms and kitchens throughout the Gila River valley, claimant Rebecca Lena Graham and her counsel prepared their challenge against her deceased father's nephews, nieces, and sisters for an estate valued at nearly $50,000 — just over $1.3 million in today's currency. Although Juana Walker eventually lost her hard-won inheritance in the Supreme Court of territorial Arizona, Graham won her father's fortune in King County Superior Court and in the Western Washington District Court, thus securing her rights before local and federal judges. The daughter of a prominent Duwamish woman and a Pennsylvania-born member of Seattle's founding elite, she was already familiar with probate proceedings in King County by the time she filed her claim in September 1893, and could count some of Puget Sound's most respected citizens and tribal leaders as her allies. Despite her respectability and legal prowess, she enjoyed no privileges of whiteness once the press seized her claim and reduced the case to "the old question of common law marriage" that had riddled Washington's state and territorial courts for nearly half a century. The press described Graham as "the half-breed daughter of Frank Matthias" and referred to her mother and namesake as a "squaw named Rebecca."[1]

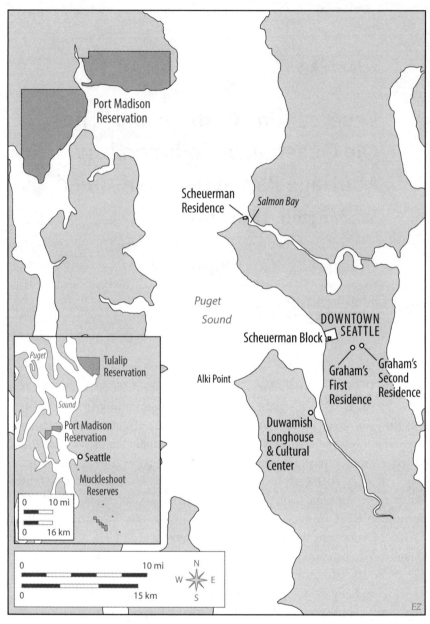

Rebecca Lena Graham's Seattle-Duwamish borderlands (Map by Ezra Zeitler)

Although it is Graham's successful claim and the remarkable contrasts and parallels between her and Juana Walker's encounters with miscegenation and probate law in the American West that make her an important figure in this study, the 1893–1894 estate case could hardly have been the most significant event in the mixed-race woman's rich and long life, though its award certainly made her more financially secure. Raised by a mother accustomed to change as a constant and vital life force that her tribe personified as Dookweebathl, the Changer, and among men foolish enough to redirect Puget Sound riverways and rearrange the shoreline, Graham would change her name and neighbors would remember her racial-ethnic affiliations differently throughout her lifetime, but in eighty-six years she never changed her origin story.[2]

Rebecca, who went by Peggy in early childhood and Lena in early adulthood because she shared her mother's name, testified before District Judge Cornelius Holgate Hanford that she was born December 29, 1859.[3] The impressive woman died Rebecca Lena Graham on April 9, 1946. In that span of years between the onset of the Civil War and the close of World War II, she married three times and was widowed, abandoned, and divorced; she lost four children in their early childhood and raised three to adulthood, but was survived by only one son; through it all, she enjoyed the close friendship of siblings and cousins who shared her legacy as the living reminders of Seattle founders' dependence on Duwamish men and women, and with them she participated in tribal efforts to seek federal recognition.

By the time she died in 1946, Seattle residents counted Graham among the descendants of their city's white founding elites, likely because they did not associate independence, legal acumen, or longevity with Indianness. Although some might have read the attribution of whiteness as a compliment to Rebecca Graham in her obituary and in earlier accounts, the erasure of her Indianness in fact served as another form of dispossession, denying her and other Duwamish descendants the persistent tribal status necessary for federal recognition in later years.[4] Rebecca's retention of Duwamish history, identity, and practice is evident in her close alliance with leaders who organized the Duwamish Tribe of Indians in 1915 and joined the Northwest Federation of American Indians, her assistance in the late 1910s to anthropologist Thomas Talbot Waterman, and her application to Charles Roblin's 1919 Census of Unenrolled Western Washington Indians as a Duwamish tribal member.[5] Despite being called white by Seattle chroniclers in anecdotes, census schedules, newspaper articles, and vital records, Rebecca continued to support Duwamish tribal leadership and descendants during her lifetime, and it would be the children and grandchildren of women like her who pursued federal claims for Duwamish recognition that continue to the present day.

Rebecca Lena Graham asserted her rights to the profits men like her father reaped because of their intimate liaisons with Duwamish women like her mother, and in doing so she pointed to the fissures in Seattle's pioneer community between those who agreed she and others deserved recognition and compensation and those who did not. Of course, many of those rifts remain today, and there are still Duwamish women lodging legal complaints and taking local action. As in Arizona and other parts of the North American West—and like Nora Jewell's before her—what Rebecca's history reveals is that the daughters of Indian women and American fathers in Puget Sound engaged the legal system as mixed-race litigants with rights and sovereignty that went well beyond debates over treaties and federal Indian policy and that remain linked to ongoing campaigns for federal recognition that continue today.[6]

Rebecca Lena Graham's resiliency in a lifetime of dramatic change should come as no surprise when we recall that her mother believed in change as a vital force in everyday life, and her father believed that he could change the Puget Sound world to his own advantage. Puget Sound genealogist Patricia Hackett Nicola wrote an eight-page article, "Rebecca Lena Graham's Fight for Her Inheritance," in the *Pacific Northwest Quarterly* in 2006. It highlights Rebecca's family history and the importance of her case in Seattle's history of pioneer-Indian intimacies. Despite the richness of Graham's story and the quality of Nicola's essay, Rebecca's life—like the lives of the other women in this book—is difficult to chronicle fully. Coll Thrush and Matthew Klingle mentioned Rebecca Graham (by other of her many names) in their excellent studies of Seattle, but only in association with either her Duwamish grandfather or her American father and not as a significant actor in Seattle's Indigenous history or Washington's legal history.[7] This chapter expands on these authors' important starts in three ways.

First, special attention is paid not only to the witnesses' relationships with Rebecca and her father, but also to the ties between Rebecca's family and the judge who ruled in her favor in the inheritance dispute. Rebecca's case is compelling because she won her inheritance claim when so few mixed-race descendants did. In her study of miscegenation law in the United States, legal historian Peggy Pascoe argued that western courts had turned against the children of Indian mothers and white fathers by 1890, but she did not include Graham's victory in her discussion of Washington.[8] Judge Hanford acknowledged that the evidence and jurisprudence gave him little to consider in Rebecca's favor, but a critical legal approach to the case reveals that he shared close ties to Graham's family and that he held deep reservations regarding federal and local policy toward her tribe. Knowing more about Graham and Hanford makes an inexplicable case an illuminating chapter in Seattle's interracial history.

Second, whereas other historians have acknowledged the social and genealogical history of the estate case, Graham's case gains greater significance as a legal history in the context of Washington's antimiscegenation and probate statutes. The 1893 case clearly pertains to Washington's state and territorial marriage laws, but Rebecca also raised questions about the nature of interracial marriages conducted in "Indian Country." Rebecca's multiple marriages and participation in the tribal recognition effort illustrate that she held a well-developed understanding of the civil and probate court system, with a clear knowledge of her rights under the law, and appreciated the importance of jurisprudence and protocol in wielding local and federal courts to her advantage. While some readers might wonder how much influence Juana Walker had in the execution of her Arizona inheritance claim, it seems clear that Rebecca Graham worked directly with her counsel and represented herself as powerfully in court as she did in her community.

A third point that others have ignored is Rebecca Lena Graham's participation in the early-twentieth-century development of the Duwamish Tribal Organization, a group that continued to pursue federal recognition into this century. Bureau of Indian Affairs records from the past forty years demonstrate that a fundamental misunderstanding of the racial-ethnic identity and social networks of women like Rebecca Lena Graham have posed a crucial barrier to the Duwamish tribe and perhaps evidence shared here will help to advance the tribe's cause before the federal government. Although small, this is a cache of records other historians have not linked to their studies of Seattle at the turn of the century, and incorporating them critically makes more apparent the essentialist notions of indigeneity and tribal status that the federal government and others have applied to Graham's tribe.[9] To fully explain all of these connections, we must turn first to Rebecca's origins, when Puget Sound remained "Indian Country," and her father was merely a young upstart in her grandfather's camp.

Some called him Chief Curley, others knew him as Duwampsh Curley, and some called him Salmon Bay Curley, but all knew him as an important

Duwamish leader. He was also Rebecca Lena Graham's maternal grandfather.[10] Curley quickly befriended the Americans that Puget Sound Indians commonly called "Boston men" when they arrived in his village in the early 1850s. Curley and the Duwamish lived on the border between the Salish Sea and the inland Cascade Mountains. Their territory along the Duwamish River gave them access to trade with Salishan tribes as far north as Alaska and with inland tribes as far west as the Great Basin. In addition to trade in commodities and foodstuffs, the Duwamish traded for slaves and songs with their Lushootseed-speaking allies. Curley and leaders like him participated in a hierarchical society with slaves at the bottom, and men who could accumulate wealth and make popular decisions at the top. High-ranking families chose their children's marriage partners carefully, selecting spouses from other tribes and villages who held equivalent authority. These incoming marriage partners brought with them sacred knowledge and access to resources. Curley's daughters no doubt grew up assured that they would continue to enjoy all the privileges appropriate to their status when they left their father's household for marriage. Curley's tribe had encountered British and American newcomers to the Salish Sea for a century by 1851, though none ever seemed to stay for long and they were more likely to leave behind confusion and disease than anything useful. Given their rich resource base and vast intertribal networks, the Duwamish might have felt they had little to gain from or lose to the Bostons until they started arriving in groups of three, then ten, then thirty, in the years after the federal government made up to 640 unceded acres available for the cost of filing a fee under the Donation Land Claims Act of 1850.[11]

Rebecca's father, Franklin Matthias, arrived in the Seattle area from Pennsylvania in 1852 and quickly joined the ranks of well-known early American settlers such as Arthur Denny, David "Doc" Maynard, Erasmus Smithers, Charles Terry, Henry Van Asselt, and Henry Yesler, among others. Like his new friends, Matthias relied on connections to Duwamish residents in order to establish himself in the tiny settlement wedged between tide flats and immense forests so far away from his birthplace in Penn's Woods. Although most readers are familiar with early arrivals' dependence on Chief Seathl's generosity and guidance, popularly celebrated in the city's name, Curley also forged close unions and mutually beneficial arrangements with the first wave of settlers that included Matthias and his neighbors. None other than Judge Hanford, who presided over Rebecca's estate trial, remembered the Duwamish man with obvious admiration, describing him as "tall and straight, not bow-legged, as were most of those whose occupation was fishing in canoes. Curley was a hunter." For eastern Americans more impressed with game on the hoof than on the hook, Curley's hunting prowess made him more manly in their eyes than other Native men who relied primarily on fishing for their families' subsistence.[12]

The men called to witness in Rebecca Lena Graham's estate trial survived their first years in Seattle because of her grandfather's generosity. Henry Van Asselt arrived at the mouth of the Duwamish River just south of Seattle's current downtown on September 14, 1851, and first camped with the Duwamish. When David Denny and Lee Terry (brothers of Matthias's close friends Arthur Denny and Charles Terry) arrived in the area a few months later, Curley brought the founding party a meal of roast duck, perhaps illustrating that they were guests in his home. For easterners new to the Sound and unaccustomed to a steady diet of salmon, Curley's initial gift of roast duck likely served to announce his ability to provide meat more familiar to the Boston palate. Curley met David "Doc" Maynard through their mutual friend Seathl, the city's namesake and first Indigenous labor broker, according to some historians. As more American men arrived in the 1850s, more Duwamish relocated to other settlements throughout the Duwamish and Puget Sound watershed, but Curley and his band continued to help and host the newcomers. Henry Yesler established a sawmill near Curley's village of thirty-some Duwamish and relied heavily on Duwamish laborers to help him fell and haul timber in his earliest days in the Sound. Duwamish women worked for Americans, too, cultivating onions and digging potatoes in the early days and later working with their families in the hop fields throughout the Sound. A carpenter by trade, Matthias had skills vital to the city's earliest settlers and likely found Curley's men to be very helpful laborers and traders. Both Yesler and Matthias would also find Curley's daughters to be valuable partners, critical in ensuring their successful transition from anonymous emigrants to founding fathers of Seattle.[13]

As Curley and his Boston neighbors negotiated their own social and economic arrangements, American men began to take donation land claims under federal provision. A look at these early claims reveals the close ties among the witnesses in Rebecca's case and their proximity to Curley's Salmon Bay settlement and each other. Henry Van Asselt, who met Curley first and who testified that Franklin had not cohabited with the Duwamish man's daughter, filed a claim on October 15, 1851. Arthur Denny filed his claim on June 12, 1852, with Henry Van Asselt among his affiants. Like Van

Asselt, Denny also testified forty years later that Franklin Matthias had no children. Henry Yesler filed his claim adjoining Doc Maynard's on November 20, 1852, with friends Maynard, Hillory Butler, and Reverend Daniel Bagley as affiants. Butler disputed Rebecca's inheritance claim, but Reverend Bagley swore that Franklin and Rebecca's mother had lived together as man and wife and that Franklin acknowledged Rebecca as his daughter. Doc Maynard's testimony would no doubt have been very compelling, but he passed away in 1873. Henry Yesler also died before Franklin Matthias, but like his friend he fathered a child with one of Curley's daughters and Rebecca Graham remained close friends with her maternal cousin Julia through adulthood. Matthias affirmed his friend Henry H. Tobin's claim on November 24, 1853, along with Dexter Horton—who would testify against Rebecca—and Moses K. Maddocks (also spelled Maddox), who may have lodged Rebecca for part of her childhood, and then served as a witness on her behalf. Erasmus Smithers, who would be a business partner of Matthias's and who testified on the side of Franklin's white relatives, filed his claim on December 1, 1853, with Arthur Denny among his affiants. Judge Cornelius Hanford's parents filed their claim when he was eleven years old on March 11, 1854. Timothy D. Hinckley affirmed their claim and later testified in Rebecca's favor. Franklin Matthias did not appear to file a donation land claim of his own, perhaps because he enjoyed Curley's hospitality and would later buy portions of his friends' claims. Though all of these men worked together in a variety of positions and projects during Seattle's first half-century, their favors for each other as donation claim affiants tended to fall along the same lines as their testimony for or against Rebecca Graham in the Matthias estate case.[14]

It is difficult to say what Rebecca's grandfather thought, or even knew, of these federally sanctioned land claims on his tribe's unceded territory, but the Duwamish would soon make their rejection of federal Indian and land policy clear to Puget Sound Americans. For the years 1851–1854, however, before the establishment of Washington Territory and territorial governor Isaac Stevens's ill-fated treaty negotiation campaign in 1854–1855, Curley and his interloping neighbors shared Duwamish land relatively peacefully. Just as in so many other communities throughout the North America West, newcomers shared intimate as well as economic exchanges with Indigenous residents. Salmon Bay Curley no doubt expected that aligning himself with key partners among the Bostons would ensure his community's leverage in economic, political, and social negotiations and in some ways he would prove right. Curley's daughter Susan, later known to *Seattle Post Intel-ligencer* readers as Skookum Susie, partnered with Henry Yesler, though Yesler was already married to a white woman who would soon join him in Seattle.[15]

Susan Curley chose a man who was already apparent to his contempo-raries as a leader among men who thought of themselves as Argonauts man-ifesting their own destiny on the fringes of society. As a man who literally felled timber, built fences, and established churches, schools, and munici-pal offices within the immediate vicinity of his frontier home, Yesler was the sort of man who inspired Frederick Jackson Turner's frontier thesis. As the woman whose ties to Indigenous landholders and laborers and whose emotional and economic contributions to their household made Yesler's early successes possible, Susan was the sort of woman Turner and others ignored in their chronicles of western history. Susan Curley gave birth to her and Henry's daughter Julia on June 12, 1855, and left Henry's house-hold when his wife Sarah arrived from the east in 1858. Henry continued to support Julia financially after his first wife Sarah joined him in Seattle, and Sarah apparently supported the liaison since it came with obvious financial benefits. Julia Yesler, more commonly known as Julia Benson Intermela, remained an important figure in Rebecca's life, just as Julia's father Henry remained important to Rebecca's father Franklin.[16]

Susan's younger sister, Rebecca's mother Peggy (also called Rebecca by some), chose Franklin Matthias as her partner sometime in 1857. Although Matthias enjoyed less renown than Yesler in the years after their deaths in the early 1890s, both men worked hand in hand to build Seattle, Yesler and his sawmill converting timber to lumber and Matthias and his carpen-try skills converting lumber to monument. Rebecca and other witnesses reported that the interracial couple lived together from 1857 to 1861 and that Rebecca was Franklin's only child, born December 29, 1859.[17] Susan and Peggy's unions with Henry and Franklin provided security not only to their husbands, but to the many vulnerable settlers vastly outnumbered by Indigenous residents in an unfamiliar world some called Indian Country. If Curley wanted his daughters to join husbands who could maintain the class status they were accustomed to, he chose well. That these unions did not last long had as much to do with his daughters' personal choices as with the legal and social frameworks their husbands were building together with other Seattle founders. The years 1854 to 1861 saw a number of signifi-cant legal and political events in addition to Susan and Peggy's marriages that would shape Duwamish and American lives dramatically as the Sound shifted from Indian Country to American territory.

Washington became its own territory set aside from Oregon in 1853, and the territorial legislature met for the first time early in 1854. Despite the name change, it would still take much effort to convert the land from Indian to American and attempt to assimilate the Indigenous people. Some Duwamish might have felt the transformative influence of Dookweebathl at work in these shifts. Governor Isaac Stevens served not only as the territory's figurehead, but also as the supervisor of Indian affairs for the region, thus tasking him with representing the conflicting interests of white settlers seeking more land and destiny for themselves and of Indigenous residents expecting the acknowledgment and protection of their land and resource rights. Stevens chose to represent his popular constituents rather than his political counterparts. With treaty terms written prior to council meetings, Stevens announced through interpreters using the Chinook jargon—a limited trade dialect widely acknowledged by both contemporary and recent chroniclers as insufficient for diplomatic communication—that Puget Sound tribes would join one another on shared reservations. The Medicine Creek Treaty of December 24, 1854, and the Point Elliott Treaty of January 22, 1855, declared that all tribal members would relocate to one of eight reserves. Although Stevens intended that some reserves would be established for particular tribes, Curley's Duwamish tribe received no specific designation of land and in subsequent years federal officials and local whites pressured Duwamish residents to join other tribes on the Port Madison, Tulalip, and Muckleshoot reserves. While those Duwamish whose families had intermarried with tribes on these reserves eventually chose to resettle, Curley's band of thirty or so remained in Seattle in defiance of federal removal. Tribal members throughout the Sound shared Curley's disapproval of the treaties and so did Congress, which refused to ratify the Point Elliott Treaty until 1859, making all American land claims a violation of tribal sovereignty for the first eight years of Puget Sound settlement, and ensuring that the region remained Indian Country at the time of Peggy and Franklin's union and of Rebecca's subsequent birth.[18]

The ratification delay also meant that tribal members who did remove to reservations and expected annuity payments and services promised in exchange for land cessions would be disappointed, as Indian agents could do little without federal appropriations. In the midst of such overt affronts to their sovereignty, Puget Sound tribes mounted an armed resistance against the American trespassers that began in the fall of 1855. Many amateur and academic historians have chronicled the Puget Sound Indian Wars that erupted in the wave of Indigenous resistance to settler-colonial incursions on unceded lands on both sides of the Cascade Mountains.[19] Most tend to blame either Isaac Stevens's hastily negotiated treaties or congressional refusals to ratify the treaties even as they authorized increasing immigration to the territory by extending the Donation Land Claims Act, and some point to incompetence at both local and federal levels as the cause of hostilities. What is clear from contemporary accounts is that, despite a low number of casualties on either side and fewer engagements than one would expect from a campaign called the Puget Sound Indian Wars, Seattle residents told themselves that they were outnumbered and surrounded by thousands of hostile Indians, that tribes east of the Cascade Mountains had turned local Indians against them, and that the federal government had first angered the tribes and then abandoned the white settlers who had heeded President Polk's call in 1845 to occupy the Pacific Northwest against British aggression and Indian belligerence.[20]

Essential to Rebecca's origin story is Judge Cornelius Hanford's account of the "Battle of Seattle" on January 26, 1856, in which Seattle residents fought unidentified Indians with the assistance of the navy sloop *Decatur* anchored in Elliott Bay. Ten when his family arrived in Seattle, and thirteen when the Indian Wars broke out, Hanford remembered that Rebecca's grandfather gave Seattle's white residents early warnings. "At the very beginning of the war, or immediately preceding it, Curley visited the homes of settlers . . . and warned them that they were to be murdered if they remained thus so isolated . . . I remember well [Curley] coming to my father's log cabin and strongly urging hasty removal of the family to the village." Curley warned residents in the vicinity of Seattle in the fall of 1855, immediately prior to the outbreak of the conflict. In a strange show of gratitude, local officials required Duwamish residents in the Seattle area to report to reservations shortly after Curley's alarm or else be considered hostile participants in the spreading violence. Although Seathl and his band followed orders and removed to the west side of Puget Sound, "a few individuals, including Curley, who were trusted by [Arthur] Denny and [Henry] Yesler and the officers of the *Decatur*, remained." Curley's ties to Yesler and other elite whites, most notably through Susan's union, had in fact proven beneficial to his band. For Hanford, in addition to his own personal knowledge of events, the fact that Seathl and his family were absent during the campaign should have been enough to dissuade rumors that Seathl or his daughter Angeline personally crossed Puget Sound to warn their white friends. "Ridiculous stories have been fabricated . . . pretending to explain the manner in which warnings had been given . . . one being that Angeline, daughter of Chief Seattle, performed a Paul Revere ride in a canoe, and gave warning, in time, to save all the inhabitants of Seattle." Hanford explains instead that Rebecca's grandfather Curley "had kept Mr. Yesler informed with respect to the assembling of hostile Indians in the vicinity." Hanford's depiction of events makes it clear that the judge held Curley in especially high regard, more so even than Seathl.[21]

What is most intriguing about Curley's participation in the siege against Seattle is that he apparently played both sides openly, such as with Klikitat fighters, whom Hanford and others believed had come from east of the Cascade Mountains to agitate local Indians. "[Curley] remained on friendly terms with the Klikitats during the Indian war, but he kept in constant communication with Mr. Yesler, giving him news of the plans and movements of the hostile Indians." Yesler paid Curley in ammunition, presumably for hunting and perhaps even with the expectation of meat in return since refugee families in Seattle could not afford to leave the barracks to hunt and some had been out of their homes since September. Curley used Yesler's payment in other ways, however. "Powder and lead were the most precious commodities that the enemy Indians had to obtain, and the few ounces that Curley could give them . . . gained . . . him free entrance into their camps. He carried news both ways; the Indians were glad to have him tell what they were doing to scare the white people, and he gave Mr. Yesler reliable information." Curley managed to trade ammunition and jokes at the expense of Seattle whites for vital intelligence regarding future attacks. Hanford remembered, "The attack [on Seattle in January 1856] was expected . . . because Curley had kept Mr. Yesler informed." As a result of Curley's duplicitous aid, the *Decatur* fired accurately on hidden attackers and residents fired small arms from barracks. The volley of fire was over within twenty-four hours, and only two Seattle residents died, including Hanford's fourteen-year-old uncle. Despite the personal loss, Hanford's account attributes his family and others' survival to Curley's interventions.[22] Perhaps the Klikitat also credit Curley for limiting their own casualties and aiding their efforts to make clear their disdain for American interlopers.

Curley's ability to sell information to Yesler in exchange for the very ammunition that other Indians used in the attacks he warned of reveals the extent to which he maintained his band's autonomy in newcomer relations. Curley's ties through leadership and marriage to Seattle residents were so strong that when whites told Seathl to leave, they asked Rebecca's grandfather to stay and provide protection even though they knew he likely laughed with the Klikitats at their expense. Curley's daughters no doubt maintained their own autonomy as well, and although Susan fades from the record after leaving Yesler's household in 1858, Peggy would come into her own as a prominent intermediary like her father in the years after the "Battle of Seattle." Perhaps it is because Peggy's older sister faced a dissolving union with Yesler that Peggy joined Franklin Matthias's household in 1857, thus allowing the family and the rest of Curley's band to maintain intimate ties to prominent Seattle builders. Intermarriage had already proven fruitful, given the band's presence in their original settlement throughout the interracial conflict in the Sound, and Curley's daughters continued to serve their community through intermarriage in the aftermath of the Indian Wars.[23]

No contemporary records document Peggy's presence in Matthias's home, but as has been shown throughout this and other scholars' work, census and vital records documented interracial intimacy inconsistently in the nineteenth century. Unlike Juana Walker's case, where research for this work uncovered trial testimony that had been misplaced in the archives, testimony from Rebecca Graham's case could not be recovered due to a district court order that the trial records be destroyed in January 1951 (thus proving that archival lightning does not strike twice).[24] Nonetheless, descriptions of Peggy and Franklin's relationship can be found in Judge Hanford's recapitulation of witness testimony in his published opinion and from press coverage of the trial—made more sensational for readers than the trial likely was for participants.

Both legal and newspaper records cite the beginning of Franklin and Peggy's union as sometime in 1857 and place Rebecca's birth in December 1859. According to witnesses and reporters, the union dissolved in 1861, and the two-year-old girl joined her mother in another wealthy man's household. What is important about the years between 1857 and 1861, though, is that the territorial legislature had banned unions between Native women and white men during this period. As mentioned in regard to Fanny and Nora Jewell's experiences in chapter 3, the first territorial legislature passed a marriage statute that made no racial exemptions on April 20, 1854, thus permitting Indian-white unions. Territorial legislators revised their seemingly progressive stance on interracial marriage on January 29, 1855, however, and barred unions between whites and persons with "one-fourth or more negro blood, or more than one-half Indian blood." The statute, although straightforward in its ban of marriages between Indigenous and white partners, also included the vague provision "that nothing in this act shall be so construed as to prevent any parties from being united in marriage, who may be living together at the time of the passage of this act."[25] For those couples who cohabited before the first month of 1855, then, it seemed the territorial legislature would sanction their marriage. Interestingly, this loophole meant that Yesler's union with Susan would have been legal had he not already been married, but made Peggy's marriage to Franklin an unsanctioned one.

Such a provision in an otherwise common rejection of interracial unions suggests that territorial legislators recognized Puget Sound Americans' early dependence on Native wives and their families, a trend that gender and legal scholars have observed broadly among the first generation of primarily male settler-colonists in the North American West. Presumably, however, legislators agreed that no more white residents would continue to form intimate unions with Indigenous women after February 1, 1855 (although we know that many citizens violated this law). For Franklin Matthias, then, who was undoubtedly familiar with the legal regime his friends established in the territorial legislature, inviting Peggy Curley into his home and bed proved defiance of the law—a tendency he shared with his Duwamish father-in-law. For Rebecca Lena Graham, however, the territorial statute made her an illegitimate child, even though in Indian Country she was the privileged child of an elite mother and father who symbolized the union of Duwamish and American interests.[26]

With Peggy Curley to manage his household and negotiate his interests among the Duwamish, Franklin Matthias worked in a number of capacities to advance his own and Seattle's economic interests in Rebecca's infancy. His interracial marriage and progeny did not seem to affect his reputation negatively among the city's white elites—indeed a number of other Seattle founders had Native wives and children as well. In 1859, the year his daughter was born, he joined Doc Maynard, Henry Yesler, David Kellogg (who would be the father of Peggy's second child, Rebecca's half-brother), and Arthur Denny to solicit funds for the establishment of a road through the Snoqualmie Pass. Timothy Hinckley became superintendent of the Snoqualmie Pass Wagon Road Committee and later testified that Franklin Matthias acknowledged Rebecca as his legitimate daughter. A year later,

Matthias and friends earned appointment as delegates on behalf of Washington Territory in negotiations for a Northern Pacific Railroad line. In response to the outbreak of the Civil War, Washington's territorial governor issued a proclamation on May 10, 1861, that all able-bodied men report to Adjutant General Franklin Matthias and be organized into militia units ready for action. While he prepared other men to fight on behalf of the Union, Matthias worked with still others to erect the first buildings on the University of Washington campus. Albert Pinkham was among the men working alongside Matthias in 1861; like Hinckley, he testified on Rebecca's behalf in later years.[27]

Peggy left Matthias in 1861 for reasons not discussed in remaining trial records or coverage, but among the Duwamish, marriage partners reserved the right to terminate unions at will. Whatever her reasons, Rebecca's mother left the carpenter and took up with accountant David Kellogg, who had worked with Matthias on the Snoqualmie Pass Wagon Road Committee. Peggy bore a son, John, in 1864 with Kellogg, but she left John's father shortly thereafter. She joined merchant and brewer Christian Scheuerman's household not long after leaving Kellogg. Scheuerman brought Peggy, Rebecca, and John into his home and gave all of them his surname. Although it was common among Seattle's elites for men to marry women with children from previous marriages, such women were usually widows—and white. Peggy and Christian had their first child together in early 1866, making their union at least as early as 1865.[28] Scheuerman, like Matthias, enjoyed prominence and wealth in the second half of the nineteenth century, but has not been widely recognized as one of Seattle's early elites—despite a tile mosaic bearing his name in the doorway of a building called the Scheuerman Block, still visible in today's Pioneer Square District.[29] Peggy's prominence proved itself in her union with Christian, who by 1865 could have joined the many other American men no longer interested in Indigenous wives. Territorial legislators did not make the choice easy for him, either, since between Peggy's partnerships with Matthias and Scheuerman, Washington's territorial senators had once again revised the antimiscegenation statutes that regulated Indian-white marriages and progeny.

As discussed earlier in the context of Nora Jewell's undisputed inheritance of her white father's estate on San Juan Island, legislators in the 1865–1866 session reiterated their ban of marriages between "a white person and . . . a negro or Indian, or a person of one-half or more negro or Indian blood."[30] Likely prompted by heightened fears of "amalgamation" between the races in the aftermath of the Civil War, this law not only made Peggy's interracial unions unlawful, it also mandated that her multiracial children could not marry white partners either. On the other hand, Matthias and Scheuerman's representatives recognized that their constituents continued to enjoy reproductive sex with Indigenous partners and so they legitimated "the issue of marriages of white men with Indian women," granting the "right of inheritance of such issue, only against parents," but barred mixed-race children's rights "from inheriting if any issue of previous lawful marriage."[31] For those concerned with the growth of a potentially dependent class of mixed-race progeny, legitimating white men's children—and it's worth noting that they did not imagine white women bearing mixed-race children—made fathers and their families responsible for the upkeep of this growing class. For Rebecca Lena Graham, born of an unsanctioned interracial marriage, the statute meant that she could press for inheritance rights against her father's estate because Franklin Matthias never married or fathered other children after Peggy left him in 1861. For Rebecca's cousin Julia Yesler Benson Intermela, however, an inheritance from Henry Yesler's estate would remain out of reach because his intraracial and state-sanctioned marriage to Sarah Yesler made the children of that union his legal heirs. If Yesler intended to remember his Duwamish daughter after his death no one would know—his legal heirs were accused of burning his will before it could be read outside the family.

As Rebecca grew up in Scheuerman's household, appearing in records then as Peggy and Lena, she and her siblings occupied a seemingly unique position between Duwamish and settler elites, but many of Curley's band members had mixed-race children and grandchildren. In fact, most of the original contributors to the Duwamish federal recognition efforts of 1925 were children of pioneer men and Duwamish women like Rebecca. For this reason the federal government proved skeptical of the mixed-race tribal petition, then and now.[32] Despite increasing hostility toward Native residents of Seattle—including an 1865 ordinance that barred Indians from living within city limits, but also required white employers of Indians to provide them with lodging, and an 1866 petition against the establishment of a Duwamish reserve on the southern edge of Seattle that Matthias and most of the witnesses in Rebecca's case signed—Curley and his band continued to live in Salmon Bay unmolested.[33] Rebecca remembered that during her early childhood, she canoed the waters intersecting Seattle that soon became rerouted and drained by her father and his friends. No doubt the girl used her canoe to visit her grandfather and other Duwamish relatives living in such close proximity to her stepfather's home. Just as Arizona men like King Woolsey and John D. Walker made Native people important parts of their personal lives and made political decisions that limited Native sovereignty, so too did men like Matthias and Yesler rely on Indigenous partnerships and then voted against tribal sovereignty.

The years immediately following the Civil War brought increasing restrictions on the personal and political sovereignty of Indigenous people in Seattle, and they brought an upsurge of growth in the city. Seattle residents sought to expand commercial, entertainment, and residential districts and link their enterprises to the growing nation via a railroad line. Perhaps he had been too busy with his duties as adjutant general to make the press, or he had taken some time to recover from losing his family to a colleague and then competitor, but by the late 1860s, Matthias reappeared as a leader in Seattle's financial and political sphere. In January of 1867, Matthias and his friend William DeShaw, who married Seathl's granddaughter and testified on Rebecca's behalf after Matthias died, served as administrators in pioneer Charles Plummer's estate, marking both men's respectability among Seattle's legal and financial elites.[34]

Having built portions of the University of Washington in 1861, Matthias served on its board of regents from 1867 to 1869 as well. In March 1867, he took on the execution and administration of his deceased friend Charles Terry's estate, along with business partner Erasmus Smithers, who testified against Rebecca. Matthias's work on the Terry estate drew him into numerous civil suits against Terry's debtors; Sheriff Louis V. Wyckoff served many of the subpoenas Matthias and Smithers issued in their estate dealings. Wyckoff died before Matthias, but Mrs. Wyckoff testified in the estate dispute that Matthias had no children. As he transitioned from a carpentry career to the full-time work of managing the substantial Terry estate, he enjoyed new political and social prominence. In 1869, Seattle residents voted Matthias to the city council, and an only slightly presumptuous editorial titled "Seattle—Past, Present, and Future" in 1871 included Rebecca's father among its list of important founding fathers. Matthias continued to serve as councilman from 1869 to 1872, gained a council seat again in 1877, and then served his last year in 1884.[35]

In 1873 Franklin Matthias helped to found the Walla Walla Railroad Company, formed in response to news that the Northern Pacific Railroad would not serve Seattle's port. Arthur Denny and Dexter Horton, among the men who testified against Matthias's daughter, also served as founding members of the railroad venture. The group attracted some criticism and the Seattle-based *Puget Sound Dispatch* came to their defense. Of Rebecca's father the editor wrote, "no man ever bore a more irreproachable character among his neighbors . . . as a careful and prudent business man, he has no superior, and for incorruptible honesty, there is not a man, woman or child among the old settlers who would not trust him implicitly, without limitation or guaranty." Of course, the unnamed person who lodged the original complaint disagreed.[36]

Four years later, in 1877, the *Dispatch* revealed that critic's identity as none other than Cornelius Hanford. When he wrote his critique in 1873, Hanford was a young law student enjoying the privileges of an upbringing in one of Seattle's most prominent families. Hanford made his protest against the Walla Walla Railroad Committee, Matthias included, on the grounds that they were "a most contemptible clique . . . trying . . . to make a good thing out of it themselves by gouging everybody else. We might consent to be gouged by these scalawags if they would build the road; they haven't got brains enough for such an enterprise." Three years later, in 1876, Hanford ran for Washington's Territorial Council on a Republican ticket and earned Seattle's vote, joining a council split five to four among Republicans and Democrats. Hanford's decision to then join the Democrats and break the Republican trust prompted the *Dispatch* to revisit the calculating politician's previous sins and reveal his earlier slander against Matthias and other city leaders.[37] Rebecca's Duwamish grandfather had saved Hanford's life when he was a thirteen-year-old boy and earned his lifelong admiration, but Rebecca's American father would face a harsh critic and political adversary in the thirty-four-year-old man. Hanford did not remain on the council for long, but he enjoyed success as a lawyer in Seattle for the remainder of the decade and served as Seattle city attorney in 1882, 1884, and 1885. He earned a prestigious appointment as chief justice of Washington Territory in March 1889; when Washington became a state later that year, he became its U.S. district judge, a post he held until his resignation in 1912.[38]

Despite their opposing views in the overlapping financial, legal, and social community of Seattle, both Hanford and Matthias did very well for themselves in the 1870s and 1880s. Franklin's success can be measured by his career trajectory over the years: carpenter in the 1860s, councilman and chief executive in the 1870s, and, according to the 1882 *Residence and Business Directory of the City of Seattle*, a capitalist in the 1880s.[39] Newspaper notices and civil suits throughout the 1870s and 1880s reveal that Matthias's management of the Terry estate did take up a lot of his time, but also made him a lot of money. No doubt he ran into Hanford when conducting his legal affairs, but he probably also ran into Christian Scheuerman when engaged in business and social dealings.

Between 1865, when Rebecca's mother joined Christian Scheuerman's household, and Peggy's death in 1884, the couple had at least nine children in addition to Rebecca and her half-brother John Kellogg. Scheuerman's home overlooked Salmon Bay, where his father-in-law's band still lived in the 1870s and 1880s. Scheuerman also invested in real estate in downtown Seattle's Pioneer Square. In 1870 and 1872, Rebecca's stepfather appeared on the federal tax assessment list as a very successful "retail liquor dealer."[40] Eleven years old in 1870, Rebecca lived with her mother and stepfather and her four half-siblings, with whom she attended Central School in Seattle's first permanent school building; she later attended a convent school in British Columbia. When Peggy's daughter turned twenty, she married John Holmes, a Massachusetts-born railroad engineer just three years her senior.[41]

In marrying John Holmes in the summer of 1879, Rebecca, who went by Lena at the time, followed a family tradition of defiance against territorial Washington's miscegenation ban. The legislature had not relaxed its stance against Indian-white marriages, and many of the territory's elites had come out against interracial unions in print and in private.[42] Despite the couple's legal and racial transgression, the *Seattle Daily Intelligencer* announced for its interested readers the marriage on July 19 of "Mr. John Holmes and Miss Lena R. Sherman" by Reverend J. A. Wirth.[43] Reverend Wirth led the First Baptist Church, which was indeed Seattle's first Baptist church, founded primarily by Cornelius Holgate Hanford's immediate family.[44] At least some of Seattle's elites, including Hanford's brother, aunts, uncles, and their reverend, continued to condone marriages among Indigenous, mixed-race, and American partners. Rebecca's ability to enjoy social prominence as the mixed-race daughter of a Duwamish woman with children from three living fathers speaks to the persistence of her family's prestige among Seattle elites. Curley continued to live in his Salmon Bay village, and despite their anti-Indian legislative pronouncements at the municipal and territorial levels of government, Seattle residents continued to rely on Duwamish wives and workers. While historians have rightly emphasized the rate of decline among Indigenous people in the years following the

Alki Point landing in 1851 and the waves of disease and dispossession that followed, some Native families maintained their prosperity by continuing to intermarry with elites from other communities who brought both sacred knowledge and valuable resources. Curley's daughters and granddaughters carried on this tradition, and their interracial marriages to notable American men with knowledge of capitalist politics and sociopolitical networking allowed Curley to protect his band's settlement, opened financial networks to his community, and gave members access to Seattle's legal system. Rebecca took advantage of all that her family connections provided.

A year after their marriage, John Holmes and Rebecca lived in Seattle's second ward, east of downtown, with Rebecca's nine-year-old half-sister Mary and a seventeen-year-old boarder attending school. Rebecca's mother and stepfather continued to live just north of the city near her grandfather in Salmon Bay. Her father Franklin lived, appropriately enough, on Commercial Street just south of Seattle's downtown, in the first ward district he represented on the city council.[45] In 1882, Rebecca bore her first child and named him George Franklin Holmes to acknowledge her father. George would be the only grandchild Peggy Curley enjoyed. Peggy died in 1884, her passing noted in the *Seattle Post Intelligencer*. The announcement referred to her as "Rebecca, wife of Christopher Sherman, aged 40 years," and reported to readers that she died on February 27 in Salmon Bay.[46] As in Juana Walker's case, mother and daughter shared names over the course of their lifetimes. Curley's daughter had been known as both Peggy and Rebecca in her forty years of life. Curley's granddaughter was called Peggy in childhood, Lena in early adulthood, and then became Lena Rebecca and Rebecca Lena in middle age, after her mother's death. Because their surnames changed often and did not always reflect parentage, Curley's female descendants could use given names to remember their lineage.

Though Curley's grandchildren had been born of banned interracial marriages, his great-grandchildren were born under a different legal regime. Rebecca's marriage to John Holmes had the blessing of Reverend Wirth's and the Hanford family's church, but not of the Territory of Washington. In 1881, however, the territorial legislature eliminated racialized language from its marriage statute.[47] This radical shift would change the terms of the debate in Rebecca's estate challenge. Although it is clear that Rebecca and her family had made a practice of ignoring the territory's efforts to limit their personal and political choices, the 1881 revision would mean that Peggy's union with Christian Scheuerman gained legal sanction and that their children could safely expect to inherit their father's estate on equal terms with other descendants of prominent Seattle men. The shift also meant that Rebecca could act as the legal partner of her husband John. She claimed this right for tragic and unexpected reasons within the decade.

After her mother's death, Rebecca continued to share close ties with her Scheuerman siblings and her maternal cousin, Julia Yesler Benson Intermela. Rebecca's own household also grew: she bore another son, Tom, the year of her mother's death, and in 1885 she gave birth to a daughter, Jola (possibly Julia), followed in 1887 by another daughter she named Lena, thus carrying on the legacy of shared names between mother and daughter. Sometime between 1885 and 1887, Rebecca's mother-in-law joined their household, making their home not only multigenerational and interracial, but likely a multilingual and interfaith one as well. John Holmes and his mother not only brought a New England outlook to Rebecca's home, the engineer had spent some time in China before arriving in Seattle via San Francisco. Although Rebecca's immediate family grew steadily, her father left Seattle shortly after her mother's death. Matthias went first to San Francisco, then to his sister's home in their Pennsylvania birthplace, and eventually resettled at Lake Tahoe.[48]

In 1888, four years after losing her mother, Rebecca faced tragedy once again. Gaps in the documentary record make it difficult to trace exactly what happened, but John and Rebecca lost one of their young children, either four-year-old Tom or two-year-old Jola.[49] For John, who may also have lost his mother that year, the grief proved devastating. Rebecca's husband fell into a depression that turned into violent rage when fueled with alcohol. Rebecca seems to have tried to control her husband's behavior within the family, but his episodes soon made him a liability and he lost his position as engineer on the Columbia & Puget Sound Railroad. Losing his job in the spring of 1889 seems to have hastened John Holmes's decline and he became a concern not only to Rebecca and his employers, but to Seattle police as well. In the last days of March, John Holmes lost his mind and Rebecca lost her husband just a year after losing her child. While the Holmes family reeled in tragedy, Cornelius Hanford celebrated his new appointment as chief justice of Washington Territory and no doubt made note of news reports chronicling the sorrows of his Duwamish hero's granddaughter.[50]

On April 4, 1889, the *Seattle Post Intelligencer* reported that "Holmes had been acting in a strange manner for several days," and "caused the train men a great deal of trouble" when he arrived at the Columbia & Puget

Sound depot. Holmes "attempted to take out an engine, laboring under the delusion that he had been employed to take 500 people free of charge on a train that cost Dexter Horton & Co. $5,000,000, and with an engine that could make the trip to New York in two hours." An officer on duty at the railyard arrested Holmes and took him to police headquarters. "While he was recording the arrest . . . Mrs. Holmes came in and said that her husband had been insane for several days and that she was afraid he would do something dangerous if allowed to remain at large. She was greatly relieved when informed that he had already been locked up, and explained that his insanity was caused by grief over the death of a favorite child."[51]

Given the sensational and public nature of Holmes's breakdown, along with its ties to a former business enterprise of Matthias and other Seattle founders who later appeared in his estate case, others who testified in the case were undoubtedly aware of the tragic episode. Although it was surely difficult, Rebecca Holmes took legal action to protect her family and her husband from himself. Fortunately, she had the support of those closest to her. Just days after her husband's arrest, Rebecca appeared in the King County Probate Court for his sanity hearing. Beside her was her maternal cousin Julia Benson, described in court records as Rebecca's sister, a label that may have more accurately reflected Duwamish kinship concepts for a maternal cousin of the same sex. Although Rebecca's testimony was not recorded, the physician's certificate reported that John Holmes had no suicidal tendencies, but that he was intemperate and had the tendency to become physically violent in sudden episodes—evidence probably gathered from Rebecca herself. The report affirmed Rebecca's explanation for her husband's apparent insanity as caused by the loss of a child.[52] The physician thus concurred with Rebecca's claim that her husband was legally insane; the court recognized the mixed-race woman as John Holmes's legal guardian when she had him committed to the Hospital for the Insane just south of Tacoma in Steilacoom. The committal proved to be a death sentence, and John Holmes died of "softening of the brain," the day after he arrived at the asylum.[53]

While no aspect of Rebecca's engagement with the King County Probate Court can be described in a positive light, the widow might have found it an immense relief to be acknowledged as John's state-sanctioned wife with rights not only as his guardian, but also to the children and property they shared. When Nora Jewell's father died on San Juan Island, she became a ward of the court because her Salish mother had no recognized maternal or spousal rights, and Rebecca's children might have faced the same disastrous fate had the territorial legislature not revoked the miscegenation ban in 1881. Although Rebecca lost her mother in 1884, a child in 1888, and her husband in 1889, she would not also face losing her three remaining children to the territorial guardianship system that had taken so many other Native and mixed-race women's progeny.[54]

The *Seattle Post Intelligencer* announcement of John Holmes's death also revealed that Rebecca and her children were not at home when the death notice arrived. According to their report, John Holmes's widow and children were "visiting in Kitsap County, so the sad news could not be communicated to them."[55] No doubt Rebecca had decided to leave Seattle and get beyond the reach of the press or nosy neighbors in light of her husband's dramatic episode and the shock it must have caused for the family. Whom she visited in Kitsap County is unknown, though she probably knew her father's business partner, William DeShaw, and his Duwamish wife and children there. The Port Madison reservation in Kitsap County was also home to many Duwamish by 1889, including family friends Chief William and his son William Rogers.[56] Perhaps one of these friends or relatives offered Rebecca and her children refuge in their difficult time, and her retreat there is evidence that she maintained intratribal kinship networks in the years following her mother's death.

When Rebecca returned to her Seattle home, she began to pick up the pieces of her life with the tenacity of a woman who knew change as a constant force, even if a sometimes chaotic one. Rebecca continued to rely on support from her "sister" Julia Benson and from her stepfather Christian Scheuerman, who still lived in Salmon Bay with seven of her half-siblings.[57] While Rebecca's own life had changed dramatically in 1889, so did the legal and social conditions shift in Seattle as Washington transitioned from territory to state, much to the delight of those whose families had begun American settlement of the Puget Sound region at Alki Point. Achieving statehood proved the "civilizing" efforts of men like Franklin Matthias, Henry Yesler, and Cornelius Hanford, but also marked the end of Puget Sound as Indian Country. Leaving territorial status behind meant that Washington's white residents had successfully outnumbered the Native and otherwise noncitizen population of Chinese, Hawaiian, and Japanese. Although the elevation in political and legal status, along with its social implications, meant much for local residents who had long been disappointed with federal interventions in territorial matters and had criticized federal appointees for corruption and incompetence, Rebecca's political life did not change nearly as much as her personal life. After statehood she remained the descendant of a prominent pioneer and a high-ranking Duwamish family, the mother of three mixed-race children, and the widow of a New Englander whose personal losses in the Pacific Northwest had driven him to mental illness and death. Although Rebecca would survive the havoc wreaked by the forces of Dookweebathl and western expansion, not all of her loved ones would be so fortunate.[58]

Rebecca remained in the home she had shared with John Holmes at Eleventh and Dearborn, an area immediately east of what was then Chinatown and what is now known as Seattle's International District. She remarried on April 2, 1890, just over a year after her first husband's death. Minister John Darrow presided over the ceremony, held at Christian Scheuerman's Salmon Bay home. Like a close and constant sister, Julia Benson witnessed Rebecca's marriage to Victor Graham, a Canadian boilermaker. Local historian Patricia Hackett Nicola's research reveals that newlyweds Victor and Rebecca, who signed her marriage certificate as Lena Graham, deeded land to George and Lena Holmes, Rebecca's surviving children from her marriage to John Holmes, just months after taking their vows. The act suggests that Victor committed himself financially as well as emotionally to Rebecca's children early in their union, a point Rebecca might have learned to insist upon from her Duwamish mother. On January 4, 1891, nine months after their wedding date, Rebecca and Victor celebrated the birth of their first son, named after his father and grandfather, Victor Matthias Graham. Six months later, however, Rebecca's daughter Lena died of spinal meningitis, and she was left with only two children, first sons from both marriages. Rebecca's only surviving daughter and namesake was just four years old when she died in July 1891, becoming the third child she had lost in as many years. It is understandable, then, that Rebecca was already preoccupied with grief when news reached Seattle from Lake Tahoe of her father's death on August 28, 1891.[59]

While Rebecca mourned the loss of her daughter, and perhaps reflected on the rapid succession of tragedy she had survived, her Matthias relatives in Pennsylvania, Illinois, Iowa, and South Dakota moved quickly to collect her father's estate. Within months of his death, Franklin Matthias's Pennsylvania property had been appraised and valued at $28,000 and his Washington property estimated at $26,800. Rebecca's paternal cousin Charles Matthias, Franklin's nephew and oldest male descendant, led legal efforts on behalf of his aunts Mary and Martha, and his cousins Frank, Alfred, Jessie, Lela, Stella, and Albert. Because Franklin Matthias died intestate, the Superior Court of King County, where Rebecca had testified to her first husband's insanity, appointed a local administrator for the estate and gave him a year to assess and appraise Matthias's personal and real property. In that year, notices appeared regularly in the *Seattle Post Intelligencer* for creditors to submit receipts and for debtors to submit payment. By September 1892, the court-appointed administrator concluded that Franklin Matthias had accumulated $26,036.90 in cash and $22,819.60 in real estate by the time he died.[60]

Given his expertise in probate and estate management, it is a surprise that Rebecca's father left no will to distribute his substantial wealth, just as Juana Walker's father's intestate death proved perplexing given his former position as probate judge in Pinal County, Arizona. Perhaps as Matthias aged he became torn between acknowledging his Indigenous daughter and disappointing his Victorian sisters. As the courts worked in the year immediately following his death to sort out exactly what he owed and owned, the Seattle press remembered him fondly as "a builder of early Seattle, and solid citizen." The *Seattle Post Intelligencer* recounted his contributions to Seattle's early history. According to their obituary, Matthias "built some of the first houses erected in the city [and] was commissary sergeant of the volunteers during the Indian war of 1855," which is no doubt what brought him closer to Curley before his marriage to Peggy. The *Intelligencer* also summarized Matthias's transition from carpenter to capitalist. "About twenty years ago he stopped working at his trade and became the manager of the Terry estate. . . . At about the same time he began dealing in real estate." Of Matthias's personal life, the obituary reported he "was not married and had no relatives here. He was well known among the early settlers and had many firm friends among them. They pronounce him to have been a man of unswerving honesty and integrity."[61]

While Rebecca mourned and read that her father had no relatives in Seattle, her sister-cousin Julia Benson also followed a personal loss in local print. Her father, Henry Yesler, died in December 1892 and she, too, found herself written out of his life in the obituaries noting his death. For the next year, disputes over Matthias's and Yesler's estates would appear side by side in the *Intelligencer,* and likely raised many eyebrows among readers who knew these founding fathers well enough to read between the lines and wonder about the fates of their Duwamish families. Rebecca and Julia, though they shared similar positions as the daughters of Duwamish and pioneer elites, occupied very different legal ground as potential heirs under Washington civil law. Because Henry Yesler had children from a state-sanctioned marriage, Julia could make no claim for inheritance. As mentioned earlier, there are many reports that Yesler had not only acknowledged Julia, but had also provided for her financially throughout his lifetime. The controversy over a will allegedly destroyed by his legitimate daughter and her attorneys suggests that Yesler might have tried to provide for Julia after his death as well. Regardless of the truth behind those suspicions, once no will could be produced, Julia lost any hope of inheritance against the claims of Yesler's white children. Rebecca, on the other hand, had the right to claim her father's estate even though she was the issue of an unsanctioned marriage because Franklin had no other children—legitimate or otherwise. Under Washington's laws of descent, direct descendants like Rebecca, even if born illegitimate, held priority over lateral descendants like her paternal cousin Charles and the other Matthias claimants. Perhaps fueled by a combined realization that Matthias's estate was indeed substantial and that she enjoyed a legal privilege few other mixed-race descendants could claim, Rebecca filed her own petition for distribution in King County Superior Court on April 1, 1893, and challenged her Matthias kin to disprove her lineage.[62]

Rebecca's petition shocked court reporters so much that they betrayed the linkage between Julia and Rebecca, Yesler and Matthias, in their own minds when first reports of Rebecca's estate challenge came out. Under the headline "Claimant to Mathias [*sic*] Estate. She Is Not Skookum Susie's Daughter—A Legal Marriage Alleged," the *Intelligencer* reported that "the claimant to the Franklin Mathias estate who has suddenly appeared proves not to be Julia [Yesler Benson] Intermela, daughter of Skookum Susie, the reputed common law wife of Mathias, but the daughter of another squaw, named Rebecca." As in Juana Walker's case, local press and readers proved unable to distinguish between the intimate Indigenous partners of their founding elites, lumping them together as degraded women, and thus faced confusion when such descendants emerged as legal actors. The article reveals some Seattle residents' uncertainty toward the Duwamish sisters who married close friends that resulted in mistaken identities between the mixed-race daughters those unions produced. What the article also shows, however, is that Seattle residents knew much more about their founding fathers' interracial households than previous reports had let on. Although the *Intelligencer* had initially reported that Matthias had no living relatives in

CLAIMANT TO MATHIAS ESTATE.

**She Is Not Skookum Susie's Daughter—
A Legal Marriage Alleged.**

The claimant to the Franklin Mathias estate who has suddenly appeared proves not to be Julia Intermela, daughter of Skookum Susie, the reputed common law wife of Mathias, but the daughter of another squaw, named Rebecca. The claimant's mother, Rebecca, went to live with Chris Scheuerman early in the sixties at his ranch on Salmon bay, and little Rebecca was raised by him. When she was about 19 years of age she married an engineer named Holmes, who worked on the Columbia & Puget Sound railway. Holmes died four or five years ago and she soon afterwards married her present husband, Victor Graham, a boilermaker. Several oldtimers say that there never was any talk of Rebecca as Mathias' child, but that Julia was so regarded by some.

Jasper N. Turner, of Turner & Behrens, who represents Mrs. Graham, declares that Mathias not only lived with and acknowledged Rebecca as his wife according to the laws of the territory, but that he expects to prove that a marriage was celebrated. The old-timers, he says, all knew the girl as Mathias' daughter, and she went by the name of Rebecca Mathias. When Rebecca was a little girl her mother left Mathias and went to live with Chris Scheuerman, but Mathias continued to provide for the girl and to acknowledge her as his daughter. This is the first time that Mrs. Graham has ever taken any steps to assert her claim upon her father's estate, says Mr. Turner, but she can bring competent witnesses from among the old settlers to establish all her claims.

"Claimant to Mathias Estate," *Puget Sound Intelligencer* (Seattle), April 5, 1893, p. 5 (Reproduced with permission from University of Washington Library Microfilm and Newspaper Collections)

Seattle, the paper now explained that "several oldtimers say that there never was any talk of Rebecca as Mathias's child, but that Julia was so regarded by some." Other "oldtimers . . . all knew the girl as Mathias's daughter, and she went by the name of Rebecca Mathias . . . [and] she can bring competent witnesses from among the old settlers to establish all her claims."[63] As in other cases chronicled in this book, "oldtimers" disagreed whether to acknowledge or obscure their friends' Native families and descendants.

Despite the sensational nature of the *Intelligencer*'s reporting of Rebecca's initial claim against her paternal relatives, the petition she submitted was actually very straightforward. She and her attorney Jasper N. Turner agreed with all previous depictions of Matthias's death and descriptions of his estate, merely adding that she was "the lawful child of [Franklin] and Rebecca Matthias his wife." Rebecca's cousin and his attorneys did not initially answer her petition. Instead, the local administrator continued his work on the estate and submitted a final report on July 20, 1893, that fully detailed Matthias's personal and real property, which included a number of lots in downtown Seattle and hundreds of acres in Island County, and advocated that the superior court distribute Franklin's estate to his lateral heirs—two sisters, three nieces, and four nephews. Rebecca and her attorney acted swiftly, submitting just a few weeks later their "answer to petition of Samuel L. Crawford, as administrator, for distribution of the estate of Franklin Matthias, deceased, and showing cause why said estate should not be distributed among the heirs and persons therein named." It is in this statement that Rebecca outlined the full history of her parents' relationship between 1857 and 1861, noting her birth in 1859. Graham and her attorney made their claim more than a personal one, however, when they included the following language outlining the political context of her origin story.

> [In] 1857, Frank Matthias . . . intermarried with an Indian woman commonly known by the name of "Peggy Curley" at what is now the County of King, then Territory of Washington, and within the limits of the Indian Country. . . . Peggy Curley belonged to and was at the time of said marriage a member of . . . the Duwamish tribe, which . . . were then possessed of the Country in which said marriage occurred, having never ceased their tribal relations, or yielded up their possession, rights or customs to that of the whites, or to the Government of the United States, or to the Territory of Washington, or to any other Power or Country whatsoever. That . . . marriage between . . . deceased and . . . Peggy Curley was . . . entered into, solemnized and celebrated according to the law, usage and custom of the said tribe of Indians, and said marriage was binding and valid and was so considered by the parties thereto.[64]

Though subtle in its approach, Rebecca and her attorney's "answer" to administrator Crawford and the King County Superior Court invoked Duwamish law in its description of the marriage between Franklin and Peggy.[65] While Juana Walker's attorneys had similarly claimed that her parents' union had taken place in "Indian Country," they referred to the Akimel O'odham reservation when they did so. Rebecca and her attorney described Seattle, King County, as Indian Country, not a federally established reservation. In addition to this bold claim, they placed Seattle's status as Indian Country as late as 1857, rejecting both the establishment of Washington Territory as American jurisdiction in 1853 and the treaties of 1854 and 1855 that the Duwamish had not accepted. Read as a description not just of Rebecca's birth and her parents' union, Graham's answer articulates Duwamish sovereignty, making her an heir of Matthias's estate because he accepted the terms of tribal law when he established himself within unceded territory and married a Duwamish woman. When also considered in light of the witnesses she called, Rebecca Graham's estate challenge, then, was not merely a personal dispute, but a tribal challenge to American dispossession. In presenting their case this way, Rebecca and her attorney sidestepped any and all reference to the miscegenation bans in place under territorial Washington law and put Matthias, and the larger Seattle community, under the jurisdiction of Indian Country.

In response to Rebecca's challenge, the Matthias claimants petitioned for the dispute to be heard in federal district court rather than in county superior court. Their reasons included the large amount of money in dispute and the fact that the litigants were living in multiple states; both legitimate grounds for federal jurisdiction. Their petition was granted and the case moved to the federal district court on October 7, 1893.[66] Soon after, Rebecca's attorneys protested the change in jurisdiction, likely because they had come so close to a ruling in King County Superior Court—a court that had already recognized Rebecca's legal authority as Holmes's wife—and would have to start over. But their efforts proved useless and they prepared for a new hearing before Cornelius Hanford: newly appointed district judge, former Seattle city attorney, sometime critic of Franklin Matthias, and longtime admirer of Chief Curley.

To bolster their case, the Matthias claimants submitted sworn affidavits from Franklin's surviving sisters Mary and Martha. Both women testified that they had visited with their brother Franklin in Blairsville, Pennsylvania, in 1890 and in St. Charles, Iowa, in 1888. In their conversations with Franklin, he apparently told them that he had never married or had children, because "there were very few women on the coast except Indian women and he had never seen a woman he cared to marry."[67] Other than this statement, the Matthias descendants could not offer any further proof to contradict Rebecca's claim, so the remainder of the evidence submitted in the case came from witnesses called to testify for both parties. Their testimony is evidence that some Seattle residents acknowledged the city's roots in Indian Country and reliance on Duwamish generosity, while others preferred to recall a history more like that espoused in the same year by

Frederick Jackson Turner: one of white male independence and ruggedness that excluded Indigenous partners and providers.

Although the district court ordered trial transcripts destroyed in 1951 —a mysterious move according to archivists consulted throughout federal, state, and county repositories in Washington—trial testimony is loosely summarized in Hanford's opinion and all witnesses are named in remaining records. Those testifying against Rebecca Graham were either witnesses who had become the wealthiest in their efforts to convert Seattle from Indian Country to industrial cosmopolis, or a few who had served as King County sheriff in the territorial years and thus had enforced laws against interracial promiscuity. Some of these men who benefited from or enforced territorial Washington's anti-Indian legal codes had worked alongside Matthias in a number of capacities over the years and based their knowledge of his intimate past on these financial and professional dealings.

Arthur Denny and Henry Van Asselt, two of Seattle's earliest arrivals and wealthiest residents, both testified that Franklin had no children, though they worked closely with him between 1859 and 1861, when Rebecca and her mother Peggy lived in Matthias's home.[68] A friend of both Denny and Van Asselt, Dexter Horton refuted Rebecca's claims as well. Perhaps because Matthias's money was deposited in his bank, Horton thought himself an authority on Franklin's personal affairs. Horton had arrived in Seattle in 1853 and probably did know as much as anyone about Matthias's business dealings, but he may also have felt that wealthy men simply did not have mixed-race heirs.[69] Hillory Butler and Erasmus Smithers also contradicted Rebecca's claims in their testimony. Both men arrived together in 1853, a year after Matthias's arrival. Smithers and Matthias worked together to administer a handful of estates, including the vast Terry estate, and Butler lived near Matthias in the 1860s.[70] As pioneer capitalists who had built much of their fortune on the backs of Indigenous laborers and their lands, Denny, Van Asselt, Horton, and Smithers might have wanted to ensure that Indian women's children could not undo the work of their fathers. If they did act to protect white men's property in the West, they would have found themselves among the majority of western jurists in the 1890s. It was not that majority that heard their testimony, however—it was Justice Hanford, a man who firmly believed his life had been saved by Rebecca's Duwamish grandfather.

Although Erasmus Smithers fit the profile of other pioneer capitalists who testified against Rebecca, Hillory Butler did not. Butler made some money in real estate, but he also served as King County sheriff in 1854, Muckleshoot Agency Indian agent in 1861–1862, and as deputy provost marshal of Washington Territory.[71] In contrast to the view ultimately taken by Judge Hanford, Butler may have taken the law-and-order stance that interracial unions banned by the territorial legislature and discouraged by Indian agents throughout Puget Sound deserved no recognition whether they happened or not. Another law-and-order view might have come from Sheriff Wyckoff's widow, who testified that Franklin had no Indian family. Lewis V. Wyckoff arrived in the years when Puget Sound remained part of Oregon Territory. He worked at first in Yesler's mill—likely alongside Duwamish laborers—and then began a blacksmith business. From 1862 to 1882, when he died, Wyckoff served as King County sheriff.[72] On what grounds his widow dismissed Rebecca's claims is unclear, but she and her husband had been longtime friends of Denny, Van Asselt, Smithers, and Horton. Finally, William Surber, King County's first sheriff, also testified against Rebecca, though little is known about him in regard to his immediate connection to Matthias. Like Wyckoff, Surber had close ties to Albert Denny, but unlike other witnesses on his side, William "Joe" Surber was rumored to have fathered a daughter with a Native woman. Since he lived his senior years with his sisters, he might have felt that Matthias's sisters deserved a part of the estate as he would have wanted his own family to share in the wealth he had accumulated in Seattle. Regardless of his motives, Surber would not be the first or last westerner to engage in private behaviors that they condemned in public.[73]

Although witnesses for Matthias's lateral relatives fell into two classes of pioneers—wealthy capitalists and territorial law enforcement—there were elites and officials on Rebecca's side of the courtroom as well. Perhaps Franklin's siblings, nieces, and nephews took a straightforward strategy in their choice of witnesses, selecting those who could speak against the legality of Peggy and Franklin's union, and then those who could speak against the likelihood of such a union among men of Matthias's capitalist class. As outsiders to Puget Sound, they might not have realized that Rebecca's witnesses would also include members of Seattle's pioneer elite class and that some of King County's law enforcement had broken the territory's laws themselves. What divided witnesses in the *Graham v. Matthias* estate case was not likely a question of the truth of Peggy and Franklin's union, but a question of whether their union, and progeny, deserved recognition and sanction. For a small class of pioneers, their friends' mixed-race children were not legitimate heirs, but for others, Rebecca and those like her were part of Seattle's past and present, and by testifying in her favor, those founding elites also acknowledged the powerful expression of Duwamish sovereignty that lay behind her claim.

Among those who testified for Rebecca were three groups: first were those who admitted only that they knew Franklin and Peggy had cohabited, but would not say whether they were married when Rebecca was born; second were those who swore not only that Franklin and Peggy lived together, but that they were in fact married; and third were Duwamish tribal members who described in great detail a marriage ceremony conducted in their community to celebrate Franklin and Peggy's union. Representing all segments of the Puget Sound population who settled on the margins of Curley's camp, their testimony convinced Justice Hanford of what he likely already knew for himself: that Rebecca was Franklin's only daughter and that many of Seattle's most respected residents had defied the miscegenation ban and crossed the color line in their private and public affairs.

Six witnesses testified that Franklin "maintained relations of intimacy with [Rebecca's] mother," but were unsure whether he did so "openly." Samuel Coombs claimed lineage to French Huguenots who arrived in New England in 1760; the family would choose the patriot side of the Revolutionary War. Coombs served in the Maine legislature before departing for California in 1859, too late to benefit from the gold rush that had sparked so much emigration, and made his way north to Yesler's mill in 1861. He worked for Henry Yesler and Timothy Hinckley—also a witness for Rebecca—before becoming a local magistrate in 1864. Coombs opened a hotel in 1867, became a justice of the peace in 1881, and enjoyed his membership in the Brotherhood of Masons. His interest in Duwamish culture and history is exhibited in his *Dictionary of the Chinook Jargon*, from 1891, in which he encouraged readers to "briefly [study] the Dictionary and then converse with Indians"—with whom he presumably remained acquainted when he testified on Rebecca's behalf. Much of his dictionary includes translations of legal transactions into Chinook, also indicating that Coombs viewed Native Puget Sounders as important legal actors in the nineteenth century—an uncommon view among western justices, but one obviously shared by Judge Hanford. His obituary in 1908 noted that Coombs knew all of the Indian leaders in the region, and if that is true, then Rebecca's grandfather Curley might have been one of the men who helped him develop his

Chinook language skills. Coombs probably knew many men who cohabited with Duwamish women in addition to Rebecca's father.[74]

Dillis B. Ward and Ed Thorndyke helped Matthias to erect some of the University of Washington's earliest buildings. Ward served as a territorial legislator and accumulated significant wealth through real estate dealings, but he ultimately suffered two bankruptcies and was forced to sell off most of his property shortly after the Matthias estate trial. Thorndyke served for a time as Seattle's police chief and shared Ward's financial fate when he lost much of his personal wealth in the 1893 panic that probably preoccupied many of the witnesses who testified in the Matthias estate trial. Thorndyke and Ward testified that Franklin and Peggy had shared a home, but that they did not know whether the couple had married.[75]

Originally from Maine, Mighill B. Maddocks also testified that he knew Rebecca's parents had cohabited at the time of her birth. Mighill enjoyed his own success in Seattle, but lived in the shadow of his brother Moses, who served as Washington's territorial representative in 1863–1864 and built the Occidental Hotel shortly after his public service. Rebecca's obituary suggests she spent parts of her childhood with "the Maddocks family," but does not indicate which brother she might have lived with. If she lived with Mighill and his wife Carrie on their White River farm, the couple would have been very familiar with Rebecca's family ties to both Seattle elites and Duwamish leaders and might have been acquainted with other White River witnesses who testified on Rebecca's behalf.[76]

If Mighill Maddocks's ties to Franklin Matthias and his daughter are difficult to trace, Timothy D. Hinckley's relationship to the case is much clearer. He served as affiant to Justice Hanford's parents' donation claim, making him familiar with the judge and his personal background. Hinckley also served in the territorial legislature, on the Seattle City Council, and made much of his money in real estate. All of these activities would have made him a frequent acquaintance of Franklin Matthias, but Hinckley knew Rebecca's father even more closely because the two men had arrived in Seattle together in March 1853. Because they shared this powerful connection in addition to their professional ties, Hinckley could reliably testify that his friend and colleague cohabited with Rebecca's mother.[77]

Although Reverend Daniel Bagley arrived in Seattle later than Matthias or Hinckley, he also knew about Franklin's shared household with Rebecca's mother. He not only served his Methodist Episcopal congregation but was also president of the University of Washington Board of Commissioners, and he likely knew Matthias through their shared interest and efforts on behalf of the university. We cannot know whether Bagley was a close confidant of Franklin or Rebecca, but his participation in the case is significant, because his son Clarence Bagley became one of Seattle's most prolific local historians, and at the time of the Matthias estate trial Clarence was already publishing regularly in local papers. The reverend's son produced a number of hefty historical volumes, including *Indian Myths of the Northwest*, which includes contributions from "an intelligent Indian woman, the wife of an 'old settler.'"[78] Because she is unnamed, it is impossible to tell which of Seattle's Native women aided Clarence Bagley, but given Rebecca's connections to the family, her willingness in later life to share Duwamish cultural practices with interested ethnohistorians, and the book's late publication date of 1930, it is probable that Clarence benefited from her knowledge just as Rebecca benefited from his father's testimony. That Judge Hanford and Dillis Ward served as Daniel Bagley's honorary pallbearers at his funeral two years after the estate case indicates that Bagley shared close ties with other of Rebecca's advocates as well.

The witnesses discussed above only acknowledged that Franklin and Peggy shared a home, but others swore that the couple in fact presented themselves as married and testified that Rebecca was Matthias's only acknowledged heir. Some of these witnesses had Native wives themselves and might have known intimate details about Franklin and Peggy's union because they shared a particular social network or knew more about Peggy's life than Franklin's. Others were law enforcement officials who worked closely with Seattle's nonwhite community and may have been familiar with Matthias as well as Rebecca's Duwamish kin. Some had worked with Matthias while he and Peggy lived together and then separated, putting them in a position to know Franklin at a vulnerable time of his life and a vital time in Rebecca's.

Like Franklin Matthias, William DeShaw, Richard Jeffs, and Alexander Spithill married Native women; unlike Matthias, these men legally acknowledged their wives and shared lifelong unions with their Native families. DeShaw married Seathl's granddaughter, described as Duwamish and Suquamish. Seathl's son-in-law served as Indian agent for Port Madison Indian Agency for some time and may have been one of the people Rebecca visited in Kitsap County while mourning the loss of husband John Holmes. DeShaw would have been well positioned to support Rebecca's genealogical testimony as well as her claim that Seattle and King County remained Indian Country as late as 1857.[79] Jeffs married a White River woman whom others described as Klikitat. He enjoyed success as a farmer with the help of his wife, but also worked as an attorney in Seattle courts, and likely knew Matthias and Hanford very well. Clarence Bagley reported that "[Jeffs] always maintained that the wife who had stood by him in the difficult days when he had to wrest a home from the wilderness should reap the rewards along with him when he attained affluence." Probably Jeffs felt the same about Rebecca and her mother Peggy, who had married Matthias before he was wealthy and enabled him to find success on Puget Sound. Jeffs also served as a member of the constitutional convention when Washington became a state, marking his prominent status within the region's legal community. Hanford no doubt weighed his testimony very carefully.[80] Spithill married a Stillaquamish woman and then a Snohomish woman's daughter after his first wife died. The pioneer served on the Tulalip, Neah Bay, and Port Madison reserves between 1859 and 1862, teaching government-sponsored agricultural and carpentry skills to resident Indians. Each of these men clearly occupied the same social world as Franklin Matthias as husbands in Indian Country.[81]

Though William Surber and L. V. Wyckoff's widow testified in accordance with the miscegenation ban that nulled Franklin and Peggy's union and might have made Rebecca an illegitimate heir, Matthias's daughter had other law enforcement witnesses on her side. David Webster and Theodore Williams both swore not only that they knew Franklin and Peggy had lived together, but that the couple lived "together as husband and wife" "for three or four years, during which time [Rebecca] was born."[82] Webster had served as Seattle's first city marshal, but apparently did not share the disregard for interracial households that his fellow police officers Surber or Wyckoff espoused in their testimony against Rebecca. Theodore Williams, described as a "gold seeker and vigilante" who "fought Indians and made desperadoes toe the mark," served as sheriff of Kitsap County and may have been familiar with Rebecca's family history through his encounters with her Duwamish relatives at Port Madison. Exactly how these men knew Franklin Matthias or Rebecca Graham is unclear, but they clearly supported Rebecca's claim that she was the product of a marriage recognized by Duwamish and American neighbors living in Indian Country.[83]

Although Washington's territorial legal code banned Indigenous witnesses from testifying against citizen defendants except when they were charged with selling alcohol to Indians, drafters of the state statutes in 1889 chose to remove racial exclusions in their description of competent witnesses.[84] Still able to bar witnesses at his own discretion, Judge Hanford decided to hear testimony from four Duwamish witnesses called on Rebecca's behalf, though he did not hear from any Indian women besides Rebecca. Their ties to the case indicate not only that Curley's granddaughter had maintained strong connections with the Duwamish community, but also that she was closely aligned with the same men who would later be acknowledged for their leadership in the Duwamish Tribal Organization's federal recognition efforts in the early twentieth century.

One of these men was Ben Solomon, a Duwamish man whom Judge Hanford would later describe as "a smart Indian boy who grew up to manhood in Seattle, and became active in religious work," and whom Daniel Bagley's son Clarence called one of the "well-known worthies" of the Seattle area's Indian community.[85] Chief William and his nephew William Rogers, both important Duwamish leaders at the turn of the twentieth century, also testified in Hanford's court on Rebecca's behalf. Along with Jake Foster, another Duwamish man well known to Clarence Bagley and other Seattle residents, Rebecca's tribal kin described an elaborate marriage ceremony between Franklin Matthias and Peggy Curley. Jake Foster claimed he was "present when Matthias obtained the consent of the relatives of the bride, and when they conducted her to his house to be married . . . and that afterwards he visited the married couple at their house." William Rogers and his uncle explained that they participated in the wedding ceremony itself, and "required each of the contracting parties to repeat twelve times the vow to assume marriage relations with each other." Though he allowed their testimony, Judge Hanford did not give his reasons for describing the Duwamish witnesses' evidence as "transparent, and manifestly false."[86] Whether their description of the marriage ceremony was true or not, the men clearly knew Rebecca and her family very intimately, and she counted on them as important witnesses in her origin story. They would later count on her to help them construct a Duwamish tribal narrative in their efforts toward federal recognition.

Rebecca Graham clearly had more witnesses on her side than her paternal cousins and aunts did, but more importantly, she had Cornelius Hanford behind the bench. Judge Hanford, who had arrived in Seattle at the age of ten in 1852, knew intimately each of the witnesses, as well as the deceased man himself. Although he represented federal authority, suggest-

ing an objective and removed perspective, Judge Hanford could not possibly have heard the testimony delivered without adding the context of his
personal knowledge and experience. Surprisingly, when he delivered his
opinion, he dismissed the testimony of most of the witnesses on both sides,
arguing that respectable elites on both sides of the case likely testified to
what they knew to be true and that Matthias had withheld certain aspects of
his life that he revealed to others. "I find in the testimony a great deal that is
mere surmise, a great deal of gossip, a great deal of rumor, and a great deal
that I regard as fiction. Some of the witnesses are not very well informed;
others are reckless. . . . [Franklin Matthias] may have been cunning with
[Mr. Smithers and Mr. Butler and others], and less guarded with others."
Hanford rejected as bald-faced lies the reports of those witnesses who had
testified most explicitly regarding the marriage ceremony between Franklin
and Peggy, and yet he concluded that Rebecca was Franklin's daughter, regardless of the fact or falsehood of marriage.[87]

Hanford referred to the 1865–1866 revision in territorial Washington's
marriage law that acknowledged the progeny of unsanctioned unions as legitimate heirs, and upheld Rebecca's claim against her father's lateral heirs,
though he did not at any point refer to the ban on interracial marriages
that made Rebecca's claim questionable in the first place.[88] That Hanford
remained silent on the miscegenation ban even though attorneys for Matthias's lateral heirs raised the contentious point might be read as his disapproval of the ban and the racial and sexual hierarchies it represented. In
fact, the legal justification he offered for his ruling that regardless of the
condition of her parents, Rebecca remained a legitimate heir is a misreading
of the miscegenation ban and its implications prior to 1865 for mixed-race
children like Rebecca. Just as jurists in Lucía Martínez's case had applied a
skewed interpretation of habeas corpus law to rule against her custody case
against King S. Woolsey, Hanford took advantage of a confusing series of
legal statutes that were no longer in effect to make a ruling that coincided
more closely with his own understanding of Seattle's and Rebecca's past and
to rule in her favor. Like other jurists who ruled on questions of race, sex,
and power in the North American West, Hanford made the Matthias estate
case seem deceptively simple in his opinion:

> The question which I have to decide on this evidence is whether it is
> proved that Frank Matthias and Peggy did so live together. . . . From
> consideration of all the evidence, I am well convinced that Matthias and

Peggy were never married. I am also convinced that Frank Matthias was the father of [Rebecca]. To entitle her to inherit his estate, being his daughter, it is not absolutely necessary that there should be proof of a marriage between her parents. . . . My conclusion is that there is a fair preponderance of the evidence . . . to the fact that [Rebecca's] mother and Frank Matthias lived together as man and wife before and after [her] birth; and . . . that . . . she is entitled to a finding in her favor.[89]

At home in Illinois, Iowa, and Pennsylvania, Rebecca's paternal cousins must have been floored when they learned of the August 1894 ruling. Not only did they lose their inheritance claim of nearly $40,000, they had to pay nearly $730 in fees associated with the case. Although they might have known Rebecca had the advantage of the 1865 statute acknowledging mixed-race children of white fathers and Indian mothers as heirs to their fathers' estates, Hanford's ruling largely discredited the witnesses who testified to Matthias's paternity and so the question of Rebecca's lineage could easily have been disputed. Without the transcripts of testimony, it is difficult to say exactly what convinced Hanford that Franklin had fathered Rebecca, but it is most likely that he knew the fact himself. Given his attachment to Curley, his shared social and professional network with Matthias, and his sustained relationships with many of the witnesses on Rebecca's side of the case, Hanford must have had his own particular insights into Franklin and Peggy's relationship, and we know he had strong opinions on the relationship between the Duwamish and Seattle's early American residents.

Hanford's role as district judge not only gave him the opportunity to rule in Rebecca's favor and perhaps show his gratitude to the woman's grandfather for saving his life during the Battle of Seattle in 1856, the case also gave him an opportunity more broadly to repay a Duwamish family for the losses they incurred in the devastating wake of American settlement and occupation of Puget Sound. Although silent on the issue in his published opinion in *Graham v. Matthias* in 1894, in *Seattle and Environs*, his history published in 1924, Hanford critiqued the treaty process that Rebecca's claim also challenged.

The treaties were prepared beforehand, and the provisions thereof were read to the Indians through an interpreter and signed by chiefs and sub-chiefs who assumed to represent and bind their people. They were unable to sign with their own hands, otherwise than by a mark, and the interpreter could at best give them only an imperfect understanding of the documents, so that in a few instances [as with the Duwamish] the identity of the signers was afterwards disputed. . . . Smart Indians were able to advance very plausible arguments against the validity of alienation of property rights. From these circumstances controversies with respect to the binding effect of the treaties arose . . . provoking resentment. But white people had claimed and taken the country, and the progress of civilization was not to be hindered by such controversies with Indians after the Government of the United States had assumed dominion over the country.[90]

Hanford's account of the controversial 1854–1855 treaties of territorial governor Isaac Stevens that led to Duwamish dispossession not only coincides with the version put forward in that tribe's century-long campaign for recognition, it also anticipates the scholarly critiques made by Pacific Northwest historians in recent years. Undoubtedly, Rebecca's case, rooted in her claim that Franklin Matthias and Hanford himself lived in Indian Country as late as 1860, informed the judge's view of the questionable taking of tribal lands in his lifetime. He may have seen Rebecca's claim as a personal opportunity to act in favor of tribal sovereignty by awarding her a share in the wealth founding elites gained with the help of Duwamish wives under the shadow of American dominion.

Whatever his reasons for ruling in Rebecca's favor when he could easily have found against her, Hanford ensured that Curley's granddaughter would have financial security for the remainder of her lifetime. The scope of his ruling was small, of course, setting precedent for other mixed-race children of Indian mothers, but not resolving the concerns of Duwamish tribal members who saw their lands quickly disappearing as the century closed. Although local journalists predicted "that several similar cases . . . will now be filed in court" in the wake of Rebecca's victory, a review of legal records does not show an increase in such cases.[91] It may be that Hanford's ambiguous opinion made other litigants hesitant to press their claims. Although attorneys on both sides of the case discussed the common-law marriage statutes of Washington Territory, the ongoing miscegenation ban would have ensured that Franklin and Peggy's marriage did not have the sanction of common-law marriage, a point neither party engaged fully in the available records. Although Rebecca's paternal kin disputed her inheritance eligibility on the grounds that no legitimate marriage had occurred between Franklin Matthias and Peggy Curley and that Matthias had not confirmed Rebecca as his daughter, their counsel also "made a strong attack upon the character and general reputation and conduct" of Rebecca's mother, no doubt suggesting that Rebecca might have been another man's daughter. Rebecca's lawyer countered those rumors, "severely scoring some of the witnesses against" Peggy, and argued that Rebecca was Matthias's "legitimate child by virtue of a . . . marriage . . . contracted at a time when [Seattle] was Indian country and Indian customs prevailed here." Her attorney also pointed to the territorial act "legitimatizing the offspring of all marriages declared null at law," though he emphasized again that the "important question . . . was whether this was 'Indian country' at the time of the . . . marriage . . . in 1857, the Indian title or right of possession not having been extinguished by treaty with the government until 1859."[92]

Because of Hanford's narrow ruling, mixed-race heirs of white fathers and Indian mothers—if others were inspired by Rebecca's legal success—would have had to subject their Indigenous families to slanderous insinuations and then hope that their case would be accepted by a sympathetic judge. Judge Hanford ultimately applied the territorial statute recognizing inheritance rights for some illegitimate children on the basis of his own knowledge that Rebecca was in fact Matthias's daughter. How many mixed-race descendants shared overlapping family histories with district judges in Washington, were in a position to assert their legal claims against potentially intimidating paternal kin, and were also eligible for inheritance under the narrow terms of the territorial statute? Not many, if the dearth of cases filed in the wake of Rebecca's success is any measure. Rebecca's legal victory is significant because it illustrates that a very specific mixture of elements had to be present for Indian women's children to achieve legal success, even if her experience is limited among those of her generation. The legal experience she accumulated during her upbringing among prominent members of Seattle's founding elite, as the granddaughter of a tribal leader who had managed to preserve his band's autonomy throughout the expulsion of the Duwamish from their Seattle homeland, and as the legal guardian of her unstable husband and then of her children after his death had given Rebecca the acumen she needed to put forward a claim that her attorneys could defend and that Judge Hanford could accept.

Juana Walker had made a similar effort in her own estate claim filed in the same year as Rebecca's, but without the benefit of a prestigious tribal background and powerful allies in Arizona's settler community. Although Juana won her lower court claim, she could not, like Rebecca, convince

Arizona's juridical elite to recognize her status as the heir of a wealthy and white father when her paternal kin challenged the ruling in higher courts. Juana took a settlement that her lawyers claimed most of, and lived the remainder of her undocumented life in Tucson's Barrio Libre district beyond the reach of legal or social scrutiny. Rebecca, on the other hand, won an impressive sum and lived the remainder of her documented life holding her family together and working to convince others that portions of Seattle remained Indian Country and that she and her Duwamish kin deserved federal recognition.

After the case, Rebecca Graham returned to the business of caring for her family and maintaining their place within the Duwamish tribal network that had spread throughout Puget Sound. In a remarkable testament to her ability to manage her personal and legal affairs seamlessly, Rebecca gave birth to her sixth child in the midst of the estate trial. Virginia Graham, Rebecca's second child with her husband Victor, was born in February 1894, just six months before Hanford ruled in the estate case.[93] Though Rebecca had lost three children and both of her parents, she focused on providing her surviving three children with a stable upbringing. She continued to manage her financial affairs after the estate trial, and in 1897 with her stepfather Christian Scheuerman and a few of her Scheuerman siblings she sold about five acres to be included in the military reserve set aside for Fort Lawton.[94] Those lands, so close to Curley's Salmon Bay village, eventually became part of the Magnolia neighborhood of northern Seattle.

In 1900, Rebecca and Victor lived near downtown Seattle around Ninth Avenue South and Dearborn Street, in the same house she had owned with John Holmes before he died. Rebecca and her second husband shared the residence with their two children, Victor Jr. and Virginia, and Rebecca's firstborn son, George Franklin Holmes, by then eighteen. The Graham family also hosted two boarders, brothers from Austria. The census enumerator who counted Rebecca's household also marked her half-sister Bertha Scheuerman, married to Joseph Bradwick, as Rebecca's neighbor. Bertha's eight-year-old daughter Lulu and Rebecca's six-year-old daughter Virginia would grow up as close cousins, much like Rebecca and her maternal cousin Julia Yesler Intermela Benson had. Although Julia no doubt provided Rebecca with moral support whenever she could, Rebecca's cousin had moved with her husband Charles Intermela to Port Townsend, across the Sound from Seattle on the tip of the Olympic Peninsula, and was busy raising her own young children, Charles, eight, and Elsie, six. Julia also cared for her former guardian and associate of her father's, Charles B. Pierce, and his wife, both of whom lived with Julia and her husband in Port Townsend. Julia died in 1907, and Rebecca likely grieved the loss of her sister-cousin deeply.[95]

By 1910 Rebecca no longer lived with Victor and had purchased a different house at 1815 South King Street, a few blocks east of her former residence. Rebecca's second husband had not gone insane, but the couple had separated and he had given in to gold fever. Victor left his family and headed to Alaska, where he remained until his death in 1938.[96] Victor Jr. and Virginia remained with their mother, along with their older brother George, who gave his occupation as "Musician," and his Iowa-born wife Hume, whom he had married in 1903. Tragically, Rebecca's oldest son died that year in a boating accident, leaving behind a son as well as his wife and mother.[97]

A year later, at the age of fifty-three, perhaps having realized her second husband was gone for good, Rebecca went to Tacoma to marry George W. Fitzhenry in a ceremony ordained by the pastor of St. John's English Lutheran Church and witnessed by the pastor's wife and another woman whose connection to the bride and groom remains unclear.[98] Rebecca and her third husband had no children, which is not surprising given her age. The couple was divorced by the end of the decade. Virginia Graham's marriage to Jack Hilliard McFadden in 1912 proved an important family event that was witnessed by her father Victor, who left for Alaska shortly after the ceremony, and by her maternal cousin Lulu Bradwick, who had grown up just a few blocks from Virginia.[99] Rebecca L. Fitzhenry celebrated her son Victor Jr.'s marriage just a few years later in 1914 to Ruth Heideman.[100] For a woman who had suffered so many family losses, including the relatively recent departure of her second husband, Rebecca must have felt some pride and perhaps security knowing that her remaining two children had begun households of their own, and that both still lived in their Duwamish homeland.

As a woman whose children had begun their own families, Rebecca earned a special place among her Duwamish friends and relatives as a respected elder who had seen their community's transition from Curley's Salmon Bay camp of thirty-odd members in the 1850s to a broad network of interracial families throughout Puget Sound by the 1910s. Even as she juggled her own legal and financial concerns, always balanced amid the tragedies and triumphs of her family life, Rebecca maintained ties to the

Duwamish men who led their community in the years after her grandfather Curley had passed. In 1915 she joined the same men who had described her parent's Duwamish marriage ceremony back in 1893 and together they worked to collect a roll of surviving Duwamish families in the area and to begin a campaign for federal recognition that was in fact a continuation of the claims they had first made during her estate trial in the 1890s. William Rogers led the impulse to organize more formally, but Ben Solomon also worked to represent Duwamish interests with local Indian agents. Along with tribal leader Charles Satiacum, they compiled a list of 361 individuals, including Rebecca's family, and they labeled their group the Duwamish Tribe of Indians.[101]

Although Rebecca's tribal community aligned with the 1916 Northwest Federation of American Indians and nominated that organization's president to advocate on their behalf, the Bureau of Indian Affairs' assumption that Duwamish concerns had only been sparked by this pantribal movement is seriously flawed. As these men had testified and Rebecca had claimed in her 1893 estate claim, the tribe's members, whether mixed-race or not, had rejected the 1854–1855 treaties and continued to insist that their leaders—Rebecca's grandfather among them—had not ceded their territory in King County. As part of their effort to document surviving Duwamish relatives in Puget Sound, Rebecca's friends also investigated the possibility of obtaining allotments or compensation for their dispossession at the hands of their American fathers' friends. These interests coincided with the Office of Indian Affairs' assignment of special agent Charles Roblin to make up a roll of off-reservation or "unenrolled" Indians throughout Puget Sound. Rebecca ensured that she and her children would be counted as Duwamish tribal members when she submitted her own affidavit of membership through Thomas Bishop—president of the Northwest Federation of American Indians—in March 1916. At the time she filed her affidavit, Rebecca was living with her only daughter Virginia, who had moved to Colorado Springs in hopes that the change in climate would ease her tubercular symptoms.[102] That Rebecca made such an effort to appear in the Roblin Rolls while caring for her ailing daughter in another state indicates that the process of registering Duwamish families for federal recognition was important to her and that she had maintained close ties to other Duwamish relatives that kept her informed of Seattle area developments while she was away.

Once Virginia and her husband were settled in Colorado Springs, Rebecca returned to Seattle and continued her efforts to share Duwamish

history and remind Seattle residents that she and her community had survived into the twentieth century and now sought recognition. Curley's
granddaughter met ethnographer Thomas T. Waterman, already famous
in the anthropological world because of his training under Franz Boas and
his work at the University of California with Alfred Kroeber after Ishi, reported to be the last survivor of his Yahi tribe, was found in 1911. Rebecca
likely met Waterman through Arthur Ballard, a prominent Seattle history enthusiast and collector of Duwamish tales, or through family friend
Clarence Bagley, also a local historian whose father had testified in 1893
that Franklin Matthias was married to Rebecca's mother Peggy. Waterman
worked with Rebecca and other Duwamish between 1916 and 1918 and described Rebecca as "a very quick and intelligent woman."[103] Though his
publications on the Duwamish and Puget Sound Indigenous practices do
not cite Rebecca directly, she and others of her generation shared a wealth of
knowledge regarding Duwamish material and cultural practices, oral traditions, and beliefs with Waterman, Ballard, and Bagley.[104]

Despite the prolific knowledge Rebecca's community shared with those
who showed interest, the Bureau of Indian Affairs to date has described her
generation as one that failed to maintain a distinct identity as Duwamish
people and ceased to associate with one another on the grounds of a shared
cultural and political history. This assessment, which the bureau uses to
withhold federal recognition for modern-day Duwamish people, apparently
does not consider the ways in which Rebecca managed to keep her extended
family closely connected throughout her lifetime.[105] Her maternal cousin
Julia Benson Intermela not only served as witness when Rebecca petitioned
to have her first husband committed to the State Hospital for the Insane
in 1889, she also witnessed Rebecca's marriage to Victor Graham in 1890.
Between the loss of one husband and her marriage to a second, Rebecca
took refuge with Duwamish relatives in nearby Kitsap County, where many
Duwamish resided on the Port Madison reserve and in the surrounding
area. Later, Rebecca asked Duwamish leaders Ben Solomon, Chief William,
and his nephew William Rogers to testify on her behalf in the estate trial in
1893. Although the state of Washington destroyed all transcripts from that
trial in the 1950s, their testimony clearly outlined a Duwamish conception
of tribal sovereignty and ongoing claims to the area surrounding Seattle and
described tribal intermarriages with newcomer whites as a practice regulated by tribal ceremony. Rebecca continued to live near her Duwamish kin
in Seattle, even if they owned homes like their American neighbors and no

longer lived in lodges on Salmon Bay as their parents and grandparents had done. Rebecca's daughter Virginia also practiced the habit of keeping close family ties, asking maternal cousin Lulu Bradwick to witness her marriage in 1912. Together, Rebecca, her surviving children Victor and Virginia, and her maternal cousins and half-siblings signed the Duwamish Tribal roll in 1915 and appeared again on the Roblin Roll compiled by the Office of Indian Affairs between 1916 and 1919. Despite these very clear assertions of a carefully maintained Duwamish communal identity, the Bureau of Indian Affairs has argued that there would be a flimsy connection between Rebecca's generation of mixed-race descendants of Duwamish and Euro-American parents and those who came after them.

Rebecca's community continued to press their claims for recognition in the face of federal officials' skepticism. Although she lost yet another of her children when Virginia died of tuberculosis in 1918, Rebecca persisted as a community leader for other Duwamish in the Seattle area.[106] In 1920 she told the federal census enumerator from her home at 1815 South King Street that she had divorced George Fitzhenry. By then nearly sixty, Rebecca lived with her twenty-nine-year-old and only remaining child, Victor Graham, who worked as a stage carpenter, and her twenty-year-old niece Adelaide McGregor. Just as she had taken in a younger sister when she first married John Holmes in 1879, Rebecca shared her home with extended Duwamish kin.[107] Although Rebecca's relatives and friends were not holding regular meetings in a designated tribal council house or openly conducting tribal ceremonies that they had learned from parents and grandparents, Seattle area Duwamish obviously knew where to find each other and how to support one another in long-standing and traditional ways.

Another sign that Rebecca and William Rogers continued to expand their efforts to gather Duwamish support for a federal recognition claim came a few years later, in February 1925, when the community published a constitution and bylaws as the Duwamish Tribal Organization, and added "an accompanying membership list" in 1926.[108] Rebecca and her son Victor, along with sixteen of her Scheuerman siblings, appeared on the 1926 list. Charles Roblin reported that he had counseled Duwamish tribal members on compiling a list of claimants during his work with them in 1917 and that "they believe that all Indians who have Duwamish blood in their veins, *no matter what their present tribal affiliations may be,* would be entitled to share in whatever settlement was made with them, as a tribe."[109] Rebecca's community recognized their relatives who had Euro-American as well as

Duwamish parentage and those who had joined relatives in other tribes to survive the hard times that had hit so many who were dispossessed in the aftermath of the Puget Sound Indian Wars and subsequent American occupation of King County. As a result of their inclusiveness, the 1926 roll included many mixed-race people and Duwamish who had enrolled as members of nearby tribes to ensure their eligibility for treaty benefits, but also, no doubt, to ensure they would not be lost to their tribe in subsequent generations of exogamy.

The Bureau of Indian Affairs has so far disregarded these 1915 and 1926 lists as evidence of the maintenance of a tribal identity, even though it is clear that individuals like Rebecca and their families had successfully retained their Duwamish identity and place within a broad tribal network throughout Puget Sound. Although we do not have direct evidence that Rebecca and her Scheuerman siblings visited relatives on nearby reservations as late as 1920, it would be naive to assume that she knew only Ben Solomon or William Rogers and no other members of their Black River bands who had relocated near and on the Tulalip and Port Madison reserves. Another important aspect of these lists is not only that their membership includes women like Rebecca, directly descended from Curley and other recognized leaders of contact-era Duwamish, but that their membership includes the great-grandparents of modern-day Duwamish leaders like Cecile Hansen, Duwamish tribal chairwoman and longtime proponent of federal tribal recognition.[110]

After 1926 Rebecca dropped the surname Fitzhenry and began using Graham again; she appeared in the 1930 census as Rebecca L. Graham, a boarder in a private home. Whether Rebecca had sold her King Street house to help her son Victor in his new start with his wife Jennie in their apartment at Pike and Ninth Avenue, or she had suffered like so many others in the financial crash the year before, or she simply felt that it was wise to scale down in her senior years, Curley's granddaughter began to rely more on others as many had counted on her in previous years. She likely called on Duwamish and perhaps non-Indian friends to help her move again in 1935, when she decided to rent a room from a different family who lived closer to Victor, who had moved with Jennie to 1515 Terry Avenue. Rebecca reported in 1940 that she relied on "income from other sources" than employment, indicating that she had managed to stretch the inheritance her father had built on Duwamish lands for nearly fifty years, and described herself as a widow since her second husband had died in Alaska in 1938.[111]

Just as Rebecca had worked to maintain her financial independence and family network on the terms she had learned from her mother Peggy, her tribal leaders insisted on the Duwamish Tribal Organization's financial and political independence. They voted to reject the Indian Reorganization Act of 1934 on the grounds that they reserved the right to distribute any funds awarded in the federal claims process rather than surrendering such decisions to the Bureau of Indian Affairs. Although the tribe had not yet won any of their claims against the federal government, they already did not trust that entity to distribute their anticipated settlement either. The U.S. Court of Claims would reject their claim later that year, though the Duwamish Tribal Organization continued to press for federal recognition.[112]

Although she had lived through the Civil War, World War I, and World War II, Rebecca Lena Graham did not live to see her tribe win its battle with the federal government. Curley's granddaughter died in 1946, remembered in the Seattle press as "One of First Whites Born Here."[113] Survived by her son Victor Matthias Graham and grandson George V. Holmes, Rebecca Graham would not likely have made such a claim herself since she had claimed her Duwamish ties much more strongly than her paternal Matthias connections. In fact, the Seattle community's unwillingness to see Rebecca and her kin as Duwamish descendants paralleled the federal government's refusal to recognize the work she, her mother, and other Duwamish women had done to maintain the matrilineal ties among their cousins and siblings that all linked back to Salmon Bay Curley, a man who had saved Seattle's founding elites in the Puget Sound Indian Wars to ensure the survival of his band. His efforts proved successful in Rebecca's lifetime, but without the acknowledgment of Seattle and D.C. politicians and residents in subsequent generations, the descendants of Curley's band continue to be legislated as white, or enrolled as members of other tribes, even as they struggle to be regarded as Duwamish.[114]

Rebecca Graham's personal victory in securing her rights to a white father's inheritance was not reflected in her tribe's efforts to secure sovereign claims to the lands they had shared with Rebecca's father and his friends. The frustrating history of Duwamish efforts toward federal recognition is better told elsewhere, but as recently as 2013, representatives from Washington State submitted petitions for Duwamish federal recognition before Congress, and Chairwoman Cecile Hansen has remained active both in Seattle and in Washington, D.C., to press the cause of her own and Rebecca's people.[115] Despite the chaotic changes overseen by Dookweebathl and wrought by settler-colonial invaders of their homeland, Cecile and the tribe's story is the same as the one Rebecca and her Duwamish and American witnesses told Judge Hanford in 1893. He believed their history of Duwamish persistence and sovereignty, not only ruling in her favor, but later publishing his own account of Duwamish history that echoed the version put forward in Franklin Matthias's estate trial. Rebecca began a campaign 120 years ago that Cecile has continued and it is this author's sincere hope that their efforts will prove fruitful very soon, marking a long and powerful chapter in Indigenous women's legal history that the Bureau of Indian Affairs and federal government can recognize as clearly as Judge Hanford did at the close of the nineteenth century.

CHAPTER 6

Dinah Hood, "The State Is Supreme"
Arizona, 1863–1935

Dinah Foote Hood's grandmother Tcha-ah-wooeha rose early on the wet morning of September 3, 1913, to gather wood for her family's morning fire. Walking along the slick banks of Granite Creek with her dogs, the elderly Yavapai widow discovered her neighbor at work on a grisly task. Less than a hundred yards from their camp in the central Arizona highlands, Juan Fernandez struggled with boulders and debris to bury the bloodied body of Jesús Esparcía, a Mexican laborer who found odd jobs in Prescott. Tcha-ah-wooeha turned away from the heinous scene and returned to the camp she shared with a dozen other Yavapai and Mexican squatters. Likely out of habitual avoidance of nearby Anglos, the elderly widow remained silent about what she saw for three months and refused to participate in the early phases of a criminal investigation that revealed much about Granite Creek residents' simultaneous presence and obscurity.[1]

Stabbed ten times, Esparcía's body fell into the crevice between state and federal jurisdiction that the Hood family had exploited throughout the region's troubled transitions from Yavapai territory to territorial capital to Yavapai County seat. Yavapai territory in 1863 spanned the entire central Arizona highlands, and band members shared alliances with neighboring tribes along the Colorado River and the Mogollon Rim. The gold rush of 1863 attracted national interest in the region, and Prescott, founded on Tcha-ah-wooeha's Granite Creek, was named territorial capital in 1864. Although Prescott would lose its status as capital, the town remained Yavapai County seat under the protection of Fort Whipple, a military fort established

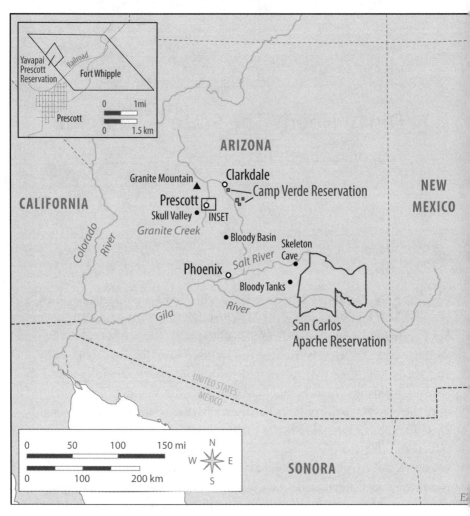

Dinah Hood's Central Arizona borderlands (Map by Ezra Zeitler)

in 1864 to launch anti-Indian campaigns. Members of the Hood family had strategically made their home along the legal borderland between the Fort Whipple military grounds and Prescott's municipal district.

Esparcía's murder threatened the refugee Yavapais' tenuous autonomy when investigators scoured the camp and claimed jurisdiction over the brush huts and their inhabitants. Dinah's English fluency and Tcha-ah-wooeha's unique vantage point on the clandestine gravesite made them targets for prosecutors; their female status made them questionable to defense attorneys. Primarily Yavapais and a few Mexicans who spoke little or no English and claimed multiple names, Granite Creek squatters confounded jurists' conceptions of state subjects. To prosecute Juan Fernandez, however, state attorneys would have to convince the superior court that Tcha-ah-wooeha, described in legal records as an "aged squaw," and her Yavapai relatives were competent witnesses subject to state authority and that the Granite Creek camp lay inside state jurisdictional bounds—both highly disputable points.[2]

At its core, the *State of Arizona v. Juan Fernandez* trial and the subsequent appeal to Arizona's supreme court brought together the diverse residents of a community struggling to reemerge from a history of racialized, territorial violence; the vestiges of that violence permeated the power dynamics in the Yavapai County superior courthouse.[3]

Like her female Indigenous contemporaries in this book, Dinah Foote Hood grew up surrounded by the prophecies and stories of her family's people. She cared for her grandmother, Tcha-ah-wooeha, and great-aunt, Tith-ri-va-ca, who were born around 1841—more than twenty years before Americans renamed their home Arizona Territory.[4] These elderly women spoke only their mother tongue and likely knew the stories that explained the sacred significance of Granite Mountain, a day's walk from the Hood family's home outside of Prescott. They might have told Dinah the stories that warned women to be wary of virile coyotes when traveling to harvesting and gathering sites throughout the year, and advised men to be cautious of young women's sexual advances lest they be fooled by vengeful murderesses.[5] Perhaps less magical, but as incredible, were the stories these matriarchs must have told about a preconquest childhood, the violent onslaught of the Indian Wars, internment among strangers on the distant San Carlos Apache Reserve, and of their eventual return with Dinah to the Prescott and Verde Valleys they knew as children. The years between 1841 and 1912 were pivotal in the region's transition from Yavapai territory to American state; Dinah's persistent ties to her Yavapai family and lands in the midst of such dramatic transformation shaped her ability to resist state interventions as an adult.

Although the women in the earlier chapters worked creatively to assert their legal challenges in district and superior courts, the women in these next two chapters—Dinah Hood and Louisa Enick—practiced evasion and petition, demonstrating less overt but no less essential legal strategies that Indigenous women used in the early twentieth century. The climactic struggles for white supremacy in the American borderlands West uprooted such women from their homes—but some like Dinah and like Louisa Enick in northwestern Washington found ways to return to and reclaim their tribal lands. Just as Washington's chroniclers have obscured the Enick family's legacy in their state's legal history, so too have historians ignored the Hood family's contributions to Arizona's juridical past. Dinah's story differs from the other women in this book because she lived to see the transition of her people from hunted "savages" to American citizens, maintained an Indian identity throughout her entire lifetime, and focused her survival efforts on avoiding legal authorities. Lucía Martínez managed to pass on citizenship to her children by claiming a Mexican identity in 1880, and Norah Jewell relied on whiteness to gain access to territorial Washington's justice system. Juana Walker became white when she died in 1916 even though courts had declared her to be Pima and she had lived somewhere in between for forty-three years. Linked to the women in chapters 2–5 because of her critique of Arizona's imperial legal regime, but unique because she launched that critique without lawyers or guardians as intermediaries and without masking her Indianness, Dinah Foote Hood's story is one that illuminates the extraordinary experiences of ordinary Indian women living in the North American West at the turn of the twentieth century.

Despite their efforts to evade white scrutiny and dodge state officials, Dinah Hood and her family quickly became the central witnesses in the investigation of Jesús Esparcía's murder. Yavapai County jurists had a vested interest in taking testimony from nonwhites like the Hood family when trying to prosecute Juan Fernandez for murder. If the state could claim authority over the Indigenous squatters, Yavapai County could safely claim jurisdiction over Granite Creek; without incorporating new subjects, the state could not incorporate new lands. Arizona had never allowed an Indian woman to testify against a white man, and the defense team hardly expected an old woman to upset legal precedent—Fernandez's attorneys would bet an appeal on this point. The following pages describe the historical and social contexts that made the Hood women contentious participants in the *Arizona v. Fernandez* trial. Their forced inclusion as witnesses could be read as an apparent expansion of rights for marginalized women in Arizona, allowed to testify for the first time against white men—but the trial also features a debate over race, space, and gender in a state still coming to terms with its territorial past.

Though she did not cross international borders, Dinah Foote Hood is considered here as a bordercrosser who traversed tribal, municipal, and federal boundaries throughout her lifetime. Expanding on the assertion by critical geographers that claiming space is claiming power, this chapter examines the spaces available to Yavapai women in central Arizona as a reflection of their shifting status from subjects to citizens in the early twentieth century. For Yavapai women of the early twentieth century, claiming space distinguishable from the areas whites had staked for themselves allowed them to transfer their Indigenous legal status, their corporeal sovereignty, to the land itself. Using the insights of critical race theorists to argue that the young state of Arizona extended limited citizenship rights to Yavapai witnesses to serve its own interest in the expansion of power makes this story an important one in western legal history. Instead of focusing on the details of Esparcía's murder, this chapter positions the trial in the longer history of Tcha-ah-wooeha and her granddaughter's transition from "squaw" to citizen between 1863 and 1924. The arguments made here suggest that Arizonans alternately acknowledged and denied the Indigenous population according to state interests.

The *Arizona v. Fernandez* trial represents a state effort to expand its authority over unregulated lands and peoples and offers historians an opportunity to measure Indigenous women's ability to ward off state scrutiny. Feminist legal critics describe the American legal system as a stronghold of white patriarchy while critical race historians explain legal decisions upholding the rights of minority subjects as the product of converging interests between state and minority parties. Other historians have shown that racial-ethnic women in the early twentieth century approached these restrictive regimes with creative resistance. Jurists sitting in the Yavapai County superior courthouse in Prescott relied on jurisprudence as enacted by white men and conducted in English, while Granite Creek residents depended on fictive kinship as enacted primarily by women and conducted in Yavapai and Spanish. In subpoenaing Yavapai women's testimony, Yavapai County jurists simultaneously established state authority over Granite Creek subjects and granted non-English-speaking women legal lengua, an authoritative voice in the courtroom. That subsequent jurists failed to uphold these women's rights to legal lengua indicates that the state offered temporary gains to minorities because it served immediate state interests to do so. Agreeing that states function "to reproduce the rule of the dominant classes," it would be naive to expect jurists to uphold a "'general interest' [in justice] that overrides all class, gender, and racial divisions."[6] Incorporating the voices of Dinah Foote Hood and Tcha-ah-wooeha allowed the state to incorporate the remaining Indigenous subjects that had survived extermination and brought their community of Yavapai squatters under state—white citizens'—authority. Dinah Foote Hood's story provides the context for such a discussion, but her story can only be understood as part of a longer history.[7]

The Yavapai living in the central Arizona highlands consisted of at least four different bands of family groups that intermarried and gathered for large harvests, but most often remained within their own regions. Dinah's family ties to the Verde Valley region indicate that she most likely belonged to the Northeastern Yavapai, or the Yavapé.[8] Prior to contact with Americans, the four Yavapai subgroups occupied a remote but vast region of Arizona's central highlands between the Salt and Gila River O'odham to their south and the Pai groups of the Grand Canyon to their north. Enemies of both the O'odham and Pais, the Yavapais aligned with Colorado River tribes to their west and Apache groups to their east, blurring Yuman and Athabaskan cultural traits through matrilineal kinship alliances.[9]

The seasonal life based upon a diverse ecological economy that Tithri-va-ca and Tcha-ah-wooeha practiced for twenty-two years gave Dinah the material knowledge she would need to support her family when they returned to their homelands at the beginning of the twentieth century. In May, women harvested "squawberry," then "the water cactus, then the palo verde tree," which yielded nutritious black seeds. In late June, Dinah's female kin picked saguaro fruit. After the summer rains, they harvested prickly pear on the desert floor. Early in the fall, families gathered to harvest acorns and piñons on foothill slopes, then later in the season they processed wild sunflower seeds. Mescal, or maguey—a type of agave—proved to be their principal food because it could be gathered year-round.[10]

Women's duties included building shelters for their families, hauling water, and making baskets and pottery necessary for storage and ceremonial uses. Men hunted game and dressed their kill, providing families with food and clothing. They also gathered firewood to aid their wives in food preparation. Men accompanied women on harvesting expeditions and were often in attendance at the birth of their children. In Dinah's band, women married as young as fifteen, but more often waited until their early twenties to take a husband.[11] Despite the pressures of conquest and removal that they would encounter, Dinah's Yavapai family would maintain these gendered economic and kinship practices into the first half of the twentieth century.

Though the state's founders recognized Yavapais as a distinct tribe well enough to rename their homeland Yavapai County, they more often labeled tribal members Apaches, Coyotero Apaches, Mojave Apaches, Tonto Apaches, or Yuma Apaches. When Tith-ri-va-ca and Tcha-ah-wooeha first appeared on tribal rolls in 1916, the agent at Camp Verde listed them as Mojave Apaches.[12] Dinah's people enjoyed relative obscurity during the first waves of American incursions into the territory recently extracted from Mexico, but when miners discovered gold along Lynx Creek in 1863, soldiers and settlers invaded their homelands and a cycle of violence began. The Yavapai called these American intruders Haiko', and responded through a combination of guerrilla warfare and desperate retreat.[13] Tribal misnomers allowed Arizonans like King Woolsey, John D. Walker, and Antonio Azul, under the guise of collective anti-Apache hysteria, to wage war against the tribe whose land held gold.[14] The war against Yavapais lasted until 1875, when Americans forced the tribe onto the San Carlos Apache reservation—removal to Apache lands being another convenient result of settler-colonists' willfully inaccurate tribal designations.

Scholars disagree as to Yavapai casualties during the Indian Wars because of the misnomers applied to the tribe, but the Haiko' killed an estimated 716 Yavapais and captured 622 survivors during that time.[15] These are significant numbers, considering estimates that in 1863 there were "between two thousand and twenty-five hundred" Yavapais.[16] Such widespread loss of life leaves no doubt that Tith-ri-va-ca and Tcha-ah-wooeha witnessed the violence that claimed nearly a third of their tribe. In their early adult years, the sacred and material landscape they knew as children became transformed by bloodshed. Places that had been a part of the Yavapais' seasonal land-use and ceremonial cycle became known for the atrocities committed there.

Site names such as Bloody Tanks, Skull Valley, Skeleton Cave, and Bloody Basin serve as stark reminders of the devastation inflicted under the banner of state-sanctioned violence. Before he found Lucía Martínez along the Mogollon Rim, King S. Woolsey invited Yavapais in the Superstition Mountains to negotiate peace for the sake of his Agua Fria Ranch in the midst of their territory. The hesitant band joined him on January 24, 1864, falling into Woolsey's ambush at a site near present-day Miami that became known as Bloody Tanks, referring to the rock pools that filled with the blood of twenty-four Yavapais killed that day.[17] Skull Valley, just twenty miles south of Prescott, designates the site where Company F members of the Arizona Volunteers killed more than seventy-five Yavapais on August 13,

1866, in a dispute over land and livestock.[18] The valley littered with skeletal remains, both human and animal, carries the name as a reminder of Haiko' cruelty or American bravery, depending on the storyteller. Skeleton Cave, so named for the bones of Dinah's kin, serves as another reminder of brutality in Yavapai homelands. On December 28, 1872, during efforts to round up all Yavapais for detention, U.S. troops opened fire on tribal members who believed they had found shelter in a cave that was ultimately too shallow to protect them from the bullets raining down from above and ricocheting off the rock walls.[19] A group of a hundred Yavapais gathering mescal agave on March 27, 1873, in a place they called Atasquaselhua, meaning "When the leaves of the sycamore turn yellow in fall," met their death at the hands of U.S. soldiers; the mescal field was renamed Bloody Basin.[20] Dinah grew up knowing the central Arizona highlands as both a reminder of suffering and a source of sustenance, but her family would be given no opportunity to recount these memories when subpoenaed before Yavapai County Superior Court.

Tith-ri-va-ca and Tcha-ah-wooeha lost friends and family during these and similar episodes of violence that made up Arizona's Indian Wars. Perhaps they were among those who began surrendering to troops in the early 1870s throughout the Prescott and Verde Valleys, seeking refuge from Haiko' citizens who drove them to starvation by keeping them on the run. In 1871—during the same spring that American, Mexican, and O'odham men participated in the anti-Apache massacre near Camp Grant—a chief identified as part of Dinah's band of "Mojave Apaches" described his people's condition. "Where that [white man's] house stands I have always planted corn; I went there this spring to plant corn, and the white man told me to go away or he would shoot me."[21] He went on to explain that there were nearby Yavapais willing to turn themselves in, but they were too weak to come in and surrender. In response, Indian commissioner Vincent Colyer set aside a reserve for the Yavapé and Wipukepa bands on October 3, 1871, to be administered through the military reserve, Camp Verde.

Within a year—likely encouraged by continued civilian threats—over two thousand Yavapais settled in the district, collecting rations that they supplemented by harvesting traditional foods outside the reservation boundary.[22] It was during such foraging expeditions that Dinah's relatives were most vulnerable, and some likely fell victim to the 1873 attack at Bloody Basin that targeted families harvesting agave. As tensions remained high between local citizens and tribal members, the federal government maintained a swath of land forty miles long and ten miles wide, divided by the Rio Verde, as a Yavapai reserve under Camp Verde protection.[23]

At the Camp Verde reserve, Yavapai men served as scouts in the service of the U.S. military, thus preserving their mobility and masculine authority despite devastating limitations on their abilities to lead and move freely throughout their tribal lands. Such men may also have sought to distinguish themselves from the Apaches whom Arizona's military forces and civilians hunted so brutally. Yavapai women like Dinah's grandmother, aunt, and mother found ways to continue gendered forms of productivity under reservation conditions. Some women found work as domestics for nearby ranching families or sold goods and crafts such as hay and baskets, while others traded wild foods. Although diseases killed nearly a third of Indigenous refugees, survivors worked hard to improve reservation conditions.[24]

Despite the Yavapais' desire to remain in their homelands, Commissioner Edward P. Smith recommended the Verde reserve be dissolved and the Indigenous refugees transferred to San Carlos, an agency established in 1871 for "hostile" Apache bands. The removal of Yavapais to the Apache reserve further contributed to the persistent misassociation of the central Arizona highlands people with a different tribe identified as enemies of the federal government and enemies of American progress in the West. Federal troops carried out the relocation in the early winter months of 1875 through a forced march that devastated those who had already endured a decade of extermination at the hands of Haiko'.[25]

Maggie Hayes, like Dinah born at San Carlos a few years after the long walk, remembered her grandmother's retelling of the terrible journey that took the tribe one hundred and eighty miles from their homeland. According to Hayes's grandmother, who would have been a member of Tcha-ah-wooeha and Tith-ri-va-ca's generation, "We were not allowed to take the time and strength to bury the dead, and who would want to bury the dying?" Hayes estimated that nearly half of her people died, a number that exceeds government estimates and that reflects the psychological trauma experienced by those who survived the terrible ordeal. When they did arrive at San Carlos, Dinah and Maggie's families "were dumped on the . . . Reservation together, unable to understand [the Apache's] languages and temperaments. They understood only vaguely, through interpreters, what was expected of them by their American captors."[26] Yavapai captives and other recently interned tribal members had difficulty settling into their new home at San Carlos, likely because some had served as anti-Apache scouts for the U.S. military at Camp Verde. The agent reported that "they several times threatened to fight rather than submit to our system of control," but this likely proved impossible once they were disarmed.[27]

Soon after Tith-ri-va-ca and Tcha-ah-wooeha's relatives arrived at their new detention center, Haiko' concerns turned from Yavapais to Cochise's Chiricahua Apaches. Men from Dinah's band enlisted once again as scouts against Apache bands, some seeking support for their families and others desiring an escape from the reservation.[28] It was around this time that Robin Hood, Dinah's future husband, enlisted as an "Apache" scout for the U.S. government. Born sometime near 1855, he was likely named Robin Hood by the American men he served with, though it is impossible to determine whether he earned the moniker by sharing the characteristics of his namesake.[29]

Despite these limited opportunities for employment, many reservation families suffered from starvation and disease.[30] There was little hope for those who wanted to return to their homelands, since Camp Verde had been opened to American settlement just months after Yavapai removal.[31] Despite continued Haiko' claims on their lands, Yavapai leaders repeatedly requested permission to return to a reserve in the Prescott and Verde Valleys.[32] Prescott residents expressed fears in 1879 that poor conditions at the agency would result in a Yavapai outbreak that could renew violence.[33] Once again, Natives and newcomers told very different stories about conquest and land claims, entitlement and incursions, but Anglo-Americans used the law to codify their imagined victimhood. It was in this context of trauma and uncertainty that Dinah Foote was born in 1881 to her father Mig-tus-gal and an unnamed mother. To her grandmother Tcha-ah-wooeha and great-aunt Tith-ri-va-ca, the infant girl and her eight-year-old sister Mary might have promised the hope of a new generation or may have added pressures to a family stretched to the brink.[34]

Desperate and fearful, Dinah's people began to seek supernatural solutions to the depression that set in at San Carlos. In August 30, 1881—the year Mig-tus-gal's daughter was born—agency officials arrested a holy man whose vision predicted the disappearance of whites and the return of dead relatives.[35] Amid poor reservation conditions, similar revitalization prophecies recurred throughout the 1880s among Dinah's neighbors and family. In 1887, when the girl was just six years old, a Yavapai shaman interpreted an earthquake as a sign that the tribe would soon be free of the Haiko'. The holy man and his followers left the agency in anticipation of a great fire that would destroy the reservation. Although the climactic vision never materialized, some Yavapai families hid in the nearby hills for nearly a year while others returned to San Carlos under the escort of soldiers.[36] Just a year later, Indian agent John L. Bullis recommended that the Yavapai—"Mojaves," as he called them—be removed "from this section of the country to a more healthy locality," although he refrained from offering a solution amenable to both Americans and Yavapais.[37] As government officials stalled Yavapai resettlement, some families trickled back to their Verde Valley homes despite the radical transformations to their territory wrought by settler-colonists, while others like Dinah's family remained at San Carlos and made do with what they had—which was mostly each other.

Like other Indian families in the North American West, Dinah's relatives fought starvation and disease throughout the 1880s; unlike their O'odham neighbors to the south, however, the Yavapai had been defined as Apache enemies of the state and suffered racialized violence similar to that experienced by Lucía Martínez's Yaqui relatives in Sonora and Louisa Enick's kin in Washington. When she was forced to go to boarding school in 1892, Dinah Foote almost fell victim to the imperial assumptions of white superiority that had impinged the rights of so many Indigenous women before her. Like the other women in this history, however, she questioned the prerogatives of white men who claimed authority over her fate.

As early as 1893, the San Carlos agent listed Dinah Foote and Maggie Hayes among ninety-one Mojave Apache children "away at school."[38] Dinah's sister Mary escaped boarding school removal by virtue of her marriage to Robin Hood in 1890. Dinah made her way with five other San Carlos children to the Santa Fe Indian Industrial School, where "former students almost always mentioned being hungry."[39] Indian Agency officials had simply transferred twelve-year-old Dinah and her Yavapai friends from one site of institutional deprivation to another.

The Santa Fe Indian School had opened in November 1890, just three years before Dinah's arrival, and serviced Southwestern tribes including those classified as Apache, Hopi, Navajo, Pima, Pueblo, and Western Shoshone.[40] Alumni "described a daily routine of marching, labor, and chores. They mentioned being homesick and hungry. But they were proud of learning English and manual labor skills."[41] Dinah became fluent and literate in her captors' language, but it is impossible to say whether doing so made her "proud."[42] As it turned out, Dinah's bilingual status actually made her more vulnerable to the whims of the state and exposed her to a settler population often unfriendly toward Native Americans.

Although many San Carlos families resisted the removal of their children, the presence of armed soldiers kept "the mothers from recovering their children."[43] In 1893, however, Dinah's parents managed to get assurance from San Carlos Indian agent Captain J. L. Bullis and the Santa Fe Indian School superintendent that their daughter could return home within five years.[44] On April 2, 1896, however, a different school official reasoned that because Dinah and the other girls from San Carlos had been removed under the authority of the United States Army, their parents had no right to negotiate the terms of their stay at Santa Fe. He further argued that returning the girls to the reservation and their families would "end their moral, physical and educational advancement." He reported that they were "well on their way to an entire condition of civilization, and in but a few years they [would] be able to take care of themselves in the exercise of their educational advantages."[45]

Perhaps Dinah took it upon herself to find another way home. On September 18, 1897, the superintendent wrote to Captain Myers, then the acting agent at San Carlos. "An Indian girl from your Agency named Dinah Foote . . . I desire to return to her home, at an early date, as her moral influence is not good on the school, and she has been here the usual [time] for them to remain at school."[46] Myers apparently never responded, and without means to ensure Dinah's transfer from Santa Fe to San Carlos, the superintendent kept the rebellious girl under his supervision. Finally, in June of 1900, eighteen-year-old Dinah returned to the San Carlos reserve, two years later than originally promised.[47]

Like other Yavapai children returning from off-reservation boarding schools, Dinah found that her family no longer resided at San Carlos.[48] Yavapais had been leaving the San Carlos Agency since the mid-1890s. Perhaps Dinah's family had requested her early release from boarding school in 1896 in anticipation of their own departure from the Apache Agency. Dinah's sister Mary had married the former Indian scout Robin Hood in 1890, and San Carlos officials began allowing Yavapai scouts to leave the reserve unofficially, while other Yavapais escaped on their own.[49] Dinah's relatives might have followed Robin and Mary Hood to the Verde Valley through his special status as a veteran—rather than victim—of the Indian Wars, although they would find that much had changed during their absence.

The tensions over race, space, and gender that complicated the Hood family's return to Prescott had started in 1863, but they continued in 1900. Despite the efforts of local and federal officials to clear the land of Indian habitants and erect a modern frontier town, a handful of Yavapais dodged internment and settled on the sliver of land between Prescott's municipal boundary and the edges of the military reservation.[50] Sufficiently outnumbered, the Granite Creek refugees no longer posed a threat to Prescott development and they eked out a marginal existence as occasional laborers and basket makers while their family members waited out their internment at San Carlos.[51] These renegade relatives ensured San Carlos detainees like the Hood family would have something to call their own in the Prescott Valley when they escaped or were released from the Apache reserve in the 1890s.

By 1900, then, when Dinah left boarding school, many San Carlos Yavapés had returned to their homelands. An Arizona newspaper reported in June 1897 that "a good many Apache-Mohaves have taken up their residence in the neighborhood of Camp Verde, and that more of them arrive from time to time from San Carlos and Globe. [T]here are a dozen camps of them containing possibly, 50 Indians." The article also noted that "[t]here has been no complaint yet on the part of the whites. These are the Indians who once occupied that section and were moved away . . . Many of them talk very good English."[52] In 1903, the *Prescott Weekly Courier* estimated that six hundred San Carlos refugees had returned to their homelands.[53] Reports from Prescott's *Journal Miner* indicate that these Yavapais found work as domestics and day laborers, lent their tracking skills to police investigations, received mail at the Prescott post office, and cultivated some of the finest land in the Verde Valley.[54]

Though the Santa Fe Indian School superintendent had sent her back to San Carlos, Dinah's family had already reestablished themselves in the Verde Valley more than 180 miles away. Probably able to relocate her relatives through word-of-mouth, Dinah somehow managed to join them at their Granite Creek camp within the year. Following Yavapai sororate marriage conventions, Robin Hood married Dinah, and he provided for both of his wives, their grandmother, and their great-aunt by working for nearby ranchers. Although only Dinah spoke fluent English, family members used traditional skills to take advantage of local trade with Prescott and Mayer residents. Mary made baskets that supplemented family income, Indian arts having recently become a novelty among "modern" Arizonans, and some of her children worked outside their traditional Yavapai home, a stick-and-brush shelter they called an *uwa*.[55]

Dinah's multigenerational household likely functioned much as other Yavapai refugee families did in the early twentieth century. A migratory, subsistence existence allowed Yavapais to supplement intermittent wage work with small-scale but reliable hunting and gathering; "several Indian groups of west-central Arizona were working as laborers in mines, on roads, and on special construction projects such as the hydroelectric plant at Fossil Creek. Indian labor, including probably Yavapai labor, may have been employed during Fort Whipple's major rebuilding episode, ca. 1905 to 1908."[56]

By 1910, Dinah Hood's household was quite large. Members of the camp included not only her husband, her sister, all eight of their children, and her great-aunt and grandmother, but also Clark and Rosy Casey, a married couple who shared their residence. Mary Hood still traded baskets and her son Jack contracted himself out as a cowboy, while his father Robin did construction work and Clark Casey found odd jobs. Dinah, Rosy Casey, and the children could have harvested "mesquite beans at Black Canyon, acorns at Granite Mountain, [and] mescal near Drake."[57] They would also have relied on the extensive food trade conducted among Native families living in the various valleys throughout Yavapai County. Although refugee families similar to Dinah's had seemingly broken free of the repressive conditions at agencies like San Carlos, life remained difficult for Indigenous men and women.[58] Yavapai County coroner's inquests from the first decade of the twentieth century show that mining and railroad accidents and alcohol-related violence claimed the lives of many Native men, as well as their citizen neighbors and co-workers.[59]

Because she left no accounts of her own, Dinah's daily life in the Prescott and Verde Valleys is hard to imagine, but her contemporary Viola Jimulla shared her experiences with a sympathetic chronicler in an as-told-to biography. Just three years older than Dinah, Jimulla returned to the Prescott area after finishing her term at the Phoenix Indian School and described the region as one in which Native women were vulnerable to white men's aggression. In the early 1910s, Viola was harvesting piñon nuts with other Yavapai women with the permission of owners of the American Ranch, who had invited the women to camp near the house. The "man of the house" returned from Prescott "thoroughly intoxicated, and headed for the girls' little camp. However, they heard him coming and ran off and hid in the brush. He and some of the others at the ranch looked for them, but they

"Yavapai Indian Woman with Water Jar and Basket, Prescott, Arizona, ca. 1900." This unnamed woman may be one of Dinah's relatives, and she certainly shared the Granite Creek camp with the Hood family in the early 1900s. (Reproduced with permission from Sharlot Hall Museum, Library and Archives, call no. iny2103pb)

remained hidden." Another time, Viola fired a shotgun in the direction of "an old white man who used to wander around the hills. [T]his character would sit and watch the girls [and] one day [she] saw the man standing on a nearby hill, watching [her]." Her warning shot warded the man off, and Viola counted two successful evasions of sexual assault.[60] Foraging in groups and with weapons would have made Yavapai women safer, but these strategies had not protected their relatives during the Indian War just two decades earlier. Women like Dinah who lived with elderly female kin must have seen the parallels between racial and sexual violence sanctioned by the federal government during the course of war and that practiced by citizens in the wake of conquest.

In September 1913, violence struck close to home for the Hood family, camped along Granite Creek just north of Prescott with about a dozen other Yavapais and a Mexican family. Dinah and her kin had been camped there for nearly a month, perhaps in preparation for the fall piñon season. The five women in camp had built four structures, shared among seven adults, four children, and an elderly couple visiting from Mayer to trade baskets in Prescott. Mexican cobbler Juan Fernandez, his partner Dolores Rodriguez, and her two young children lived next to Robin Hood's camp, though a language barrier kept them from knowing their neighbors intimately.[61]

On the afternoon of September 2, Dinah's son Harry, twelve, and cousin Kelly Wilson, twenty-two, witnessed an altercation between their neighbor Juan Fernandez and two Mexican men they did not know along the railroad tracks near their camp. The men were yelling and throwing rocks at Fernandez, but the boys chose not to get involved and turned away from them toward their settlement along the creek. Later that evening, after everyone had gone to bed, Robin Hood heard someone "hollering quite sorry," directly across the creek from Fernandez's tent. Although the sounds disturbed his sleep all night, like his son he chose not to investigate.[62]

Dinah's grandmother, Tcha-ah-wooeha, rose in the early dawn of September 3 to gather wood—her usual contribution to the camp as an elderly, widowed woman. She stepped carefully along the slippery bank of Granite Creek, wet from a misty rain that was still falling, and saw her neighbor Juan just a hundred feet or so up the hill moving brush and rocks, burying the body of Jesús Esparcía, one of the men Harry and Kelly had seen chasing Juan the day before. Tcha-ah-wooeha simply turned around and returned to the camp, perhaps reminded of the quick and shallow burials she had seen on the long march to San Carlos a quarter century before.[63]

Four members of the Granite Creek squatter community witnessed events tied to Esparcía's murder, but none of them volunteered to report what they had seen. Watarama, an elderly Yavapai man who had served as an interpreter and informant in E. W. Gifford's ethnographic studies of the Yavapai early in the twentieth century, had been visiting the Granite Creek camp and was on his way back to Mayer.[64] Perhaps deferring to the elder male's authority, the Yavapais camped along Granite Creek agreed that Watarama would report the incident to local officials and leave the investigation to them.[65] Within hours of the elder's report, however, the Hood family and their relatives found themselves pulled into the coroner's inquest and the coroner pressed Dinah into service as their interpreter.[66] Witnesses to and survivors of genocide and the agony of internment, Dinah and her family were not to be granted an opportunity to describe the violence that Arizonans had unleashed upon the Yavapai; instead, they would find themselves compelled to serve as state's witnesses to a murder they knew little about.

It is difficult to know how the Hood family understood their participation in the murder trial, or what they thought about the justice system that had defended the life of an anonymous Mexican laborer even though it had denied the humanity of their Yavapai relatives. No one would ask the Yavapai witnesses to describe the violence they experienced during the Indian Wars, at Camp Verde, or at San Carlos. No man stood trial for the murder of their kin even though so many sites in their homeland now bore names that recorded episodes of bloodshed. Instead, they would be pressured to testify as state's witnesses against a neighbor who shared their marginal subsistence and had lived and worked with them for three years. Prescott residents' desire to silence such alternative versions of their city's violent past is evidenced by the questions they did and did not ask of their Yavapai witnesses, and by the cultural distance they imagined between themselves as citizens and Yavapais as Indians in spite of the geographic proximity they shared.

Before the *Arizona v. Fernandez* trial brought county officials into the camp, Prescott residents treated Granite Creek squatters ambivalently and knew very little about anything other than the economic aspects of their lives. In 1913, many of the white Prescott residents continued to honor local veterans of the Indian Wars even as they alternately pitied, ignored, and despised the Yavapai survivors in their midst. A matrilineal kinship society integrating traditional subsistence and cultural practices with a modern economy and new sociopolitical geography, the Yavapai at Granite Creek and their makeshift huts stood as a stark contrast to the expanding grid of civic, commercial, and residential development that manifested the consolidation of state power in downtown Prescott, the Yavapai County seat. The Fernandez murder trial offered Prescott officials the opportunity to expand their municipal jurisdiction over the Granite Creek community and granted the state an opportunity to more clearly define the status of unincorporated Indians within the fledgling legal system. In other words, *Arizona v. Fernandez* offered Prescott residents an opportunity to put Granite Creek Yavapais on the map and at the same time expand Prescott's municipal power grid.[67]

The jurisdictional ambiguities at play in *Arizona v. Fernandez* represent the legal borderlands that separated Prescott residents from the people living along Granite Creek. Yavapai County jurists almost immediately recognized the dilemma posed by the land and loyalties that Granite Creek dwellers claimed: Was the camp on state or federal land? Were the squatters state or federal subjects? The *Prescott Journal Miner* reported inaccurately to its readers that "Arizona was admitted as a state . . . on the same basis as the original thirteen states; that the United States reserved no judicial jurisdiction over any of the military or Indian reservations in Arizona and, therefore, the state is supreme in this question."[68] Even if it required jurists to deny the fact that the federal government had retained jurisdiction over much of the state's lands, answering this juridical dilemma in favor of state power offered Yavapai County jurists an opportunity to flex newly established state authority over noncitizen subjects like the Hood family, and in so doing, to abrogate tribal sovereignty.[69] As described in chapter 4, the territorial supreme court that claimed the authority to void John D. Walker's tribal marriage to Churga used a similarly faulty juridical logic when it trumped federal recognition of marriages conducted in Indian Country.

Although Yavapai County jurists claimed the Granite Creek lands under municipal, and thus state, jurisdiction, Watarama did not initially report Esparcía's death to city officials. Instead, the Yavapai elder approached A. J. Oliver, the Fort Whipple groundskeeper. Watarama may have chosen Oliver as a representative of federal rather than local or state authority. In doing so, Watarama would have acknowledged his band's unique tribal status under federal jurisdiction.

According to the Major Crimes Act of 1885, a murder committed by a tribal member on tribal land falls under federal authority rather than state authority.[70] When Yavapais reported the murder to Fort Whipple personnel, they may have been claiming Juan Fernandez as a member of their Indian community and the Granite Creek camp as tribal land. Of course, it is difficult to say whether Watarama or the Hood family knew the legislation that defined their relationships to federal and state officials. Watarama, however, was a tribal leader recognized by his Yavapai peers and Anglo officials alike, making it likely that he had become familiar with the jurisdictional issues regarding Indians in Arizona. Robin Hood had served as a scout in the U.S. military and Dinah had been educated in a boarding school, suggesting that they would have gained some understanding of the guardian-ward relationship between tribal members and the federal government even if they did not choose to see themselves as wards. The Major Crimes Act diminished tribal sovereignty by denying tribes the ability to administer justice, but for the Granite Creek squatters who had no recognized sovereignty, claiming the Major Crimes Act would have initiated federal recognition of their right to call the Granite Creek camp Indian land. As discussed in chapter 2, Lucía

Martínez sought federal jurisdiction when she filed her petition for habeas corpus to retain custody of the children King S. Woolsey fathered and then indentured, indicating that Arizona's off-reservation Indians carefully selected the jurisdictional authorities they appealed to in times of need.

The U.S. attorney general, U.S. district attorney, and Yavapai County jurists who answered the jurisdictional question in favor of Yavapai County used a flawed legal argument that reflected the prevailing assimilationist attitude toward Indians at the time.[71] Attorney General James Clark McReynolds, who later served as a U.S. Supreme Court justice, argued that "the United States has no jurisdiction over any land unless the jurisdiction is given it by the state . . . the United States reserved no judicial jurisdiction over any of the military or Indian reservations in Arizona and, therefore, the state is supreme in this question."[72]

McReynolds's convoluted logic illustrated the conundrum he and Yavapai County jurists faced. The most obvious justification for state jurisdiction in the case was that victim Esparcía and defendant Fernandez were, legally, white Mexicans and therefore did not fall under the Major Crimes Act even if the land where the crime occurred might be deemed Yavapai land. That McReynolds and others actually failed to raise this argument shows their discomfort in classifying Esparcía and Fernandez, two non-English-speaking Mexicans, as white men.[73] The second argument available to state officials required that they claim the land on which Granite Creek squatters lived as part of Yavapai County; this argument would prove difficult because Yavapais had backed themselves up to the federal Fort Whipple reserve and could seek federal jurisdiction even without recognition of aboriginal title.

McReynolds's abdication of federal authority in favor of state supremacy indicated how far he was willing to go to support the expansion of juridical authority over Indian subjects in the young state of Arizona. Just as the federal government had erected Fort Whipple in 1864 to protect mining and ranching claims against Yavapais in territorial Arizona, the federal government now conceded Fort Whipple to protect Yavapai County residents' jurisdictional claims.[74] The attorney general's view that states should incorporate Indians and that the federal government should dissolve the guardian-ward relationship that had been constructed in nineteenth-century Indian policy echoed the opinions of many politicians and reformers of the early twentieth century who felt that Indian wardship slowed assimilation and discouraged tribal members from seeking the "privileges" of citizenship—which often put tribal lands at risk.[75] In essence, when Indians became American citizens, their lands fell under state authority; when Indians remained tribal wards, their lands were disposable only at the whim of the federal government. In states with substantial Indian populations, Indigenous citizenship status prior to the Indian Citizenship Act of 1924 was a debate over land as much as civic inclusion.[76]

The prosecution team claiming jurisdiction over Granite Creek consisted of Yavapai County assistant district attorney Joseph H. Morgan, working under the tutelage of Yavapai County district attorney P. W. O'Sullivan. O'Sullivan had lived in Prescott since 1894, while Morgan, who would administer much of the state's case, had lived in Prescott for only three years. Juan Fernandez's hopes would be pinned on the appointed counsel of Ralph J. Tascher, working with the firm of Clark, Tascher, and Clark. Elias S. Clark, territorial attorney general between 1905 and 1909, headed the firm, but only sat in on the trial occasionally to oversee the efforts of Tascher, his newly certified partner, and his son Neil, who assisted Tascher. Neil Clark had graduated from Prescott High School and was described in 1914 as "a man of much promise." The prosecution and defense sat before the Honorable Frank O. Smith, "one of the most scholarly men of Prescott's bar." Smith shared his alma mater, Northwestern University, with Tascher and the younger Clark, and sat as an accomplished superior court judge who had won the position as a Republican in a Democratic county.[77] Together these respected, educated, and well-connected members of Yavapai County's patriarchal elite worked to ensure that justice would be served at Granite Creek.

Just a few hours after Tcha-ah-wooeha discovered Fernandez's bloody secret, Fort Whipple groundskeeper A. J. Oliver—informed of the crime by Yavapai elder Watarama—notified Prescott justice of the peace Charles McLane. With remarkable haste, the county official called a coroner's inquest to conduct an investigation. McLane and local sheriff Charles C. Keeler ventured with Oliver to Granite Creek to encounter a crime scene in the middle of a jurisdictional gray zone dominated by non-English-speaking and nonwhite women whose loyalties to each other eclipsed their loyalties to state and patriarchal authority. They found that many Granite Creek residents had heard the struggle between Esparcía and Fernandez, a few had seen evidence of Esparcía's death, but only under subpoena would any of the Granite Creek residents testify against their neighbor. Dinah's grandmother evaded the coroner's inquest altogether, and emerged unexpectedly

"Yavapai Indian Dwellings, Showing Anglo Photographers, Prescott, Arizona, ca. 1900." This photograph was likely taken as part of the coroner's investigation of Jesús Esparcía's murder, because it coincides with the notes describing that event in the coroner's inquest. The two Yavapai women at far right are fleeing the camp to avoid photographers and investigators. (Reproduced with permission from Sharlot Hall Museum, Library and Archives, call no. iny2101p)

during the trial in December 1913—evidence that McLane and Keeler did not expect to rely so heavily on an elderly Indian woman to convict Fernandez of Esparcía's murder.

Once they secured the crime scene and apprehended Fernandez and Rodriguez, McLane called a coroner's jury to hear the examination of witnesses and to determine whether there was sufficient evidence to call for a trial. A handful of Granite Creek residents testified willingly, their statements translated for the coroner's jury by Dinah Foote Hood, selected because of her English fluency. Harry Hood and Kelly Wilson testified that they saw Fernandez and Esparcía arguing the day before the murder and that Esparcía and another unidentified Mexican male attacked Fernandez. Non-Indian witnesses testified that Fernandez and his Granite Creek neighbors worked occasional shifts at the local railroad depot and that Fernandez had been seen arguing with other males in the "Mexican saloon."[78]

The first round of witnesses gave their testimony before the coroner's jury just hours after Oliver had been notified of the crime. A little after noon, jurymen and Prescott officials returned to Granite Creek to explore the crime scene for themselves. For many, this would prove a rare opportunity to scrutinize recently pacified Indians' homes and domestic relations, and to cross borders between Anglo and Indian worlds. Social and language barriers had minimized contact, limited to economic transactions, between Prescott Americans and Granite Creek Yavapais, but as jurors, white men gained full access into their employees' domestic and private domain. Investigators found men and women's tracks between the simple shelters and Esparcía's shallow grave, footprints matching Fernandez's shoes, and noted piles of wine bottles outside of Fernandez's tent. In their invasion of Granite Creek residents' privacy, Prescott jurists entered a zone unclaimed by the federal military presence of nearby Fort Whipple and largely unknown to Prescott municipal officials. Here, Apache, Yavapai, and Spanish predominated and McLane, Keeler, and their jurors encountered the stares of Yavapai men, women, and children who had never fully surrendered to white supremacy, but had instead established their own geopolitical boundaries around the Granite Creek camp. Wasting little time, McLane and his jurors found sufficient evidence to indict Juan Fernandez for the Granite Creek murder and sent the case to superior court judge Frank O. Smith.[79]

In the Yavapai County superior courthouse, just a mile from the Hood family's camp, Assistant District Attorney Morgan subpoenaed non-English-speaking noncitizens to serve as state's witnesses against the defendant. Ironically, defense attorney Tascher would be the one to challenge the state's authority to call such witnesses, but Judge Smith upheld the remarkable measure. Tascher later based his appeal of Fernandez's conviction on grounds that Smith erred in accepting testimony from Indian women usually deemed incompetent under the law; Tascher had the power of jurisprudence behind his appeal.[80] Perhaps sensing that the strength of his appeal rested in the vulnerability of Native women in particular, Tascher did not appeal the court's decision to accept testimony from male members of the Hood family. Likely he wanted to avoid any encounters with post-Reconstruction and post–Allotment Act concepts of the universal male citizen that could include Yavapai witnesses such as Robin Hood, who had, after all, served as an Indian scout for the U.S. military. In challenging the legal competence of male Granite Creek squatters, Tascher would also have raised doubts regarding the competence of his own defendant, who was described as a non-English-speaking Mexican with a purported tendency to drink, living with a dishonest woman and her illegitimate children—characteristics that made him more Indian than white, in the attitudes that prevailed in early-twentieth-century Arizona toward Mexican racial ambiguity. The defense chose then to cast suspicion on Tcha-ah-wooeha in the appeal announced immediately after Judge Smith delivered a life sentence for their client.

In the initial trial held in December, three months after Esparcía's murder, prosecutors for the state of Arizona called seventeen Anglo witnesses, one Mexican witness, and four of Dinah's Yavapai relatives to testify against Juan Fernandez. The defense added three Anglos and their Mexican defendant to that list of witnesses. Three of the Anglos testifying for the state included A. J. Oliver and his family, all of whom had heard—from their residence on the grounds of Fort Whipple—sounds indicating a violent disturbance.[81] Defense attorney Tascher conducted a voir dire examination—designed to determine the legal and mental competency of minor and otherwise unreliable witnesses—of Tcha-ah-wooeha, Harry and Robin Hood, and Kelly Wilson, through translator Indian Dick. The defense failed to conduct voir dire examinations against any English-speaking witnesses, although at least two Anglo witnesses were under the age of eighteen and voir dire protocol would have suggested that these witnesses might not have fully understood the implications of their testimony against Fernandez. More telling, neither the state nor the defense conducted a voir dire examination of Fernandez, who seemingly enjoyed the fullest potential of his legal whiteness only as a defendant for murder even as he testified in Spanish through a translator. Such tactical decisions by the defense, highly touted in the press coverage of the trial, show that Tascher and Clark aimed to defend Fernandez's claim to white patriarchy at the cost of Indian and female witnesses.

Anglo witnesses in the trial, all of middle-class or elite status in the Prescott community, delivered rather noncontroversial testimony throughout their interrogations and showed a relative degree of familiarity with legal proceedings and the expectations of them held by Judge Smith and the prosecution and defense teams. Likewise, defense and state attorneys questioned the Anglo witnesses respectfully, prodding for details but not insulting their morality or intelligence. Granite Creek witnesses, on the other hand, showed signs of resistance, confusion, and frustration during testimony that revealed fundamental differences in worldview between themselves and Anglos present in the courtroom. Furthermore, both legal teams attacked Yavapai speakers' mental competence because of their inability or unwillingness to testify in English and to fully submit to an oath of loyalty to the state and God. Cousin Kelly Wilson exhibited embarrassment and shame, while Tcha-ah-wooeha's frustration and hostility was so evident that reporters included it in their coverage of the trial.[82]

Dinah's grandmother, elderly and widowed, gave the defense little opportunity to question her sexual morality (though they did imply that Fernandez's female Mexican housemate engaged in promiscuous and immoral behavior), so they interrogated her to try to disprove mental competence instead. The court transcriber mistyped her name as "Chachawawa," and it was her Yavapai interpreter who furnished an English name, Mary Woolsey, for the court. Tcha-ah-wooeha explained that her deceased "husband" had given her the name Mary Woolsey; otherwise, she preferred Tcha-ah-wooeha. Attorneys failed to solicit information on the husband, and neither the translator nor the widow offered any further explanation. Among Yavapai County jurists the surname might have barred further questioning because of its legacy—familiar to Prescott residents in 1913 and today.[83]

In response to questions Tascher did ask, Tcha-ah-wooeha plainly stated that she was prepared to tell the truth regarding her knowledge of the murder, but defense attorney Tascher proved unwilling to accept her oath because the elderly survivor would not explicitly confirm that she knew she could be jailed for perjury. The widow's testimony revealed a fundamental commitment to the truth, but also a radically different worldview than that held by members of the court. To the frustration of the court, Dinah's grandmother articulated a sense of time based on a seasonal, lunar calendar, rather than the Gregorian calendar, and defined her living quarters in relation to the crime scene only through locative description—in relation to particular trees or structures—rather than with spatial measurements such as feet or yards. Tcha-ah-wooeha refused to say that she saw Fernandez burying Esparcía's body, and admitted only that she saw Fernandez moving brush and debris from one place to another—an omission that would have served defense attorneys better had they chosen not to batter her on the witness stand. Although she answered the questions put to her, the Yavapai woman's resentment of her rough treatment came through even in the trial transcripts, and an observant reporter summarized her testimony best: "The squaw's . . . testimony was offered through an interpreter and the wit-

SAW HIM COVER UP GRAVE, SQUAW SWEARS

Prosecution Springs Surprise in Fernandez Murder Trial by Putting New Witness on Stand

"Saw Him Cover Up Grave, Squaw Swears," *Prescott Journal-Miner*, December 11, 1913, p. 1 (Reproduced with permission from University of Arizona Library Microfilm and Newspaper Collection)

ness became at times frustrated, especially when asked whether she knew what the truth meant."[84]

Defense attorneys did not badger female witnesses only. Kelly Wilson, Dinah's twenty-five-year-old cousin, endured a hostile interrogation as well. Although Dinah translated Wilson's examination during the coroner's inquest, the defense objected to an interpreter during Wilson's trial testimony, insisting that he knew enough English to testify. The transcripts captured Wilson's apparent linguistic helplessness as defense attorneys fired questions he seemed to not fully comprehend and demanded answers he could or would not articulate. It seems the defense felt justified in expecting English fluency from Wilson because of his anglicized name and his experience as a laborer in the Prescott vicinity, but when they found that his language skills seemed to be lacking, the defense challenged his competency through a voir dire examination that barraged Wilson with legal terminology regarding perjury and sworn oaths that drove Wilson into silence. Eventually, the state convinced the court to provide an interpreter, and the interrogation proceeded with the assistance of Indian Dick. As in the case of Tcha-ah-wooeha's testimony, which did not actually describe Fernandez engaged in a murderous act, Wilson's testimony could have helped the defense. Wilson testified that he saw Fernandez fighting with Esparcía and another Mexican and that the forty-two-year-old Fernandez might have been the victim of younger men's harassment.[85]

When the jury convicted Fernandez of Esparcía's murder, Tascher and Clark declared their intent to appeal almost immediately. Within months, they presented their appeal before the Arizona Supreme Court on the grounds of Justice Frank O. Smith's error in accepting Rodriguez and Tcha-ah-wooeha's testimony. The appellants claimed that the "aged squaw" had failed her voir dire testimony (though she had in fact fared better than Wilson), and that Indian women were without legal standing in state courts. They presented jurisprudence from cases in nearby western states that had dismissed Indian testimony on the grounds of incompetence and ambiguous citizenship—both grounds that the state of Arizona later used to deny Indians suffrage after 1924.[86]

The state supreme court's ruling upheld the county court's decision against Fernandez, and in so doing bolstered the state's authority to incarcerate and extract testimony from Indian women like Dinah's grandmother and to subpoena Indigenous knowledge without fully acknowledging the legal competency of Indian subjects in Arizona. A superficial reading of these decisions could lead observers to assume that the court's ruling would encourage Yavapais to report violent crime in their community—an important privilege of civic inclusion. A closer reading of each woman's testimony, however, reveals that the court pressured Tcha-ah-wooeha to describe a violent murder when she had witnessed only the concealment of a crime that may have involved at least three others besides Fernandez and Esparcía. That the defense struggled to affirm Fernandez's whiteness and innocence through their objections to non-English-speaking women, while the court upheld white patriarchy through their wresting of such women's testimony illustrates the interdependence of white patriarchy and female subjectivity.

Critical race historian and legal scholar Derrick Bell describes court decisions enacted in juridical self-interest but resulting in the expansion of rights for women and minorities as "interest convergence." Bell argues that judicial decisions affirming minority rights ought to be viewed in terms of white interests. When applied to *Arizona v. Fernandez*, we see that Tascher and Clark's expert and aggressive defense of Fernandez in fact solidified all

white men's access to a vigorous, state-funded defense and that the court's
acceptance of Tcha-ah-wooeha's testimony served the state's interest in upholding order; indeed, Fernandez's ambiguous status as white and Mexican
allowed both the defense and the state to uphold white patriarchy in their
pursuit of justice. Bell's theory about interest convergence not only points
to an expansion of minority rights to suit the needs of dominant members
of society, but notes the frequent abandonment or reversal of decisions affirming minority rights once the interests of white stakeholders fade. Although the Arizona Supreme Court affirmed Yavapai women's mental competency to serve as state's witnesses in 1914, the same court ruled in 1928
that Arizona Indians had insufficient mental competency to exercise the
vote, so tribal members remained disfranchised until 1948. By 1928, Arizona's juridical authority and white patriarchy had sufficiently taken hold
in the young state and the court no longer needed to include tribal members
in courtroom proceedings to showcase its own power over Indigenous and
female subjects.[87]

The case of *State of Arizona v. Fernandez* unified a segregated Yavapai
County community in concretely gendered and racialized ways. White male
jurists sought to ensure racial justice in their courtroom in order to illustrate their own racial and juridical superiority. For young defense attorneys
Neil Clark and Ralph Tascher, securing an equitable trial for a working-
class Mexican defendant showcased their courtroom prowess and legal acumen. For the Honorable Frank O. Smith, subpoenaing the testimony of
noncitizens and resistant witnesses strengthened his and the state of Arizona's jurisdictional virility. Male Indian, Mexican, and white residents of
Prescott and Granite Creek affirmed their communal and domestic masculine authority through legal testimony that validated their dominant status
over female residents and family members. Jurists and reporters shared suspicions toward nonwhite women's sexuality and national loyalties in their
demeaning treatment and pejorative depictions of non-English-speaking
female witnesses.

Courtroom proceedings and local coverage upheld the racial and gendered hierarchies fundamental to Prescott municipal development and Arizona state formation. Dinah and her grandmother resisted such hierarchies
in distinctive ways, some successful and others less so. Hood translated
for the coroner, but gave no indication that she herself retained knowledge
valuable to the state. Tcha-ah-wooeha steadfastly challenged the court's
condescension and presumption of authority. The critical questions in the

appeal had nothing to do with Fernandez's guilt or innocence. The ruling depended on Tcha-ah-wooeha's ability to determine the truth, to weigh the penalty of perjury, and to swear an oath of loyalty to the superior court and the state of Arizona. In appealing Fernandez's conviction to the Arizona Court of Appeals, Tascher and Clark asked: Can an Indian tell the truth; can a "squaw" be expected to act like a citizen?

Members of the Hood family and other Arizona Indians did not gain national or state citizenship status until 1924, eleven years after *Arizona v. Fernandez;* the question of Native peoples' competence as members of the body politic had not yet been settled in 1913. Territorial Arizonans had excluded Indians from testifying for or against white residents under the Howell Code that ruled Yavapai County until 1912, just as they had largely excluded Indians from their conceptual maps of the borderlands world they had built.[88] Had Fernandez been charged with murder just eighteen months earlier, none of his Yavapai neighbors would have been permitted to serve as state's witnesses, because they would not have been recognized as state subjects. After achieving statehood on February 14, 1912, however, Arizona statutes identified "all persons who can perceive and express their perceptions" as eligible witnesses, and established voir dire examinations subject to judicial opinion as the accepted determinant for the legal competency of a witness.[89] Voir dire examinations, used primarily for minor and unsound witnesses, allowed jurists to determine whether witnesses understood the obligations of an oath, the consequences of perjury, and the risk of self-incrimination. Applied to non-English-speaking witnesses, however, voir dire examinations could become an opportunity to badger witnesses and exploit differing ideologies regarding truth and higher authority. The change in state statutes did not necessarily reflect a change in state attitudes, however, and women like Dinah and Tcha-ah-wooeha remained "squaws" and squatters in the eyes of most Arizonans.

In addition to the juridical importance of the trial, courtroom testimony also made clear the complex social relationships among Anglo, Mexican, and Yavapai witnesses. What their inconclusive testimony indicates is the existence of a multiracial community of marginalized people living together on the outskirts of Prescott. Kelly Wilson had lived along Granite Creek for eight years and knew his neighbor Fernandez from their work together on area construction crews.[90] Mexican and Yavapai men worked intermittently at the nearby depot, collected scrap metal and firewood to barter or sell, and hunted horses to sell to area ranchers. These men lived with women who shied away from contact with whites, likely motivated by self-preservation, and who practiced household economies that relied on Indigenous botanical knowledge, craft production, and technological innovation. Dinah and her female relatives foraged wild edibles, sold baskets, and used Prescott residents' trash to supply household needs. Women who spoke English could do laundry and other domestic errands for Prescott residents less than a mile away. These gendered economic practices made up a meager subsistence that allowed the Hood family and others to reside within their tribal homelands in the aftermath of the Indian Wars and relocation.[91] Their reluctance to attract the attention of county officials suggests that these Yavapai squatters knew they lived in a jurisdictional borderland and wanted to maintain a marginality through acts of evasion that actually granted them freedom from incarceration on foreign reservations.

In the aftermath of the traumatic trial, Dinah's family continued to live in the multiracial communities that had become characteristic in the Sonoran borderlands. Robin Hood died sometime in 1915, a year after he appeared before the Yavapai County District Court. Dinah reported to the Camp Verde Indian agent in 1916 that she was a widow supporting her seventy-five-year-old great-aunt and grandmother along with her five children: Harry, fifteen years of age; Mabel, twelve; Jim, five; Hiawatha, three; and Louise, one. The family may have collected rations but did not live permanently at Camp Verde, since nearby mining towns like Clarkdale, Cottonwood, Jerome, and Mayer offered wage opportunities for herself and her children. The Hoods appeared consistently in Camp Verde Agency census schedules between 1916 and 1927, making it possible to reconstruct the next decade of Dinah's life. Tcha-ah-wooeha died sometime between 1918 and 1920; Tith-ri-va-ca died between 1923 and 1926, making her at least sixty-eight years old when she passed. The young widow worked near Clarkdale—a United Verde Copper Company town—as a "washwoman," perhaps living in the small southwestern part of town set aside as the "Indian Village."[92]

In Clarkdale, a company town conceived by William A. Clark to house his United Verde Copper Company employees, Dinah Hood occupied a jurisdictional borderland similar to that along Granite Creek. Clarkdale census records affirm the incorporation of families like Dinah's, enumerating "Indian Village" households even though these Yavapais also appeared in Indian census records for Camp Verde, suggesting that Dinah and her neighbors crossed bureaucratic, geographical, and sociocultural borders on a daily basis. As overseers of a corporate mining town, Clarkdale municipal officials may have been more willing than their Prescott counterparts to recognize Indigenous members of their population because to do so allowed them to claim Indian laborers. Dinah's Indian agent reported that her children attended public school in nearby Clarkdale, though they likely attended the company town's Indian School rather than the school for mineworkers' children.[93] Washing miners' laundry in the shadows and fallout zone of the smelter could not have been easy for the widow, but she managed to keep her family intact—a remarkable testament to the woman's ability to merge capitalist and Indigenous subsistence strategies.

Census records imply that life was difficult for Dinah after her husband's death, but it is a 1920 birth certificate that reveals the extent of Dinah's vulnerability as a female and Indigenous household head. Dr. George Laben, physician and superintendent of the Havasupai Indian Reservation, filed a certificate that described Dinah as a forty-year-old Indian housewife living in Clarkdale under the supervision of the Camp Verde Agency. Although he did not attend the birth of the Yavapai woman's sixth child, Dr. Laben typed "1/2 white" in the box marked "Legitimate?" and gave the male infant's father's name as "Possibly a white man" aged "30–35" who lived in Dinah's community and whose occupation he designated as "Farmer may work for Smelters (copper)." In the box assigned to the father's race the superintendent marked "4/4 White Mistrust," which raises as many questions as Dinah refused to answer. The Verde Valley community where she worked as a laundress was a small one—home to less than eight hundred white residents, a dozen or so Mexicans, and just under one hundred Yavapais—where interracial sexual liaisons, consensual or otherwise, would have been difficult to conceal.[94] Despite the mixed-race classification on his birth certificate, Solomon Hood's mother reported him to agency officials as Indian for the remainder of her life and never revealed his father's identity to state officials.

Dinah's reluctance to report her sexual history shows that she was unconvinced of tribal and legal officials' capacity to administer justice for women living in the marginal spaces between "squaw" and citizen, and that she refused to allow colonial counters to designate the racial status of her offspring. Although her experiences in boarding school and in the Yavapai County justice system would have introduced her to notions of legal authority and the criminal codes that defined sexual assault, adultery, and bastardy, the Yavapai widow withheld her story from Dr. Laben just as she and

DEPARTMENT OF COMMERCE—BUREAU OF THE CENSUS   State File No. **632**

STANDARD CERTIFICATE OF BIRTH   Registered No.

1. PLACE OF BIRTH—
   County ____ Yavapai ____   State ____ Arizona.
   Township ____   or Village ____
   City ____ Clarkdale,   No. ____   St. ____ Ward
   (If birth occurred in a hospital or institution, give its NAME instead of street and number)

2. Full name of child ____ Name of child unknown
   (If child is not yet named, make supplemental report, as directed)

3. Sex of child Male
   To be answered ONLY in event of plural births.
   4. Twin, triplet or other ____
   5. Number, in order of birth ____ 6
   6. Legitimate? white
   7. Date of birth Oct 23/24 (Month, day, year)

8. Full name FATHER Possibly a white man
   14. Full maiden name MOTHER Dinah Hood.

9. Residence (Usual place of abode) If nonresident, give place and State
   Clarkdale, Ariz. Camp Verde, Ariz.
   15. Residence (Usual place of abode) If nonresident, give place and State
   Clarkdale on Camp Verde, Ariz

10. Color or race 4/4 White Mistrust a Possibly 30-35 Age at last birthday ____ (Years)
   16. Color or race 4/4 Ind
   17. Age at last birthday 40 ____ (Years)

12. Birthplace (city or place) Clarkdale, Ariz. (State or country) Camp Verde, Ariz.
   18. Birthplace (city or place) San Carlos, Ariz. (State or country)

13. Occupation Farmer may work for Nature of Industry Smelters(Copper)
   19. Occupation House-wife Nature of Industry

20. Number of children of this mother
   (Taken as of time of birth of child herein certified and including this child.)
   (a) Born alive and now living 6
   (b) Born alive but now dead 1
   (c) Stillborn

CERTIFICATE OF ATTENDING PHYSICIAN OR MIDWIFE*
I hereby certify that I attended the birth of this child, who was Did not attend (Born alive or stillborn) at ____ m. on the date above stated.

* When there was no attending physician or midwife, then the father, householder, etc., should make this return. A stillborn child is one that neither breathes nor shows other evidence of life after birth.

Signature George ____
Physician.
(Physician or Midwife)

Given name added from a supplemental report 084-023-484 (Month, day, year)
Address Camp Verde, Arizona.

____ Registrar.
Filed ____, 19__
Registrar.

State of Arizona birth certificate issued to Dinah Hood, mother, October 23, 1924 (State of Arizona Vital Statistics)

her relatives had attempted to withhold their stories from Yavapai County jurists. Perhaps because legal authorities had not asked her the right questions, she had claimed her right to withhold answers.

Harry Hood, Robin and Dinah's first-born child, lived with his mother through the 1920s, though he had attended Phoenix Indian School in his adolescence and enlisted in the army during World War I. Perhaps it was in her son's absence that Dinah had become vulnerable to the desires of local working-class white men, since Solomon was born in 1920, suggesting she had become pregnant while Harry was away. In 1928, after his sister Mabel married and left their home, Harry started a new household with his Yavapai wife, Ruby Beauty, and shortly after had a son they named Lawrence. They continued to live near Dinah in the Verde Valley and the 1930 federal census listed Harry as a household head supporting his wife, two children, mother, and sister Louise in the "Indian Village" section of Clarkdale.

Dinah continued work as a "laundress" and her eldest son found employment as a "yard worker" at the United Verde Copper Company smelter.[95]

Dinah and her children became American citizens through federal legislation in 1924, though evidence suggests this transformation in legal status did not immediately alter their economic strategies or kinship practices. Their combined reliance on ethnobotanical knowledge of the landscape and extended kinship networks that spanned the Verde and Yavapai Valleys gave them a foundation upon which to maintain their Yavapai identity as they attended government schools and joined capitalist communities that sprang up in their tribal homelands during the early twentieth century. Twenty-first-century Hood family descendants recall personal stories of allotments, military service, the fight for Indian suffrage—tribal economic and political developments that are part of Yavapai tribal history in the years following Dinah's death after 1932. This ordinary woman's extraordinary experiences in the central Arizona highlands provide historians with an opportunity to ask questions about sex, space, and citizenship during Arizona's transition from Indian Country to American state. Those questions focus on the Hood family and others who claimed space in the Verde and Yavapai Valleys as well, revealing that the towns of Prescott and Clarkdale were experienced and perceived differently by the Anglo-Americans, Mexicans, and Yavapais who lived there together.

Those Yavapai women who claimed space along Granite Creek and in Clarkdale's "Indian Village" continued to recognize portions of the central Arizona highlands as Indigenous space in the midst of debates regarding Indian civic inclusion and citizenship. Although many acknowledged their jurisdictional ties to the Camp Verde reserve established for Yavapais in 1903, they did not live there—preferring instead spaces that had belonged to their bands before the 1875 removal. In 1935, the U.S. government recognized the Granite Creek encampment as a federal Indian reservation and the community of Dinah's relatives who had remained there after 1913 became known as the Yavapai-Prescott Indian Tribe—even though they had been made invisible in state and federal records.[96] Clarkdale Yavapais continued to claim their "Indian Village" after the Phelps Dodge Company bought out the United Verde Copper Company in 1935, and their persistence paid off. Historian Helen Palmer Peterson noted that Yavapai residents of the "Indian Village" were removed "from 'squatter' status to legitimate residents" in 1969, when Phelps Dodge granted the space they claimed to the Camp Verde Agency, making their small community a federal reservation.[97] Dinah Foote Hood's persistent claims to off-reservation lands demonstrated that Indian presence could transform the lands they occupied from American to Indian, even if state and federal politicians were working to transform her tribe from Yavapai to American.

Unlike the women chronicled in previous chapters, Dinah's legal history is one of avoidance and silence rather than filing suit or submitting evidence. Nonetheless, the result of her and other Yavapai women's persistence in holding traditional lands can be seen in the modern-day recognition of the Yavapai-Prescott Indian Tribe and the Yavapai-Apache Reserves on the very lands she occupied in the early twentieth century. Dinah's story, in tandem with the other Yavapai women chronicled here in a generational composite, reflects poignantly the poetics and politics of Indigenous women's legal history as a "return from the enemy." Again distinct from the other women in this book because she was born on a federal Indian reserve and bound to attend federal Indian boarding school until the age of eighteen, Dinah knew fluently the enemy's language and practices, but she did not forget her own. Difficult to depict as an ardent leader for Yavapai recognition or an activist for corporeal sovereignty, Dinah's strategy of avoiding state officials and focusing her energies inward toward the maintenance and protection of her family may be more characteristic of Indigenous women's legal history than the more overt strategies used by other women in this book. That she managed to keep her family intact on traditional Yavapai lands throughout her adulthood is a sign of success in claiming authority over her body, progeny, and lands, though she clearly faced great obstacles in doing so. Dinah Foote Hood's descendants remain integral members of the Yavapai community, promoting tribal sovereignty and traditional practices in ways that reflect the range of strategies Dinah invoked in her lifetime. Dinah's imprint on Arizona and Yavapai history may be more poetic than political, but there can be no doubt that she staked an important claim to her people's land and to her children that ensured her family's survival through the tumultuous period between Yavapai removal and recognition.

CHAPTER 7

Louisa Enick, "Hemmed In on All Sides"

Washington, 1855–1935

The letter that Louisa Enick dictated to her friend and future son-in-law William Salter on November 30, 1920, reveals as much as it obscures. Louisa's letter, written on her behalf because she was illiterate, narrates her lifelong struggle to retain tribal lands in the Sauk and Suiattle River valleys of the Cascade mountain range. Perhaps she did not want U.S. officials at the Bureau of Land Management's General Land Office (GLO) headquarters in Washington, D.C., to know more than necessary about her family when she wrote to claim the public domain allotment lands being seized by the U.S. Forest Service just over one hundred miles away. Or perhaps her limited English and her friend's limited literacy made it possible to convey only the most essential details. Still, Enick's letter offers powerful evidence of Indigenous women's resistance to exploitative federal legal maneuvers. Salter, a young man from Illinois, wrote for her:

> She has raised six children on that place and her-herself has been there since a child and she is now at least fifty years old her Husband being dead something like seven years ago she all ways worked a crew of men in the Timber and worked it out to the best of her advanidge [*sic*] farmed what ground she could work up planted some fruit trees and so forth put up a house allso a barn and she has witnesses to prove that she was on that place long before it ever came under the head of Washington National Forest her Husbands Father and Mother both lived on that land from children up her Husband all so died on that place.

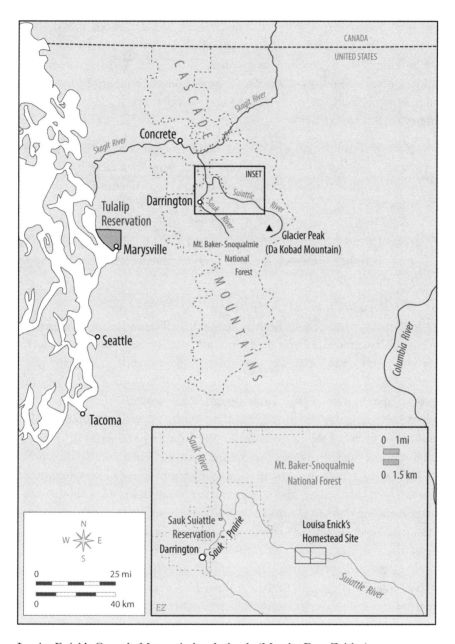

Louisa Enick's Cascade Mountain borderlands (Map by Ezra Zeitler)

The Sauk-Suiattle widow did not ask her friend to reveal that she was late in her third trimester with a seventh child, or explain why she had taken up lodging at the Elgin Hotel in Tacoma, Washington. Writing the letter in a loose longhand on hotel letterhead from Louisa's birthing bed, twenty-four-year-old William Salter closed Louisa's letter with his own assessment of her land claims struggle:

> therefor I can not see why she can not get a clear deed for her place she has been at least two years trying to get some satisfaction about her place as she has no other way in the world to make her living with all those children at large she has been fooled out of lots of money trying to get Back her place Mr. W. F. Dickens Superintendent of the Tulalip school treated her something awfull as I was [illegible word] there the poor lady has been sick for over two years now please and give this prompt attention.[1]

The details of Louisa Enick's story are recounted in this chapter to illustrate that some Indigenous women pursued legal claims outside the courts, which became more difficult for individual Native women to enter as territorial legal structures gave way to state and federal governments more interested in confining Indigenous people to reservations. Louisa and her family proved able to defend their lands against settler-colonial incursions in the nineteenth century, but in the twentieth century their autonomy toppled under the growing weight of bureaucratic authority and national interests embodied in the U.S. Forest Service and Government Land Office—arms of the Departments of Agriculture and Interior. Their history highlights the rarely chronicled experience of nonreservation Indigenous families who sought public domain allotments rather than reservation lands, a distinction made more clear throughout this chapter. Louisa and her family suffered the grievous loss of their lands even though the law was on their side; their plight prompted tribal leadership to embark on a multigenerational and eventually successful campaign for federal acknowledgment and reclamation of tribal lands, and Louisa's descendants continue to live in the river valleys of the Cascades.

We learn from women like Louisa Patrick Enick and Dinah Foote Hood, both barred from legal venues to air their grievances against settler-colonialism, that Indigenous women made critical legal arguments even when federal and state officials failed to hear them. Louisa's letter highlights her understanding of legitimate land claims as simultaneously rooted in her

William Salter to Tulalip Indian Agency on behalf of Louisa Enick, November 30, 1920 (RG 75, Records of the Bureau of Indian Affairs, Western Washington Agency, Tribal Operations Branch, General Correspondence [Old Taholah / Tulalip] ca. 1914–1951, IRA-921, Folder 380, Public Domain Allotments, Skagit and Whatcom Counties [Tulalip], 1914–1937; reproduced with permission from National Archives at Seattle) own reproductive and productive labors—raising children and a barn, burying seeds and a husband. She cites her own ancestral claims to the land through parents and kin, and offers to produce witnesses able to testify that she owned land improperly surveyed by the Land Office, illegally claimed by the U.S. Forest Service, and inappropriately policed by the U.S. Office of Indian Affairs. Her savvy understanding of the wrongs she suffered and the rights she demanded were the result of a lifelong battle against dispossession that she would pass on to her daughters—including the one she bore just weeks after dictating her letter to Washington officials.

Louisa Enick's understanding of her ancestral landholding rights and her legal property rights (or lack thereof) in contrast to federal, state, and territorial land policies and laws had been an issue for the Sauk-Suiattle people since the Treaty of Point Elliott in 1855. They made their homes in the Sauk, Skagit, and Suiattle River valleys that carved through the Cascade Mountains. They traveled widely along Puget Sound, crossed the U.S.-Canadian border, crossed the Cascades to the Plateau country, and intermarried with tribes on the Plateau, in Canada, and on Puget Sound. Amid such extensive geographic and intertribal mobility, the Sauk-Suiattle gathered annually for winter settlement and summer celebrations on the Sauk Prairie. There, Louisa's female relatives harvested camas tubers that they cultivated on the vast expanse in family plots, managed the winter-long distribution of dried berries and salmon that they had processed through the summer months, and practiced extensive craft production from cedar and other regional resources. Louisa's people hunted, harvested, and fished, accessing resources through kinship networks and in well-established seasonal migrations. Individuals and families also maintained spiritual connections to specific sites that gave them and their families property and use rights. For the Enick family, those sites were on the banks of the Suiattle River.[2]

By the time the Sauk-Suiattle began encountering growing numbers of Americans in the mid–nineteenth century, they had already grown accustomed to the British and American fur trades, had incorporated the cultivation of potatoes to supplement camas production and adopted horses from Plateau relatives as markers of wealth and esteem, and had begun the selective integration of Catholic tenets into their spiritual beliefs. They practiced careful relations with incoming settler-colonists in the early years of Oregon and Washington territorial growth, choosing to rely on neighboring tribes as intermediaries in newcomer relations. This caution allowed Sauk-Suiattle groups to avoid the devastating waves of epidemic disease and stave off the social disruption that affected coastal Puget Sound tribes so heavily in the nineteenth century. Like other Sauk-Suiattle families, Louisa's parents were discriminating—and taught their children to be thus—in their incorporation of newcomers to the valley beneath Da Kobad (Great White Mother Mountain), the breathtaking mountain that Americans would call Glacier Peak.[3]

Perhaps this carefully managed distance explains why Enick's tribe refused to recognize the Point Elliott Treaty, one of a flurry of Puget Sound treaties negotiated by Washington's first territorial governor, Isaac Stevens.[4] The Point Elliott Treaty assumed federal jurisdiction over Indigenous people from twenty-two tribes, and established five reservations in exchange for the remainder of their ceded lands. A widely contested document, the Point Elliott Treaty lists the "Sahkamenu" as a signatory tribe to the agreement over land cessions and reservation internment. Some Sauk-Suiattle and some ethnographers agree that "Sahkamenu" was a nineteenth-century term used to refer to the tribe, but many scholars and tribal members disagree that the tribal delegate consented to the treaty. Despite this and other points of contention, territorial and federal officials proceeded to ratify the Point Elliott Treaty in 1859. The treaty assigned Sauk-Suiattle tribal members to the authority of the Tulalip Agency and opened Puget Sound Indian lands to white settlement; it marked the beginning of a century-long tendency of federal officials to mistake the Sauk-Suiattle people for Skagit and other tribal groups assigned to the Tulalip Agency.[5]

Due to the slow penetration of territorial citizens into the densely forested and daunting peaks of the Cascade mountain range, Louisa's parents remained largely undisturbed on the Sauk Prairie and throughout their seasonal settlements in the years immediately following the 1855 treaty. Other tribes fought in the Puget Sound Indian Wars of 1855–1856, but twentieth-century Sauk-Suiattle members claimed their families did not take up arms in that conflict because their lands remained unceded and unclaimed by newcomers in spite of the Donation Lands Act.[6] A rush of gold fever crept up the Cascade range via the Skagit River and across the U.S.-Canadian border in 1858, but the Sauk-Suiattle seem to have dodged the full brunt of its effects in their lands just south of Mount Baker.[7]

Although reservation agencies represented an encroaching federal presence from the Tulalip and Swinomish reserves particularly, the Sauk-Suiattle continued to carry out seasonal rounds from their permanent Sauk Prairie village. The years including the buildup and breakout of the

Civil War granted the tribe another reprieve from westering citizens and corporations, but the painful effects of the Homestead Act in 1862 and Reconstruction-era railroad grants soon became a very real hardship for Louisa's parents and their tribe. Facing an onslaught of engineers, farmers, loggers, and miners, the Sauk-Suiattle quickly learned the vital importance of surveys and titles in the shifting imperial legal regime that engulfed them by the end of the nineteenth century. That Louisa was able to articulate the legal and personal aspects of her land claim despite being illiterate and marginalized in the American legal system demonstrates the extent to which Indigenous women both comprehended and critiqued the legal regime that incorporated their bodies and lands in less than a generation. The settler-colonial forces that threatened her corporeal autonomy began to take shape in the late 1860s and early 1870s, about a decade before she was born.[8]

The same cautious management of settler-colonial relations that had spared their tribe from epidemic diseases in the Puget Sound region also protected the Sauk-Suiattle from exploratory surveys in the first twenty-odd years of Pacific Northwest settler-colonial history. That changed in 1870, when D. C. Linsley served as a locating engineer for the Northern Pacific Railroad. In his survey of the Sauk-Suiattle homelands, Linsley found himself completely dependent on the paid work of Skagit and Sauk-Suiattle guides.[9] His efforts to identify a route through the passes of the Cascade mountain range coincided with a growing interest among Louisa's people and their Skagit neighbors to establish surveyed boundaries demarcating their lands against settler-colonial intrusion. Once again, Louisa's tribe managed to mediate and maneuver outsider interventions to suit their own needs.

Indian men led Linsley's survey and Indian women supplied it, taking the opportunity to direct the potentially chaotic travel and settlement of incoming entrepreneurs, farmers, loggers, and miners. In doing so, both tribes successfully asserted their sovereign authority over the region. Linsley's reports describe extensive debates among Skagit and Sauk-Suiattle tribal members regarding the survey. On May 27, 1870, the engineer waited until "after a long talk participated in by nearly every grown member of the [Skagit] tribe present we succeeded in procuring canoes and Indians to continue the ascent of the river."[10] A few days later, on June 1, Linsley again "remained in camp all day," while "the Indians [made] great objections to going. . . . A grand 'powwow' is going on tonight among them in relation to this matter and speech making for half a dozen political meetings is be-

ing done." On June 2, the railroad man reported "another long 'powwow'
this morning which finally resulted in a new trade by which I am to give
the Indians an advance of 30 cents per day for canoe work after this date."[11]
Having renegotiated the terms of their payment, the Skagit delivered Linsley into Sauk-Suiattle territory, where he described the tribal leader Wawetkin's brother as "one of the best looking Indians I have seen. He received
us with a set speach [sic]. Expressed great gratification at our coming and
promised any assistance his tribe could render."[12] Linsley would spend the
remainder of his summer voyage among the Sauk-Suiattle, who continued
to display their extensive knowledge of the region's resources and to extract
payment for "assistance" they offered him.

Although the Northern Pacific Railroad ended up taking none of the
routes Linsley suggested, his published survey triggered new interest in
the region among land-hungry newcomers. As early as 1873, the Tulalip
Indian agent E. C. Chirouse reported that Indians on the reservation complained "against the Department for not having their lands surveyed and
secured to them, and thus save them from the trouble and annoyance they
are continually receiving at the hands of the white settlers."[13] As was true
elsewhere in the American West, reserved Indian lands were not safe from
citizen exploitation and trespass. Indian agents' reports from Washington
Territory include repeated complaints about white citizens squatting on Indian lands and exploiting Indian resources—primarily fishing grounds and
timber stands.

These illegal incursions affected not only the Sauk-Suiattle's reservation-
bound kin. Chirouse explained in 1874 that the Indians assigned to his
jurisdiction, which according to the Office of Indian Affairs included the
Sauk-Suiattle, refused to submit to federal authority and were willing to
surrender tribal affiliation in order to retain traditionally held lands under
the Homestead Act's amendments of 1865. "Many Indians, unwilling to
leave their country and to reside on reservations, have taken homesteads. . . .
They took such steps merely to prevent white settlers occupying the land;
they make no improvements on the land, but are causing great and con-
tinual trouble among the whites (their neighbors). . . . They only ask from
the Government a good and written title to a piece of land on their respec-
tive reservations."[14] Three years after making lands available for a song to
white citizens, Congress revised the act to include Indians as eligible homestead applicants. The homesteading Indians that Chirouse described likely
did not feel their ancestral homes needed "improvements" to conform to

the Homestead Act, and perceived the provision as an opportunity for gaining title.[15]

Though their attention was sidetracked by concerns about liquor sales to off-reservation Indians who claimed an ambiguous and contentious sort of American citizenship, Indian agents on Puget Sound consistently reported that Indigenous residents asked for secure land titles throughout the 1870s. Historians of the Dawes Act and the implementation of Indian allotment have maintained that agents often distorted their representation of tribal needs, but for Indians like the Sauk-Suiattle, private ownership of land provided title to traditional lands not granted through treaty and implied they would not have to relocate to reservations outside of their homelands. Although the federal government had offered limited homesteading opportunities to Indians in 1865, legislators opened homesteading to all Indians in 1875, provided they abandoned tribal relations.[16] For Indigenous Puget Sounders unwilling to live on reservations and who had not recognized the legitimacy of the 1855 treaties, such an option might have seemed palatable, especially in the linkage of homeland to identity. Homesteading required General Land Office surveys, however, and despite accepting payment for the guide work they provided D. C. Linsley in 1870, the Sauk-Suiattle had not yet agreed to open their lands to outsiders.

By the late 1870s, Louisa's tribe saw waves of fortune-seeking and largely unwelcome newcomers. A familiar story in the North American West, most of these men came as miners, but failing that they stayed as farmers. On December 11, 1879, the editor of the *Vancouver Independent* reported that "Seattle is now happy because . . . there is gold [on the Skagit gold field] in paying quantities; the people of Seattle are going to open a trail for the mines through the mountains, from the head of navigation on the Skagit river."[17] The Sauk-Suiattle were soon overwhelmed with miners, along with the surveyors and soldiers that accompanied them. Together these men would drastically change the world Louisa was born into.[18]

Born in 1878, the second daughter of Sam Patrick and his wife Adsuiltsa, Louisa's early girlhood coincided with a new era of Sauk-Suiattle resistance. The tribe had thus far avoided violent conflict with settler-colonists and government troops, but the second gold rush that came through their country in 1880 included the added momentum of homesteading hopefuls, and brought the Sauk-Suiattle to arms. In October of 1880, eight months after accounts of gold had circulated throughout the Pacific Northwest and at the time of year when Louisa's people gathered together in large numbers on their Sauk Prairie winter settlement, a deadly encounter with miners in the Skagit River region left two Indians dead and prompted the Sauk-Suiattle and Skagit tribes to demand that federal surveying parties abandon their homelands. The U.S. deputy surveyor sent a telegram to the surveyor general reporting that "the Indians have stopped the survey on Skagit River. They threaten to kill the whole party. Everett and Baker were attacked yesterday and shot two Indians in self defense. The upper settlements are in danger. We cannot work unless protected by the government."[19] Just as the federal government had removed Yavapais in central Arizona to protect the gold-seekers and ranchers in Dinah Foote Hood's homelands, the U.S. military provided troops to ensure the rights of white Americans to "work" in Louisa's tribal territory.

Two accounts of the violent disruption and standoff published in the *Puget Sound Weekly Argus* out of Port Townsend (which also reported smugly on Nora Jewell's rape trial in 1880) reveal that some territorial Washington citizens understood, even if they did not empathize with, the claims of Sauk-Suiattle tribal members defending their lands. Of the initial dispatch of federal troops the territorial paper reported:

> The Indian demonstrations of hostility . . . are subsiding. The presence of a company of troops from Fort Townsend has a tendency to impress the noble siwash with a wholesome regard for the laws. The cause of the trouble was the presence of a party of surveyors to extend the surveys up the river as far as Sauk. There is a large body of very inviting and desirable land on the Sauk river, the principal tributary of the Skagit, which the whites desire surveyed for the purpose of settling thereon. This place having for generations been a favorite resort with the roving bands of Indians outside of the reservations, they naturally protested against the encroachments of the "Boston men" on their happy camping grounds, so a few of them got together and protested against the surveys being extended any further up the river. They threatened the surveyors with violence and the latter called on the Government for protection; and hence the presence of the troops.[20]

C. W. Philbrick, editor and publisher of the *Puget Sound Weekly Argus*, demonstrates the complex attitudes of readers of his elite class toward resident Indians. His use of the phrase "noble siwash" expresses a derogatory view of tribal members' humanity that undercuts the perceived legitimacy of their sovereign claims to the land. Philbrick notes explicitly the importance of using force to impose a "wholesome regard for the laws," revealing that the hegemonic weight of federal Indian policy and land legislation had not impressed the Sauk-Suiattle into compliance. The editor goes on to state very accurately, if not sympathetically, "the cause of the trouble": that the tribe held lands valuable to settler-colonists and that troops were necessary to impose land cessions supposedly negotiated through treaty. The problematic tone of the Port Townsend journalist's coverage accompanied a ruthless understanding of the stakes involved in the land dispute. His readers could not possibly misunderstand that their demands for land and resources invoked the use of federal force against Indigenous people, and in fact this relationship between settler and soldier underscored the process of settler-colonialism throughout the North American West.[21]

Readers continued to get reports from Philbrick's paper that illustrate a savvy understanding of the Sauk-Suiattle's sovereignty and land claims. In an article Philbrick reprinted from the *Vancouver Independent* (which had also announced the promise of gold in that area the previous year), readers learned that the Sauk-Suiattle viewed themselves as a nonsignatory tribe in the Point Elliott Treaty, argued their lands had not been ceded, and that the Sauk-Suiattle sometimes allied with, but were separate from the Skagit tribe:

> Lieut. T. W. Symons, engineering corps . . . returned to headquarters from the Skagit river where he proceeded with . . . the 21st Infantry, under orders to settle . . . trouble with the Indians. Lieut. Symons found the Indians had gathered about 150 warriors in anticipation of a fight. Lieut. Symons reports some able men and smart talkers among those Indians, who are the remnants of the Sauk and Skagit tribes, and closely related by marriage and otherwise to the Indians in the neighborhood of Camp Chelan. They claimed the lands being surveyed had never been traded by them to the whites, and they were not going to let them go without some equivalent. They seemed to understand that once surveyed they would soon be settled. After much talk . . . these Indians finally agreed with Lieut. Symons to allow the survey to proceed as far up the Skagit as the mouth of Sauk river which is about the limit of the contract. Lieut. Symons is to properly represent this case to the Indian department. The Indians seemed to have plenty of money and arms, and were disposed to stand on their dignity, so that it would have been very easy to have kicked up a big row. All is safe now until another spring.[22]

The article once again demonstrates that the local press kept readers well informed about the Sauk-Suiattle's land claims and tribal history. In this encounter, the "able men and smart talkers" of both tribes effectively negotiated their own agreement with representatives of the General Land Office and U.S. military, and no doubt viewed the arrangement as legally binding. The terms of their agreement included the establishment of a geographic boundary between white and Indian settlement and tribal members expected Symons to make that boundary official in his report to the Office of Indian Affairs. Finally, the Sauk-Suiattle and their Skagit allies used the threat of force to impose their own law of the land, indicating that they fully understood how to communicate their "wholesome regard for the laws" in terms the federal government and local territorial residents would understand, and that they had yielded their sovereignty, described here as "dignity," to no one. Given the significance of these events to her family and tribe, it is likely that Louisa heard accounts of Sauk-Suiattle self-determination from birth and understood herself to be born into an era of resistance and autonomy. Her tribe had ably demonstrated their sovereign independence and savvy interpretations of federal Indian law despite their carefully protected isolation from Washington's territorial communities and legal networks.

In March 1881, the local press reported that investigators for the Office of Indian Affairs had visited the Skagit and Sauk-Suiattle and had "thoroughly mastered the Indian problem" there.[23] Tulalip Indian agent John O'Keane's reports to the Board of Indian Commissioners make that claim questionable. O'Keane acknowledged the 1880 conflict involving the Skagit, but made no mention of the Sauk-Suiattle. His omission is important because federal officials, in spite of the understandings of territorial citizens and the Sauk-Suiattle themselves, continued to identify the Sauk-Suiattle as members of the Skagit tribe, and this misrepresentation of tribal affiliation justified the denial of federal recognition for Louisa Enick's tribe throughout most of the twentieth century. O'Keane's explanation of events differed from those of the local press in other ways as well. In the first place, he did not even mention that miners had killed two Indians or that the two tribes had taken up arms against Lt. Symons and his surveying crew. Instead, he emphasized the effect of the standoff on Indians living on the Tulalip Agency. "There is . . . a small band or remnant of a tribe, under the leadership of John Campbell, living on the Upper Skagit River, who refuse to live on the reservations or adopt the customs of civilization. . . . They make it a point on every occasion when practicable to taunt the Indians here about their docility, and encourage an outbreak as the only means by which to gain favors from the government."[24] Those "favors" would include, presumably, federal recognition of their lands and secure title against the incursions of homesteaders and miners—both contentious aspects of late-nineteenth-century federal Indian policy. Agent O'Keane did not make a report on the establishment of the Sauk River as a boundary line between white and Sauk-Suiattle lands negotiated by Symons and Louisa's tribe in any of his subsequent reports from the Tulalip Indian Agency, making her people still vulnerable to the trespasses of local citizens.

Despite the ignorance of the Indian Office, whether malignant or benign, Louisa undoubtedly grew up knowing about her people's successful pushback against GLO surveyors and the establishment of the Sauk River as the defining marker of their territory. The tribe continued to gather in the winter villages on Sauk Prairie after 1880 and relied on their extensive seasonal rounds and intertribal kinship networks on both sides of the Cascades to sustain themselves throughout Louisa's early childhood. Like many of their Puget Sound kin and neighbors, the tribe incorporated wage-labor in the territory's hopfields as part of their annual migrations.[25] When they returned to their Sauk Prairie home after the fall hop harvest in 1884, tribal members found their homes burned and looted, and the lands occupied by white "claim jumpers," armed with guns and homesteading papers. That the tribe had not secured title to their lands and individuals had not filed homestead claims to communally held property made them defenseless against the legally sanctioned and violent dispossession they suffered. Tribal members took what belongings they could and moved less than ten miles north along the lands between the Sauk and Suiattle Rivers and prepared for what must have been a devastating winter.[26] Seven-year-old Louisa's parents, Sam and Adsuiltsa, sought refuge at the Tulalip Agency, perhaps because they had kin there or because they wanted the security of government subsidies to support their four children, the oldest thirteen and the youngest only an infant.[27] The Tulalip Indian agent recorded Louisa's family in his annual census for 1885, 1886, and 1887, but made no reference to the Sauk Prairie arson and eviction or to the status of Sauk-Suiattle refugees in its aftermath. The tribe's ordeals continued to go unacknowledged among resident federal officials, although the growing settler-colonial population remained cognizant of the tribe's tenuous land status along the Sauk and Suiattle Rivers.[28]

While Louisa's people worked to retain their autonomy and reestablish themselves on traditional lands, Indian agents in Washington Territory repeatedly advocated in general terms for the issuance of secure land title to Indians off the reservation and reported to their superiors that Indigenous people continued to live off-reservation whether they "owned" their lands or not.[29] As Louisa grew up between the Tulalip Indian Agency and her Suiattle River people, momentum in Washington, D.C., began to build toward the development of an allotment law that would divide reservation lands into individual land holdings and open remaining acreage to white settlement. The development, ratification, and implementation of the Allotment Act in 1887 has been well historicized by others, but not as it pertained to groups such as the Sauk-Suiattle, who had no reservation lands to allot in severalty and whose greatest hope stemmed from a provision buried in the fourth section of the act that has largely escaped historians' attention.[30]

Section 4 of the Allotment Act provided that Indians "not residing upon a reservation, or for whose tribe no reservation has been provided . . . shall make settlement upon any surveyed or unsurveyed lands of the United States not otherwise appropriated, [and] he or she shall be entitled, upon applications to the local land-office . . . to have the same allotted to him or her . . . as provided in this act for Indians residing upon reservations."[31] The legislation outlined the procedural and financial steps necessary for Indians to acquire what would become known as public domain allotments, which included federal responsibility for the costs of locating and filing such claims. That the act put the onus of filing paperwork on the agents of the Office of Indian Affairs and the General Land Office is perhaps mundane, but it is also acutely important, since later disputes over land would place the blame for misplaced and incomplete paperwork on illiterate and Indigenous applicants like Louisa Patrick Enick. In its conception, however, the provision seemed perfectly suited to the special needs of women like Louisa, who came of age under the combined storm of settler-colonial pressures to make private claims to "public" (and still unceded) lands and a growing concern among eastern reformers about the conservation of those same lands.

Legislators in the early 1890s simultaneously jeopardized and protected Sauk-Suiattle homes, perhaps without even realizing the double-edged and contradictory nature of their acts. In 1891, as Louisa began her teenage years, a revision of the Timber Culture Act of 1878 allowed the president of the United States to "set apart and reserve . . . public land having forests . . . as public reservations."[32] This legislative shift was noted by Indian commissioners, who were no doubt concerned about its effects on their efforts to serve those Indians still living on "public land having forests." Though not seeming to acknowledge that Indians were living on forested public lands, Congress authorized the expenditure of funds in 1893 to pursue section 4 of the Allotment Act granting public domain allotments. The Indian commissioner applauded this move, explaining that "the public domain is rapidly disappearing [and] contests against Indian entries have become frequent. The endeavor of this office to defend Indians against cases initiated by whites and to save them their homes has shown that, in most cases, the Indians are too poor to defray the expenses incurred in such proceedings, and are ignorant of the regulations and laws governing in such matters."[33]

It is clear that these laws would have been useful in defending the Sauk-Suiattle against the 1884 seizure of their Sauk Prairie lands by white homesteaders, but even in 1893 the tribe still stood to benefit from federal expenditures on behalf of nonreservation Indians as they resettled just a few miles north along the Suiattle and Sauk Rivers. Although Washington personnel of the Office of Indian Affairs continually failed to name Louisa's tribe as a beneficiary, the Tulalip Indian agent began to request the services of a special allotting agent in 1891; by 1893 the commissioner of Indian Affairs assigned special agents to carry out section 4 provisions throughout the western states and territories—at the same time that fledgling conservationists began traipsing through western forests seeking trees in need of presidential protection.[34]

The work of the special allotting agents took much time and effort, but by 1895, Agent Bernard Arntzen made his way to the Sauk-Suiattle families struggling to stave off homesteaders in growing towns that encroached upon their homes. Arntzen had already been "making allotments to nonreservation Indians" for two years by the time he arrived in Louisa's refugee community. His work reflected the concern of the commissioner of Indian Affairs and nonreservation Indians who, "realizing the fact that the unappropriated public lands are rapidly disappearing, are making efforts to find lands which may be secured as their homes. Whites have settled everywhere, and circumscribed [the Indians'] territory; they are hemmed in on all sides and must adopt the ways of civilization or perish."[35]

Only fifteen when Arntzen arrived, Louisa was not among the Sauk-Suiattle who made allotment claims to their Suiattle River lands in 1895, nor were her parents. The exact number of Sauk-Suiattle allotments made with Arntzen's assistance is difficult to determine, but families filed for public domain allotments on April 9 and April 12 of that year. That the applications share the same tribal leaders as witnesses, bear Agent Arntzen's signature, and were all filed on the same two days suggests that these individual allotments were undertaken as a communal process.[36]

Tribal members no doubt celebrated their public domain allotment applications as an empowering way to mark the ten-year anniversary of their violent Sauk Prairie eviction. That more of Louisa's people were eager to obtain public domain allotments is clear, but their efforts were stopped short by the death of Agent Arntzen in November, 1895. In his two years of public domain allotment work, Arntzen had submitted 795 applications on behalf of nonreservation Indians like the Sauk-Suiattle. Unfortunately for Louisa and other young tribal members like her, Indian commissioners reassigned Arntzen's replacement to Minnesota and suspended his work in Washington.[37]

The Office of Indian Affairs, remaining concerned about nonreservation Indians, reported in 1895 that efforts were being made to correct errors in public domain allotments that resulted from inaccurate surveys and urged federal agents in the Indian Office and the Land Office to move quickly to approve Indians' public domain allotments that were vulnerable to "whites in some sections of the country [who] seem to have very little respect for the rights of Indians."[38] The commissioner of Indian Affairs noted astutely in 1896 that "it would seem that Indian lands have peculiar attraction for a certain class of white men. They seek the home of an Indian because they apprehend that the land contains valuable minerals, water facilities, timber, or a soil better adapted to the purposes of agriculture or grazing than other portions of the surrounding country."[39] Without mentioning the Sauk-Suiattle specifically, the commissioner perfectly described the difficulties Louisa's tribe had experienced in 1880 and 1884, when white settlers and surveyors took up tribal lands like the Sauk Prairie, which offered excellent agricultural potential because of the tribe's caretaking over generations, and lands along the Skagit River, which promised gold, timber, and water. No doubt the tribe felt the same pressures again in 1895 to establish secure titles that would finally protect the remaining lands they claimed in the midst of growing white settlements in towns like Concrete, Darrington, Perley, and Sauk. Some of Louisa's neighbors had managed to file allotments with Agent Arntzen's help, but she would have to wait for almost another decade.

Continuing their trend of disregard for Sauk-Suiattle interests, local Indian agents and other officials expressed dramatically different concerns about nonreservation public domain allotments near the Tulalip Indian

Agency. Without naming tribal affiliations, the Tulalip Indian agent complained about Arntzen's allotment work in the region. "The promiscuous
issuance of patents of Indians of the agency [which included the Skagit and
Sauk-Suiattle under the terms of the 1855 Point Elliott Treaty] without
any regard to the fact as to whether or not they are living upon the land,
improving it, and honestly intend to make homes for themselves and their
families is not only a detriment to the service, but an injury as well to the
Indian."[40] While Agent D. C. Govan claimed that such Indians sought allotments only in order to gain citizenship rights to alcohol consumption,
undoubtedly Sauk-Suiattle and Skagit families applied for allotments that
allowed them to maintain their traditional territory and the seasonal camps
necessary in their diverse terrain; it is likely that Govan failed to recognize
the lodges and processing camps allottees built as improvements or homes.
Given the communal nature of these allotments, it is possible that Louisa
and her kin came to understand allotment applications as both a ritualized
and legal mechanism that connected them to their tribe and the land. In addition to linking land and identity through the spiritual practices that her
people continue to this day, Louisa and her relatives could use allotment
applications as an opportunity to secure legal title to the land they already
held through traditional use and occupancy.

In the midst of local and national concerns about the public domain and
Indian assimilation, Louisa made an important shift in her private domain
in 1896. Somewhere between the age of sixteen and seventeen, she married
Samuel Enick and the Sauk-Suiattle couple joined Samuel's family along
the Suiattle River. As they established their own families, Samuel Enick
and his brother John Enick—who also married a woman named Louisa—
would carry on the same seasonal use of the land as their parents' generation, establishing summer and winter camps that allowed them to utilize the
widely varied resources available in the mountainous and riverine terrain
they occupied. In addition to the traditional tasks Sam and Louisa continued, they also participated in the expanding timber industry that grew
up around them in neighboring towns and camps, primarily through the
processing and sale of cedar shingle bolts. Soon Louisa Enick bore her first
child, Agnes, and the family worked to negotiate the growth of an industrial
and extractive economy and the maintenance of a sustainable and sacred
connection to tribal lands.

Though the Enicks managed to benefit from wage and cash opportunities the timber trade offered, federal officials and conservation reform-

ers grew more convinced that the western forests required protection from exploitative and wasteful logging carried out by citizens and corporations alike, and they set their eyes on Louisa Enick's homelands. Just when Bernard Arntzen had been surveying and signing the Sauk-Suiattle public domain allotments, elite conservationists had gathered in the state to consider its vast forests as candidates for protection. At a time when tribal members had seemingly managed to leverage federal Indian policies and personnel to their advantage, another threat to their lands emerged.

As the Enick family celebrated Agnes's birth in 1898, President Cleveland established "Washington's Birthday Reserves," thirteen forest reserves that reflected Cleveland's executive authority to withdraw public forests from private settlement. The Enick family's Suiattle River home fell within the Washington Forest Reserve.[41] Effectively gifting Louisa's lands to national interests, this executive decision coincided with the seemingly innocuous campaign to reorganize federal agencies and land use policies in the American West. While the move roused critics in Washington State and in Washington, D.C., Sauk-Suiattle residents of the land appear not to have been notified of the move that dispossessed them of their homes once again.[42]

Readers should not be surprised that Louisa Enick found herself in the crosshairs of federal Indian and conservation policy at the turn of the twentieth century. Federal authority over the nation's Indians and forests had long been held in the Department of the Interior, and both the Indian allotment and forest reserve systems shared an early advocate in Secretary of the Interior Carl Schurz in the 1870s. Native people in the American West suffered from the ill effects of both policies. The allotment program took off in the 1880s and 1890s with the support of eastern reformers hoping to civilize Indians and western residents hoping to seize Indian lands, but the forest reserve system split eastern and western Americans. Cleveland's seizure of public lands for the Washington's Birthday Reserves on his way out of presidential office upset Americans not because the move violated Indigenous land rights, but because the establishment of national forests curtailed citizens' ability to drain, log, and mine substantial swaths of western lands, even as federal Indian allotment policy opened more western lands to citizen settlement. To assuage angry citizens of the American West—and a number of them were in Washington State—Cleveland and his advisers added a "lieu land" clause to the act establishing an unprecedented number of reserved acres. Called the "Forest Lieu" provision, the amendment allowed settlers within forest reserve boundaries to exchange their reserved acreage for public domain lands outside of the reserve at no cost. This policy led to extensive land fraud, but not among the Sauk-Suiattle, who did not take up lieu land applications and instead remained on their settlements within the Washington Forest. The Washington Forest, which contained Louisa Enick's home along the Suiattle River, comprised 3,594,240 acres in the Cascade Mountains, few of which had ever been surveyed, thanks to the resistance of Louisa's tribe.[43]

While westering and conservation icon Teddy Roosevelt championed federal management of western lands, Louisa and Sam bore a second child, Francis, and raised him along with Agnes in lands they used to cultivate berries and potatoes, cut cedar bolts, practice traditional rites, and process fish and game. Too young to benefit from Special Agent Arntzen's public domain allotment work in 1895, Sam and Louisa eagerly met his replacement George A. Keepers in 1903. By then, the couple had borne two more children, a sign that they were able to sustain good health and enjoyed some prosperity in their early years of marriage on the Suiattle River. For his part, Keepers had much work ahead of him: not only did he need to allot lands to the families who had clung tenaciously to their lands for the eight years since Arntzen's visit, but many of the allotment applications Arntzen filed on tribal members' behalf in 1895 had not been completed in the GLO. The Office of Indian Affairs had complained in 1897 that "great difficulty is experienced in effecting the delivery of [public domain patents for nonreservation Indians] by local land officers, and most of the patents in the hands of such officers [in 1896], awaiting delivery, still remain undelivered." Keepers's job in 1903 would include "the procurement of additional proofs" for the allotment applications Louisa Enick's neighbors had already filed, in addition to the task of submitting applications for public domain allotments on behalf of the remaining Suiattle River inhabitants.[44]

From Ohio, George A. Keepers had spent two years investigating public domain allotment applications among Minnesota Ojibwe and found that, although they did not know their actions contradicted federal law, nonreservation Indians there had claimed timber lands rather than agricultural lands for their allotments.[45] Keepers took up special allotment work among the Blackfeet in the Helena, Montana, land district in 1900 and recommended the cancellation of nearly fifty-two public domain allotment applicants who "were Indian women married to white men and their half-blood children . . . not therefore entitled to allotments under the rulings and decisions of the Department."[46] The next year, Keepers went to Washington State, "cautioned to exercise the utmost care in making further allotments and to consider Indian character, settlement, and suitability of the land as an Indian home, etc."[47]

Certainly more familiar with potential pitfalls in public domain allotments for nonreservation Indians than his predecessor, Special Agent Keepers nonetheless found Louisa Enick and her neighbors suitable candidates for public land claims. In a section of his report titled "Sauk Valley, Washington," the Indian commissioner reported in 1903 that "Mr. Keepers has been engaged in making allotments to the Indians in Sauk Valley, Washington." Although local Indian agents had not ever mentioned the tribe directly, their public domain allotments made it into the commissioner's annual report, marking their significance in the work of the national Office of Indian Affairs. The commissioner continued to explain,

> in 1895 Special Allotting Agent Bernard Arntzen visited the locality and made some allotments, but was ordered elsewhere before the work was completed. Mr. Keepers has made 60 more allotments . . . The lands allotted are embraced for the most part in townships included, or withdrawn from settlement with a view to being included, in a forest reservation. As the Indians were, however, in occupancy of and had improved the lands prior to the [1897] date of the order creating the forest reserve, they were no doubt entitled to have their lands allotted to them in severalty.[48]

The significance of the commissioner's endorsement of Sauk-Suiattle land claims over Washington National Forest jurisdiction cannot be overstated. His report makes clear that Office of Indian Affairs and Department of the Interior officials by 1903 understood the potential conflicts in land claims along the Suiattle River, but that they intended to resolve them in favor of Louisa Enick and her tribe, thus recognizing their autonomy. To assure the secretary of the interior that Louisa Enick and her neighbors truly deserved the lands they occupied even if they had been contained within federal lands, "Mr. Keepers reports that these Indians are intelligent and progressive; that they took great interest in the [allotment] work and assisted in its performance, and that the lands are well suited for Indian allotments and homes, all containing at least small patches susceptible of cultivation. None of the lands allotted are particularly valuable for the timber thereon."[49] For a man who had spent years canceling disputed timber allotments in

Minnesota and allotting lands along racial and surveyed lines in Montana, Keepers ought to have been able to sort out any complications regarding the Sauk-Suiattle allotments. As a representative of the federal government, his sound endorsement undoubtedly convinced the Sauk-Suiattle that their lands would be securely patented under Keepers's signature.

Samuel Enick filed an application for an eighty-acre allotment for himself, one for Louisa, and one each for his daughters Agnes and Mabel on August 14, 1903.[50] As a married woman, Louisa could not file on her own accord, though she and her daughters were eligible for secure title to their allotments in their own right. Revealing the vestiges of coverture laws within American imperialism, federal allotment policy limited Indian women's ability to advocate for corporeal sovereignty on their own terms, but Louisa worked with her husband to ensure her own and her daughters' land claims.[51] The plat description of their allotments, though technically within the boundaries of the Washington National Forest, described their location within "unsurveyed lands," indicating that federal and local officials had taken possession of lands they had not even charted—an imperial gesture if ever there was one.

In filing applications for himself and each of his family members, Louisa's husband acted as a head of household under the auspices of the Allotment Act, which granted individual, but usually conjoining, allotments to each family member of the household. In this way, Indian applications for public domain allotments differed from the public domain homesteads that citizens could apply for within national forest reserves, since only heads of households earned patents and not each member of the household. This and other crucial distinctions between public domain allotments and homesteads were no doubt obvious to Special Agent Keepers, the Enick family, and other Sauk-Suiattle allottees, even if these distinctions would become lost among Land Office, Indian Office, and Forest Service officials after 1905.

By the time Louisa Enick had borne her fourth child at home along the banks of the Suiattle River, President Theodore Roosevelt, an outspoken proponent of conservation, established the U.S. Forest Service within the Department of Agriculture in 1905. Roosevelt's move separated the administration of the nation's forests from the GLO, responsible for the transfer of lands from public to private domain, and from the Office of Indian Affairs, responsible for administering Indigenous land rights and federal treaty obligations.[52] Under the direction of Gifford Pinchot (the same man who

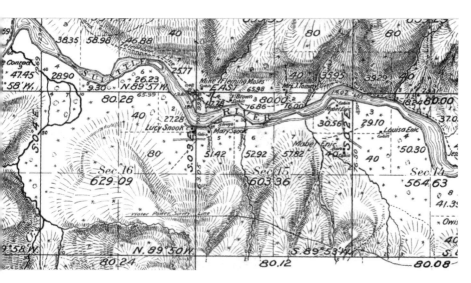

Plat map showing Louisa and Mabel Enick's allotments (General Land Office plat map of T. 32 N., R. 11 E., W.M., Washington, approved June 3, 1918; reproduced with permission of the Bureau of Land Management Land Status and Cadastral Survey Records of Oregon and Washington)

had actually selected Louisa's family lands for inclusion in the Washington Forest), the Forest Service would employ a cadre of rangers, trained to police and preserve the nation's forest reserves. Roosevelt's move revealed that he and others viewed the nation's forests as an important natural resource commodity, and that they understood little about the people—Native and newcomer—who actually occupied those forests.[53]

The confusion over land transfer and use that characterized forest policy at the turn of the twentieth century knotted itself most tightly in the continued work toward securing public domain allotments for nonreservation Indians and the concessions conservationists made in allowing citizens and Indians to apply for homesteads inside forest reserves. Office of Indian Affairs personnel demonstrated that they were perfectly aware by 1903 that the Sauk-Suiattle and Skagit occupied forest reserve lands; they continued to authorize public domain allotments there because they supported the primacy of Indigenous land rights and, frankly, had nowhere else to put the allottees. The Department of the Interior, however, suspended public domain allotment applications the same year that Special Agent Keepers prepared the Sauk-Suiattle applications, while the Indian Office continued to submit new applications. That suspension was waived two years later in 1907, when it became clear that there were not enough personnel in the Land Office or the Indian Office to investigate the backlog of public domain allotment applications. The Indian commissioner continued to advocate for special allotment work, "owing to the rapidity with which the public land available for allotment to Indians is being appropriated, this work should be prosecuted without the interruptions which have been so frequent during the last three or four years, so that the Indians on the public domain may be provided with homes before all suitable and available lands have passed into the possession of white settlers," or, in the case of the Sauk-Suiattle, into the possession of the federal government.[54]

With the Department of the Interior and Department of Agriculture working at cross-purposes in forest reserve lands, the administrators of public domain allotment applications and patents proved obscenely incompetent, and Louisa Enick and the rest of the Sauk-Suiattle allottees found themselves in the grip of bureaucratic imperialism. Of course, Louisa and her family found none of the federal government's contradictory or complex policies confusing: their Suiattle River lands were their own. Once they filed their public domain allotment applications in 1903, they proceeded to work the land as they and their parents' generation had done, and prepared themselves and their homes for the subsequent Land Office surveys that would determine the proof of their improvement on and claims to their allotments—proof that was only required of homesteads and not allotments, but that they managed to provide nonetheless.

Acting on the authority invested in the newly constituted Forest Service in 1905 to determine whether the Enick family's allotments constituted agricultural rather than timber lands, deputy forest ranger C. L. Farrar surveyed the Enick family's allotments in 1905 and 1907. Farrar reported to his Forest Service supervisor that Sam and Louisa had made unconventional use of their lands, but that he felt they had sufficiently developed the Suiattle River properties to be approved for perfected title to their public domain allotments. Farrar noted that the family made their home on Louisa's allotment tract, cultivated crops on Samuel's plot, and had built barns and planted berries, potatoes, and orchards on their daughters' lands. His report indicates that Farrar observed the continuation of Indigenous land use practices within Louisa's family, but viewed their incorporation of agricultural and domestic practices such as barn raising, husbandry, and mono-cropping as satisfactory evidence that they had indeed proved their claims and deserved perfect title. Farrar described Louisa's tract in particular as "a valuable piece of farming land . . . and well suited for the purpose for which it is now used, and being allotted by a duly authorized agent of the government [George Keepers] it would be an injustice to the allottee to now cancel it."[55] Aware, then, of the importance of his report's endorsement of allotted lands within forest reserve boundaries, Farrar advocated for Samuel and Louisa Enick and their children. Farrar made his recommendation even as he acknowledged that the family had not built homes on each plot, rotated their settlements seasonally, and did not cultivate all of the allotments, suggesting that he understood that the family's Indigenous knowledge and use of the land met "the spirit of the law if not the letter."[56]

Although the forest ranger recognized the Enicks' legitimate claims to their land, there were early signs that Forest Service and GLO agents questioned the legitimacy of Sauk-Suiattle residency along the Suiattle River. In 1906, after Farrar's first survey of the Enick family allotments, GLO commissioner W. A. Richards notified the Portland Area Office Register of Lands J. Henry Smith (who had signed most of the 1903 and 1905 allotment applications) that Mabel and Agnes Enick's allotment applications would be canceled on the grounds that children under eighteen could not meet the requirements of settlement on allotment lands and should be considered as residents on their parents' allotments. While it appears that Smith notified Samuel of the cancellation of his daughters' allotments, the Enick family continued to live on and work the four allotments they held within the family.[57] Also ignoring the cancellation order, Farrar surveyed Agnes's allotment in 1907 and noted that Louisa's eldest daughter's tract was "good agricultural land when cleared, well suited for an Indian homestead as to location, etc., and being allotted by an agent of the Government, I believe the allotment should stand." He "recommended that the allottee be allowed to perfect title without protest."[58] Farrar's endorsement stood unacknowledged for nine years, though no one acted to evict the Enicks either, and the family continued to live through the cycles of blessings and crises that made up their days and years on the Suiattle River. Like the establishment of the Washington Forest Reserve in 1897, the cancellation of Agnes and Mabel Enick's allotments in 1906 initially proved insignificant as the measure had only been enacted on paper, not in person. Once more federal personnel became available, however, Louisa and her daughters would feel the brunt of paper removal.

Farrar's report demonstrates that some Forest Service officials recognized the primacy of Indigenous land claims over forest reserves, but as the

Land Office cancellation action indicates, not all of Farrar's bureaucratic colleagues agreed. Farrar's national supervisor Gifford Pinchot became known as the father of the U.S. Forest Service after working with President Theodore Roosevelt to build the bureau and manage America's forests "for the greatest good for the greatest number for the long run," but it was the Sauk-Suiattle who were expected to surrender their interests to the "greatest good."[59] Pinchot and his supporters insisted that the federal government could better manage western lands and drew the ire of Washington residents, who targeted Pinchot in their complaints about the Washington forest reserves in 1909. "[Gifford Pinchot] . . . has bottled up the . . . lands of Washington, hindered the development of our water powers, harassed the Suiattle Indians in using their orchards planted more than 20 years ago, and precluded settlement of much unoccupied land."[60] That the editor of *The Ranch: A Journal of the Land and the Home in the New West* included the misappropriation of Sauk-Suiattle lands in his critique of Pinchot suggests that ranching Americans aligned with Indigenous neighbors when federal forces threatened both tribal and citizen interests. The editorial, echoing the ambivalent tone of press coverage of tribal land disputes in the 1880s, also demonstrates once again that local residents understood Louisa Enick and her tribe's historical and legal claims to the land quite clearly. *The Ranch* readers may only have posited Sauk-Suiattle concerns because they echoed their own, but the example indicates once again that local citizens recognized Louisa Enick's longstanding claims to the land against the more recent National Forest claims.

In 1910, Forest Service officials like Pinchot campaigned for conservation on the national circuit and local agents like Farrar concerned themselves with professionalization and fire prevention once they had surveyed the Sauk-Suiattle allotments. Office of Indian Affairs personnel continued the work of implementing the Dawes Act, in place for more than twenty years by 1910 and already a failure in the eyes of many Progressive Era critics. While reform-minded senators and Indian Office agents worked to improve upon the Allotment Act, Louisa Enick and her Sauk-Suiattle neighbors continued to occupy lands they perceived as securely their own since they had been allotted by Indian Office agents and surveyed by Forest Service officials. Tribe members' resistance to the Point Elliott Treaty of 1855, their rejection of pressure to move to the Tulalip Agency, and their refusal to surrender lands along the Suiattle and Sauk Rivers even when threatened with arson and armed troops seemed to have paid off. Louisa and Sam Enick had built a comfortable home, erected a barn and some outbuildings (likely smokehouses for processing fish and game), and with their children worked their own potato fields, maintained berry patches, and cared for livestock. Sam would take up seasonal work in lumber camps throughout the Cascade mountain region and Louisa would work their land with their many children.

Like many other Indigenous women responding to the increasing risk of losing their children to state and federal boarding schools and sanitoriums at the turn of the twentieth century, Louisa did not share her family's secrets indiscriminately with census enumerators, Indian agents, or Land Office employees. Census and allotment records vary widely and contradict one another when chronicling the births, deaths, and names of Louisa's children, but by 1910 Agnes was at least seven and helped to supervise her younger siblings Francis, Dick, Mabel, and Susan. With relatives and tribal members living nearby and still practicing the sacred and seasonal rites that made them the Sauk and the Suiattle, Louisa's children grew up understanding that they shared a profound connection to their birthplace along the Suiattle River. They learned that they could find in the cathedral firs and towering cedars around them a strength and power that would guide them for a lifetime.

Louisa's people espoused a worldview that emphasized the importance of individual fasting and isolation at sacred sites to encourage spiritual relationships with the beings that shared the Cascade valleys and mountains with the original human inhabitants. In addition to this shared belief in personal relationships with nonhuman teachers, some in animal form, and their powers, Sauk-Suiattle people recognized the significance of specific sites in a person's lifetime—namely birthplace, for both mother and child, cedar groves and fishing sites, the places where spiritual relationships were established, and burial grounds. Maintaining spiritual relationships and sacred sites was a matter of life and death, not just a question of property ownership, since tribal members also believed that illness and even death would result from an extended absence from their Sauk and Suiattle River homelands. That some of these places were highly individualized and others were shared among the community may explain why Sauk-Suiattle allottees embraced the concept of public domain allotments. Tribal members could own land individually, but such private ownership was authorized by nominating tribal leaders to sign allotment applications as witnesses and by filing such applications together on the same day as a communal event. As

Land Office agent Farrar noted, families shared their individual allotments, and modern-day tribal members recall that families also shared the yields from their individual allotments with relatives and friends throughout the community, making collective use of their private lands.[61]

Though Louisa Enick and her family occupied their lands without concern or confusion, the commissioner of Indian Affairs continued to express concerns about Indian rights to forest reserve allotments and the Forest Service and GLO continued to confuse policies regarding such land claims. In response, Congress revised the 1887 Allotment Act on June 25, 1910:

> Allotments in National Forests. The Secretary of the Interior is authorized, in his discretion, to make allotments within the national forests . . . to any Indian occupying, living on, or having improvements on land included within any such national forest who is not entitled to an allotment on any existing Indian reservation, or for whose tribe no reservation has been provided, or whose reservation was not sufficient to afford an allotment to each member thereof. All applications for allotments under the provisions of this section shall be submitted to the Secretary of Agriculture who shall determine whether the lands applied for are more valuable for agricultural or grazing purposes than for the timber found thereon; and if it be found that the lands applied for are more valuable for agricultural or grazing purposes, then the Secretary of the Interior shall cause allotment to be made as herein provided.[62]

Sauk-Suiattle allottees qualified for National Forest allotments as members of a tribe not provided with reservation lands. Even if bureaucrats believed the Sauk-Suiattle ought to have accepted the terms of the Point Elliott Treaty and surrender to the Tulalip Indian Agency, Indian agent Edwin Eells allotted the Tulalip and Swinomish reserves in 1885, and by 1910 the off-reservation Sauk-Suiattle were no longer "entitled to an allotment on any existing Indian reservation."[63] This important legislation made clear that Sauk-Suiattle allottees in the Washington National Forest like the Enick family had only to "occupy" such lands and "improvements" were not mandatory to perfect title on allotted lands. Additionally, the statute granted minors in addition to their parents the right to claim an allotment. Finally, if the land could be found to have agricultural value greater than the timber assessment, the Indian claim would trump Forest Service interests. Although this congressional measure should have resolved any lingering questions regarding the Enick family allotments after Farrar's report, federal officials continued to mishandle Sauk-Suiattle claims in the Washington National Forest.

While it is unclear whether the Enicks understood the extent to which federal officials were misinterpreting the legislative changes that should have secured their legal land claims, other events very clearly strengthened and reaffirmed the family's cultural and physical ties to the Washington forests. In the early spring of 1913, Agnes and her brother Francis were gathering firewood within earshot of their home when a nine-foot cougar leaped from the soggy forest and tackled the boy. Agnes wielded a stick to defend her brother and screamed at the giant cat. As the predator mauled the boy's face, pawing and gnawing at his ear and eye, the girl struck the cougar with all her might. The children's father heard the screams and ran out of the cabin to rescue his first-born daughter and son. The beast released its hold on Francis's head and bounded back into the dense underbrush. Once he was assured his children would survive, Sam Enick and his hound dogs pursued the animal and returned shortly with their kill. Louisa nursed Francis and soothed Agnes, and her husband traveled to Everett, some sixty miles away, to tell their remarkable story and collect his bounty on the massive cougar. The *Tacoma Times* found the story newsworthy, and on the first page of its Saturday edition it declared that "there is no more courageous little girl in the Northwest than the . . . daughter of Sam Enick, full-blooded Indian, who . . . beat a . . . cougar into retreat by wielding a . . . stick on the brute as he tore at her little brother's eye."[64]

The graphic story no doubt enthralled and entertained readers in its celebration of Indian mastery over the savage beast. For Louisa's family, however, the encounter marked the beginning—or perhaps the continuation—of a powerful spiritual relationship to cougars and to the specific site where their lives had been spared. Louisa's tribe encouraged children to "know themselves" by the age of nine or ten through "self-discipline, discomfort, and sometimes fear and danger." Parents in prosperous families like the Enicks encouraged their sons and daughters to "recognize supernatural premonitory signs" and to be "familiar with . . . classes of spirits appropriate . . . to their real achievement and position in later life."[65] In light of their beliefs in the importance of individual relationships to flora and fauna, this event designated, or perhaps reaffirmed, the Enick family as the dramatically chosen guardians of the land and hunters of cougars for those who knew how to read the signs in the Cascade river valleys. Enick descendants' ties to the cougar and the river continue to this day, and they know their relative Agnes as "cougar woman," defender of her family and her land.[66]

Although the Enicks emerged victorious from the cougar attack, their luck did not hold. About a year after she had nearly lost her two oldest children, Louisa lost her daughter Mabel to undocumented causes. Just eleven years old when she died, Mabel had been allotted along with Agnes in 1903. Although the sisters' plots had both been targeted for cancellation in 1906, they remained in family possession in 1914 when Mabel passed away.[67] Two years after he took down the cougar that mauled his son, Samuel Enick also died of undocumented causes.[68] His work in timber camps and throughout the Cascade mountain range was undoubtedly dangerous, but his family members believe he may have died in a logging accident in 1915 that was not prevented by white co-workers jealous of Enick's skill and unwilling to share wages with Indians. Local autobiographies confirm tribal members' memories of interracial animosity among logging men in the early twentieth century.[69] In the wake of their grief, Louisa and her remaining children had to face the bureaucratic onslaught of allotment cancellations—no less brutal than a Cascade mountain lion—that escalated in the year after Samuel's death.[70]

In 1916, Forest Service and Indian Office agents began an investigation of the ambiguous allotments, since it had become clear that there were conflicting claims on the Sauk, Skagit, and Suiattle Rivers. What had once been an isolated part of Washington's Cascade mountain range had by then become an increasingly valuable agricultural and timber zone for federal, private, and tribal landholders alike. In January, acting forester A. F. Potter wrote in regard to eighteen-year-old Agnes's allotment: "Since it is reported by the Forest Supervisor that this applicant has never made settlement on the land nor cultivated any portion of it, nor erected any buildings thereon, it is suggested that steps should be taken to reject the application and close the case."[71] Under such reasoning, all minors' allotment applications would fail to meet Forest Service standards for forest reserve allotments. It is important to point out once again that public domain allotments for Indians differed from public domain homestead claims for citizens in that allotments could be made in minors' names, and that there were no specific requirements for improvements on allotted lands like there were on homestead lands. The Forest Service and GLO acted as if they were working to approve homesteads even though they used allotment terminology; Office of Indian Affairs officials protested the cancellation of Sauk-Suiattle allotments but never explained the very important distinctions between allotment and homestead law.[72]

The forest supervisor also recommended that Louisa Enick's public domain allotment be canceled for reasons of nonoccupancy, but then suggested that she reapply for the same allotment under the 1910 "Allotments in Forest Reserves" law, since she had in fact made use of the land and continued to camp "along the river," making it clear that the Forest Service's definition of "occupancy" was filtered by expectations of a built environment rangers could recognize.[73] Apparently willing to allow Louisa but not her daughter to remain on the land, the Forest Service nonetheless wanted to cancel her application and require that the paperwork be resubmitted under a different legal clause. Such bureaucratic maneuvers effectively constituted removal by red tape.

Of course, where legislators and bureaucrats are ambiguous on the fine points of Indian law, historians can rely on Felix Cohen, renowned scholar of federal Indian policy, to provide clarity. Cohen's explanation of public domain allotments generally cites cases like the Sauk-Suiattle's, in which "government officials apparently assisted applications for public domain allotments in clusters to provide a land base for landless Indian communities." To be approved, such public domain allotments "must be valuable for agricultural purposes and capable of supporting an Indian family," which Farrar took pains to affirm for the Enick family allottees. Because "public domain allotments have the same status as allotments created from tribal land," agricultural and architectural improvements are not a requirement of public domain allotments.[74] Should the secretary of the interior, responsible for both the Indian Office and the Land Office, not approve an Indian application for a public domain allotment, Indian applicants could challenge the ruling in federal court. That court challenge would eventually happen, but in the early months of 1916, Forest Service and Land Office agents treated Louisa Enick's land as a homestead application and came to varying conclusions regarding the fate of Louisa's claims.

The Office of Indian Affairs sent special allotting agent Charles Roblin to make a report before they weighed in on the controversy, but he too failed to distinguish between allotment and homestead laws, making his endorsement of the allottees weaker than it might have been. Louisa Enick's family received a visit from Roblin in the fall of 1916. Most known to scholars of Indian and western history for his 1919 census of unenrolled Indians, Roblin arrived in the Pacific Northwest with special orders to clarify the conflicting claims regarding the Sauk-Suiattle allotments in the Washington National Forest. He interviewed Indians and Indian agents, forest rangers and loggers, and Land Office registrars and surveyors. Roblin's investigation proved a pivotal moment in the allotment cancellation process. His general report indicates that certain Forest Service and Land Office officials expressed a willingness to concede lands to the Suiattle River allottees as long as the surveys could be clarified and the paperwork finalized, a stance that both departments would reverse just a few years later. Other Forest Service officials, however, particularly the local forest ranger (unnamed), used physical violence and verbal harassment against Suiattle River allottees to prevent them from working their lands. Roblin explained that before making his investigation, he held a meeting with tribal members and asked Suiattle River allottees to simply move south, beyond the Washington National Forest boundaries, but he faced immediate and ardent opposition. He noted that "the Indians all understood that [George Keepers's 1903 and 1905 allotments] were final and confirmed the title to them. They have carefully preserved the certificates of selection which Mr. Keepers issued, regarding them as evidence of their titles." Roblin acknowledged the contradictory legislation regulating the Sauk-Suiattle allotments. He found that tribal allottees had done their part to preserve the records that proved their land claims and that they understood the importance of maintaining legal title to the land. To ascertain which of the Suiattle River allottees held lands suitable for forest reserve allotments, Roblin proceeded to meet individually with families and interview heads of households throughout the valley.[75]

Rather than interviewing Louisa or any of her older children, Charles Roblin recorded an affidavit on the Enick family allotments from Dick Enick, Louisa's second-oldest son, aged about sixteen at the time of Roblin's investigation. Perhaps Louisa's English-language skills limited her ability to answer the special agent's questions and she preferred to be represented by her son, or perhaps Roblin was more accustomed to addressing male members of households in his allotment work. Either way, Dick's description of his family's allotments revealed the vast extent of female labor invested in the Enicks' lands. Describing his father's allotment to Roblin, Dick explained that his father had built a house on the land and that "a clearing was made and garden has been raised on this each year; raspberry bushes and [currant] bushes were also set out and are still there." The gendered division of Sauk-Suiattle labor at the turn of the twentieth century put cultivation and berry harvesting under women's purview, and Dick Enick's affidavit emphasized the work of Louisa and her daughters as evidence of their improvements upon the land.

Of Agnes's plot, Roblin explained, "this tract of land was and is part of the original tract settled upon by Samuel Enic and family over twenty years ago [prior to the establishment of the Washington National Forest]. . . . A house was built on this particular allotment ten years ago. A clearing was also made . . . and . . . has been used by the family ever since for raising garden truck for their maintenance. Nine sacks of potatoes were raised on this place in one year . . . Fruit trees and raspberry bushes have been planted on this allotment. . . . The allotment should be confirmed to this claimant."[76] Not only did the special allotting agent affirm Louisa and Agnes's claim, Roblin emphasized once again the female contributions to the land as evidence that their plots has been properly utilized. Because Louisa's tribe viewed berry harvesting as a sign of spiritual prowess manifested as a material skill, the repeated references to berries on her allotments is an important aspect of Indigenous perspectives on laws regarding land ownership. Planting camas tubers had also been a traditionally female practice that included the matrilineal bequest of planting grounds from generation to generation.[77] In Sauk-Suiattle eyes, digging tubers and picking berries made the land distinctively Louisa's own because of a sacred and tangible connection that just happened to coincide with the federal government's misperception that "improvements" upon the land justified ownership. In the eyes of federal law, occupancy alone should have affirmed Louisa and Agnes Enick's title to their public domain allotment. Despite this fundamental mistake in his interpretation of the "Allotments in Forest Reserves" law, Roblin nonetheless endorsed Louisa Enick's legal claim after his visit in September 1916.

Just as Forest Service and GLO administrators ignored deputy forest ranger Farrar's recommendation in favor of the Enick allotments in 1905 and 1907, they dismissed special allotting agent Roblin's report in 1916 as well. Two years after Roblin's investigation, the assistant commissioner of the GLO notified the Portland Area Land Office that they had canceled Samuel Enick's allotment because his death constituted nonoccupancy and that without action on Louisa's part to reapply for her allotment lands under the 1910 forest reserves allotment law, the GLO would cancel her allotment as filed under section 4 of the Allotment Act. Of course, had Samuel's title been perfected, the land would have descended to Louisa, and had federal officials accurately applied federal Indian land policy her title would also have been perfected. On November 26, 1918, the Register of Lands wrote to

Photographs of Sallie Sauk public domain allotment and improvements: dwelling, smokehouse, and timber. The improvements are similar to those described on Louisa Enick's allotment. (RG 75, Bureau of Indian Affairs, Portland Area Office, Land Transaction Case Files 1946–1965, 1957, 310 Western Washington US-W, 312 W Wash A, Box 122, Folder WW 310; Vognild, Henry, Allotment Public Domain Seattle 81, Sallie Sauk; reproduced with permission from National Archives at Seattle)

his commissioner that the letter informing Louisa Enick of the cancellation of her allotment had been "returned unclaimed," though service had been made to Tulalip Indian agent Charles Buchanan. He closed his letter to the commissioner's office in Washington, D.C., with words now typical of Louisa Enick's allotment dispute: "No action has been taken in the case."[78] Perhaps the Register of Lands was distracted by relief over World War I having just ended, or by news of the devastating global flu pandemic, but whatever slowed his hand, Louisa would take advantage of the delay.

Although bureaucrats failed to act on their cancellation threats, Louisa Enick dictated a letter to an unidentified ally (most likely her friend William Salter) on December 8, 1919. While other women her age celebrated their right to vote in national elections and looked forward to the election year of 1920, Louisa Enick—not included in suffrage because of her Indianness— nonetheless laid claim to her corporeal sovereignty when it was threatened. The hastily scrawled note explained that Louisa failed to reply earlier to the cancellation notices because she was "bed fast," but that once well enough she visited the Land Office in Seattle and "fixed up the papers but never got any reply."[79] The letter indicates that the widow complied with Forest Service and Land Office requests that she resubmit her application for the allotment under the 1910 legislation despite their incomprehensible reasons for requiring her to do so. Her actions are also evidence that she understood the legal maneuvers necessary to successfully obtain title to her allotment as well or better than the bureaucrats whose correspondence reveals their incompetence.

Louisa managed to overcome these bureaucratic hurdles with the support of William Salter, himself a widower, and Tulalip Indian Agency farmer Joe Shell, who wrote a letter of introduction for her business with the Land Office in Seattle. Such allies, in tandem with the favorable reports from Farrar and Roblin, mean that there were white male advocates of Indigenous women's corporeal sovereignty who opposed federal efforts to dispossess women like Louisa Enick. Though somewhat tangential, it is important to note that, unlike Dinah Hood in central Arizona, Louisa did not have to face sexual vulnerability at the hands of those who could help her. Perhaps this was because by 1919, Washington had long ago repealed its antimiscegenation statutes and allowed Indians to testify on their own behalf against white citizens. Even though Louisa's body might have been safer than Dinah Hood's, her lands remained in dispute and, depending on who you asked, she was a mere squatter on federal lands just as Dinah had been on the Granite Creek Fort Whipple Reserve in Arizona.

Apparently ignorant of the lengthy correspondence and cancellation threats that Louisa's allotment had already generated, the assistant commissioner of the GLO responded to Enick's letter two days before Christmas 1919 and informed her that her application will "be considered by this office in due course of business. In the meantime, there is nothing that can be done in this matter and should any action thereon be required, you will be promptly advised."[80] Forced to wait until the winter snows melted to make a survey of Louisa Enick's application for an allotment inside forest reserve lands, no further action would be taken until May 1920. When they did finally arrive to inspect Louisa's allotment lands, Forest Service agents determined—in direct contradiction to both Farrar and Roblin's descriptions of the Suiattle River plot—that the tract proved far more valuable for timber than for agriculture and therefore failed to meet the requirements of the 1910 forest reserve allotment provision. The GLO commissioner explained that unless Louisa Enick could prove settlement prior to the establishment of the Washington National Forest in 1897—a point she had tried to make in her original section 4 allotment application and that Roblin had affirmed explicitly in his report on her settlement—her application would be closed.

A brief period of silence followed in the summer months of 1920, but at the end of August the special agent in charge of the Tulalip Indian Agency wrote to the GLO commissioner that he had submitted an appeal on Louisa Enick's behalf through the commissioner of Indian Affairs and that he hoped to get some assistance from the Land Office in reviewing the allotment. The frustrating consequences of dividing the administration of national forests and sovereign Indians between the Department of Agriculture and the Department of the Interior are evident in these files containing multiple copies of letters sent to multiple offices in Washington State and in Washington, D.C. Will Salter wrote his own letter to the GLO commissioner in October of that year, explaining that Louisa had been ill—vital records show that she was pregnant—and was trying to "get her land affairs straightened up."[81] In November 1920 he wrote the letter that opened this chapter, transcribing Louisa's defense of the lands where she had borne and buried children, healed wounds and hauled water, picked berries, and pruned trees. The letter-writing campaign of 1920 apparently had an effect, and on January 12, 1921, the GLO commissioner allowed additional time for Louisa Enick and her allies to make proof on the allotment lands she had occupied since childhood and before the laws that regulated her use of the land had even been passed.[82]

Even though it must have been a relief to earn a stay of cancellation, the standards by which Louisa's land claim were measured remained skewed. Regardless of bureaucratic misperceptions regarding the stipulations that regulated public domain and forest reserve allotments and homesteads, the Office of Indian Affairs conceded to the Forest Service designation of the land as a timber stand not suitable for agricultural use or Indian occupation, and Louisa Enick's case was closed on February 5, 1921. No one in the Department of the Interior or the Department of Agriculture asked how Louisa's plot had transformed from the rich agricultural land planted with potatoes, fruit trees, and berries that Roblin described in 1916 to a timber stand with no agricultural value just four years later. Louisa's case was closed eighteen years after she and her husband had filed their claims, fourteen years after deputy forest ranger Farrar had recommended that she be granted secure title, five years after special allotting agent Roblin endorsed her allotment, and the same year her youngest daughter Marie was born. Although available records are silent regarding the nature of Louisa Enick and William Salter's friendship, Marie Enick eventually married the man who wrote to the GLO on her mother's behalf, affirming his affectionate commitment to the family and their land struggles.

Although Louisa's letters, written by William Salter on her behalf, came from the small settlement of Gold Bar, Washington, in 1919, and from the Elgin Hotel in Tacoma, where she rested while pregnant in 1920, Louisa and her children appeared in the Tulalip Indian Agency census between 1921 and 1923. Indian agent W. F. Dickens included Louisa Enick, widow, in his schedule of "Suiattle Indians" for those years, though she likely lived, like others who had lost their allotments, "along the Sauk River in the vicinity of Mansford, Sauk, [and] Darrington." Louisa's final appearance in the census in 1923 is explained by her death in 1924; she was at least fifty years old.[83] Louisa died the same year that Congress passed the American Indian Citizenship Act. She had personally felt and fought the brutal results of half a century of federal Indian policy in the Pacific Northwest. She did not succeed in maintaining her lands and passing property on to her children, but she instilled in them and inspired among members of her tribe a commitment to taking legal action in the face of federal intransigence and in the spirit, as well as the letter, of the law.

Agnes's allotment application had been canceled with far less bureaucratic fanfare, or red tape, than her mother's. The Land Office and Forest Service colluded to cancel Agnes's allotment for the combined reasons that Agnes was born after the 1898 establishment of the Washington National

Forest and was therefore not old enough to claim prior settlement, and that her status as a minor allottee living with parents made it impossible for her to improve upon the allotted lands and she therefore failed to meet the requirements for secure title. Of course, as explained above, the laws regulating public domain and forest reserve allotments allowed minors to hold allotment separate from those of their parents, and if Agnes was too young to make a section 4 allotment claim under the Allotment Act, she was old enough to make a claim under the 1910 forest reserve allotments law. As in her mother's case, however, no one raised these specific challenges at the time of her 1918 cancellation and her case was closed.

Just as her mother wrote letters with William Salter's help, Agnes Enick inquired about her family's allotments with the aid of her part-Cowlitz husband, Leo Metcalf.[84] On December 26, 1922, Leo wrote to the superintendent of the Tulalip Indian School and explained, "my wife asked me to write you and ask about her claim." Agnes's husband asked for the section numbers of the Enick family allotments and also asked where the Enick siblings would be allotted if their original applications had indeed been canceled. Early in January 1923, the superintendent replied that the Enick allotments had been canceled because the family had not proven settlement prior to the 1897 order establishing the Washington National Forest. Of course, as this chapter has shown, there is and was a substantial body of evidence proving the family's prior settlement along the Suiattle River. The superintendent closed his letter to Agnes's husband with promising news, however. He told Agnes's family that "this office is now engaged in obtaining data and information concerning the claims of unallotted Indians which, when completed, will be presented to the commissioner of Indian Affairs for the purpose of asking Congress to allow these Indians to present their claims before the Court of Claims for settlement. The papers in connection with your wife's claim will be placed with others of like nature and will be given consideration at the proper time."[85]

Although he could not act alone to reverse the cancellation of Louisa and others' Suiattle River allotments, the superintendent of the Tulalip Indian Agency had already protested the GLO and Forest Service actions in May 1921. He submitted a report—very similar to the one Roblin filed five years earlier—that quite plainly explained the false logic of the cancellations and entreated the commissioner of Indian Affairs to intervene on behalf of the tribe, whose members "have been unfairly treated. The local Forestry Officials are prejudiced, and the Indians have no more chance than the proverbial 'snowball.' While he should be assisted in making proof under the most liberal construction of the law, just the opposite has applied and the most exacting requirements of the law have been demanded and technicalities resorted to as the grounds for cancellation."[86]

Louisa Enick's land remains part of the Washington National Forest even though she met every requirement put to her by government agents. Even though she had ample evidence to support her legal title, her protests were never heard in court because incompetent bureaucrats bungled her claims. Other women in this book forced their way into nineteenth-century courtrooms, but the halls of justice had narrowed by the twentieth century, and Louisa found herself barred from local or federal legal venues. Although her name cannot be found in any legal journals or court records, proof of Louisa Enick's legacy can be found in the letters her daughters and sons-in-law wrote to inquire about the cancellation of her allotment and in tribal efforts led by Louisa's nephew George Enick to achieve compensation and recognition in the Court of Claims in the 1930s and 1950s. George Enick, Agnes and Marie's cousin, would serve as the Sauk-Suiattle tribal chairman and work with lawyers and empathetic reformers to press the first claim against the U.S. Court of Claims in 1936. Agnes and Marie both wrote letters in their own hand during the 1930s, still asking pointed questions about their family's dispossession at the hands of federal officials.[87] The displacement and desperation of Louisa's daughters illustrates the dire consequences of federal cancellation of the family's public domain allotments.

Agnes's letter, written from Taholah, Washington, on February 13, 1932, recounts her family's dispossession and seeks recourse:

> My mother in 1920 received a letter threw [*sic*] your office which stated she would have to take her children to some reservation where there was land still open for allotment where we would come to live and there settle. Would you please search your records and send me a duplicate of this letter. It is of great importance to me. Please answer as soon as possible as the (page 2) allotting agent is here and we need this letter to get a claim. We are Suattle [*sic*]. I am the daughter of Sam Enick, my mother was Louisa Enick. . . . Have you ever heard anything about my people in the Suattle Reservation now known as the Washington National Forest? Please answer soon. Respectfully yours, Mrs. Agnes Metcalf.[88]

The letter stresses that the family understood the importance of documenting their legal allotment claims and that they identified the Washington

(2)

aloting agent is here and
we need this letter to get a
claim, we are suattls
I am the daughter of sam
Enick my mother was Jouisa
Enick, my name before marrage
was agnes Enick, have you
ever heard any thing about
my people in the suattle
resewation now known as
the washington national
forest. please answer soon
respectfully yours
mrs agnes metcalf
Tahola
Wash.

Letter from Mrs. Agnes Metcalf to Tulalip Indian School, February 13, 1932 (RG 75, Records of the Bureau of Indian Affairs, Western Washington Agency, Tribal Operations Branch, General Correspondence [Old Taholah/Tulalip] ca. 1914–1951, IRA-921, Folder 380, Public Domain Allotments, Skagit and Whatcom Counties [Tulalip], 1914–1937; reproduced with permission from National Archives at Seattle)

National Forest as occupying Suiattle lands—and not the inverse. Agnes expected the Tulalip agent to be able to provide her with assistance in claiming lands on the Quinault Reservation on Washington's Olympic Peninsula as a consequence of his inability to preserve her original lands. Agnes's grandchildren explained her 1930s residence so far from the Suiattle River as the consequence of her husband Leo's employment as a fireguard.

Louisa's youngest daughter Maria, born just months after Louisa dictated the letter that opened this chapter, married her mother's friend William Salter sometime in the mid-1930s; she wrote the Tulalip Indian Agency five years after her oldest sister Agnes:

> I wish to get some information as to the allotment number of the land my mother, Mrs. Louisa Enick, was living on up in the Suattle [*sic*] valley up at Skagit, and as I know you have this on record, I wish to get it as it may be of some importance to me. I was very small the time of my mother's death and I have been told that Mr. Dickens was the man that was the Superintendent at that time [and he] was fully to blame for her leaving the land as she was one of the first to get up in that country. And furthermore had proven up on it a hole [*sic*] lot as she sold shingle [bolts] off the placed and so on. She was unedgecated [*sic*] and Mr. Dickens from what I have learned from different ones, he scared her off from the land. All I am asking of you is to give me the number of the allotment. I wish an early reply. Very Respt. Marie Salter.[89]

Addressed from Tacoma, Marie's letter also bears the stamp of relocation in the wake of dispossession, but she takes on a tone and formality reminiscent of the letter her mother dictated and her sister sent before her. Again, Marie recounts the family's history on the land, arguing that her mother was "one of the first up in that country," and naming those responsible for her eviction. She requests documentation, affirming that Louisa's daughters had learned from their mother the importance of proving land claims through paper title as well as oral tradition. While her cousin George Enick led the tribe's first formal lawsuit against the federal government, Marie continued her family's individual pursuit of justice.[90]

The tribe lost its court cases throughout the 1930s and 1950s, but achieved federal acknowledgment in 1972. Modern descendants still live on the fringes of the Washington National Forest, raising families and working, sometimes picking berries and tracking cougars. Agnes and Marie's life stories and those of their siblings are beyond the purview of this chapter, but

Jan 18 – 1937

Mr Upchurch

Dear Sir:

I wish to get some information as to the allotment number of the land my mother. Mrs Louisa Enick was living on, up in the Suattle valley up at Skagit. And as I know you have this on record. I wish to get it as it may be of some importance to me, I was very small the time of my mothers death and I have been told that Mr Dickens was the man that was the Superintendent at that time was fully to Blame for her leaving the land as she was one of the first to get up in that country. and further more had proved up on it a hole lot as she sold shingle Blots off the place and so on. she was unedgecated, + Mr Dickens from what I have learned from different ones. He scared her off from the land, all I am asking of you is to give me the number of the allotment. I wish an early Reply Very Respt

Marie Salter

1107½ So J St. Tacoma Wash.

Letter from Marie Salter to Mr. Upchurch at Tulalip Indian Agency, January 18, 1937 (RG 75, Records of the Bureau of Indian Affairs, Western Washington Agency, Tribal Operations Branch, General Correspondence [Old Taholah/Tulalip] ca. 1914–1951, IRA-921, Folder 380, Public Domain Allotments, Skagit and Whatcom Counties [Tulalip], 1914–1937; reproduced with permission from National Archives at Seattle) they are often shared among their grandchildren and great-grandchildren still living in the Sauk and Suiattle River valleys, in the Tacoma area, and on the Olympic Peninsula. Tribal leaders and their lawyers continue to untangle the legislation and correspondence that outline the tribe's legitimate titles. Louisa's descendants can still revisit the place where she lived. Together they tell the stories of their family's century-long struggle to retain their Sauk and Suiattle River homes in the midst of cedars and cougars, in the face of soldiers and surveyors, in the courts of law and in the ceremonies of spirit. As a collective oral tradition recounting the transition from physical to bureaucratic violence and its aftermath, such stories are both case law and testament to the tribe's survival that Louisa Enick's generation ensured.[91]

This history does not end with Louisa Enick's dispossession, of course, and readers should not reflect on this case as merely one episode in a long history of Indigenous losses. Louisa Enick's experiences demonstrate that even when legislation aligns like celestial bodies in support of Indigenous land rights, those policies are susceptible to the whims of federal agents and local actors. The law itself carries insufficient force to uphold Indian women's sovereignty. Without the compliance of surveyors general, land registrars, forest supervisors, Indian agents, lawyers, and judges, section 4 of the Allotment Act held no teeth. When federal policy contradicted itself to the benefit of the federal government and the detriment of women like Louisa Enick, the support of citizen friends, local ranchers, and regional news editors could not press legal challenges into federal courts. Louisa's tribe did not gain legal traction until the 1930s: after her death in 1924, after the Meriam Report in 1928 exposed widespread incompetencies and abuses in the Bureau of Indian Affairs (formerly the Office of Indian Affairs), and after the Indian Reorganization Act of 1934 ended allotment and offered tribes an opportunity to reestablish political relations with the federal government.[92]

To some readers it may be obvious that the law does not operate as a well-oiled machine, intuiting and responding to social needs for justice, progress, and transparency. Skepticism toward legal objectivity and neutrality is, after all, a basic tenet of critical legal history.[93] For newcomers to Native women's western legal history, however, it may be a surprise that Indian women could lose their lands even with the law on their side. It is the accounts of dispossession through violence and fraud, through treachery and corruption, that capture our historical attention, not the more subtle histories of sovereignty eroded through bureaucratic inaction and incompetence. And yet, by the early 1920s when Louisa Enick voiced her legal claims and in the 1930s when her daughters wrote pointed letters, Indian women no longer defended their lands from surveyors, soldiers, or settler-colonists. Instead, Louisa and her daughters faced clerks and bureaucrats, lawyers and judges. These men did not wield rifles or burn homes; they stamped papers and shuffled pages, but with devastating results. The battlefields of Indigenous sovereignty changed dramatically during Louisa Enick's lifetime, from prairie to courtroom, but she and her tribe managed to redirect their resistance from physical violence to bureaucratic violence, and the Sauk-Suiattle remained creative in their efforts to assert tribal sovereignty.

Like the other women in this book, Louisa's loss is significant because of the legal critiques she articulated against those who threatened her corporeal sovereignty—her autonomy over her body, progeny, and lands. Like the women in Joy Harjo's poem, Louisa Enick lost her country to the "purveyors of law." Nonetheless, she responded with an articulation of gendered and embodied sovereignty: she had become a person on her land, she had borne children on her land, and she had raised crops on her land. Louisa's words are echoed in Harjo's depiction of Indian women's return from the enemies who dispossessed them:

> The law of the gods I claim state:
> *When entering another country do not claim ownership.*
> *It is important to address the souls there kindly, with respect.*
> *And ask permission.*
> I am asking you to leave the country of my body, my mind, if you have
> anything other than honorable intentions.[94]

It was not until 1972 that Louisa's tribe found the legal, political, and social traction to enforce these words, but Louisa and her daughters rehearsed them as early as 1916, and they are whispered in the conifers of the Mount Baker–Snoqualmie National Forest even today.

CHAPTER 8

"The Acts of Forgetfulness"

Indigenous Women's Legal History in Archives and Tribal Offices Throughout the North American West

Chronicling the lives of the women in this book during some very formative years of my own life has been a tremendously personal and inspiring experience. Learning from their strategies of recovery and efforts toward personal sovereignty has made me think about alliance building, direct communication, and persistent advocacy in new ways. The skills they exhibited in working among diverse and sometimes adversarial communities have given me much to consider as I hone my own approaches in sharing their histories with a sometimes skeptical audience. Rather than drawing overarching or summative claims about the worlds these women lived in, this conclusion does more to describe the worlds these women are remembered in. I invoke Joy Harjo's poem once again to characterize the archival and community work that made these intimate and important depictions of Native women's legal history possible. In describing the "acts of forgetfulness" that have placed Indian women's legal history beyond the scope of western historians, this chapter encourages scholars to find more evidence of Indian women's contributions to western history in local and state archives. The chapter also chronicles my experience working with the tribes and communities represented in this book, who have participated in its writing on a broad scale ranging from disinterest to direct editorial assistance. My hope in sharing the process that allowed me to overcome many archival and interpersonal hurdles is to convince skeptical historians that legal archives contain a female Indigenous perspective and to encourage others in their efforts to work with tribal communities.

I began this project with a fairly straightforward goal: to find evidence of Native women's use of territorial legal systems in the North American West and to put their strategies into a historical context. My interest in doing so came from my appreciation of Native authors' critiques of the law and history in creative nonfiction and fictional works. Combining my training in American Indian studies and history, I hoped to write a book that intermingled the poetics and politics of Indigenous women's legal history. That goal turned out to be incredibly fraught with tensions that I have certainly not resolved, but also laced with obligations that I can only hope I have met. Joy Harjo's poem "Returning from the Enemy" addresses some of the tensions I encountered and obligations I incurred in carrying out this project. On one hand, there is a sorrow, and for some a shame, in stories of loss in Indigenous communities, and certainly some people's "shoulders bear each act of forgetfulness," when left-behind stories like those told in this book are recalled. On the other hand, the women in this book and members of their contemporary communities have worked hard in their lifetimes to reclaim their histories and their losses from the enemies who "called themselves priests, preachers, and the purveyors of law." In that light, there is a powerful resistance that I read in these histories and that Joy Harjo's poem also expresses in her closing stanza: "I am asking you to leave the country of my body, my mind, if you have anything other than honorable intentions." It has been a great privilege to observe how tribal communities are gathering the political, economic, and cultural strength to expel those without honorable intentions from their homelands and their institutions. This final chapter explains how honorable intentions granted me entry into some remarkable Indian women's legal histories, guided my choices in government archives, and graced my conversations in tribal offices throughout the North American West.

Although some readers might anticipate that tribal members occasionally met me with skepticism when I first contacted them about this project, others might be surprised to learn that my research efforts attracted the most resistance from those guardians of historical knowledge in small archival branches in remote corners of their states. My initial research queries were made over the phone to determine the availability of archival material related to Indian women's legal encounters in off-reservation communities, so I contacted repositories of some of Arizona's and Washington's earliest territorial legal records. When I explained my project, archivists gave me two blanket rejections to explain why they could not help me: either they held no Indian material because they were state repositories and Indians were either federal or ethnographic subjects, or Indians were "treated well" and "well liked" in their communities and therefore had no cause to use the legal system.

The first assertion proved easy to overturn once more friendly archivists in other repositories helped me to navigate the intricacies of territorial legal records and I developed a process of searching civil and criminal records for evidence of Indigenous plaintiffs. Those initially resistant archivists remained convinced that their collections held no Indian material, however, even after I ordered hundreds of pages of copies that proved Native people engaged their region's legal systems—some even expressed regret that I had wasted a trip to visit them. The second assertion proved impossible to overcome in those institutions not yet catalogued online—and there are many repositories still based in paper indexes known primarily by the sole archivist on staff. Historians rely heavily on archivists' assistance in planning their research ventures, and when those professionals commit their own "acts of forgetfulness," we all suffer from notable gaps in our past. There are archives I did not consult for this project for the simple reason that I could not afford a trip to a repository without the promise of potential material or archival assistance, and I learned, as others surely have before me, that I must craft my initial research questions very carefully when approaching repositories for the first time.

Although this book has chronicled the experiences of only six women, there is a vast legal record available for scholars interested in pursuing other arenas of Indigenous women's legal history. My interest has been in Native women as litigants, with the exception here of Dinah Foote Hood and her grandmother, who proved resistant when Arizona jurists tried to coerce their testimony. There are many other cases tied to Indigenous women as defendants, or as named parties in crimes charged against other defendants. Of course, in the archives, none of these records are tagged as "Indian" cases particularly. For this reason, I stress to scholars and archivists that there is much more work to be done in what is sometimes a chaotic set of material. The Washington State Archive's Frontier Justice records are at least indexed by case type and name, but the Arizona records are simply in chronological order and are not actually indexed at all.[1] In the work I am doing toward my next book project, I have found that most federal district court records are not indexed and that most western states' legal records are equally uncategorized. My experience in this project makes it clear that

there are Native women in those materials, and a vast history remains un-
told while those records are left unsorted. Miroslava Chávez-García's work
on Indigenous and Mexican women as litigants in Spanish, Mexican, and
early-American California reveals that much can be found there as well, and
I hope this book convinces western legal historians that there is much opportunity in building the field of Indigenous women's legal history. Indeed,
until that work is done, one folder and one box at a time, our understandings of western legal history are remarkably incomplete.

As noted above, there were archivists and librarians who proved im-
mensely helpful as I stumbled over myself in the early phases of this project.
The staff at the Arizona State Library, Archives, and Public Records not
only patiently advised me on how Arizona's legal records had been organized and could be searched, but they took it upon themselves to trace leads
for me and to find complementary material in their collections that I would
never have found on my own. The budget cuts they have suffered are a tragedy to residents and historians of that state, and I hope the Arizona legislature sees the value of their work. Another Arizona institution whose staff
has been tremendously supportive is the Sharlot Hall Museum Library and
Archives. Sharlot Hall administrators and staff not only helped me to answer some of my earliest questions in sorting out the identities of Indian
women who bore multiple names throughout their lifetimes, but they also
introduced me to local history enthusiasts and tribal members whose interest in the project has proven both informative and motivating. In Washington I found out that the staff at the Seattle branch of the National Archives
and Records Administration is an amazing group of advocates for public
history who are superb ambassadors of their vast collection. I have benefited
from their input at every stage of this project. The research assistants at the
Puget Sound Regional Branch of the Washington State Archives are also an
incredible group of people who have faced their own onslaught of losses due
to budget cuts. The materials in their collection are vital for those pursuing innovative approaches to western legal history and I hope they become
more accessible in the near future. Finally, with enthusiasm and patience,
the staff at the Center for Pacific Northwest Studies has helped me to navigate their rich ethnographic collection.

Researchers of Native legal histories will find much support at these
institutions, although the financial and personal resources it required to
visit all of them made it clear how fortunate I was to be able to carry out
my seemingly straightforward goal. State archives and special collections

throughout the North American West contain important evidence of Indian women's legal history that has been buried in the acts of forgetfulness. Academic credentials and a wide array of funding sources make it possible for me to visit archives that these women's community members could only attempt to access from afar. Whether Native or not, people invested in the histories in this book are engaged in full-time work and holding together families and communities, which makes it difficult to spend money and time in archives not always friendly or approachable. Thinking of those who cannot visit archives makes the work even more meaningful, and it is my hope that more resources can be directed toward the distribution and publication of archival material online in the form of digital and public history. It has been a relief to see more diverse professionals hired as administrators and archivists in private and public repositories, and I know that as these changes occur, their collections will become more accessible to professional and amateur historians alike.

Once I was equipped with hundreds of pages of archival material and a more nuanced understanding of the historical and contemporary networks of Indian and immigrant relations in the Arizona and Washington regions that became the focus of this study, my second step in researching this manuscript was to contact the communities that all six women had claimed as their own. Based in Tucson for my graduate work at the University of Arizona, I began with Lucía Martínez's Yaqui tribe at Pascua Yaqui. Robert Valencia, then vice chairman of the Pascua Yaqui tribe, responded to my e-mail queries and met with me to discuss Lucía's ties to the tribe's transnational history in Sonora and Arizona. Though Valencia commended the project and listened to my recounting of Lucía's story with enthusiastic interest, he saw no need for official tribal involvement in the manuscript, and at the time the tribe had no place to house the archival material I had collected in her case. I promised to report back when the book was complete, and moved on feeling flattered that a member of the tribal council had taken the time to meet with me and pursued other venues for engagement with local community members.

While I sent out e-mails to members of the Cultural Resources Management Program at the Gila River Indian Community of Akimel O'odham about my work on Juana Walker and to the director of Culture and Research for the Yavapai Prescott Indian Tribe regarding Dinah Hood's history, Viola Romero contacted me with interest in her great-great-grandmother Lucía Martínez. She had found my work through an online announcement about a talk I gave at the Sharlot Hall Museum in Prescott and wanted to discuss her family's history. Viola and her family proved to be kind supporters of the project and shared their own memories and photographs, some of which appear in these pages with their generous permission. Their inspiring interest helped me to accept the critique I received from the Gila River Indian Community's (GRIC) Cultural Resources Subcommittee of the Tribal Council a few months later.

Barnaby Lewis, tribal historic preservation officer, and Andrew Darling of the GRIC Cultural Resources Management Program met with me to discuss Juana Walker's chapter and arranged for me to present my work in its early phase before the Cultural Resources Subcommittee to determine whether the tribe had a vested interest in the manuscript. The overwhelming message I received there was that my efforts to share Juana Walker's history were misguided and that the work I was doing would be much better carried out by a scholar from the Akimel O'odham community. Members of the subcommittee expressed resentment at outsider scholars who researched and published their community's history without consultation with the tribe and without consideration for the gap between modern challenges facing tribal members and the privileged positions that academics enjoyed. They acknowledged that my research was based in public records and did not contain confidential or sacred material, but made it clear they wanted no involvement or affiliation with the project in its subsequent stages.

While their response obviously disappointed me, I also realized that the subcommittee's goal of protecting and preserving tribal cultural resources—which includes historical knowledge—required stopgap measures that can seem severe, but that constitute an important part of claiming cultural sovereignty as well as political sovereignty. Many non-Native scholars contemplate their relationship to the Native people they write about, but one of the important aspects of this outsider identity is to accept—and in my opinion, to accept without argument—the potential rejection of tribal communities. Members of the subcommittee were right, after all, that many outsider histories of Indigenous people are misguided and tribes like the Akimel O'odham can point to many exploitative relationships with academic researchers in the past. My ability to tell Juana Walker's story is limited without the input or feedback of tribal members fluent in their community's history, but I offer it here with good intentions, still respecting the decision of the GRIC Cultural Resources Subcommittee to disassociate themselves from the project and from me. Their choice means that Juana Walker's chapter is not an

Akimel O'odham history, it is her story alone, and a version of her story limited by my own interpretation of the archival record her life generated. The GRIC subcommittee's response to my proposal reinforced the importance of applying a number of analytical lenses to archival materials that include empathy and compassion. Tsianina Lomawaima writes that "the emotional ties—and responsibilities that knit scholars to the communities we 'study' and serve also apply to the personalities behind life histories and archival documents. The analytic strategies of comparison, cross-checking, and verification are not vitiated by affection. Offering our sources the affection they deserve implies our respect for *their* emotions."[2] Juana Walker, like all of the women in this narrative, suffered deeply at the hands of those who failed to recognize and protect her interests. My affection for her requires that I honor those seeking to protect her community's interests today, even if it means that I am excluded from that community. Perhaps as more scholars integrate empathy in their analysis of deeply emotional events in history, tribal communities can feel more confident that their histories will be contemplated with critical care.

The Yavapai-Prescott Indian Tribe's director of culture and research chose another approach to preserving her community's historical knowledge when she learned about this project. I contacted Linda Ogo, along with the tribe's archaeologist Scott Kwiatkowski, after the talk I had given at Sharlot Hall in Prescott. Linda invited me to share the work on Dinah Hood and her grandmother's participation in the Fernandez murder trial and their important role in maintaining Yavapai land claims near Prescott. I provided her office with copies of the archival material I had obtained and shared early drafts of the chapter with Linda Ogo and members of the Yavapai Elders' Speaker's Group. The group offered suggestions for revision that helped me to more deftly describe the complex relationship Yavapai tribal members shared with Prescott residents in the years before federal recognition in 1935. I also enjoyed the stories members shared about their own families and the extraordinary history of their tribe's persistent survival. Scott showed me ongoing digs at sites near Dinah Hood's Granite Creek home, and it gave me a closer relationship to her story knowing that we had stood on the same ground and shared the same views of Granite Mountain and the boulder-topped valleys that she and her family knew so intimately. Today the tribe is becoming a stronger contributor to Prescott's economic growth and political community, and it has been a tremendous pleasure to work with them.

Not only did Dinah Hood's chapter benefit from the insights of Linda Ogo and the YPIT elders' group, but Hood descendants also contributed their own input on their family's history. Katherine Marquez, who until recently worked as director of the Yavapai Nation Cultural Preservation Office, contacted me when she learned of my work on her relatives and invited me to join other family members on the Fort McDowell Nation. Together we looked through the records Dinah Hood and her grandmother's legal actions generated, and I turned over copies of archival records to Marquez for family safe-keeping. Katherine and others shared fond memories of their Hood relatives, and I learned that many members of the family continue to work in formal and unofficial ways to preserve and protect Yavapai practices throughout central Arizona. When writing has proven difficult or publication seemed too distant a reality, remembering my time spent with Dinah Hood and Lucía Martínez's relatives has motivated me to continue this important work. Although I have referred in some instances throughout this book to family versions of their history, I have not included in detail the conversations I shared with Marquez and others who met with me to discuss each chapter. I found our conversations more fruitful without the pressure of potential publication, and I am sure those families and community members are doing an excellent job ensuring that those who should hear them know their histories. This book can supplement their family stories but is not meant to subsume them.

It took much longer for me to establish ties to communities on Washington's Puget Sound, since I was never in residence there. I did, however, benefit tremendously from connections among staff in county and regional records offices when the current owners of Nora Jewell's San Juan Island property contacted me because they learned I was tracing the title history of their property. Connie and Guard Sundstrom have become wonderful friends and have shared many of the intricacies of San Juan Island local history with me in visits over the years. Their devoted care of Nora Jewell's land, including their stewardship of a Garry Oak that stood in Nora's time, is only one aspect of their commitment to the island's tumultuous and intimate past and future. With their permission, Nora's tree is pictured in these pages as a marker of her presence at the center of San Juan Island's history and geography. Shortly after I met them, Connie and Guard nominated a road that passes the tree to be named "Jewell Lane," so now there is a testament to Nora's family history mapped onto the very island itself.

It has been difficult to know what tribal community might claim Nora's history, but after learning that some of her cousins registered as Lummi tribal members in the early twentieth century I reached out to Al Scott Johnnie, cultural administrative policy assistant to the Lummi Tribe's Cultural Commission. We met in the tribal offices near Bellingham, and I shared drafts of Nora Jewell's chapter with him for his and the Cultural Commission's review. The work Al and others are doing to preserve Lummi cultural and political sovereignty is both exciting and innovative and will no doubt do much to enhance their community's standing in the immediate area. The commission made no comment on the drafts I submitted, perhaps because Nora Jewell did not join the Roblin Rolls and no records indicate her tribal affiliation in modern-day terms. Still, my meeting with Al Scott Johnnie was a rewarding one. Readers should know that it took more than a year for me to arrange this meeting at Lummi and that the conversation was at first a one-sided series of e-mails in which I introduced myself and my work with patient—and perhaps annoying—persistence. Fellow scholars have complained to me repeatedly that tribal communities do not respond to their queries, so they give up, but I would advise repeated efforts that include phone calls as well as e-mails. I can only assume that tribal officials fail to reply promptly for at least two reasons: first, they are incredibly busy with the daily work of responding to their community's needs, and second, they receive a wide range of queries regarding tribal history that include the horribly offensive as well as those sent with "honorable intentions." If we are truly approaching such leaders respectfully, we will give them repeated opportunities to respond and will respect their rapidly shifting schedules and priorities—which may not always include us in the end. You will improve your odds of a response if you can show that you have something to share—like a collection of archival material tied to their community's history—and that you are hoping to have a conversation rather than deliver a speech or lecture to an audience likely more knowledgeable than yourself.

Perhaps because my e-mails were from Lincoln, Nebraska, and might have seemed to come from nowhere, or more likely because she had more urgent priorities, Sauk-Suiattle tribal chairwoman Norma Joseph also took some time to respond to my many e-mails. By asking around the Darrington community between hikes in the Mount Baker–Snoqualmie National Forest, however, I did manage to get hold of archaeologist Astrida Onat, who has worked very closely with Louisa Enick's tribe. Astrida has provided immeasurable support, both as a mentor in Pacific Northwest ethnohistory, and as a friend I can visit when researching in Seattle. She encouraged me to keep trying to get in touch with the tribal chairwoman, and when Norma Joseph did reply, she invited me to visit the Sauk-Suiattle community and share Louisa Enick's records with tribal members and Enick descendants. Norma's generous invitation allowed me to share the history I had collected in archives with Louisa's family and community and to learn from tribal members how her story fit into their own experiences of maintaining tribal lands and upholding their community's sovereignty in the river valleys of the North Cascades. Over the course of a week I was able to visit with Louisa Enick's relatives and especially enjoyed the hospitality of Ronda Metcalf and others who joined me for community lunches prepared by "Chef Dave," also an Enick descendant. Particularly special was a guided tour of the area with tribal elder Mary Jack, who pointed out public domain allotments and community gathering sites along the roadsides that crisscross the tribe's homelands. I left copies of Louisa Enick's archival material with Norma Joseph in hopes of a future Sauk-Suiattle tribal archive collection and have enjoyed being able to stay in touch with tribal members since my visit. Their losses in the Oso mudslide in February 2014 have taken up much of the tribe's energies, and Sauk-Suiattle leaders are finding themselves once again in the position of raising complaints and making demands of federal and state agents who have acted with disregard and ineptitude in the face of crisis in Indian Country.

Meeting Duwamish tribal chairwoman Cecile Hansen to discuss my work on Rebecca Lena Graham's historic contribution to the tribe's legal history and recognition efforts proved fortuitous rather than formally scheduled. Like other tribal leaders, Cecile is working tirelessly to serve her community's immediate and long-term needs and had little time to reply to e-mails from an unknown historian not likely to deliver much assistance in the ongoing federal recognition campaign. While in Seattle researching Rebecca Lena Graham's case, however, I visited the Duwamish Longhouse and unexpectedly found Cecile there. My brief meeting with her left the distinct impression that she has maintained remarkable humor and grace in her nearly fifty years of working in and then leading the tribe's recognition efforts. Other authors write more expertly on the inherent problems in the government's standards for tribal recognition than I can, but Cecile can make you laugh and cry about the seeming idiocy of that process in seconds. I would be remiss if I did not remind readers that they can learn how to support this ongoing campaign financially and politically on the tribe's website at duwamishtribe.org or by joining their Facebook page. As strange as it seems, I think even Rebecca Lena Graham would want me to include that plug here.

Cecile and others that this book has helped me to meet spend much of their time working with tribal members and non-Native allies to repair the "acts of forgetfulness" that continue to make Native women and their families vulnerable actors in the state and federal legal regimes that overlap in the North American West. These gatherings have reminded me very much of the ones I attended as a child growing up in northern Wisconsin during the spearfishing controversy of the 1980s and 1990s. While members of my community slapped bumper stickers on their cars and trucks that proclaimed "Save a Walleye, Spear an Indian," and sold "Treaty Beer" to fund their occasionally violent and always racist protests of Ojibwe treaty rights at boat landings where Native families fished, my mother took me to Was-Wa-Gon Treaty Association meetings and Honor the Earth pow-wows on the Lac Courte Oreilles and Lac du Flambeau reserves. There I listened to tribal leaders and area activists speak on the longstanding traditions of Ojibwe spearfishing, the importance of fishing to families and their communities, and the long history of violated treaties in the Great Lakes region and the United States in general. I spent most of my time with the women who attended these meetings, some of whom spoke powerfully in front of large crowds and stood defiantly before hostile protestors on boat landings. Often I helped in the kitchens, doing dishes or delivering plates of food to elders and their families while women cooked and told stories. The stories they told were those of subtle and overt resistance of the longstanding legal regimes that Native women have faced in their struggles to protect their bodies, their children, and their lands against the whims of men and women more empowered by the law. I learned much about the ways families tell their communities' legal histories and in the naïveté of childhood, I assumed that their references to treaties, tribal sovereignty, and jurisdictional problems that put Native women in particularly vulnerable positions, were common knowledge. That was not especially true in the 1990s, but the work of Indigenous leaders throughout the United States like Sarah Deer, recipient in 2014 of a MacArthur "Genius Grant," and Winona LaDuke, executive director of the White Earth Land Recovery Project and inductee of the National Women's Hall of Fame, is helping to bring some of those contemporary issues to light. Scholars of Indigenous women's legal history can do much to provide historical context for the discussions such leaders are pushing forward in journals such as *Indian Country Today* and through organizations such as Idle No More.

Because of my childhood experiences throughout Wisconsin's Indian Country, I went into undergraduate and graduate classrooms and public and private archives expecting to find evidence of the grandmothers' challenges that I had heard described over wild rice and venison. With some persistence and the invaluable mentorship of many along the way, my expectations have been surpassed, and I hope this book goes a long way toward reversing the acts of forgetfulness that have plagued Native and newcomer communities alike. I am grateful for this experience, and the opportunity to practice a history that has meaning beyond these pages. For some readers, these are histories that were never forgotten, and for others, these histories are painful to remember. For all of us, though, they are an important step toward acknowledging, as other authors have also made clear, that Indigenous women have defended the "country of [their] mind, [their] body," since the first trespassers arrived. This book chronicles their efforts to do so within exploitative legal regimes as evidence that Native women did not accept the limitations settler-colonists imposed upon them.

Renowned Indigenous intellectuals like Elizabeth Cook-Lynn, Mishuana Goeman, J. Kehaulani Kauanui, Devon Mihesuah, and Luana Ross, to name a few, provide ongoing evidence of the rigorous challenges Native women pose before exploitative laws and ideologies that are remnants of North American colonialism.[3] Native women's legal history continues to unfold before us, and western legal historians are uniquely positioned to make sense of the tensions embedded in debates over the Violence Against Women Act or the building outrage over missing Indigenous women in the militarized border zones between the United States and Mexico, in an increasingly well-developed sex trade linking reservations and urban centers in the United States, and in the border towns surrounding First Nations communities in Canada. The women in this book fought the same forces that promote a disregard for Native women's political and corporeal sovereignty today. Although their stories are ended here by the first half of the twentieth century, their families and communities are still dealing with the legacies of inequality that remain embedded in the law. Our collective acts of forgetfulness allow such trends to continue, but we must all "return from the enemy" together.

Notes

Chapter 1. "Returning from the Enemy"

1. Larry Evers and Felipe S. Molina, *Yaqui Deer Songs, Maso Bwikam: A Native American Poetry*, 3rd ed. (Tucson: University of Arizona Press, 1993), 37. David Delgado Shorter, *We Will Dance Our Truth: Yaqui History in Yoeme Performances* (Lincoln: University of Nebraska Press, 2009), 22, 112–130. Edward Spicer, prominent scholar of Yaqui culture, estimates that the Talking Tree story predates the Jesuit period in New Spain, putting it as early as the 1680s. Edward H. Spicer, *The Yaquis: A Cultural History* (Tucson: University of Arizona Press, 1980).

2. Rev. Myron Eells, *The Twana, Chemakum, and Klallam Indians of Washington Territory*, extract from Smithsonian Annual Report, 1887, facsimile reproduction (Seattle: Shorey Book Store, 1971), 679–681. Ella Clark, *Indian Legends of the Pacific Northwest* (Berkeley: University of California Press, 2003). M. Terry Thompson and Steven M. Egesdal, eds., *Salish Myths and Legends: One People's Stories* (Lincoln: University of Nebraska Press, 2008). Wayne Prescott Suttles, "The Economic Life of the Coast Salish of Haro and Rosario Straits," in *Coast Salish and Western Washington Indians* (New York: Garland, 1974), 1:446–499. Crisca Bierwert, *Brushed by Cedar, Living by the River: Coast Salish Figures of Power* (Tucson: University of Arizona Press, 1999), 71–73.

3. James W. Zion, "Searching for Indian Common Law," in *Indigenous Law and the State*, ed. Bradford W. Morse and Gordon R. Woodman (Providence: Forse, 1988), 121–150. Sidney L. Harring, *Crow Dog's Case: American Indian Sovereignty, Tribal Law, and United States Law in the Nineteenth Century* (London: Cambridge University Press, 1994). David E. Wilkins, *American Indian Sovereignty and the U.S. Supreme Court: The Masking of Justice* (Austin: University of Texas Press, 1997). Robert A. Williams Jr., *The American Indian in Western Legal*

Thought: The Discourses of Conquest (New York: Oxford University Press, 1990). Miroslava Chávez-García, *Negotiating Conquest: Gender and Power in California, 1770s to 1880s* (Tucson: University of Arizona Press, 2006). Nancy Shoemaker, ed., *Negotiators of Change: Historical Perspectives on Native American Women* (London: Routledge, 1995).

4. Joy Harjo, "Returning from the Enemy," *A Map to the Next World* (New York: Norton, 2000), 69–96. Amelia V. Katanski, "Writing the Living Law: American Indian Literature as Legal Narrative," *American Indian Law Review* 33:53 (2008–2009), 53–76.

5. Harjo, "Returning from the Enemy," 75, 77. Quoted with permission. Italics are as in original. *The law of the gods I claim state* is as Harjo wrote the line.

6. Gerald Vizenor, ed., *Survivance: Narratives of Native Presence* (Lincoln: University of Nebraska Press, 2008).

7. Luana Ross, "From the 'F' Word to Indigenous/Feminisms," *Wicazo Sa Review* 24:2 (Fall 2009), 39–52. Laura Tohe, "There Is No Word for Feminism in My Language," *Wicazo Sa Review* 15:2 (Fall 2000), 103–110. "Forum: Native Feminisms Without Apology," special issue, *American Quarterly* 60:2 (June 2008). "Native Feminisms: Legacies, Interventions, and Indigenous Sovereignties," special issue, *Wicazo Sa Review* 24:2 (Fall 2009). Paula Gunn Allen, *The Sacred Hoop: Recovering the Feminine in American Indian Traditions* (Boston: Beacon, 1986). Elizabeth Cook-Lynn, *Notebooks of Elizabeth Cook-Lynn* (Tucson: University of Arizona Press, 2007), 170–177. Devon Abbott Mihesuah, *Indigenous American Women: Decolonization, Empowerment, Activism* (Lincoln: University of Nebraska Press, 2003). Leslie Marmon Silko, *Yellow Woman and a Beauty of Spirit: Essays on Native American Life Today* (New York: Simon & Schuster, 1996). Theda Perdue, *Cherokee Women: Gender and Culture Change, 1700–1835* (Lincoln: University of Nebraska Press, 1998). Winona LaDuke, *All Our Relations: Native Struggles for Land and Life* (Cambridge, Mass.: South End, 1999).

8. Julie Evans et al., *Equal Subjects, Unequal Rights: Indigenous Peoples in British Settler Colonies, 1830–1910* (Manchester: Manchester University Press, 2003), 1–16. Victoria Haskins and Margaret Jacobs, eds., "Domestic Frontiers," special issue, *Frontiers* 28:1–2 (2007). Tracey Banivanua Mar and Penelope Edmonds, eds., *Making Settler Colonial Space: Perspectives on Race, Place and Identity* (New York: Palgrave Macmillan, 2010), 1–24, 179–197. Hamar Foster, Benjamin L. Berger, and A. R. Buck, eds., *The Grand Experiment: Law and Legal Culture in British Settler Societies* (Vancouver: University of British Columbia Press, 2008).

9. Harjo, "Returning from the Enemy," 75, 77.

10. Ned Blackhawk, *Violence over the Land: Indians and Empires in the Early American West* (Cambridge: Harvard University Press, 2006). Brian DeLay, *War of a Thousand Deserts: Indian Raids and the U.S.-Mexican War* (New Haven: Yale University Press, 2008). Pekka Hämäläinen, *The Comanche Empire* (New Haven: Yale University Press, 2008). Elizabeth Jameson et al., "If Not Now, When? Gender, Power, and the Decolonization of Western History," *Pacific Historical Review* 79:4 (November 2010), 573–628.

11. David Roediger, *The Wages of Whiteness: Race and the Making of the American Working Class* (New York: Verso, 1991). Ian Haney López, *White by Law: The Legal Construction of Race* (New York: New York University Press, 2006).

12. Harjo, "Returning from the Enemy," 75, 77. Coll Peter Thrush and Robert H. Keller Jr., "'I See What I Have Done': The Life and Murder Trial of Xwelas, a S'Klallam Woman," in *Writing the Range: Race, Class, and Culture in the Women's West,* ed. Elizabeth Jameson and Susan Armitage (Norman: University of Oklahoma Press, 1997), 173. Lillian Schlissel, Vicki L. Ruiz, and Janice Monk, eds., *Western Women: Their Land, Their Lives* (Albuquerque: University of New Mexico Press, 1988), 227. Genevieve Chato and Christine Conte, "The Legal Rights of American Indian Women," in *Western Women: Their Land, Their Lives* (Albuquerque: University of New Mexico Press, 1988), 229–257.

13. Amnesty International, *Maze of Injustice: The Failure to Protect Indigenous Women from Sexual Violence in the USA* (London: Amnesty International, 2007). Federal responses to Indian women's susceptibility to violence can be found online through the Department of Justice: www.ovw.usdoj.gov/tribal.html (accessed May 22, 2012). Sarah Deer, "Decolonizing Rape Law: A Native Feminist Synthesis of Safety and Sovereignty," *Wicazo Sa Review* 24:2 (Fall 2009), 149–167.

14. Harjo, "Returning from the Enemy," 75, 77. Wilkins, *American Indian Sovereignty and the U.S. Supreme Court,* 20–21. Kristen A. Carpenter, "Interpretive Sovereignty: A Research Agenda," *American Indian Law Review* 33:1 (2008–2009), 111–152.

15. Alexandra Harmon, "Coast Salish History," in *Be of Good Mind: Essays on the Coast Salish,* ed. Bruce Granville Miller (Vancouver: University of British Columbia Press, 2007), 30–54, 33. Giovanni Levi, "On Microhistory," in *New Perspectives on Historical Writing,* ed. Peter Burke (Cambridge: Polity, 2001), 2nd ed., 97–120, 101. James Brooks, Christopher R. N. DeCorse, and John Walton, eds., *Small Worlds: Method, Meaning, and Narrative in Microhistory* (Santa Fe, N.M.: School for Advanced Research Press, 2008). Richard D. Brown, "Microhistory and the Post-Modern Challenge," *Journal of the Early Republic* 23:1 (Spring 2003), 1–20. Jill Lepore, "Historians Who Love Too Much: Reflections on Microhistory and Biography," *Journal of American History* 88:1 (June 2001), 129–144. Natalie Zemon Davis, *Women on the Margins: Three Seventeenth-Century Lives* (Cambridge: Harvard University Press, 1995). Carlo Ginzberg, *The Cheese and the Worms: The Cosmos of a Sixteenth-Century Miller* (Baltimore: Johns Hopkins University Press, 1980). Paige Raibmon, "Unmaking Native Space: A Genealogy of Indian Policy, Settler Practice, and the Microtechniques of Dispossession," in *The Power of Promises: Rethinking Indian Treaties in the Pacific Northwest,* ed. Alexandra Harmon (Seattle: University of Washington Press, 2008), 56–85. Laurel Thatcher Ulrich, *A Midwife's Tale: The Live of Martha Ballard, Based on Her Diary, 1785–1812* (New York: Knopf, 1990). David Sweet and Gary Nash, *Struggle and Survival in Colonial America* (Berkeley: University of California Press, 1982).

16. Loretta Fowler, *Wives and Husbands: Gender and Age in Southern Arapaho History* (Norman: University of Oklahoma Press, 2010).

17. James F. Brooks, *Captives and Cousins: Slavery, Kinship, and Community in the Southwest Borderlands* (Chapel Hill: University of North Carolina Press, 2002).

18. Robert E. Ficken, *Washington Territory* (Pullman: Washington State University Press, 2002). John A. Hemphill and Robert C. Cumbow, *Westpointers and Early Washington* (Seattle: West Point Society of Puget Sound, 1992). Sherry L. Smith, *The View from Officers' Row: Army Perceptions of Western Indians* (Tucson: University of Arizona Press, 1995, 1990). Martha Summerhayes, *Vanished Arizona: Recollections of the Army Life of a New England Woman* (Lincoln: University of Nebraska Press, 1979). Andrew Wallace, "Fort Whipple in the Days of the Empire," *The Smoke Signal* 26 (Fall 1972), 113–140.

19. Robert E. Ficken, *Unsettled Boundaries: Fraser Gold and the British-American Northwest* (Pullman: Washington State University Press, 2003). Pauline Henson, *Founding a Wilderness Capital: Prescott, A.T., 1864* (Flagstaff, Ariz.: Northland Press, 1965). Daniel P. Marshall, "No Parallel: American Miner-Soldiers at War with the Nlaka'pamux of the Canadian West," in *Parallel Destinies: Canadian-American Relations West of the Rockies,* ed. John M. Findlay and Ken S. Coates (Seattle: University of Washington Press, 2002), 31–79.

20. Brad Asher, *Beyond the Reservation: Indians, Settlers, and the Law in Washington Territory, 1853–1889* (Norman: University of Oklahoma Press, 1999). Timothy Braatz, *Surviving Conquest: A History of the Yavapai Peoples* (Lincoln: University of Nebraska Press, 2003). Andrew H. Fisher, *Shadow Tribe: The Making of Columbia River Indian Identity* (Seattle: University of Washington Press, 2010). Alexandra Harmon, *Indians in the Making: Ethnic Relations and Indian Identities Around Puget Sound* (Berkeley: University of California Press, 1998). Eric Meeks, *Border Citizens: The Making of Indians, Mexicans, and Anglos in Arizona* (Austin: University of Texas Press, 2007). Paige Raibmon, *Authentic Indians: Episodes of Encounter from the Late-Nineteenth-Century Northwest Coast* (Durham, N.C.: Duke University Press, 2005). Jeffrey P. Shepherd, *We Are an Indian Nation: A History of the Hualapai Nation* (Tucson: University of Arizona Press, 2010). Margaret D. Jacobs, *White Mother to a Dark Race: Settler Colonialism, Maternalism, and the Removal of Indigenous Children in the American West and Australia, 1880–1940* (Lincoln: University of Nebraska Press, 2009).

21. Chávez-García, *Negotiating Conquest.* Susan Gray, *Lines of Descent: Family Stories from the North Country* (Chapel Hill: University of North Carolina Press, forthcoming). Catherine Denial, *Making Marriage: Husbands, Wives, and the American State in Dakota and Ojibwe Country* (St. Paul: Minnesota Historical Society Press, 2013).

22. Davis, *Women on the Margins.* Martha Hodes, *The Sea Captain's Wife: A True Story of Love, Race, and War in the Nineteenth Century* (New York: Norton, 2006). Hayden White, *Metahistory: The Historical Imagination in Nineteenth-Century Europe* (Baltimore: Johns Hopkins University Press, 1973). Kerwin Lee Klein, *Frontiers of Historical Imagination: Narrating the European Conquest of Native America, 1890–1990* (Berkeley: University of California Press, 1997).

23. Harjo, "Returning from the Enemy," 75, 77.

24. These hundreds of other women appear in legal records maintained in Arizona and Washington's state archives and in the legal records available through the RG 75 Records of the Bureau of Indian Affairs and RG 21 Records of District Courts of the United States that the author has exhaustively searched at the National Archives and Records Administration (NARA) regional branches in Riverside, formerly in Laguna Niguel, and in Seattle. The concentration of this study on Native women's engagement with local and state legal regimes resulted in a focus on the material available primarily in state archives with limited use of federal archival material.

25. Katrina Jagodinsky, "'I'm in Family Way': Guarding Indigenous Women's Children in Washington Territory," *American Indian Quarterly* 37:2 (Spring 2013), 160–177; and "Territorial Bonds: Indenture and Affection in Intercultural Arizona, 1864–1894," in *On the Borders of Love and Power: Families and Kinship in the Intercultural American West,* ed. David Wallace Adams and Crista DeLuzio (Berkeley: University of California Press, 2012), 380–412.

26. Two commendable exceptions to this trend include Brad Asher, *Beyond the Reservation: Indians, Settlers, and the Law in Washington Territory* and Deborah A. Rosen, *American Indians and State Law: Sovereignty, Race, and Citizenship, 1790–1880* (Lincoln: University of Nebraska Press, 2007).

27. Quintin Hoare and Geoffrey Nowell Smith, *Selections from the Prison Notebooks of Antonia Gramsci* (New York: International, 1971).

28. Robert J. C. Young, *Colonial Desire: Hybridity in Theory, Culture, and Race* (New York: Routledge, 1995), 162.

29. Antonia I. Castaneda, "Women of Color and the Rewriting of Western History: The Discourse, Politics, and Decolonization of History," *Pacific Historical Review* 61:4 (November 1992), 501–533. Kimberlé Crenshaw et al., *Critical Race Theory: The Key Writings That Formed the Movement* (New York: New Press, 1995). Richard Delgado and Jean Stefanic, *Critical Race Theory: An Introduction* (New York: New York University Press, 2001). Micaela Di Leonardo, *Gender at the Crossroads of Knowledge: Feminist Anthropology in the Postmodern Era* (Berkeley: University of California Press, 1991). López, *White by Law.*

30. Devon A. Mihesuah, "Commonality of Difference: American Indian Women and History," *American Indian Quarterly* 20:1 (Winter 1996), 15–27.

31. Benjamin H. Johnson and Andrew R. Graybill, eds., *Bridging National Borders in North America: Transnational and Comparative Histories* (Durham, N.C.: Duke University Press, 2010), 4.

32. The terms *métis* and *mestizo* are used throughout the text interchangeably with "mixed-race" to designate persons with Indigenous and European or Euro-American backgrounds. As used here, *métis* should not be read as a specifically French and Indian racial mixture or as reference to the Métis people formally recognized by the Canadian government; *mestizo* does not imply Mexican nationality, although I generally use *métis* in chapters based in the Pacific Northwest and *mestizo* to describe mixed-race persons in the Sonoran Southwest, since these terms have developed historical regional significance. I also refer to Americans, Mexicans, and Indigenous actors in this book distinctively: I do so to emphasize that all three

of these terms are simultaneously racial and national categories in the period between 1854 and 1946 (and arguably still are today). The conflation of whiteness and citizen is intentional in my usage of the term "American" in some contexts in the narrative, as is the racialization of Mexican and Indigenous Americans in the contextual exclusion of those racial groups from the category of "American." Although the Treaty of Guadalupe Hidalgo granted citizenship to Mexicans remaining in the United States after 1848, few Spanish-speaking Mexicans achieved equal status in the eyes of white Americans at the time. As for the Native people featured in this book, citizenship came only after 1924 and even then proved limited for most and unwanted for some. Distinguishing "Indigenous" from "American" not only highlights the disenfranchisement of Native people in U.S. history; it also emphasizes that "Indian" is a political as well as racial category; when Native people became American citizens, they maintained political distinction as tribal members. All of this is to say that my usage of "American," "Mexican," and "Indigenous" throughout the book is meant to expose the hierarchies that separated these groups, but not to obscure the efforts of marginalized groups to claim U.S. citizenship at the turn of the twentieth century. For histories that emphasize Indigenous women as cultural and political border-dwellers in contemporary and colonial contexts, see Gloria Anzaldúa, *Borderlands/La Frontera: The New Mestiza* (San Francisco: Spinsters/Aunt Lute, 1987). Martha Hodes, *Sex, Love, Race: Crossing Boundaries in North American History* (New York: New York University Press, 1999). Elizabeth Jameson and Sheila McManus, eds., *One Step Over the Line: Toward a History of Women in the North American Wests* (Edmonton: University of Alberta Press, 2008). Ann Laura Stoler, *Carnal Knowledge and Imperial Power: Race and the Intimate in Colonial Rule* (Berkeley: University of California Press, 2002).

33. Mary L. Dudziak and Leti Volpp, "Introduction, Legal Borderlands: Law and the Construction of American Borders," special issue, *American Quarterly* 57:3 (September 2005), 593–610.

34. Gray H. Whaley, *Oregon and the Collapse of Illahee: U.S. Empire and the Transformation of an Indigenous World, 1792–1859* (Chapel Hill: University of North Carolina Press, 2010). David A. Chang, "Borderlands in a World at Sea: Concow Indians, Native Hawaiians, and South Chinese in Indigenous, Global, and National Spaces," *Journal of American History* 98:2 (2011), 384–403. Natale A. Zappia, *Traders and Raiders: The Indigenous World of the Colorado Basin, 1540–1859* (Chapel Hill: University of North Carolina Press, 2014), and "Indigenous Borderlands: Livestock, Captivity, and Power in the Far West," *Pacific Historical Review* 81:2 (May 2012), 193–220. Joshua Reid, *The Sea Is My Country: The Maritime World of the Makah* (New Haven: Yale University Press, 2015). Richard White, *The Middle Ground: Indians, Empires, and Republics in the Great Lakes Region, 1650–1815* (New York: Cambridge University Press, 1991). Colin Calloway, *One Vast Winter Count: The Native American West Before Lewis and Clark* (Lincoln: University of Nebraska Press, 2003). Hämäläinen, *The Comanche Empire.*

35. Anzaldúa, *Borderlands.*

36. Norma Basch, "Marriage and Domestic Relations," and Barbara Young Welke, "Law, Personhood, and Citizenship in the Long Nineteenth Century: The

Borders of Belonging," in *The Cambridge History of Law in America: The Long Nineteenth Century, 1789–1920,* ed. Michael Grossberg and Christopher Tomlins (New York: Cambridge University Press, 2008), 2:245–279, 345–386. E. Wayne Carp, ed., *Adoption in America: Historical Perspectives* (Ann Arbor: University of Michigan Press, 2002). Michael Grossberg, *Governing the Hearth: Law and the Family in Nineteenth-Century America* (Chapel Hill: University of North Carolina Press, 1985). Jacquelyn Dowd Hall et al., *Like a Family: The Making of a Southern Cotton Mill World* (Chapel Hill: University of North Carolina Press, 1987), particularly 152–153. Leslie J. Harris, "Law as Father: Metaphors of Family in Nineteenth-Century Law," *Communication Studies* 61:5 (2010), 526–542. David Wallace Adams and Crista DeLuzio, eds., *On the Borders of Love and Power: Families and Kinship in the Intercultural American Southwest* (Berkeley: University of California Press, 2012). Anne F. Hyde, *Empires, Nations, and Families: A History of the North American West, 1800–1860* (Lincoln: University of Nebraska Press, 2011).

37. Penelope Edmonds, *Urbanizing Frontiers: Indigenous Peoples and Settlers in 19th-Century Pacific Rim Cities* (Vancouver: University of British Columbia Press, 2010). Erin Hogan Fouberg, "Understanding Space, Understanding Citizenship," *Journal of Geography* 101 (2002), 81–85. Bettina Koschade and Evelyn Peters, "Algonquin Notions of Jurisdiction: Inserting Indigenous Voices into Legal Spaces," *Geografiska Annaler:* Series B, *Human Geography* 88:3 (September 2006), 299–310. Mar and Edmonds, eds., *Making Settler Colonial Space*. Sherene H. Razack, ed., *Race, Space, and the Law: Unmapping a White Settler Society* (Toronto: Between the Lines, 2002). Raibmon, "Unmaking Native Space," 56–85. Jane Samson, ed., *The Pacific World: Lands, Peoples and History of the Pacific, 1500–1900,* vol. 8: *British Imperial Strategies in the Pacific, 1750–1900* (Burlington, Vt.: Ashgate, 2003). Wendy S. Shaw, R. D. K. Herman, and G. Rebecca Dobbs, "Encountering Indigeneity: Re-Imagining and Decolonizing Geography," *Geografiska Annaler:* Series B, *Human Geography* 88:3 (September 2006), 267–276. Edward W. Soja, *Postmodern Geographies: The Reassertion of Space in Critical Social Theory* (New York: Verso, 1989).

38. Thrush and Keller, "'I See What I Have Done,'" 172–187. Chávez-García, *Negotiating Conquest*. Rose Stremlau, *Cherokee Family: Kinship and the Allotment of an Indigenous Nation* (Chapel Hill: University of North Carolina Press, 2011).

39. Harjo, "Returning from the Enemy," 5, 77.

40. Young, *Colonial Desire,* 162.

41. Ibid.

42. Walter Johnson, "On Agency," *Journal of Social History* 37:1 (2003), 113–124.

43 Harjo, "Returning from the Enemy," 75, 77.

Chapter 2. Lucía Martínez and the "Putative Father"

1. Federal and Indian census data gathered for this project has been accessed through Ancestry.com and can be reviewed through both the name search and browsing features. 1880 U.S. Census, Arizona Territory.

2. 1880 U.S. Census, Arizona Territory. MS 296 Catholic Church, Diocese of Tucson Records, 1721–1957, vol. 12: Yuma—Church of the Immaculate Conception, 1866–1880, p. 75, baptismal record 768, September 10, 1877. Robert Nelson, *Images of America: Early Yuma* (Charleston: Arcadia, 2006), 59, 89. Frank Love, *A Prayer, A Poultice, A Pall: Life and Death in Yuma, Arizona Territory, 1854–1893* (private press, 1994), 19. Robert P. Broadwater, *General George H. Thomas: A Biography of the Union's "Rock of Chickamauga"* (Jefferson, N.C.: McFarland, 2009), 39.

3. Sources that did not name Lucía specifically, but seem to refer to her, alternately described her as an "Apache captive" or "Mexican," both of which might have made sense to the contemporary authors since Lucía had lived among her Apache captors, was from Sonora, and likely spoke more Spanish than English.

4. Edward H. Spicer, *The Yaquis: A Cultural History* (Tucson: University of Arizona Press, 1980), 125–127.

5. Larry Evers and Felipe S. Molina, *Yaqui Deer Songs, Maso Bwikam: A Native American Poetry*, 3rd ed. (Tucson: University of Arizona Press, 1993), 7, 18, 37, 44, 45, 47, 54–55, 73, 194.

6. Spicer, *The Yaquis*, 60, 120, 137, 153.

7. Rosalio Moisés, Jane Holden Kelley, and William Curry Holden, *A Yaqui Life: The Personal Chronicle of a Yaqui Indian* (Lincoln: University of Nebraska Press, 1971) 17, 21–24. Kirstin C. Erickson, *Yaqui Homeland and Homeplace: The Everyday Production of Ethnic Identity* (Tucson: University of Arizona Press, 2008), 48–49.

8. Moisés et al., *A Yaqui Life*, 3, 17, 40. Spicer, *The Yaquis*, 153, 160.

9. Erickson, *Yaqui Homeland and Homeplace*, 42.

10. David Delgado Shorter, "Yoeme to Yaqui," in *Vachiam Eecha: Planting the Seeds*, http://hemi.nyu.edu/cuaderno/yoeme/content.html (accessed April 20, 2010).

11. Ned Blackhawk, *Violence over the Land: Indians and Empires in the Early American West* (Cambridge: Harvard University Press, 2006). James F. Brooks, *Captives and Cousins: Slavery, Kinship, and Community in the Southwest Borderlands* (Chapel Hill: University of North Carolina Press, 2002). Pekka Hämäläinen, *The Comanche Empire* (New Haven: Yale University Press, 2008). Katrina Jagodinsky, "Territorial Bonds: Indenture and Affection in Intercultural Arizona, 1864–1894," in *On the Borders of Love and Power: Families and Kinship in the Intercultural American West*, ed. David Wallace Adams and Crista DeLuzio (Berkeley: University of California Press, 2012), 380–412. Margot Mifflin, *The Blue Tattoo: The Life of Olive Oatman* (Lincoln: University of Nebraska Press, 2009). Victoria Smith, *Captive Arizona, 1851–1900* (Lincoln: University of Nebraska Press, 2009).

12. Felipe Molina and Larry Evers, *Seyewailo, The Flower World: Yaqui Deer Songs* (Tucson: University of Arizona Radio-TV-Film Bureau, 1978).

13. Moisés et al., *A Yaqui Life*, 10.

14. Anne F. Hyde, *Empires, Nations, and Families: A History of the North American West, 1800–1860* (Lincoln: University of Nebraska Press, 2011).

15. *Phoenix Herald,* July 2, 1879, 2: 2, 3, King S. Woolsey Biographical File, Benjamin Sacks Collection of the American West, Arizona Historical Foundation (AHF).

16. Robert E. May, *Manifest Destiny's Underworld: Filibustering in Antebellum America* (Chapel Hill: University of North Carolina Press, 2002), xiii, 14–16, 20–36, 39, 87.

17. John S. Goff, *King S. Woolsey* (Cave Creek, Ariz.: Black Mountain, 1981), 2.

18. Colonel (Ret.) John L. Johnson, ed., "Arizona Army National Guard: The First One Hundred Years," *Pamphlet No. 870–5* (Phoenix, Ariz.: 180th Field Artillery Regiment Association, 2002), 12.

19. King Woolsey Papers, CM MSM 640, Hayden Arizona Collection, Department of Archives and Special Collections, Arizona State University Libraries. Karl Jacoby, *Shadows at Dawn: A Borderlands Massacre and the Violence of History* (New York: Penguin, 2008).

20. King Woolsey Papers.

21. MS 93 Brichta, Augustus, box 1, folder 2, "Reminiscences of an Old Pioneer," 10, Arizona State Historical Society, Tucson (ASHS).

22. "Letter from Lieutenant Colonel King S. Woolsey, Arizona Volunteers, to General James H. Carleton, Department of New Mexico and Arizona, March 29, 1864," King Woolsey Papers; emphasis in original.

23. Karl Jacoby, "'The Broad Platform of Extermination': Nature and Violence in the Nineteenth-Century North American Borderlands," *Journal of Genocide Research* 10:2 (June 2008), 249–267.

24. Thomas Edwin Farish, *History of Arizona* (San Francisco: Filmer Brothers Electrotype, 1915–1918), 3:277.

25. Charles D. Poston, *Building a State in Apache Land: The Story of Arizona's Founding Told by Arizona's Founder* (Tempe, Ariz.: Aztec, 1963), 117.

26. Goff, *King S. Woolsey,* 52.

27. Ibid., 48.

28. Daniel Ellis Conner, *Joseph Reddeford Walker and the Arizona Adventure* (Norman: University of Oklahoma Press, 1956), 181–184. These accounts contradict each other in ways that reflect the romanticization of American men's dominance over Indian women during this period. Subsequent depictions of Woolsey and Martínez's relationship marked the girl as Apache or Mexican, despite Woolsey's identification of her as Yaqui.

29. George H. Kelly, *Legislative History: Arizona, 1864–1912* (Phoenix: Manufacturing Stationers, 1926), 1–2. Goff, *King S. Woolsey,* 23, 57.

30. Kelly, *Legislative History,* 6.

31. Ibid., 9.

32. Mifflin, *The Blue Tattoo.*

33. Brooks, *Captives and Cousins.* Juliana Barr, "From Captives to Slaves: Commodifying Indian Women in the Borderlands," *Journal of American History* 92:1 (June 2005), 19–46. Albert Hurtado, "'Hardly a Farm House—a Kitchen

Without Them': Indian and White Households on the California Borderland Frontier in 1860," *Western Historical Quarterly* 13:3 (July 1982), 245–270. Jagodinsky, "Territorial Bonds," 380–412. Mifflin, *The Blue Tattoo*. Smith, *Captive Arizona*.

34. William T. Howell, *Howell Code Adopted by the First Legislative Assembly of the Territory of Arizona, 1864* (Prescott: Office of the Arizona Miner, 1865). Amy S. Greenberg, *Manifest Manhood and the Antebellum American Empire* (New York: Cambridge University Press, 2005), 12–13.

35. Howard R. Lamar, *The Far Southwest, 1846–1912: A Territorial History* (Albuquerque: University of New Mexico Press, 2000), 380, 384–385.

36. John S. Goff, "William T. Howell and the Howell Code of Arizona," *The American Journal of Legal History* 11:3 (July, 1967), 221–233.

37. Jagodinsky, "Territorial Bonds," 380–412.

38. The native-born white population in 1864 Arizona was not over 600 and ethnic Mexicans made Arizona's white population more like 6,500, a slim majority over the territory's 4,000 "civilized" Indians; these demographics threatened Arizona's prospects for statehood. Farish, *History of Arizona* 2:322–323. Katherine Benton-Cohen, *Borderline Americans: Racial Division and Labor War in the Arizona Borderlands* (Cambridge: Harvard University Press, 2009), 7–16.

39. Brooks, *Captives and Cousins*. Albert Hurtado, *Intimate Frontiers: Sex, Gender and Culture in Old California* (Albuquerque: University of New Mexico Press, 1999). Jacoby, *Shadows at Dawn*.

40. "Offences Against the Persons of Individuals," ch. 10, 5th div., sec. 47, Howell Code, 1865 Ariz. Terr. Sess. Laws, 54. "Of Marriages," ch. 30, sec. 7, Howell Code, 1865 Ariz. Terr. Sess. Laws, 231. Leslie K. Dunlap, "The Reform of Rape Law and the Problem of White Men: Age of Consent Campaigns in the South, 1885–1910," in *Sex, Love, Race: Crossing Boundaries in North American History*, ed. Martha Hodes (New York: New York University Press, 1999), 352–372.

41. "Who May Be a Witness in a Criminal Case," art. 10, 3rd div., sec. 14, Howell Code, 1865 Ariz. Terr. Sess. Laws, 50. "Offences Against the Persons of Individuals," art. 10, 5th div., secs. 45, 47, Howell Code, 1865 Ariz. Terr. Sess. Laws, 53–54. "Of Witnesses, and of the Manner of Obtaining Evidence of Witnesses," art. 48, sec. 396, Howell Code, 1865 Ariz. Terr. Sess. Laws, 354. "Who May Be a Witness in Criminal Cases," art. 10, 3rd div., sec. 14, 1871 Ariz. Terr. Sess. Laws, 72. "Witnesses and the Mode of Enforcing Their Attendance," pt. 10: Evidence, ch. 1, sec. 1677, 1913 Revised Statutes of Arizona, 588. *Fernandez v. State of Arizona* (1914), Case No. 360, Arizona Court of Appeals, Division One; Criminal Files, Briefs and Records, Arizona State Library, Archives and Public Records (ASLAPR); this case is discussed at length in the chapter on Dinah Foote Hood, and in Katrina Jagodinsky, "A Testament to Power: Mary Woolsey and Dolores Rodriguez as Trial Witnesses in Arizona's Early Statehood," *Western Legal History* 26:1 and 2 (2013), 69–96.

42. "Of Marriages," art. 30, sec. 3, Howell Code, 1865 Ariz. Terr. Sess. Laws, 230.

43. Martha Menchaca, "Chicano Indianism: A Historical Account of Racial Repression in the United States," *American Ethnologist* 20:3 (1993), 583–603. Peggy Pascoe, "Race, Gender, and Intercultural Relations: The Case of Interracial Marriage," *Frontiers: A Journal of Women Studies* 12:1 (1991), 5–18.

44. Norma Basch, "Marriage and Domestic Relations," in *The Cambridge History of Law in America: The Long Nineteenth Century, 1789–1920*, ed. Michael Grossberg and Christopher Tomlins (New York: Cambridge University Press, 2008), 2:245–279.

45. Kathleen Brown, *Good Wives, Nasty Wenches, and Anxious Patriarchs: Gender, Race, and Power in Colonial Virginia* (Chapel Hill: University of North Carolina Press, 1996). Jennifer Morgan, *Laboring Women: Reproduction and Gender in New World Slavery* (Philadelphia: University of Pennsylvania Press, 2004). Joshua K. Rothman, *Notorious in the Neighborhood: Sex and Families Across the Color Line in Virginia, 1787–1861* (Chapel Hill: University of North Carolina Press, 2003). Peter Wallenstein, *"Tell the Court I Love My Wife": Race, Marriage, and Law—An American History* (New York: Palgrave Macmillan, 2002).

46. Peggy Pascoe, *What Comes Naturally: Miscegenation Law and the Making of Race in America* (New York: Oxford University Press, 2009). Ariela Gross, *What Blood Won't Tell: A History of Race on Trial in America* (Cambridge: Harvard University Press, 2010).

47. "Of the Support of Minor Indians," art. 56, sec. 14–16, Howell Code, 1865 Ariz. Terr. Sess. Laws, 428.

48. Sondra Jones, "'Redeeming the Indian': The Enslavement of Indian Children in New Mexico and Utah," *Utah Historical Quarterly* 67:3 (1999), 220–224. Michael Magliari, "Free Soil, Unfree Labor: Cave Johnson Couts and the Binding of Indian Workers in California, 1850–1867," *The Pacific Historical Review* 73:3 (August 2004), 349–389.

49. Stacey Leigh Smith, *Freedom's Frontier: California and the Struggle over Unfree Labor, Emancipation, and Reconstruction* (Chapel Hill: University of North Carolina Press, 2013). "An Act to Provide for the Adoption of Children, Approved February 14, 1873," ch. 20, 1877 Ariz. Terr. Sess. Laws, 315. "Repeal of Laws, Rights, Preserved Construction of Revised Statutes," ch. 1, sec. 1, 1887 Ariz. Terr. Sess. Laws, 568.

50. Smith, *Captive Arizona*.

51. Morgan, *Laboring Women*.

52. Evelyn Nakano Glenn, "From Servitude to Service Work: Historical Continuities in the Racial Division of Paid Reproductive Labor," *Signs* 18:1 (Autumn 1992), 1.

53. Peter Boag, *Re-Dressing America's Frontier Past* (Berkeley: University of California Press, 2011) and *Same-Sex Affairs: Constructing and Controlling Homosexuality in the Pacific Northwest* (Berkeley: University of California Press, 2003). Pablo Mitchell, *West of Sex: Making Mexican America, 1900–1930* (Chicago: University of Chicago Press, 2012) and *Coyote Nation: Sexuality, Race, and Conquest in Modernizing New Mexico, 1880–1920* (Chicago: University of Chicago Press,

2005). Nayan Shah, *Stranger Intimacy: Contesting Race, Sexuality and the Law in the North American West* (Berkeley: University of California Press, 2012).

54. Goff, *King S. Woolsey*, 25. "Reminiscences of an Old Pioneer," 4.

55. John Nicolson, ed., *The Arizona of Joseph Pratt Allyn, Letters from a Pioneer Judge: Observations and Travels, 1863–1866* (Tucson: University of Arizona Press, 1974), 81. Justice Allyn's reference to a "Mrs. W" and her "Indian girl" are problematic, but do indicate that King Woolsey and his friends included racial distinctions to describe domestic and intimate relationships.

56. Morgan, *Laboring Women*. Kirsten Fischer, *Suspect Relations: Sex, Race, and Resistance in Colonial North Carolina* (Ithaca: Cornell University Press, 2002).

57. Moisés et al., *A Yaqui Life*, 17.

58. MS 296 Catholic Church, Diocese of Tucson Records, 1721–1957, vol. 12: Yuma—Church of the Immaculate Conception, 1866–1880, p. 75, baptismal record 768, September 10, 1877. Clara Woolsey Marron Death Certificate, State File No. 265, July 25, 1947; Arizona State Department of Health, Division of Vital Statistics.

59. *Arizona Miner* (Prescott), March 14, 1866, 3:1, King S. Woolsey Biographical File, Benjamin Sacks Collection, AHF.

60. *Arizona Miner* (Prescott), May 23, 1866, 3:1, King S. Woolsey Biographical File, AHF.

61. *Arizona Miner* (Prescott), June 1, 1867, 3:4; June 15, 1867, 4:3; September 21, 1867, 2:3, King S. Woolsey Biographical File, AHF.

62. *Arizona Miner* (Prescott), August 7, 1869, 3:1, King S. Woolsey Biographical File, AHF.

63. *Arizona Miner* (Prescott), February 8, 1868, 3:2, King S. Woolsey Biographical File, AHF.

64. MS 296 Catholic Church, Diocese of Tucson Records, 1721–1957, vol. 12: Yuma—Church of the Immaculate Conception, 1866–1880, p. 75, baptismal record 769, September 11, 1877.

65. *San Diego Union*, October 27, 1870, 1:7, King S. Woolsey Biographical File, AHF.

66. *San Diego Union*, November 24, 1870, 2:3, King S. Woolsey, Arizona Pioneer Biographies, Arizona Historical Foundation (AHF) Microfilm Collection, 783.

67. *Arizona Sentinel* (Yuma), October 5, 1878, 2:2, King S. Woolsey Biographical File, AHF.

68. Greenberg, *Manifest Manhood*.

69. *Weekly Arizona Miner* (Prescott), October 18, 1878, 2:4, King S. Woolsey Biographical File, AHF.

70. *Arizona Enterprise* (Florence), August 10, 1878, 2:4, King S. Woolsey Biographical File, AHF.

71. Goff, *King S. Woolsey*, 20. Book of Marriages, Maricopa County, Book 1A, 127, Arizona State Library, Archives and Public Records (ASLAPR).

72. Spicer, *The Yaquis*, 144–160, 284. Clifford E. Trafzer, *Yuma: Frontier Crossing of the Far Southwest* (Wichita: Western Heritage Press, 1980).

73. Evers and Molina, *Yaqui Deer Songs, Maso Bwikam*, 194.

74. Juan Silverio and Jaime Leon, *Testimonio de una Mujer Yaqui* (Hermosillo: Conaculta, 2000). Thanks to Andrew Offenburger for sharing this reference.

75. Trafzer, *Yuma: Frontier Crossing*. Moisés et al., *A Yaqui Life*, 20. Spicer, *The Yaquis*, 241, 284.

76. Not relevant to the discussion here, but perhaps of interest to readers is a dispute over Apache children named Guadalupe and Bonifacio Woolsey between Woolsey's friend A. T. Ammerman, named as a codefendant in Lucía's probate claim, and Jack Swilling, another prominent Maricopa County neighbor. Those cases remain difficult to explain. They are discussed in my anthology chapter, Jagodinsky, "Territorial Bonds: Indenture and Affection in Intercultural Arizona," in *On the Borders of Love and Power: Families and Kinship in the Intercultural American West* (Berkeley: University of California Press, 2012), 380–412. Possible explanations are explored later in this chapter as well.

77. James M. Murphy, *Laws, Courts, and Lawyers: Through the Years in Arizona* (Tucson: University of Arizona Press, 1970), 23.

78. Kelly, *Legislative History*, 49. *Lucía Martínez v. Thomas Barnum, K. S. Woolsey, John Ammerman, Mrs. Ammerman*, Maricopa County Superior Court of Probate Bonds (1871), 6–8, ASLAPR. Marcus D. Dobbins, *Memorial and Affidavits Showing Outrages Perpetrated by the Apache Indians, in the Territory of Arizona, for the years 1869 and 1870* (San Francisco: Francis and Valentine, 1871). Jacoby, *Shadows at Dawn*.

79. Basch, "Marriage and Domestic Relations," 245–279.

80. Mark E. Neely Jr., *The Fate of Liberty: Abraham Lincoln and Civil Liberties* (New York: Oxford University Press, 1991), xiv.

81. Lamar, *The Far Southwest*, 6.

82. William M. Wiecek, "The Great Writ and Reconstruction: The Habeas Corpus Act of 1867," in *Civil Rights in American History: Major Historical Interpretations*, ed. Kermit L. Hall (New York: Garland, 1987), 760.

83. David E. Wilkins, "Federal Policy, Western Movement, and Consequences for Indigenous People, 1790–1920," in *The Cambridge History of Law in America: The Long Nineteenth Century, 1789–1920*, ed. Michael Grossberg and Christopher Tomlins (New York: Cambridge University Press, 2008), 2:204–244.

84. Maricopa County Superior Court of Probate Bonds, 1871, p. 7, ASLAPR.

85. *Lucía Martínez v. Thomas Barnum, K. S. Woolsey, John Ammerman, Mrs. Ammerman*, 1871. Farish, *History of Arizona* 1:91, 139. Alsap, Barnum, and Swilling were partners in the Phoenix Ditch Company. *Weekly Arizona Miner* (Prescott), August 8, 1870, 3:3, King S. Woolsey Biographical File, AHF.

86. Maricopa County Superior Court of Probate Bonds, 1871, 8, ASLAPR.

87. Ibid., 15–17.

88. E. Wayne Carp, ed., *Adoption in America: Historical Perspectives* (Ann Arbor: University of Michigan Press, 2002), 5.

89. Murphy, *Laws, Courts, and Lawyers,* 17. Lamar, *The Far Southwest,* 384.

90. The blunted language and blundered protocol observed in Alsap's courtroom means that historians would be hard-pressed to find similar disputes over illegitimate Indigenous children—but not because they do not exist. For a discussion of race-neutral language in racially discriminatory laws, see Barbara Young Welke, "Law, Personhood, and Citizenship in the Long Nineteenth Century: The Borders of Belonging," in *The Cambridge History of Law in America: The Long Nineteenth Century, 1789–1920,* ed. Michael Grossberg and Christopher Tomlins (New York: Cambridge University Press, 2008), 2:345–386.

91. MS 296 Catholic Church, Diocese of Tucson Records, 1721–1957, vol. 12: Yuma—Church of the Immaculate Conception, 1866–1880, baptismal records 768 and 769, September 10, 1877. Lucía gave 1866 and 1869 as their birth years, indicating that she was twelve when she bore Clara and fifteen when she delivered Concepción. Despite interest in the importance of *compadrazgo* among southwestern women in the nineteenth century, no data on Lucía's comadres could be found. Erickson, *Yaqui Homeland and Homeplace,* 116–117. Erika Perez, "Colonial Intimacies: Interethnic Kinship, Sexuality, and Marriage in Southern California, 1769–1885" (Ph.D. diss., University of California–Los Angeles, 2010).

92. Editorial, *Arizona Sentinel* (Yuma), October 5, 1878, 2:2, King S. Woolsey Biographical File, AHF.

93. MS 296 Catholic Church, Diocese of Tucson Records, 1721–1957, vol. 12: Yuma—Church of the Immaculate Conception, 1866–1880, p. 75, baptismal record 769, September 11, 1877. 1880 U.S. Census, Arizona Territory.

94. Moisés et al., *A Yaqui Life,* xl–xlvi. Spicer, *The Yaquis,* 160. Erickson, *Yaqui Homeland and Homeplace,* 73–112.

95. *Salt River Herald* (Arizona), June 1, 1878, 2:1, King S. Woolsey Biographical File, AHF.

96. Marshall Trimble, *Roadside History of Arizona* (Mountain Press, 1986), 394, 396.

97. *Arizona Republican* (Phoenix), April 13, 1927, sec. 2, 1:4, King S. Woolsey Biographical File, AHF.

98. Interview with Mary Woolsey Baxter, ca. 1927, 3, King S. Woolsey Biographical File, AHF.

99. Goff, *Woolsey,* 19–20. Interview with Mary Woolsey Baxter, ca. 1927, 3, King S. Woolsey Biographical File, AHF.

100. *Weekly Arizona Miner* (Prescott), June 14, 1873, 1:4; *San Diego Union,* June 25, 1874, 2:9; *Weekly Arizona Miner* (Prescott), April 27, 1877, 1:3, King S. Woolsey Biographical File, AHF.

101. *Arizona Sentinel* (Yuma), July 18, 1874, 2:2, King S. Woolsey Biographical File, AHF.

102. *Arizona Citizen* (Tucson), April 10, 1875, 2:2, King S. Woolsey Biographical File, AHF.

103. Patricia Blaine, "Jose Maria Redondo: Yuma Pioneer and Entrepreneur, 1830–1878" (M.A. thesis: Arizona State University, 2003), 102. Blaine also notes that Redondo and other Mexican elites in Yuma hired Yaqui servants and laborers, indicating that Lucía might have found employment there rather easily.

104. *Arizona Sentinel* (Yuma), May 25, 1878, 2:1; *Arizona Enterprise* (Florence), May 11, 1878, 1:4, King S. Woolsey Biographical File, Arizona Historical Foundation (AHF).

105. Lamar, *The Far Southwest.* James E. Officer, *Arizona's Hispanic Perspective* (Tucson: University of Arizona Press, 1981).

106. Editorial, *Arizona Sentinel* (Yuma), October 5, 1878, 2:2, King S. Woolsey Biographical File, AHF.

107. King S. Woolsey Estate, Maricopa County Probate Case No. 32, 1879, 46–50, ASLAPR. 1880 U.S. Census, Arizona Territory.

108. Goff, *King S. Woolsey,* 73. *Phoenix Herald,* April 30, 1879, 3:1, King S. Woolsey Biographical File, AHF.

109. *Phoenix Herald,* July 2, 1879, 2:2, 3, King S. Woolsey Biographical File, AHF.

110. Robert Nelson, *Images of America: Early Yuma,* 52.

111. Ibid., 52, 91. The Martínez and Fitzgerald households are numbered 156 and 170 in the 1880 U.S. Census for District 13: Yuma, Yuma County, Arizona Territory.

112. Farish, *History of Arizona* 6:268–269. Maricopa County, Arizona Territorial Marriages Book 1, 11, ASLAPR.

113. Yuma County Board of Registers Bonds and Agreements, 1873, 1878, ASLAPR. David Neahr Biographical File, Benjamin Sacks Collection, AHF. King S. Woolsey Estate, Maricopa County Probate Case No. 32, 1879, 4–5, ASLAPR.

114. King S. Woolsey Estate, Maricopa County Probate Case No. 32, 1879, 20–21, 24–30, ASLAPR.

115. Ibid., 46–50.

116. Ibid., 15–19. "Of Title to Real Property by Descent," art. 26, sec. 2, Howell Code, 1865 Ariz. Terr. Sess. Laws, 183.

117. King S. Woolsey Estate, Maricopa County Probate Case No. 32, 1879, 16–17, ASLAPR.

118. Ibid., 18.

119. Case No. 37, Record Group (RG) 114, Yuma County Superior Court Probate Division and Maricopa County Probate Court Record Book (1871–1874), 575, RG 107, Maricopa County, Subgroup 8, Superior Court, ASLAPR. Only a handful of indentures have been found, though the author is inclined to believe that indenture records do not accurately reflect the numbers of minor Indians laboring in citizen households because white authority over Indian children often went unquestioned and undocumented. For the informal and frequent nature of Indigenous child removal among Arizona settler-colonists, see Smith, *Captive Arizona.*

120. *Arizona Miner* (Prescott), June 1, 1867, 3:4; June 15, 1867, 4:3; September 21, 1867, 2:3, King S. Woolsey Biographical File, AHF.

121. *Clara Woolsey et al. v. M. W. Kales, Administrator of King S. Woolsey Estate,* Maricopa County Superior Court Civil Case No. 146 (1880), RG 107, Maricopa County, Subgroup 8, Superior Court, Civil Cases No. 146, 1880–1881, film-file 4, ASLAPR.

122. Ibid.

123. Ibid.

124. Ibid.

125. *Phoenix Herald,* October 24, 1881, 4:1, King S. Woolsey Biographical File, AHF.

126. MS 296 Catholic Church, Diocese of Tucson Records, 1721–1957, vol. 12: Yuma—Church of the Immaculate Conception, 1866–1880, p. 75, baptismal record 768, September 10, 1877.

127. Death and birth certificates for Lucía Martínez's children and grandchildren are available online via http://genealogy.az.gov. It is in these documents that her descendants' preference for the Woolsey surname is evidenced.

128. Al Bates describes "Lucy" as Mexican, not Yaqui, and as the servant of Prescott residents John and Mary Dickerson until her "common-law marriage" to Woolsey. His evidence is culled from the remembrances of Yavapai County settlers that do not correspond to the legal and civil records used here. Bates's confusion is matched by those his works are based on, and is somewhat understandable given the significant number of adolescent and female captives circulating in territorial Arizona. Bates claims that "Lucy's" Indian identity was fabricated by Woolsey's widow so that she could protect her inheritance from illegitimate mixed-race heirs. Bates does not explain the other indications of Lucía's Indian identity that are cited throughout this chapter, and dismisses King Woolsey's own identification of Lucía as Yaqui with no explanation. For his sentimental depiction of Woolsey's "first wife," see "Lucy Martinez's Love Story, pt. 1," *Days Past,* April 6, 2013, and "Lucy Martinez's Love Story, pt. 2," *Days Past,* April 13, 2013, accessible at www.sharlot.org/library-archives.

Chapter 3. Nora Jewell "In Family Way"

1. *Territory of Washington v. James Smith,* Jefferson County, Washington Territory, 1880, Criminal Case 1088, Washington State Archive.

2. "Brief Local Items," *Puget Sound Weekly Argus* (Port Townsend), March 4, 1880, 5:1.

3. "Western Washington," *Spokane Times,* April 1, 1880, 4:1.

4. Brad Asher, *Beyond the Reservation: Indians, Settlers, and the Law in Washington Territory, 1853–1889* (Norman: University of Oklahoma Press, 1999). Andrew H. Fisher, *Shadow Tribe: The Making of Columbia River Indian Identity* (Seattle: University of Washington Press, 2010). Alexandra Harmon, *Indians in the Making: Ethnic Relations and Indian Identities Around Puget Sound* (Berkeley: University of California Press, 1998). Paige Raibmon, *Authentic Indians: Episodes of Encounter from the Late-Nineteenth-Century Northwest Coast* (Durham, N.C.: Duke University Press, 2005). Coll Thrush, *Native Seattle: Histories from the Crossing-*

Over Place (Seattle: University of Washington Press, 2007). Lissa K. Wadewitz, *The Nature of Borders: Salmon, Boundaries, and Bandits on the Salish Sea* (Seattle: University of Washington Press, 2012).

5. U.S. Census, 1880. Robert E. Ficken, *Washington Territory* (Pullman: Washington State University Press, 2002), 57–58. John A. Hemphill and Robert C. Cumbow, *Westpointers and Early Washington* (Seattle: West Point Society of Puget Sound, 1992), 186–196.

6. Julie K. Stein, *Exploring Coast Salish Prehistory: The Archaeology of San Juan Island* (Seattle: University of Washington Press, 2000). Mike Vouri, Julia Vouri, et al., *Images of America: San Juan Island* (Charleston: Arcadia, 2010), 9, 52, 54.

7. Lelah Jackson Edson, *The Fourth Corner: Highlights from the Early Northwest* (Bellingham: Whatcom Museum of History and Art, 1968), 106–115.

8. Scott Kaufman, *The Pig War: The United States, Britain, and the Balance of Power in the Pacific Northwest, 1846–1872* (Lanham, Md.: Lexington, 2004). Mike Vouri, *Outpost of Empire: The Royal Marines and the Joint Occupation of San Juan Island* (Seattle: Northwest Interpretive Association / University of Washington Press, 2004).

9. Joshua Reid, *The Sea Is My Country: The Maritime World of the Makah* (New Haven: Yale University Press, 2015).

10. 1870 U.S. Census. Coast Salish band identity is difficult to determine in the nineteenth-century record, and for women like Fanny and Ellen, who intermarried with white men and did not draw ethnohistorians' attention in the twentieth century, it is impossible to determine exactly which Salish bands they claimed. For excellent scholarship on the complexity of Salishan identity and their relationship to American, British, and Canadian governments during this period, see Penelope Edmonds, *Urbanizing Frontiers: Indigenous Peoples and Settlers in 19th-Century Pacific Rim Cities* (Vancouver: University of British Columbia Press, 2010). Alexandra Harmon, "Lines in Sand: Shifting Boundaries Between Indians and Non-Indians in the Puget Sound Region," *Western Historical Quarterly* 26:4 (Winter 1995), 429–453. Alexandra Harmon, ed., *The Power of Promises: Rethinking Indian Treaties in the Pacific Northwest* (Seattle: University of Washington Press, 2008). Bruce Granville Miller, ed., *Be of Good Mind: Essays on the Coast Salish* (Vancouver: University of British Columbia Press, 2007). Ann Nugent, ed., *Lummi Elders Speak* (Lynden, Wash.: Lynden Tribune, 1982), 70.

11. Notices of port business and traffic appeared weekly in the *Puget Sound Weekly Argus* (Port Townsend) during this period. Robert E. Ficken, *Unsettled Boundaries: Fraser Gold and the British-American Northwest* (Pullman: Washington State University Press, 2003). Daniel P. Marshall, "No Parallel: American Miner-Soldiers at War with the Nlaka'pamux of the Canadian West," in *Parallel Destinies: Canadian-American Relations West of the Rockies*, ed. John M. Findlay and Ken S. Coates (Seattle: University of Washington Press, 2002), 31–79.

12. Victoria Freeman, "Attitudes Toward 'Miscegenation' in Canada, the United States, New Zealand, and Australia, 1860–1914," *Native Studies Review* 16:1 (2005), 41–69. Hemphill and Cumbow, *Westpointers and Early Washington*,

74-75. Mary-Ellen Kelm and Lorna Townsend, eds., *In the Days of Our Grand-mothers: A Reader in Aboriginal Women's History in Canada* (Toronto: University of Toronto Press, 2006). John Lutz, "Making 'Indians' in British Columbia: Power, Race, and the Importance of Place," in *Power and Place in the North American West*, ed. Richard White and John Findlay (Seattle: University of Washington Press, 1999), 61-86. Adele Perry, *On the Edge of Empire: Gender, Race, and the Making of British Columbia, 1849-1871* (Toronto: University of Toronto Press, 2001).

13. Peggy Pascoe, *What Comes Naturally: Miscegenation Law and the Making of Race in America* (New York: Oxford University Press, 2009). Debra Thompson, "Racial Ideas and Gendered Intimacies: The Regulation of Interracial Relationships in North America," *Social and Legal Studies* 18:3 (2009), 353-371. Sylvia Van Kirk, *Many Tender Ties: Women in Fur-Trade Society, 1670-1870* (Norman: University of Oklahoma Press, 1990). My depiction of Indigenous and Euro-American families on San Juan Island between 1860 and 1900 as métis is based on their documented maintenance of "a new cultural, political, and racial identity distinct from Indian and European parents' generation," and their shared characteristics with métis in other U.S.-Canadian borderlands: "an expansive geographic familiarity [and] tremendous physical and social mobility," throughout the island chain in this context and between Anglo and Indian communities in Washington and British Columbia, and their "maintenance of strong family ties across time and space," in the words of Nicole St.-Onge, Carolyn Podruchny, and Brenda Macdougall, eds., *Contours of People: Metis Family, Mobility, and History* (Norman: University of Oklahoma Press, 2012), 7-8. See also Chris Andersen, *Metis: Race, Recognition, and the Struggle for Indigenous Peoplehood* (Vancouver: University of British Columbia Press, 2014). Agreeing with Andersen's argument that being métis is not just a matter of being part white and part Indian, but rather a matter of maintaining a distinctive identity from those who claim whiteness and those who claim indigeneity, I would argue that these San Juan Island families remained racially métis after 1900, but that the opportunity to enroll in area tribes convinced some to reclaim the Indigenous identities of their mothers and grand-mothers after 1910.

14. Vouri et al., *Images of America: San Juan Island*, 10, 11, 52, 54, 91, 101. Harmon, *Indians in the Making*. Karen Jones-Lamb, *Native American Wives of San Juan Settlers* (n.p.: Bryn Tirion, 1994).

15. Edson, *The Fourth Corner*. Ficken, *Washington Territory*. Mike Vouri, Julia Vouri, et al., *Images of America: Friday Harbor* (Charleston: Arcadia, 2009).

16. "An Act Relating to the Construction and Maintaining of Roads," *Statutes of the Terr. of Washington 1855*, sec. 26-41, 348-353. *John Keddy v. Peter Jewell*, Jefferson County Civil Case 913 (1875). Washington State Archive, Northwest Regional Branch.

17. 1900 U.S. Census. Archambault appears in legal notices in the *Puget Sound Weekly Argus* twenty times between 1876 and 1883; digitized territorial newspapers are available at the Washington State Archive. *John Keddy v. Peter Jewell*, Jefferson County Civil Case 913 (1875).

18. *John Keddy v. Peter Jewell,* Jefferson County Civil Case 913 (1875).

19. San Juan County Probate Case No. 4, Peter Jewell Estate, 1876.

20. Ibid.

21. Ibid.

22. Ibid.

23. "An Act to Regulate Marriages," *Statutes of the Terr. of Washington 1855,* 404–405. "An Act to Amend an Act, Entitled, 'An Act to Regulate Marriage,' Passed April 20th, 1854," *2nd Regular Session Laws of Washington, 1855,* 33. "An Act Declaring Legitimate the Issue of Marriages of White Men with Indian Women," *13th Annual Session Laws of Washington Territory, 1865–1866,* 85. "Of Offenses Against Morality and Decency," *2nd Biennial Session Laws of Washington Territory, 1869,* ch. 7, sec. 119–120, 225.

24. "Half Breeds," *Walla Walla Statesman* March 13, 1868, 2:3.

25. Katrina Jagodinsky, "'I'm in Family Way': Guarding Indigenous Women's Children in Washington Territory," *American Indian Quarterly* 37:2 (Spring 2013), 160–177.

26. "Administrator's Notice," *Puget Sound Weekly Argus* (Port Townsend), February 2, 1877, 4:3.

27. Cole Harris, *Making Native Space: Colonialism, Resistance, and Reserves in British Columbia* (Vancouver: University of British Columbia Press, 2002). Robert Admoski et al., eds., *Contesting Canadian Citizenship: Historical Readings* (Peterborough, Ontario: Broadview, 2002). Greg Russell Hubbard, "The Indian Under the White Man's Law in Washington Territory, 1853–1889" (M.A. thesis, University of Washington, 1972). Marcia Langton et al., eds., *Honour Among Nations? Treaties and Agreements with Indigenous People* (Victoria: Melbourne University Press, 2004). Keith D. Smith, *Liberalism, Surveillance, and Resistance: Indigenous Communities in Western Canada, 1877–1927* (Edmonton: Athabasca University Press, 2009). Angela Wanhalla, "Women 'Living Across the Line': Intermarriage on the Canadian Prairies and in Southern New Zealand, 1870–1900," *Ethnohistory* 55:1 (Winter 2008), 29–49.

28. Beryl Mildred Cryer, *Two Houses Half-Buried in Sand: Oral Traditions of the Hul'Q'umi'Num' Coast Salish of Kuper Island and Vancouver Island,* ed. Chris Arnett (Vancouver: Talonbooks, 2007). Raibmon, *Authentic Indians.*

29. Caroline Andrew and Sandra Rodgers, eds., *Women and the Canadian State* (Montreal: McGill-Queen's University Press, 1997). Sarah Carter, *The Importance of Being Monogamous: Marriage and Nation Building in Western Canada to 1915* (Edmonton: University of Alberta Press, 2008). Thomas Flanagan et al., *Beyond the Indian Act: Restoring Aboriginal Property Rights* (Montreal: McGill-Queen's University Press, 2010).

30. "An Act to Regulate the Practice and Proceedings in Civil Actions," *Statutes of the Terr. of Washington 1855,* sec. 6–7, 132.

31. Daniel Wright Clayton, *Islands of Truth: The Imperial Fashioning of Vancouver Island* (Vancouver: University of British Columbia Press, 2000). Perry, *On the Edge of Empire.* Stephen Royle, *Company, Crown and Colony: The Hudson's*

Bay Company and Territorial Endeavour in Western Canada (London: I. B. Tauris, 2011).

32. Wayne Prescott Suttles, "The Economic Life of the Coast Salish of Haro and Rosario Straits," in *Coast Salish and Western Washington Indians* (New York: Garland, 1974), 1:51.

33. Nugent, ed., *Lummi Elders Speak*, 70.

34. Paige Raibmon, "Unmaking Native Space: A Genealogy of Indian Policy, Settler Practice, and the Microtechniques of Dispossession," in *The Power of Promises: Rethinking Indian Treaties in the Pacific Northwest*, ed. Alexandra Harmon (Seattle: University of Washington Press, 2008), 56–85.

35. Jagodinsky, "'I'm in Family Way,'" 160–177.

36. Bruce G. Miller and Daniel L. Boxberger, "Creating Chiefdoms: The Puget Sound Case," *Ethnohistory* 41:2 (Spring 1994), 267–293.

37. San Juan County Probate Case No. 4, Peter Jewell Estate, 1876.

38. Edson, *The Fourth Corner*. Phoebe Goodell Judson, *A Pioneer's Search for an Ideal Home, by Phoebe Goodell Judson Who Crossed the Plains 1853 and Became a Resident on Puget Sound Before the Organization of Washington Territory* (Lincoln: University of Nebraska Press, 1984 [1925]). Peyton Kane, "The Whatcom Nine: Legal and Political Ramifications of Metis Family Life in Washington Territory," *Columbia Magazine* 14:2 (Summer 2000), 39–44.

39. Frederick Hoxie, *A Final Promise: The Campaign to Assimilate the Indians, 1880–1920* (Lincoln: University of Nebraska Press, 1984).

40. Valerie Matsumoto and Blake Allmendinger, eds., *Over the Edge: Remapping the American West* (Berkeley: University of California Press, 1999). David D. Smits, "'Squaw Men,' 'Half-Breeds,' and Amalgamators: Late Nineteenth-Century Anglo-American Attitudes Toward Indian-White Race-Mixing," *American Indian Culture and Research Journal* 15:3 (1991), 29–61. Patrick Wolfe, "Land, Labor, and Difference: Elementary Structures of Race," *The American Historical Review* 106:3 (June 2001), 866–905.

41. "Pocahontas at a Discount," *Puget Sound Courier*, May 31, 1855, 2:6. "Poetry: Lines by a Klootchman," *Puget Sound Herald*, December 17, 1858, 1:2; circulated in a number of Pacific Northwest papers, it mocked the romantic relationship between a Native woman and her white lover. "Murder and Suicide," *Puget Sound Weekly Gazette*, April 22, 1867, 3:1; reported that a Whidby Island Indian woman killed her mixed-race children and herself after being abused by a second white male partner. "Marriage Law," *Walla Walla Statesman*, February 14, 1868, 2:1; an editor condemned the removal of racial language from the marriage law as "an advance step toward white-nigger-Indian equality." "Died from a Christmas Carousal," *Yakima Herald*, January 1, 1891, 3:1; a story of a Yakima woman who traded sex to white men for alcohol. Such portrayals and attitudes frequently appear in the papers of Indian agent Edwin Eells from 1871 to 1878: Eells, MS 76, box 2, folder 37, Washington State Historical Society Research Center, Tacoma, Wash.

42. San Juan County Probate Case No. 4, Peter Jewell Estate, 1876. 1880 U.S. Census.

43. Hemphill and Cumbow, *Westpointers and Early Washington.*

44. *Territory of Washington v. James Smith,* Jefferson County, Washington Territory (1880), Criminal Case 1088, Washington State Archive.

45. Ibid.

46. "Coroner's Inquest," *Puget Sound Herald,* September 26, 1861, 2:3.

47. Lucía and Nora's sexual vulnerability under servitude also corresponds with the analysis of enslaved women's vulnerabilities in colonial Barbados and Carolina in Jennifer Morgan, *Laboring Women: Reproduction and Gender in New World Slavery* (Philadelphia: University of Pennsylvania Press, 2004).

48. *Territory of Washington v. James Smith,* Jefferson County, Washington Territory (1880), Criminal Case 1088, Washington State Archive.

49. Ibid. Vouri et al., *Images of America: San Juan Island,* 36–37, 79, 81.

50. The clerk's notes are the only trial record, and they do not include a full testimonial account, making it difficult to determine the trial proceedings. What they do include, however, are summaries of testimony that center on the key points in the trial raised by both defense and prosecuting witnesses. John R. Wunder, *Inferior Courts, Superior Justice: A History of the Justices of the Peace on the Northwest Frontier, 1853–1889* (Westport, Conn.: Greenwood, 1979).

51. *Territory of Washington v. James Smith,* Jefferson County, Washington Territory (1880), Criminal Case 1088, Washington State Archive. "An Act to Regulate the Practice and Proceedings in Civil Actions," *Statutes of the Terr. of Washington 1855,* ch. 31, sec. 293, 186–187.

52. *Territory of Washington v. James Smith,* Jefferson County, Washington Territory (1880), Criminal Case 1088, Washington State Archive.

53. Ibid.

54. Ibid.

55. Ibid.

56. Ibid.

57. Ibid.

58. Ibid.

59. "Questions Suggested by Judge Greene's Decision in the Indian Marriage Cases," *Puget Sound Mail* (LaConner, Wash.), September 25, 1880, 2:3. Robert E. Bieder, "Scientific Attitudes Toward Indian Mixed-Bloods in Early Nineteenth-Century America," *Journal of Ethnic Studies* 8:2 (Summer 1980), 17–30. Kane, "The Whatcom Nine," 39–44. Cynthia L. Nakashima, "An Invisible Monster: The Creation and Denial of Mixed-Race People in America," in *Racially Mixed Peoples in America,* ed. Maria P. P. Root (Newbury Park, Calif.: Sage, 1992), 162–178.

60. *Territory of Washington v. James Smith,* Jefferson County, Washington Territory (1880), Criminal Case 1088, Washington State Archive.

61. David Wallace Adams and Crista DeLuzio, eds., *On the Borders of Love and Power: Families and Kinship in the Intercultural American Southwest* (Berkeley: University of California Press, 2012). Jennifer S. H. Brown, *Strangers in Blood: Fur Trade Company Families in Indian Country* (Vancouver: University of British Columbia Press, 1980). Carter, *The Importance of Being Monogamous.* Albert Hurtado,

Intimate Frontiers: Sex, Gender, and Culture in Old California (Albuquerque: University of New Mexico Press, 1999). Anne F. Hyde, *Empires, Nations and Families: A History of the North American West, 1800–1860* (Lincoln: University of Nebraska Press, 2011). Elizabeth Jameson and Sheila McManus, *One Step Over the Line: Toward a History of Women in the North American Wests* (Edmonton: University of Alberta Press, 2008). Sheila McManus, *The Line Which Separates: Race, Gender, and the Making of the Alberta-Montana Borderlands* (Edmonton: University of Alberta Press, 2005). Van Kirk, *Many Tender Ties.*

62. Antonia Castaneda, introduction, "Gender on the Borderlands," *Frontiers: A Journal of Women Studies* 24:2–3 (2003), xi–xix. Antonia Castaneda, "Women of Color and the Rewriting of Western History: The Discourse, Politics, and Decolonization of History," *Pacific Historical Review* 61:4 (November 1992), 501–533. Hurtado, *Intimate Frontiers.*

63. Hyde, *Empires, Nations, and Families,* 89–146, 409–450.

64. Judson, *A Pioneer's Search.* Robert E. Ficken, "The Fraser River Humbug: Americans and Gold in the British Pacific Northwest," *Western Historical Quarterly* 33:3 (Autumn 2002), 297–313. Joseph Kinsey Howard, "Manifest Destiny and the British Empire's Pig," *Montana: The Magazine of Western History* 5:4 (Autumn, 1955), 19–23. J. Orin Oliphant, "The Cattle Trade on Puget Sound, 1858–1890," *Agricultural History* 7:3 (July, 1933), 129–149. Suttles, "The Economic Life of the Coast Salish." Carroll Riley et al., *Coast Salish and Western Washington Indians,* vol. 2 (New York: Garland, 1974). Commission Findings, Indian Claims Commission, in *Coast Salish and Western Washington Indians,* vol. 5.

65. Robin Fisher, "Indian Warfare and Two Frontiers: A Comparison of British Columbia and Washington Territory During the Early Years of Settlement," *Pacific Historical Review* 50:1 (February 1981), 31–51. Harmon, ed., *The Power of Promises.* Frank W. Porter III, "In Search of Recognition: Federal Indian Policy and the Landless Tribes of Western Washington," *American Indian Quarterly* 14:2 (Spring 1990), 113–132. Robert H. Ruby and John A. Brown, *Indians of the Pacific Northwest: A History* (Norman: University of Oklahoma Press, 1981), 100–182.

66. Kim Anderson, "Native Women, the Body, Land, and Narratives of Contact and Arrival," in *Storied Communities: Narratives of Contact and Arrival in Constituting Political Community,* ed. Hester Lessard, Rebecca Johnson, and Jeremy Webber (Vancouver: University of British Columbia Press, 2011), 167–188. Hamar Foster, Benjamin L. Berger, and A. R. Buck, eds., *The Grand Experiment: Law and Legal Culture in British Settler Societies* (Vancouver: University of British Columbia Press, 2008). Bettina Koschade and Evelyn Peters, "Algonquin Notions of Jurisdiction: Inserting Indigenous Voices into Legal Spaces," *Geografiska Annaler: Series B, Human Geography* 88:3 (September 2006), 299–310. Hester Lessard, Rebecca Johnson, and Jeremy Webber, eds., *Storied Communities: Narratives of Contact and Arrival in Constituting Political Community* (Vancouver: University of British Columbia Press, 2011). Jon'a F. Meyer and Gloria Bogdan, "Co-habitation and Co-optation: Some Intersections Between Native American and Euroamerican

Legal Systems in the Nineteenth Century," *American Transcendental Quarterly* 15:4 (December, 2001), 257–273. Bradford W. Morse and Gordon R. Woodman, eds., *Indigenous Law and the State* (Providence: Foris, 1988).

67. Cryer, *Two Houses Half-Buried in Sand*. Crisca Bierwert, *Brushed by Cedar, Living by the River: Coast Salish Figures of Power* (Tucson: University of Arizona Press, 1999). Colleen E. Boyd, "'You See Your Culture Coming Out of the Ground Like a Power': Uncanny Narratives in Time and Space on the Northwest Coast," *Ethnohistory* 56:4 (Fall 2009), 699–731. Hermann Haeberlin and Franz Boas, "Mythology of Puget Sound," *Journal of American Folklore* 37:145–146 (July–December 1924), 371–438.

68. M. Terry Thompson and Steven M. Egesdal, eds., *Salish Myths and Legends: One People's Stories* (Lincoln: University of Nebraska Press, 2008), 3, 13, 155–176, 328–329.

69. Thompson and Egesdal, eds., *Salish Myths and Legends*, 285.

70. Suttles, "The Economic Life of the Coast Salish," 394–411, 500.

71. Ibid., 105.

72. James W. Zion, "Searching for Indian Common Law," in *Indigenous Law and the State*, ed. Bradford W. Morse and Gordon R. Woodman (Providence: Foris, 1988), 139, 132.

73. Notable exceptions to this oversight include Himani Bannerji, "Age of Consent and Hegemonic Social Reform," in *Gender and Imperialism*, ed. Clare Midgley (New York: Manchester University Press, 1998), 21–44. Leslie K. Dunlap, "The Reform of Rape Law and the Problem of White Men: Age of Consent Campaigns in the South, 1885–1910," in *Sex, Love, Race: Crossing Boundaries in North American History*, ed. Martha Hodes (New York: New York University Press, 1999), 352–372. Nayan Shah, *Stranger Intimacy: Contesting Race, Sexuality and the Law in the North American West* (Berkeley: University of California Press, 2012). Nicholas L. Syrett, "'I Did and I Don't Regret It': Child Marriage and the Contestation of Childhood in the United States, 1880–1925," *Journal of the History of Childhood and Youth* 6:2 (Spring 2013), 314–331.

74. "An Act Relative to Crimes and Punishments, and Proceedings in Criminal Cases," *Statutes of the Terr. of Washington 1855*, ch. 2, sec. 33, 80. In 1880, territorial legislators raised the age of consent to eighteen, illustrating the influence of middle-class and women reformers in the early stages of the national WCTU campaign to raise age of consent. Today, the age of consent in Washington is sixteen, reflecting the mainstream perception that teenaged girls are sexually active before they are legal adults.

75. Shah, *Stranger Intimacy*, 129–152.

76. These cases can be found through the Frontier Justice Index, www.digital archives.wa.gov/Collections#RSID:13.

77. "An Act to Regulate the Practice and Pleadings in Prosecutions for Crimes" and "An Act to Regulate the Practice and Proceedings in Civil Actions," *Statutes of the Terr. of Washington 1855*, ch. 10, sec. 95, 117; ch. 31, sec. 293, 186–187. Hubbard, "The Indian Under the White Man's Law," 41, 186. When Indians

were allowed in 1881 to testify against white defendants in Washington's territorial courts, it was exclusively for the prosecution of liquor sales to Indians.

78. *Territory of Washington v. Joseph Roberts,* Snohomish County Criminal Records, Washington Territory (1878), Case No. 105, Washington State Archive. Laura F. Edwards, *Gendered Strife and Confusion: The Political Culture of Reconstruction* (Urbana: University of Illinois Press, 1997). Ariela Gross, *What Blood Won't Tell: A History of Race on Trial in America* (Cambridge: Harvard University Press, 2010).

79. *Territory of Washington v. James Smith,* Jefferson County, Washington Territory (1880), Criminal Case 1088, Washington State Archive.

80. Suttles, "The Economic Life of the Coast Salish," 517. Kathleen Brown, *Good Wives, Nasty Wenches, and Anxious Patriarchs: Gender, Race, and Power in Colonial Virginia* (Chapel Hill: University of North Carolina Press, 1996).

81. Washington Marriages, 1802–1902 database at Ancestry.com (accessed March 5, 2012). 1880 U.S. Census; 1883 and 1885 Washington Territorial Census.

82. Copies of land sale records provided to me by Guard Sundstrom, current owner of the Jewell family property.

83. 1887 Washington Territorial Census, San Juan County, San Juan Island. San Juan County Marriage Records, vol. 2, p. 31, San Juan County Auditor, Marriage Records, 1864–1939, Washington State Archives. Vouri et al., *Images of America: San Juan Island,* 9, 17. Vouri et al., *Images of America: Friday Harbor,* 17.

84. Nora Jewell is an uncommon name; I found Jewell in Tacoma in 1910 by scouring census schedules for Washington and British Columbia that spanned the range of Nora's possible lifetime. See Harmon, *Indians in the Making,* Raibmon, *Authentic Indians,* and Coll Thrush, *Native Seattle* on racial-ethnic-national ambiguities in particular. On the decreasing influence of mixed-race Puget Sounders, see Kane, "The Whatcom Nine," 39–44, and Pascoe, *What Comes Naturally,* 98–103.

85. James C. Scott, *Domination and the Arts of Resistance: Hidden Transcripts* (New Haven: Yale University Press, 1990).

86. 1887 Washington Territorial Census. Robert J. C. Young, *Colonial Desire: Hybridity in Theory, Culture and Race* (New York: Routledge, 1995).

87. Perry, *On the Edge of Empire.* Raibmon, *Authentic Indians.*

88. Data drawn from the 1910 U.S. Census and Tacoma, Washington, City Directory, 1910, both accessed via Ancestry.com.

89. Charles E. Roblin, *Application for Enrollment and Allotment of Washington Indians, 1911–1919* (Washington, D.C.: National Archives and Records Administration, General Services Administration), RG 75, microfilm available at the NARA branch in Seattle.

90. Cryer, *Two Houses Half-Buried in Sand.* Harmon, ed., *The Power of Promises.* Miller, ed., *Be of Good Mind.* Nugent, ed., *Lummi Elders Speak.* Wadewitz, *The Nature of Borders.*

91. Gordon Bakken, ed., *Law in the Western United States* (Norman: University of Oklahoma Press, 2000). Julie Evans et al., *Equal Subjects, Unequal Rights: Indig-*

enous Peoples in British Settler Colonies, 1830–1910 (Manchester: Manchester University Press, 2003). Ficken, *Washington Territory*. Foster, Berger, and Buck, eds., *The Grand Experiment*. Hubbard, "The Indian Under the White Man's Law."

Chapter 4. Juana Walker's "Legal Right as a Half-Breed"

1. Frank Russell, *The Pima Indians* (Tucson: University of Arizona Press, 1975), 53–55. David H. DeJong, "'See the New Country': The Removal Controversy and Pima-Maricopa Water Rights, 1869–1879," *Journal of Arizona History* 33:4 (1992), 379–380. For Akimel O'odham history and place names, see www .gilariver.org. George Webb, *A Pima Remembers* (Tucson: University of Arizona Press, 1959), 34. Churga's name is spelled a variety of ways, but this version will be used because it seems to have been the most common manifestation. *In re* Walker Estate, 1893, Pinal County Probate Case No. 128, p. 198, Isaac Smith 1894 testimony, Arizona State Library, Archives and Public Records (ASLAPR). *Arizona Citizen* (Tucson), January 3, 1874, 1:2, John D. Walker Biographical File, Arizona Historical Foundation (AHF) Microfilm Collection, reel 42.

2. *Arizona Republican* (Phoenix), October 1, 1892, 1:5, 6, John D. Walker Biographical File, AHF Microfilm Collection, reel 42.

3. John D. Walker to Eleanor Rice, October 15, 1890, *In re* Walker Estate, 1893, Pinal County Probate Case No. 128, p. 593, ASLAPR. Walker's enlistment record can be found on Ancestry.com in their American Civil War Soldiers database.

4. Karl Jacoby, *Shadows at Dawn: A Borderlands Massacre and the Violence of History* (New York: Penguin, 2008), 194, 195, 201.

5. *Arizona Weekly Enterprise* (Florence), July 9, 1887, 3:1, John D. Walker Biographical File, AHF Microfilm Collection, reel 42.

6. Sidney L. Harring, *Crow Dog's Case: American Indian Sovereignty, Tribal Law, and United States Law in the Nineteenth Century* (New York: Cambridge University Press, 1994). Frank Pommersheim, *Broken Landscape: Indians, Indian Tribes, and the Constitution* (New York: Oxford University Press, 2009). Wendy L. Wall, "Gender and the 'Citizen Indian,'" in *Writing the Range: Race, Class, and Culture in the Women's West*, ed. Elizabeth Jameson and Susan Armitage (Norman: University of Oklahoma Press, 1997), 202–229. David E. Wilkins and K. Tsianina Lomawaima, *Uneven Ground: American Indian Sovereignty and Federal Law* (Norman: University of Oklahoma Press, 2001). Robert A. Williams, *Like a Loaded Weapon: The Rehnquist Court, Indian Rights, and the Legal History of Racism in America* (Minneapolis: University of Minnesota Press, 2005).

7. Gila River Indian Community, "Surveying the Pima Reservation: 1859," Pima-Maricopa Irrigation Project Education Initiative, 2005–2006, www.gilariver .com (accessed January 7, 2011). *Gila River Pima-Maricopa Indian Community et al. v. The United States of America*, 27 Ind. Cl. Comm. 11 (1972), 11–15, http://digital .library.okstate.edu/icc/v27/iccv27p011.pdf (accessed January 7, 2011).

8. DeJong, "'See the New Country,'" 367.

9. Malcolm L. Comeaux, "Creating Indian Lands: The Boundary of the Salt River Indian Community," *Journal of Historical Geography* 17:3 (1991), 244.

10. DeJong, "'See the New Country,'" 379. David H. DeJong, *Stealing the Gila: The Pima Agricultural Economy and Water Deprivation, 1848–1921* (Tucson: University of Arizona Press, 2009).

11. Russell, *The Pima Indians*, 49.

12. Thanks to Bernard and Regina Siquieros, Ronald Geronimo, and Joe Joaquin for their kind assistance with the translation. Ruth M. Underhill, *Papago Woman* (Long Grove, Ill.: Waveland, 1985), 36. Russell, *The Pima Indians*.

13. Thomas Edwin Farish, *History of Arizona* (San Francisco: Filmer Brothers Electrotype, 1915–1918), 4:93–116. Jacoby, *Shadows at Dawn*.

14. Lord's correspondence quoted in letter from Indian agent F. E. Grossman to Brevet Colonel George L. Andrews, Superintendent of Indian Affairs for Arizona Territory, October 31, 1869, in Benjamin Sacks Collection, B43, F8, AHF. Presbyterian minister Charles H. Cook took up the position as agency teacher when he arrived in 1870.

15. John D. Walker, *Arizona Pioneer Biographies*, AHF Microfilm Collection, reel 78, 3.

16. DeJong, "'See the New Country,'" 370.

17. Comeaux, "Creating Indian Lands," 241. Marjane Ambler, *Breaking the Iron Bonds: Indian Control of Energy Development* (Lawrence: University of Kansas Press, 1990), 10.

18. Comeaux, "Creating Indian Lands," 242–244.

19. "Of Marriages," art. 30, sec. 3, Howell Code, 1865 Ariz. Terr. Sess. Laws, 230.

20. "Of Marriages," ch. 30, sec. 3, Howell Code, 1877 Ariz. Terr. Sess. Laws, 295–296.

21. Martha Menchaca, "The Anti-Miscegenation History of the American Southwest, 1837–1970: Transforming Racial Ideology into Law," *Cultural Dynamics* 20:3 (2008), 301, 304. Peggy Pascoe correctly points out that the 1887 statutes dropped Indians from marital exclusions, but they were quickly reinstated under the miscegenation clause and the brief exemption did not actually legitimate Indian-white marriages. Peggy Pascoe, *What Comes Naturally: Miscegenation Law and the Making of Race in America* (New York: Oxford University Press, 2009), 102.

22. These include the Trade and Intercourse Acts of the 1790s and 1800s, renewed and revised repeatedly, but ultimately incorporated into federal Indian law as the general rule that only federally appointed agents and licensed traders could contract with tribes for lands, trade, and treaties. These acts are available in full text online via Yale Law School's Avalon Project, http://avalon.law.yale.edu/subject_menus/namenu.asp.

23. Ambler, *Breaking the Iron Bonds*. Stuart Banner, *How the Indians Lost Their Land: Law and Power on the Frontier* (Cambridge: Harvard University Press, 2005). Thomas Biolsi, *Deadliest Enemies: Law and Race Relations On and Off Rose-*

bud Reservation (Minneapolis: University of Minnesota Press, 2001, 2007). Francis Paul Prucha, *American Indian Policy in the Formative Years: The Indian Trade and Intercourse Acts, 1780–1834* (Lincoln: University of Nebraska Press, 1970, 1962). Stephen J. Rockwell, *Indian Affairs and the Administrative State in the Nineteenth Century* (New York: Cambridge University Press, 2010).

24. Sylvester Mowry, *Arizona and Sonora: The Geography, History, and Resources of the Silver Region of North America* (New York: Harper, 1864). Gila River Indian Community, "Surveying the Pima Reservation: 1859," Pima-Maricopa Irrigation Project Education Initiative. Comeaux, "Creating Indian Lands," 242. F. E. Grossman, "The Pima Indians of Arizona," *Annual Report of the Board of Regents of the Smithsonian Institution* (Washington: Government Printing Office, 1873), 412.

25. Grossman, "The Pima Indians of Arizona," 412, 415.

26. Ibid., 415.

27. Pascoe, *What Comes Naturally*, 70. David D. Smits, "'Squaw Men,' 'Half-Breeds,' and Amalgamators: Late Nineteenth-Century Anglo-American Attitudes Toward Indian-White Race-Mixing," *American Indian Culture and Research Journal* 15:3 (1991), 29–61.

28. Donald Bahr et al., *Ants and Orioles: Showing the Art of Pima Poetry* (Salt Lake City: University of Utah Press, 1997), 28, 30, 139, 141. Donald Bahr, ed., *O'odham Creation and Related Events, As Told to Ruth Benedict in 1927 in Prose, Oratory, and Song* (Tucson: University of Arizona Press, 2001), 11, 25, 57, 69–77, 123.

29. Russell, *The Pima Indians*, 185. Anna Moore Shaw, *A Pima Past* (Tucson: University of Arizona Press, 1974), 14–16, 154.

30. Russell, *The Pima Indians*, 184.

31. Grossman, "The Pima Indians of Arizona," 415.

32. Farish, *History of Arizona* 4:93–116.

33. Letter from J. D. Walker to Eleanor Rice, October 9, 1890, *In re* Walker Estate, 1893, Pinal County Probate Case No. 128, p. 531, ASLAPR.

34. Letter from Indian agent F. E. Grossman to Brevet Colonel George L. Andrews, Superintendent of Indian Affairs for Arizona Territory, May 23, 1870, in Benjamin Sacks Collection, B43, F8, AHF.

35. Webb, *A Pima Remembers*, 89. MS 1174 Pinal County Legal Documents, folder 1, "1892 Estate of John D. Walker," vol. 1, Arizona State Historical Society, Tucson (ASHS).

36. For a description of Akimel O'odham marital practices, see Webb, *A Pima Remembers*, 29, and Shaw, *A Pima Past*, 69.

37. Joshua K. Rothman, *Notorious in the Neighborhood: Sex and Families Across the Color Line in Virginia, 1787–1861* (Chapel Hill: University of North Carolina Press, 2003).

38. Carroll D. Wright, *The History and Growth of the United States, Prepared for the Senate Committee on the Census* (Washington, D.C.: Government Printing Office, 1900), 159.

39. *Phoenix Herald,* May 27, 1891, 1:2, John D. Walker Biographical File, Benjamin Sacks Collection, box 28, folder 34, AHF. 1870 U.S. Census, Arizona Territory.

40. Isaac Smith 1894 testimony and in *Arizona Citizen* (Tucson), January 3, 1874, 1:2, John D. Walker Biographical File, AHF Microfilm Collection, reel 42. Testimony of Isaac D. Smith, MS 1174 Pinal County Legal Documents, folder 5: 1894 Estate of John D. Walker, Appeal by William H. Walker, pp. 78–113. *Arizona Citizen* (Tucson), August 24, 1872, 2:2, John D. Walker Biographical File, AHF Microfilm Collection, reel 42.

41. Testimony of Isaac D. Smith, MS 1174 Pinal County Legal Documents, folder 5: 1894 Estate of John D. Walker, Appeal by William H. Walker, pp. 78–113.

42. Ibid.

43. Ibid. Shaw, *A Pima Past.*

44. Russell, *The Pima Indians,* 58. Gila River Indian Community, "Pima-Maricopa Irrigation Project Education Initiative," www.gilariver.com/lessons/waterlosslesson08.pdf, pp. 30–31.

45. John S. Goff, *Arizona Biographical Dictionary* (Cave Creek, Ariz.: Black Mountain, 1983), 13. Brady had been a Texas Ranger and fought in the U.S.-Mexican War. He served as a Spanish interpreter for the 1855 U.S. Boundary Commission while dabbling in mining interests throughout southern Arizona. He served later as an Indian interpreter and was Pima County sheriff twice, then was a territorial legislator for three nonconsecutive sessions. He died in 1899 in Tucson.

46. *Arizona Weekly Enterprise* (Florence), July 26, 1886, John D. Walker Biographical File, AHF Microfilm Collection, reel 42. Nell Murbarger, *Ghosts of the Adobe Walls: Human Interest and Historical Highlights from 400 Ghost Haunts of Old Arizona* (Los Angeles: Westernlore, 1964), 242. *Arizona Weekly Enterprise* (Florence), March 15, 1884, 3:3, John D. Walker Biographical File, AHF Microfilm Collection, reel 42.

47. *Arizona Citizen* (Tucson), May 22, 1886, 3:3, 4, John D. Walker Biographical File, box 28, folder 34, AHF.

48. James H. McClintock, *Mormon Settlement in Arizona: A Record of Peaceful Conquest of the Desert* (Phoenix: Manufacturing Stationers, 1921), 212, 213–215, 217. McClintock describes the Pomeroys as founding members of the Mormon town of Mesa City, which would eventually become modern-day Mesa. The Pomeroy home was the first one built in Mesa City in 1878. Mormon induction of Indian children into their households as servants was common in the late nineteenth century and Juana may have been seen as an ideal helpmeet to the Pomeroy matriarch faced with raising eleven children on the frontier. Sondra Jones, "'Redeeming the Indian': The Enslavement of Indian Children in New Mexico and Utah," *Utah Historical Quarterly* 67:3 (1999), 220–224. *In re* Walker Estate, 1893, Pinal County Probate Case No. 128, pp. 508–513, 514–518, ASLAPR.

49. Correspondence filed in *In re* Walker Estate, 1893, Pinal County Probate Case No. 128, ASLAPR.

50. Ibid.

51. Testimony given in *In re* Walker Estate, 1893, Pinal County Probate Case No. 128, ASLAPR.

52. *Arizona Weekly Enterprise* (Florence), November 23, 1889, 3:1 (undated newspaper transcription), John D. Walker Biographical File, AHF Microfilm Collection, reel 42.

53. *In re* Walker Estate, 1893, Pinal County Probate Case No. 128, ASLAPR.

54. Ibid. *Arizona Weekly Enterprise* (Florence), July 26, 1890, 3:1, John D. Walker Biographical File, AHF Microfilm Collection, reel 42.

55. *In re* Walker Estate, 1893, Pinal County Probate Case No. 128, ASLAPR.

56. Letter from J. D. Walker to A. J. Doran, October 22, 1890, *In re* Walker Estate, 1893, Pinal County Probate Case No. 128, ASLAPR.

57. Letters from J. D. Walker to Eleanor Rice, December 21, 1890; January 7, 1891; January 16, 1891; January 23, 1891, *In re* Walker Estate, 1893, Pinal County Probate Case No. 128, ASLAPR. *Arizona Weekly Enterprise* (Florence), November 15, 1890, 3:1, and January 10, 1891, 3:1, John D. Walker Biographical File, AHF Microfilm Collection, reel 42.

58. Little is known about Eleanor Rice before or after her tragic marriage to John D. Walker. She was living with a married sister when she moved to California and had inherited some of her brother's estate when he died in 1879. *Woodruff v. Williams*, 1905, in *Colorado Reports: Cases Adjudged in the Supreme Court of Colorado*, Irving B. Melville (Denver: Mills, 1907), 37:28–67.

59. *In re* Walker Estate, 1893, Pinal County Probate Case No. 128, ASLAPR. *Arizona Weekly Enterprise* (Florence), April 25, 1891, 3:2, John D. Walker Biographical File, AHF Microfilm Collection, reel 42.

60. *In re* Walker Estate, 1893, Pinal County Probate Case No. 128, ASLAPR. *Phoenix Herald,* April 23, 1891, 3:4, John D. Walker Biographical File in Benjamin Sacks Collection, box 28, folder 34, AHF.

61. *Arizona Daily Star* (Tucson), April 24, 1891, 2:1, 2, John D. Walker Biographical File, AHF Microfilm Collection, reel 42.

62. *Arizona Daily Citizen* (Tucson), April 9, 1891, 2:1, John D. Walker Biographical File, AHF Microfilm Collection, reel 42.

63. *In re* Walker Estate, 1893, Pinal County Probate Case No. 128, ASLAPR. *Arizona Weekly Enterprise* (Florence), May 16, 1891, 2:2, John D. Walker Biographical File, AHF Microfilm Collection, reel 42.

64. William T. Day and Dr. Choate testimony, *In re* Walker Estate, 1893, Pinal County Probate Case No. 128, ASLAPR. *Arizona Daily Citizen* (Tucson), May 22, 1891, 2:1, John D. Walker Biographical File, AHF Microfilm Collection, reel 42.

65. *Arizona Weekly Enterprise* (Florence), September 5, 1891, 2:1, 3:1, John D. Walker Biographical File, AHF Microfilm Collection, reel 42.

66. *Graham County Bulletin* (Solomonville), September 11, 1891, 3:4, John D. Walker Biographical File, AHF Microfilm Collection, reel 42. *Los Angeles Times,* quoted in *Weekly Phoenix Herald,* September 10, 1891, 2:2, John D. Walker Biographical File, AHF Microfilm Collection, reel 42.

67. *Arizona Republican* (Phoenix), October 1, 1892, 1:5, 6, John D. Walker Biographical File, AHF Microfilm Collection, reel 42.

68. MS 1174 Pinal County Legal Documents, folder 1, "1892. Estate of John D. Walker," vol. 1, ASHS. Dr. Sabin Testimony, 144, 147.

69. Ibid., Dr. Choate Testimony, 216–217, 221.

70. Ibid., W. T. Day Testimony, 77, 131, 135–136.

71. MS 1174 Pinal County Legal Documents, folder 1, "1892. Estate of John D. Walker," vol. 1, ASHS.

72. Ibid., James J. Choate Testimony, 239–241; Sabin Testimony, 196.

73. Ibid., L. C. Hughes, 1–37.

74. Ibid., W. J. Osborn, 134–136.

75. Ibid., J. C. Harris, 90.

76. J. C. Harris's intercultural family can be found in the 1880, 1900, and 1910 U.S. Census schedules for Pinal County through Ancestry.com.

77. After the Pinal County court failed to recognize her as Walker's heir, Eleanor continued to use the Walker surname and claim the status of widow. The U.S. Census for 1900 shows her living in San Francisco as a "lodger." In 1910 she was living with her widowed sister (the same sister she had lived with before joining John D. in Arizona) in Quincy, Illinois. In 1920, at the age of sixty-eight, she continued to live among family members as a widow in her hometown.

78. MS 1174 Pinal County Legal Documents, folder 1, "1892. Estate of John D. Walker," vol. 1, ASHS. James Choate, 241.

79. *Arizona Republican* (Phoenix), October 1, 1892, 1:5, 6, John D. Walker Biographical File, AHF Microfilm Collection, reel 42.

80. Clare V. McKanna Jr., *White Justice in Arizona: Apache Murder Trials in the Nineteenth Century* (Lubbock: Texas Tech University Press, 2005) for a discussion of H. N. Alexander's defense of Gonshayee, an Apache man charged with murdering a white man in Pinal County in 1888. G. C. Israel's questionable management of his client's finances is in "Over the Line in Arizona," *Los Angeles Herald*, June 13, 1895.

81. *Arizona Republican* (Phoenix), October 1, 1892, 1:5, 6, John D. Walker Biographical File, AHF Microfilm Collection, reel 42.

82. *Arizona Gazette* (Phoenix), June 28, 1896, 5:1, John D. Walker Biographical File, AHF Microfilm Collection, reel 42.

83. In O'odham, parents refer to their own children differently than they would other children. As Juana's father, Walker would have referred to the girl as his *alida:g,* child, or his *uv alida:g,* daughter. "March Community Gathering Features O'odham Imik (Relations)," *Ak-Chin O'odham Runner* 23:7 (April 3–16, 2009), 4.

84. *In re* Walker Estate, 1893, Pinal County Probate Case No. 128, pp. 78–113, Isaac D. Smith, ASLAPR.

85. Ibid., 240–241, 245–247, Lucien E. Walker Testimony.

86. Ibid., 242–244, 248–250.

87. RG 111, Pinal County, SG 8, Superior Court, Civil and Probate, Case No. 128, Estate of John Walker (1891), John D. Walker Correspondence, 655, ASLAPR.

88. *In re* Walker Estate, 1893, Pinal County Probate Case No. 128, pp. 229–230, 233–234, Isabel Cosgrove Testimony, ASLAPR.

89. Ibid., 231–232, 235–236.

90. *In re* Walker Estate, 1893, Pinal County Probate Case No. 128, ASLAPR.

91. Ibid.

92. Peggy Pascoe, "Race, Gender, and the Privileges of Property: On the Significance of Miscegenation Law in the U.S. West," in *Over the Edge: Remapping the American West*, ed. Valerie Matsumoto and Blake Allmendinger (Berkeley: University of California Press, 1999), 215–230.

93. Bernie D. Jones, *Fathers of Conscience*, 4. Smits, "'Squaw Men,' 'Half-Breeds,' and Amalgamators," 56.

94. Everett E. Putnam, 1920 Federal Census, Mammoth District, Pinal County, Arizona.

95. Freeman A. Chamberlin, 1920 Federal Census, Florence District, Pinal County, Arizona. Peggy Pascoe, "Race, Gender, and Intercultural Relations: The Case of Interracial Marriage," in *Writing the Range: Race, Class, and Culture in the Women's West*, ed. Elizabeth Jameson and Susan Armitage (Norman: University of Oklahoma Press, 1997), 69–80.

96. Rufus E. Kohler, 1880 Federal Census, Hanvers District, Frederick County, Maryland.

97. Lucius Swingle, 1900 Federal Census, Precinct 5, Pinal County, Arizona Territory.

98. Willis Black, 1900 Federal Census, Precinct 5, Pinal County, Arizona Territory.

99. Edward A. Clark, 1900 Federal Census, Precinct 5, Pinal County, Arizona Territory.

100. Herbert Pinching, 1880 Federal Census, Vulture Mine, Maricopa County, Arizona Territory; 1910 Federal Census, Yavapai County, Arizona Territory.

101. Isaac Parkey, 1900 Federal Census, Townships 1, 3–5, Pinal County, Arizona Territory.

102. Charles French, 1910 Federal Census, Colorado River Indian Reservation, Yuma, Arizona Territory; 1910, Prescott, Yavapai County, Arizona Territory.

103. Case No. 128, *Walker v. Territory* (1893), 271–275, ASLAPR.

104. *In re* Walker Estate, 1893, Pinal County Probate Case No. 128, pp. 344–414, ASLAPR.

105. Ibid., 415–444.

106. Act of August 9, 1888 (25 Stat., 392). The act seems mostly to have protected the land rights of allotted Indian women married to white men and was not invoked in Juana Walker's case.

107. Estate of John D. Walker, Dec'd. *In re* Application of Juana Walker Civil No. 429. Filed September 8, 1896, 5 Ariz. 71, 46 Pac. 67 (1896).

108. *Globe Times,* reprinted in the *Prescott Courier,* August 8, 1901, 1:6, John D. Walker Biographical File, AHF Microfilm Collection, reel 42.

109. Eric Meeks, *Border Citizens: The Making of Indians, Mexicans, and Anglos in Arizona* (Austin: University of Texas Press, 2007).

110. *Tucson Citizen,* August 30, 1907, 8:1, John D. Walker Biographical File, AHF Microfilm Collection, reel 42.

111. *Prescott Courier,* August 29, 1907, 1:7, John D. Walker Biographical File, AHF Microfilm Collection, reel 42.

112. *Tucson Citizen,* August 30, 1907, 8:1, John D. Walker Biographical File, AHF Microfilm Collection, reel 42.

113. *Arizona Daily Star* (Tucson), September 15, 1907, 6:1, John D. Walker Biographical File, AHF Microfilm Collection, reel 42.

114. Arizona State Board of Health, Bureau of Vital Statistics, Original Certificate of Death for Juana Walker, http://genealogy.az.gov (accessed March 22, 2010).

115. College of Architecture "Urban Rehabilitation" Class Project, *Barrio Historico Tucson* (Tucson: University of Arizona Press, 1971), 5–6.

116. Arturo W. Carrillo's address, ethnicity, and profession are in the 1920 U.S. census; he is also listed in the 1936 Tucson City Directory.

117. *The Messenger* (Phoenix), July 15, 1916, ASLAPR (previously published as *El Mensajero* by J. M. Melendrez).

118. Bethany Ruth Berger, "After Pocahontas: Indian Women and the Law, 1830 to 1934," *American Indian Law Review* 21:1 (1997), 1–62. Sharon Block, "Lines of Color, Sex, and Service: Comparative Sexual Coercion in Early America." Hannah Rosen, "'Not That Sort of Women': Race, Gender, and Sexual Violence," in *Sex, Love, Race: Crossing Boundaries in North American History,* ed. Martha Hodes (New York: New York University Press, 1999), 141–158, 268. Sarah Deer, "Decolonizing Rape Law: A Native Feminist Synthesis of Safety and Sovereignty," *Wicazo Sa Review* 24:2 (Fall 2009), 149–167. Deena J. Gonzalez, *Refusing the Favor: The Spanish-Mexican Women of Santa Fe, 1820–1880* (New York: Oxford University Press, 1999). Merrill D. Smith, ed., *Sex Without Consent: Rape and Sexual Coercion in America* (New York: New York University Press, 2001). Amy Dru Stanley, *From Bondage to Contract: Wage Labor, Marriage, and the Market in the Age of Slave Emancipation* (New York: Cambridge University Press, 1998), x, 135, 175–217, 218–263.

119. Maria P. P. Root, ed., *Racially Mixed Peoples in America* (Newbury Park, Calif.: Sage, 1992), 5, 7.

120. Cynthia L. Nakashima, "An Invisible Monster: The Creation and Denial of Mixed-Race People in America," in *Racially Mixed Peoples in America,* ed. Maria P. P. Root (Newbury Park, Calif.: Sage, 1992), 177.

121. Mario Barrera, *Race and Class in the Southwest: A Theory of Racial Inequality* (Notre Dame, Ind.: University of Notre Dame Press, 1979). Laura E. Gómez, *Manifest Destinies: The Making of the Mexican American Race* (New York: New York University Press, 2007). Martha Menchaca, *Recovering History, Recon-*

structing Race: The Indian, Black, and White Roots of Mexican Americans (Austin: University of Texas Press, 2001). James E. Officer, *Arizona's Hispanic Perspective* (Tucson: University of Arizona Press, 1981).

Chapter 5. Rebecca Lena Graham and "The Old Question of Common Law Marriage Raised by a Half-Breed"

1. *Seattle Post Intelligencer,* July 24, 1894, 5.

2. Coll Thrush, *Native Seattle: Histories from the Crossing-Over Place* (Seattle: University of Washington Press, 2007), 24–25.

3. "*In re* the Estate of Franklin Matthias, deceased, Facts Submitted," April 1, 1893, folder 1 of 4: case 331 *In re* Estate of Franklin Matthias, deceased, box 48: Seattle Civil and Criminal Case Files 1890–1911, 326–331, RG 21, U.S. District Court, Western District of Washington, Northern Division, National Archives and Records Administration, Seattle. Rebecca Lena Graham Death Certificate, Washington State Digital Archives, www.digitalarchives.wa.gov (accessed July 29, 2014). Many census records and newspaper accounts record Graham's birth as 1862, but Rebecca testified in the *Graham v. Matthias* estate case that she was born in 1859.

4. Paige Raibmon, "Unmaking Native Space: A Genealogy of Indian Policy, Settler Practice, and the Microtechniques of Dispossession," in *The Power of Promises: Rethinking Indian Treaties in the Pacific Northwest,* ed. Alexandra Harmon (Seattle: University of Washington Press, 2008), 56–85. Bureau of Indian Affairs, "Summary Under the Criteria and Evidence for Proposed Finding Against Acknowledgment of the Duwamish Tribal Organization" (Washington, D.C.: Government Printing Office, 1996), www.bia.gov/cs/groups/xofa/documents/text/idc-001381.pdf (accessed July 29, 2014).

5. Rebecca Lena Graham obituary, Rebecca Graham Biographical File, University of Washington Special Collections. Bureau of Indian Affairs, "Summary Under the Criteria and Evidence for Proposed Finding Against Acknowledgment of the Duwamish Tribal Organization." Rebecca Fitzhenry Affidavit, Dwamish Tribal Register, M1343: Roblin Rolls, Roll 3, NARA Seattle.

6. Vincent Schilling, "Duwamish Chairwoman Speaks About Fighting for Federal Recognition and Getting Another Chance," *Indian Country Today,* March 28, 2013. Andrew Graybill, *The Red and the White: A Family Saga of the American West* (New York: Norton, 2013).

7. Patricia Hackett Nicola, "Rebecca Lena Graham's Fight for Her Inheritance," *Pacific Northwest Quarterly* 97:3 (Summer, 2006), 139–147. Thrush, *Native Seattle.* Matthew Klingle, *Emerald City: An Environmental History of Seattle* (New Haven: Yale University Press, 2007).

8. Peggy Pascoe, *What Comes Naturally: Miscegenation Law and the Making of Race in America* (New York: Oxford University Press, 2009).

9. At the heart of the Bureau of Indian Affairs' denial of Duwamish federal recognition is their conclusion that the tribe's membership changed between 1915 and 1926 and that 1926 members did not maintain community ties to 1915

members. Rebecca's case shows that the same Duwamish witnesses who testified on her behalf in 1893 and members of her extended family appeared in both the 1915 and 1926 rolls (unless deceased by then), and that her descendants continued to be involved in the Duwamish Tribal Organization into the 1950s. Disturbingly, the Bureau of Indian Affairs has other evidence that indicates these longstanding interpersonal connections, but their interpretation of that evidence has not led to a positive ruling on Duwamish federal recognition at this date. "*In re* the Estate of Franklin Matthias, deceased, Facts Submitted," April 1, 1893, folder 1 of 4: case 331 *In re* Estate of Franklin Matthias, deceased, box 48: Seattle Civil and Criminal Case Files 1890–1911, 326–331, RG 21, U.S. District Court, Western District of Washington, Northern Division, NARA Seattle.

10. Patricia Hackett Nicola's article on Rebecca Lena Graham refers to Curley as Rebecca's great-uncle. "Rebecca Lena Graham's Fight for Her Inheritance." Duwamish genealogical data recorded for federal recognition indicates, however, that Rebecca's mother Peggy was Curley's daughter. Bureau of Indian Affairs, "Summary Under the Criteria and Evidence for Proposed Finding Against Acknowledgment of the Duwamish Tribal Organization."

11. Catherine D. Lucignani, "Seattle's First People: An Ethnohistory of Washington's Duwamish, 1850–1900" (M.A. thesis, University of Wyoming, 2005). Wayne Suttles, *Coast Salish Essays* (Seattle: University of Washington Press, 1987). Kenneth D. Tollefson, "Political Organization of the Duwamish," *Ethnology* 28:2 (1989), 135–149; "The Political Survival of Landless Puget Sound Indians," *American Indian Quarterly* 16:2 (1992), 213–235; "Tribal Estates: A Comparative and Case Study," *Ethnology* 35:4 (1996), 321–328.

12. Cornelius Holgate Hanford, *Seattle and Environs, 1852–1924* (Chicago and Seattle: Pioneer Historical Publishing, 1924), 1:148.

13. *Tacoma Ledger,* December 8, 1902, Henry Van Asselt Biographical File, University of Washington Special Collections. Clarence B. Bagley, *History of King County, Washington* (Chicago and Seattle: S. J. Clarke, 1929), 1:48–49. Hanford, *Seattle and Environs,* 141. Thrush, *Native Seattle,* 28–29. Klingle, *Emerald City,* 29–30. Bureau of Indian Affairs, "Summary Under the Criteria and Evidence for Proposed Finding Against Acknowledgment of the Duwamish Tribal Organization."

14. Marie Freeman et al., *Washington Territory Donation Land Claims: An Abstract of Information in the Land Claim Papers of Persons Who Settled in Washington Territory Before 1856* (Seattle: Seattle Genealogical Society, 1980), Newberry Library Local History Reference Collection. Henry Van Asselt: secs. 27, 28, 32 and 34 of T 24N R 4E, p. 89; Arthur Denny: secs. 31 and 32 of T 25N R 4E, p. 68; Erasmus M. Smithers: secs. 13, 14, 23, and 24 in T 25N R 3E, p. 90; Henry Yesler: secs. 4, 5 and 6 of T 24N R 4E and secs. 33 of T 25N R 4E, p. 96; Judge Cornelius Hanford's parents, Edward and Abigail Jane Hanford: secs. 8, 9, 16, and 17, T 24N R 4E, p. 97; Henry H. Tobin: secs. 17, 18, and 20 of T 23N R 5E, p. 108. Though Matthias does not appear as a claimant in the Donation Lands index, he does appear as an estate administrator and as an affiant for other claimants, and is also listed as a King County official.

15. "Claimant to Mathias [*sic*] Estate. She Is Not Skookum Susie's Daughter—A Legal Marriage Alleged," *Seattle Post Intelligencer,* April 5, 1893, 3.

16. John Mack Faragher, ed., *Rereading Frederick Jackson Turner: The Significance of the Frontier in American History, and Other Essays* (New York: Holt, 1994). Patricia Limerick, "Turnerians All: The Dream of a Helpful History in an Intelligible World," *American Historical Review* 100:3 (1995), 697–716. Kathie Zetterberg, "Henry Yesler's Native American Daughter Julia Is Born on June 12, 1855," www.historylink.org/index (accessed August 4, 2014). Klingle, *Emerald City,* 27.

17. "The Mathias Heirs. Close of Argument on an Indian Marriage Case. A $50,000 Estate Involved. The Old Question of Common Law Marriage Raised by a Half-Breed Claimant," *Seattle Post Intelligencer,* July 24, 1894, 5.

18. Bureau of Indian Affairs, "Summary Under the Criteria and Evidence for Proposed Finding Against Acknowledgment of the Duwamish Tribal Organization." Kristen A. Carpenter, "Interpretive Sovereignty: A Research Agenda," *American Indian Law Review* 33:1 (2008–2009), 111–152. Hanford, *Seattle and Environs,* 100. Frank W. Porter III, "In Search of Recognition: Federal Indian Policy and the Landless Tribes of Western Washington," *American Indian Quarterly,* 14:2 (Spring 1990), 113–132. Robert H. Ruby and John A. Brown, *Indians of the Pacific Northwest: A History* (Norman: University of Oklahoma Press, 1981), 130–135.

19. Robert E. Ficken, *Washington Territory* (Pullman: Washington State University Press, 2002). Charles Edwin Garretson, "A History of the Washington Superintendency of Indian Affairs, 1853–1865" (M.A. thesis, University of Washington, 1962). John A. Hemphill and Robert C. Cumbow, *Westpointers and Early Washington* (Seattle: West Point Society of Puget Sound, 1992). Richard Kluger, *The Bitter Waters of Medicine Creek: A Tragic Clash Between White and Native America* (New York: Alfred A. Knopf, 2011). Ruby and Brown, *Indians of the Pacific Northwest.*

20. Bagley, *History of King County.* George Pierre Castile, *The Indians of Puget Sound: The Notebooks of Myron Eells* (Seattle: University of Washington Press, 1985). Ezra Meeker, *Pioneer Reminiscences of Puget Sound* (Seattle: Lowman and Hanford Printing, 1905). Thomas Phelps, *Reminiscences of Seattle, Washington Territory, and of the U.S. Sloop-of-War Decatur During the Indian War of 1855–1856* (Fairfield, Wash.: Ye Galleon Press, 1970 [1881]). Amy S. Greenberg, *Manifest Destiny and American Territorial Expansion: A Brief History with Documents* (New York: Bedford/St. Martin's, 2012). John C. Pinheiro, *Manifest Ambition: James K. Polk and Civil-Military Relations During the Mexican War* (Westport, Conn.: Praeger Security International, 2007).

21. Hanford, *Seattle and Environs,* 148, 107, 113, 117.

22. Ibid., 148, 118.

23. According to descendant Kathie Zetterberg, Susan partnered with Jeremiah Benson after leaving Yesler. Federal census records confirm that Susan's fifteen-year-old daughter Julia lived in Jeremiah's household in 1870, but not afterward, and that Jeremiah had a mixed-race daughter named Hannah, born in 1865, living with Julia and Jeremiah in 1870. Hannah lived with her father at least until

the age of nineteen. Hannah's death certificate from 1917 reports Susan Curley and Jeremiah Benson as her parents. I have confirmed these records, relying on Zetterberg's article as a guide to find them via Washington State's online database of vital records. See Kathie Zetterberg, "Henry Yesler's Native American Daughter Julia Is Born on June 12, 1855," www.historylink.org/index (accessed August 4, 2014).

24. "Order for the Withdrawal of Transcript of Testimony and Exhibits," dated January 29, 1951, folder 3 of 4: case 331 *In re* Estate of Franklin Matthias, deceased, box 48: Seattle Civil and Criminal Case Files 1890–1911, 326–331, RG 21, U.S. District Court, Western District of Washington, Northern Division, NARA Seattle.

25. "An Act to Regulate Marriages," *Statutes of the Terr. of Washington 1855*, 404–405. "An Act to Amend an Act, Entitled, 'An Act to Regulate Marriage,' Passed April 20th, 1854," *2nd Regular Session Laws of Washington, 1855*, 33.

26. Pascoe, *What Comes Naturally.*

27. Bagley, *History of King County*, 1:262, 196–197. "Snoqualmoo Pass Wagon Road," *Puget Sound Herald* (Steilacoom, Wash.), September 2, 1859, 2:4. "Railroad Convention at Vancouver," *Pioneer and Democrat* (Olympia, Wash.), February 24, 1860, 1:5. "Proclamation by the Governor of Washington Territory," *Pioneer and Democrat* (Olympia, Wash.), May 17, 1861, 2:3, 3:3.

28. Proving how effective her genealogical skills are, Patricia Hackett Nicola found the evidence that Peggy lived with David Kellogg between her partnerships with Matthias and Scheuerman, bearing a son named John by him in 1864. "Rebecca Lena Graham's Fight for Her Inheritance." John Kellogg's death certificate names Peggy Curley and David Kellogg as parents and is indexed online through the Washington State Digital Archives, www.digitalarchives.wa.gov (accessed August 12, 2014). John is included in the Scheuerman household in census records in the 1870s, however, as John Sherman. The 1880 U.S. census for Seattle lists Peggy and Christian Scheuerman's children Lissette, Bertha, Frederick, and Walter along with John Kellogg, by then fifteen and working as a farm laborer. They are recorded as Salmon Bay residents, evidence of Scheuerman's residence near his father-in-law's settlement. Strangely, Peggy's children are all listed without either parent in this census schedule.

29. Pioneer District application for the National Register of Historic Places, 1970, http://pdfhost.focus.nps.gov/docs/NRHP (accessed August 12, 2014).

30. "An Act to Regulate Marriages," *13th Annual Session Laws of Washington Territory, 1865–1866*, sec. 2, 81.

31. "An Act Declaring Legitimate the Issue of Marriages of White Men with Indian Women," *13th Annual Session Laws of Washington Territory, 1865–1866*, 85.

32. James Clifford, *The Predicament of Culture* (Cambridge: Harvard University Press, 1988), 277–346. Brian Klopotek, *Recognition Odysseys: Indigeneity, Race, and Federal Tribal Recognition Policy in Three Louisiana Indian Communities* (Raleigh: Duke University Press, 2011). Sarah Krakoff, "Inextricably Political:

Race, Membership, and Tribal Sovereignty," *Washington Law Review* 87:4 (2012), 1041–1091.

33. Bureau of Indian Affairs, "Summary Under the Criteria and Evidence for Proposed Finding Against Acknowledgment of the Duwamish Tribal Organization." Thrush, *Native Seattle*, 54–55. The petition that Matthias and others signed is available at www.historylink.org (accessed August 11, 2014). Curley's household is included in the 1880 U.S. census for Seattle.

34. "Pay Up! Pay Up!" *Puget Sound Weekly* (Seattle), January 14 and 21, 1867, 3:1.

35. "Washington Territory Things," *Vancouver Register* (Washington), February 16, 1867, 2:4. Washington (State), *Legislative Assembly. Council. Journal of the Proceedings of the Council, of Washington Territory, During the . . . Regular Session, Olympia, 1855*, 59, 99. *Puget Sound Weekly* (Seattle), March 25, 1867, 3:5. "Seattle—Past, Present, and Future," *Puget Sound Dispatch* (Seattle), December 18, 1871, 2:1. *Puget Sound Business Directory, 1872*, Graff Collection 2936, Newberry Library, Chicago. Hanford, *Seattle and Environs*, 134, 143. Bagley, *History of King County*, 1:624.

36. Bagley, *History of King County*, 1:375. "The Seattle 'Scalawags,'" *Puget Sound Dispatch* (Seattle), September 25, 1873, 2:2. "Seattle's Opportunity," *Puget Sound Dispatch* (Seattle), July 24, 1873, 1:3.

37. "An Old Sore," *Puget Sound Dispatch* (Seattle), October 6, 1877, 6:3.

38. MsSC 68 Hanford, Judge Cornelius Hanford, box 1, folder 1, Washington State Historical Society Research Center, Tacoma, Wash.

39. *Residence and Business Directory of the City of Seattle, 1882*, 47, Graff Collection 4967, Newberry Library, Chicago.

40. The Scheuerman property now makes up the current neighborhood of Lawton Wood and portions of Fort Lawton. "Seattle Neighborhoods: Magnolia—Thumbnail History," www.historylink.org (accessed August 11, 2014). "East Coast capitalists invest in Seattle and King County for the first time in July 1871," www.historylink.org (accessed August 11, 2014). Lewis W. Call, *Military Reservations, National Cemeteries, and Military Parks: Title, Jurisdiction, Etc.* (Washington, D.C.: Government Printing Office, 1907). National Archives and Records Administration, Washington, D.C.; Internal Revenue Assessment Lists, Oregon District, 1867–1873, Series: M1631, Roll: 2; Description: Annual, Monthly and Special Lists, April 1870–April 1873, RG 58, Records of the Internal Revenue Service, 1791–2006.

41. 1870 U.S. Census for Seattle. Rebecca Lena Graham obituary, Rebecca Graham Biographical File, University of Washington Special Collections. 1880 U.S. Census for Seattle.

42. Bagley, *History of King County*, 1:226.

43. "Married," *Seattle Daily Intelligencer*, July 20, 1879, 2:3.

44. Frederic James Grant, ed., *History of Seattle, Washington: With Illustrations and Biographical Sketches of Some of Its Prominent Men and Pioneers* (New York: American Publishing and Engraving, 1891), 338.

45. All of Rebecca's family members appeared in the 1880 U.S. Census for Seattle, suggesting that the city's ban on Indigenous residents had been applied very selectively.

46. "Died," *Seattle Post Intelligencer*, March 2, 1884, 2:3.

47. "Offenses Against Public Policy," *8th Biennial Session Laws of Washington Territory, 1881*, sec. 949, 184. Some sources claim that Washington Territory dropped its miscegenation ban as early as 1869. A close reading of the annual session laws and the regularly published statutes, however, reveals that the legislature did not actually revise the marriage statute to eliminate racial bans until 1881. Changes to marriage law between 1869 and 1881 include an expansion of the defined rights and obligations of marital partners, and of the penalties for persons violating the marriage law, but no removal or revision of the miscegenation ban can be found in those years.

48. 1885 and 1887 Washington Territorial Census. "An Old Settler Dead," *Seattle Post Intelligencer*, October 7, 1891, 2.

49. Neither Tom nor Jola appear in vital records after their births are noted in the 1885 and 1887 Washington territorial censuses.

50. Because there is not another family appearance in the census until 1892 and neither of them appears there, it is impossible to tell whether Tom or Jola is the "favorite child" referred to in accounts associated with Holmes's sudden and tragic episode of mental illness. John Holmes Probate Case, King County, Washington Territory, Case No. 838, 1889. Washington State Archive, Puget Sound Regional Branch. "An Insane Engineer," *Seattle Post Intelligencer*, April 4, 1889, 3. "Death of John C. Holmes," *Seattle Post Intelligencer*, May 25, 1889, 5. C. H. Hanford, "The Orphan Railroad and the Rams Horn Right of Way," *Washington Historical Quarterly* 14:2 (April 1923), 83–99. Before 1880, the Columbia & Puget Sound Railroad had been the Seattle and Walla Walla Line that Franklin Matthias and friends Arthur Denny, Henry Yesler, and Dexter Horton had founded with others in 1873, on a line that Cornelius Hanford had predicted would never be built.

51. "An Insane Engineer," *Seattle Post Intelligencer*, April 4, 1889, 3. "Death of John C. Holmes," *Seattle Post Intelligencer*, May 25, 1889, 5.

52. John Holmes Probate Case, King County, Washington Territory, Case No. 838, 1889, Washington State Archive.

53. "Death of John C. Holmes," *Seattle Post Intelligencer*, May 25, 1889, 5.

54. Katrina Jagodinsky, "'I'm in Family Way': Guarding Indigenous Women's Children in Washington Territory," *American Indian Quarterly* 37:2 (Spring 2013), 160–177.

55. "Death of John C. Holmes," 5.

56. 1889 Territorial Washington Census and 1918 Tulalip Agency Census, Indian Census Rolls, 1885–1940.

57. 1889 Washington Territorial Census.

58. Ficken, *Washington Territory*, 2, 106, 203. Kenneth N. Owens, "The Prizes of Statehood," *Montana: The Magazine of Western History* 37:4 The Centennial

West: Politics (Autumn, 1987), 2–9. Carlos A. Schwantes, *The Pacific Northwest: An Interpretive History* (Lincoln: University of Nebraska Press, 1996), 251–270.

59. April 2, 1890, marriage certificate, Washington State Digital Archives. Nicola, "Rebecca Lena Graham's Fight for Her Inheritance," 140. Victor Matthias Graham draft registration, 1942, via Ancestry.com. "The Mortuary Record," *Seattle Post Intelligencer*, July 17, 1891, 5. "An Old Settler Dead," *Seattle Post Intelligencer*, October 7, 1891, 2. "The Administration Is Finished," *Seattle Post Intelligencer*, July 29, 1893, 5.

60. "Samuel Crawford's Petition for Distribution Before Judge J. W. Langley," July 20, 1893, folder 1 of 4: case 331 *In re* Estate of Franklin Matthias, deceased, box 48: Seattle Civil and Criminal Case Files 1890–1911, 326–331, RG 21, U.S. District Court, Western District of Washington, Northern Division, NARA Seattle.

61. "An Old Settler Dead," *Seattle Post Intelligencer*, October 7, 1891, 2.

62. "Informations Against Jordan and Van Buren May Fail. Claimant to Mathias Estate. A Mysterious Woman Who Claims To Be the Daughter of the Late Rich Pioneer—Court News," *Seattle Post Intelligencer*, April 4, 1893, 5. "Petition for Distribution To the Honorable I. W. Langley, Judge of the Superior Court of King County *In re* the Estate of Franklin Matthias, dec'd," April 1, 1893, folder 1 of 4: case 331 *In re* Estate of Franklin Matthias, deceased, box 48: Seattle Civil and Criminal Case Files 1890–1911, 326–331, RG 21, U.S. District Court, Western District of Washington, Northern Division, NARA Seattle.

63. "Claimant to Mathias Estate. She Is Not Skookum Susie's Daughter," *Seattle Post Intelligencer*, April 5, 1893, 3.

64. "Answer to Petition of Samuel L. Crawford, as administrator, for distribution of the estate of Franklin Matthias, deceased, and showing cause why said estate should not be distributed among the heirs and persons therein named," August 3, 1893, folder 1 of 4: case 331 *In re* Estate of Franklin Matthias, deceased, box 48: Seattle Civil and Criminal Case Files 1890–1911, 326–331, RG 21, U.S. District Court, Western District of Washington, Northern Division, NARA Seattle.

65. Law Commission of Canada, *Indigenous Legal Traditions* (Vancouver: University of British Columbia Press, 2007). Maria Morellato, ed., *Aboriginal Law Since Delgamuukw* (Aurora, Ontario: Cartwright Group Canada Law Book, 2009). Bradford W. Morse and Gordon R. Woodman, eds., *Indigenous Law and the State* (Providence: Foris, 1988). Justin B. Richland and Sarah Deer, *Introduction to Tribal Legal Studies* (Lanham, Md.: AltaMira, 2010).

66. "Petition for removal of this cause to the United States Circuit Court for the District of Washington, Northern Division, Ninth Circuit," September 23, 1893, folder 1 of 4: case 331 *In re* estate of Franklin Matthias, deceased, box 48: Seattle Civil and Criminal Case Files 1890–1911, 326–331, RG 21, U.S. District Court, Western District of Washington, Northern Division, NARA Seattle.

67. Mary Matthias Affidavit, folder 4 of 4: case 331 *In re* estate of Franklin Matthias, deceased, box 48: Seattle Civil and Criminal Case Files 1890–1911, 326–331, RG 21, U.S. District Court, Western District of Washington, Northern Division, NARA Seattle.

68. Marjorie Rhodes, *Biography Notes on Pioneers of Puget Sound* (Seattle: self-published, 1992), 64–65, 184–187. Arthur Denny Biographical File; Henry Van Asselt Biographical File, University of Washington Special Collections.

69. "In the matter of the Estate of Franklin Matthias, dec'd., No. 1391 in the Superior Court of King County, State of Washington, Probate Jurisdiction, Honorable I. J. Lichtenberg, submitted by Charles Matthias of Chicago," October 8, 1891, folder 1 of 4: case 331 *In re* estate of Franklin Matthias, deceased, box 48: Seattle Civil and Criminal Case Files 1890–1911, 326–331, RG 21, U.S. District Court, Western District of Washington, Northern Division, NARA Seattle. Rhodes, *Biography Notes,* 91–92. Dexter Horton Biographical File, University of Washington Special Collections.

70. 1860 U.S. Census.

71. Rhodes, *Biography Notes,* 50–51. Hillory Butler Biographical File, University of Washington Special Collections.

72. Rhodes, *Biography Notes,* 198–199. L. V. Wyckoff Biographical File, University of Washington Special Collections.

73. Rhodes, *Biography Notes,* 179. William Surber Biographical File, University of Washington Special Collections.

74. Samuel Coombs Biographical File, University of Washington Special Collections. Samuel Coombs, *Dictionary of the Chinook Jargon as Spoken on Puget Sound and the Northwest, with Original Indian Names for Prominent Places and Localities with Their Meanings, Historical Sketch, Etc.* (Seattle: Lowman & Hanford, 1891), Ayer Collection PM848.C7, Newberry Library, Chicago.

75. Dillis B. Ward, *Across the Plains in 1853* (Seattle: University of Washington Library, 1911), Graff Collection 4530, Newberry Library, Chicago. Dillis Ward Biographical File, University of Washington Special Collections. Rhodes, *Biography Notes,* 187–188. Ed Thorndyke Biographical File, University of Washington Special Collections. Bagley, *History of King County,* 1:197.

76. Rhodes, *Biography Notes,* 115–116.

77. Ibid., 87. Timothy Hinckley Biographical File, University of Washington Special Collections.

78. Clarence B. Bagley, *Indian Myths of the Northwest* (Seattle: Lowman and Hanford, 1930), 110.

79. William DeShaw Biographical File, University of Washington Special Collections.

80. Richard Jeffs Biographical File, University of Washington Special Collections. Rhodes, *Biography Notes,* 65, 97. Hanford, *Seattle and Environs,* 143. Bagley, *History of King County,* 1:121, 705.

81. Alexander Spithill Biographical File, University of Washington Special Collections. Alexandra Harmon, *Indians in the Making: Ethnic Relations and Indian Identities Around Puget Sound* (Berkeley: University of California Press, 1998), 141–144.

82. Hanford opinion, *In re* Matthias' Estate, *Graham v. Matthias et al.,* n.d., 63 F. 523 (1894 U.S. App.).

83. "Pioneer of '49 Days Dies in Seattle," *Seattle Times*, September 10, 1909. David Webster and Theodore Williams Biographical Files, University of Washington Special Collections.

84. "Relating to Evidence," *2nd Legislature, Regular Session Laws of Washington State, 1891*, ch. 19, sec. 1, 33.

85. Hanford, *Seattle and Environs*, 149. Bagley, *History of King County*, 1:142.

86. Hanford opinion, *In re* Matthias' Estate, *Graham v. Matthias et al.*, n.d., 63 F. 523 (1894 U.S. App.).

87. Ibid.

88. Ibid.

89. Ibid.

90. Hanford, *Seattle and Environs*, 100.

91. "She Is an Heiress. Matthias' Half-Breed Daughter's Claim Allowed. Other Similar Claims Likely," *Seattle Post Intelligencer*, September 1, 1894, 5. That such estate cases often do not indicate the racial-ethnic backgrounds of involved parties makes it very possible that there are more cases.

92. "The Mathias Heirs. Close of Argument on an Indian Marriage Case," *Seattle Post Intelligencer*, July 24, 1894, 5.

93. 1900 U.S. Census.

94. *United States Military Reservations, National Cemeteries, and Military Parks* (Washington, D.C.: United States Army Office of the Judge Advocate General, 1916), 449.

95. 1900 U.S. Census. Zetterberg, "Henry Yesler's Native American Daughter Julia Is Born on June 12, 1855."

96. Rebecca Graham Biographical File, University of Washington Special Collections.

97. Nicola, "Rebecca Lena Graham's Fight for Her Inheritance," 145.

98. Marriage certificate April 11, 1911, Washington State Digital Archives. "Church Services," *Tacoma Times*, July 17, 1909, 8:4.

99. King County, Washington, marriage certificate, Washington State Digital Archives.

100. King County, Washington, marriage certificate for Victor Graham Jr. and Ruth Heideman, November 30, 1914, Washington State Digital Archives.

101. Bureau of Indian Affairs, "Summary Under the Criteria and Evidence for Proposed Finding Against Acknowledgment of the Duwamish Tribal Organization" (Washington, D.C.: Government Printing Office, 1996).

102. Rebecca Fitzhenry Affidavit, Dwamish Tribal Register, M1343: Roblin Rolls, Roll 3, NARA Seattle. Nicola, "Rebecca Lena Graham's Fight for Her Inheritance," 145.

103. Thomas Talbot Waterman, 1920, as quoted in Bureau of Indian Affairs, "Summary Under the Criteria and Evidence for Proposed Finding Against Acknowledgment of the Duwamish Tribal Organization."

104. Bagley, *Indian Myths of the Northwest*. Arthur C. Ballard, "Some Tales of the Southern Puget Sound Salish," *University of Washington Publications in*

Anthropology 2:3 (1927), 57–81. Thomas Talbot Waterman, *Notes on the Ethnology of the Indians of Puget Sound* (New York: Museum of the American Indian, 1973; originally written in 1921).

105. Bureau of Indian Affairs, "Summary Under the Criteria and Evidence for Proposed Finding Against Acknowledgment of the Duwamish Tribal Organization."

106. Nicola, "Rebecca Lena Graham's Fight for Her Inheritance," 145.

107. 1920 U.S. Census.

108. Bureau of Indian Affairs, "Summary Under the Criteria and Evidence for Proposed Finding Against Acknowledgment of the Duwamish Tribal Organization."

109. Charles Roblin, 1917, as quoted in Bureau of Indian Affairs, "Summary Under the Criteria and Evidence for Proposed Finding Against Acknowledgment of the Duwamish Tribal Organization," emphasis in original.

110. Bureau of Indian Affairs, "Summary Under the Criteria and Evidence for Proposed Finding Against Acknowledgment of the Duwamish Tribal Organization."

111. 1930 and 1940 U.S. Census.

112. Bureau of Indian Affairs, "Summary Under the Criteria and Evidence for Proposed Finding Against Acknowledgment of the Duwamish Tribal Organization." *Duwamish et al. v. U.S.*, 79 C. Cls. 530, filed in 1926 and rejected in 1934.

113. Rebecca Graham Biographical File, University of Washington Special Collections.

114. As a result of denied federal recognition as Duwamish, some tribal members with relatives from other local tribes have enrolled in other tribes, so they are viewed as Indian by the federal government, but not as Duwamish.

115. The Duwamish federal recognition effort is ongoing and readers will find the most current information on that process on the tribe's website, duwamish-tribe.org.

Chapter 6. Dinah Hood, "The State Is Supreme"

1. *State of Arizona v. Juan Fernandez* (1913), Arizona Superior Court of Yavapai County. Coroner's Inquest on September 2, 1913 (Records of Yavapai County, 1913), SG3 Coroner, microfilm 50.25.5, Case No. 769 (hereafter Coroner's Inquest). "Two Murder Suspects Are Now in Custody: Husband of Woman Detained as Witness, Is Thought to Know Something of Monday Night Tragedy," *Prescott Journal Miner*, September 4, 1913, 1.

2. It is always worth pointing out that my inclusion of the word "squaw" is based on the primary sources themselves and is valuable in stressing the views that *Arizona v. Fernandez* jurists held toward the women in Dinah's family. Similarly, I use the identification American, Mexican, or Yavapai throughout this chapter to highlight the national and racial hierarchies in play throughout central Arizona at the turn of the twentieth century. Despite the transmission of American citi-

zenship by the Treaty of Guadalupe Hidalgo to Mexicans remaining north of the U.S.-Mexico border after 1848, Anglo Arizonans persisted in viewing themselves as Americans but ethnic Mexicans and Yavapais as racialized noncitizens. This was especially true for ethnic Mexicans like the ones described in this chapter who did not speak English fluently. Considered more "Yankee" than cities like Tucson in southern Arizona, Prescott was particularly segregated and maintained social as well as legal and physical distinctions between white Americans, ethnic Mexicans, and resident Yavapais. I also use the term "American" in contradistinction to "Indigenous" or "Yavapai" to highlight that these suggest national and racial categories; "American" at the time implied white U.S. citizens. "Yavapai" invokes Indian and tribal citizen; Yavapais would be leaders in efforts to push for American Indian citizenship rights and served in the U.S. military during World War I and World War II.

3. Timothy Braatz, *Surviving Conquest: A History of the Yavapai Peoples* (Lincoln: University of Nebraska Press, 2003). Gerhard Grytz, "Culture in the Making: The Yavapé of Central Arizona, 1860–1935," *American Indian Culture and Research Journal*, 24:3 (2000): 111–129. "The Yavapai; The Yavapai-Apache Indian Community; The Fort McDowell Mohave-Apache Community, Petitioners v. The United States of America, Defendant," 15 *Indian Claims Commission* 68 (March 3, 1965), Docket No. 22-E. James C. Scott, *Seeing Like a State: How Certain Schemes to Improve the Human Condition Have Failed* (New Haven: Yale University Press, 1999). Samuel Truett, *Fugitive Landscapes: The Forgotten History of the U.S.-Mexico Borderlands* (New Haven: Yale University Press, 2006). Katherine Morrissey, *Mental Territories: Mapping the Inland Empire* (Ithaca: Cornell University Press, 1997). Paul Reeve, *Making Space on the Western Frontier: Mormons, Miners, and Southern Paiutes* (Urbana: University of Illinois Press, 2006). Edward W. Soja, *Postmodern Geographies: The Reassertion of Space in Critical Social Theory* (New York: Verso, 1989). Derrick A. Bell Jr., "Comment: Brown v. Board of Education and the Interest-Convergence Dilemma," *Harvard Law Review* 93 (1979–1980), 518–533. Irene Silverblatt, "Interpreting Women in States: New Feminist Ethnohistories," in *Gender at the Crossroads of Knowledge: Feminist Anthropology in the Postmodern Era*, ed. Micaela di Leonardo (Berkeley: University of California Press, 1991), 140–171. Robert Porter, "The Demise of the Ongwehoweh and the Rise of the Native Americans: Redressing the Genocidal Act of Forcing American Citizenship upon Indigenous Peoples," 107–183.

4. 1916 U.S. Indian Census Schedule, Camp Verde.

5. Granite Mountain is about ten miles from the camp Dinah's family shared, and therefore inside the eighteen-kilometer distance that anthropologists have estimated for round-trip day trips among Native people. Robert Drennan, "Long Distant Transport Costs in Pre-Hispanic Mesoamerica," *American Anthropologist* 86:1 (1984), 105–112. David R. Willcox et al., "Early Pueblo III Defensive Refuge Systems in West-Central Arizona," in *In Deadly Landscapes: Case Studies in Prehistoric Southwestern Warfare*, ed. Glen E. Rice and Steven A. LeBlanc (Salt Lake City: University of Utah Press, 2001), 109–140. E. W. Gifford, "Northeastern and

Western Yavapai Myths," *Journal of American Folklore* 46:182 (October–December 1933), 347–415.

6. Elizabeth Dore and Maxine Molyneux, eds., *Hidden Histories of Gender and the State in Latin America* (Durham, N.C.: Duke University Press, 2000), 148.

7. Martha Minow, "Feminist Reason: Getting It and Losing It," *Journal of Legal Education* 38 (1988), 47–60. Patricia Smith, ed., *Feminist Jurisprudence* (New York: Oxford University Press, 1993). Patricia A. Cain, "Feminist Jurisprudence: Grounding the Theories," *Berkeley Women's Law Journal* 4 (1989–1990), 191–214. Cornelia Hughes Dayton, *Women Before the Bar: Gender, Law, and Society in Connecticut, 1639–1789* (Chapel Hill: University of North Carolina Press, 1995). Linda Kerber, *No Constitutional Right to Be Ladies: Women and Obligations of Citizenship* (New York: Hill & Wang, 1998). Susan Kellogg, *Law and the Transformation of Aztec Culture, 1500–1700* (Norman: University of Oklahoma Press, 1995). Robert A. Williams Jr., "Gendered Checks and Balances: Understanding the Legacy of White Patriarchy in an American Indian Cultural Context," *Georgia Law Review* 24 (1989–1990), 1019–1044.

8. Braatz, *Surviving Conquest*, 25–52.

9. Ibid., 25–52. Dick Glenn Winchell, "Space and Place of the Yavapai" (Ph.D. diss., Arizona State University, 1982), 62.

10. Mike Burns, *All of My People Were Killed: The Memoir of Mike Burns (Hoomothya), a Captive Indian* (Prescott, Ariz.: Sharlot Hall Museum, 2010), 133.

11. E. W. Gifford, "Northeastern and Western Yavapai," *University of California Publications in American Archaeology and Ethnology* 34:4 (June 1936), 247–354, 296, 298–299.

12. 1916 U.S. Indian Census Schedule, Camp Verde.

13. Ethnologist E. W. Gifford reports that the literal meaning of *Haiko'* is unknown, but that *-ko* means to hold something in one's hand. Gifford, "Northeastern and Western Yavapai," 252.

14. Sigrid Khera, ed., *The Yavapai of Fort McDowell: An Outline of Their History and Culture* (n.p., 1977), 1–2.

15. Albert II. Schroeder, "A Study of Yavapai History" in *Yavapai Indians*, ed. David Agee Horr (New York: Garland, 1974), 23–354, 34.

16. Braatz, *Surviving Conquest*, 49–50.

17. Charles D. Poston, *Building a State in Apache Land: The Story of Arizona's Founding Told by Arizona's Founder* (Tempe, Ariz.: Aztec, 1963), 116–117; Braatz, *Surviving Conquest*, 94–95.

18. Orick Jackson, *The White Conquest of Arizona: History of the Pioneers* (Los Angeles: West Coast Magazine, 1908), 23. Braatz, *Surviving Conquest*, 105–106.

19. Braatz, *Surviving Conquest*, 138–139, 10–11.

20. United States Office of Indian Affairs, *Annual Report of the Commissioner of Indian Affairs to the Secretary of the Interior* (Washington, D.C.: Government Printing Office, 1872), 66–67.

21. John Williams interview published in unknown periodical in "Apache Indians" folder at Sharlot Hall Library and Archive, Prescott, Arizona.

22. United States Office of Indian Affairs, *Annual Report*, 1873, 342.

23. United States Office of Indian Affairs, *Annual Report*, 1874, 60.

24. United States Office of Indian Affairs, *Annual Report*, 1873, 288; 1874, 60, 298–299. Braatz, *Surviving Conquest*, 160–62. Trudy Griffin-Pierce, *Native Peoples of the Southwest* (Albuquerque: University of New Mexico Press, 2000), 295.

25. United States Office of Indian Affairs, *Annual Report*, 1874, 62, 299. Braatz, *Surviving Conquest*, 170. Jay J. Wagoner, *Arizona Territory, 1863–1912: A Political History* (Tucson: University of Arizona Press, 1970), 122, 144. Griffin-Pierce, *Native Peoples of the Southwest*, 296.

26. John Perkins and Maggie Hayes, "Our Thanksgiving Story Begins," *The Arizona Republic* (Phoenix), November 23, 1959, 6:2, 6:3.

27. United States Office of Indian Affairs, *Annual Report*, 1875, 215; 1876, 10; 1875, 216.

28. Perkins and Hayes, "Our Thanksgiving Story," 6:4. United States Office of Indian Affairs, *Annual Report*, 1876, xviii.

29. Original data: *General Index to Pension Files, 1861–1934*, Washington, D.C.: National Archives and Records Administration, T288, 544 rolls. *Civil War Pension Index: General Index to Pension Files, 1861–1934*, NARA database online. Robin and Dinah Hood's family refer to this record as evidence of his service as an Indian Scout in 1881–1882 and 1885–1886, though Robin Hood is misspelled as "Robert Hoth" and the widow applying for her pension in 1928 is Julia "Hoth," who would have been Robin's daughter, not widow.

30. Perkins and Hayes, "Our Thanksgiving Story," 6:4.

31. United States Office of Indian Affairs, *Annual Report*, 1878, 230.

32. Winchell, "Space and Place of the Yavapai" 95.

33. Mary Lee Spence, *The Arizona Diary of Lily Fremont, 1878–1881* (Tucson: University of Arizona Press, 1997), 69.

34. 1910 U.S. Census, Arizona Territory; the census enumerator indicated that Robin's wives Dinah and Mary were sisters, but there are no other records to confirm a relationship that the Hood family may have offered to explain their household as one joined in sororal polygamy—a practice ethnographers and Indian officials tolerated more than nonsororal polygamy. Modern-day Hood descendants do affirm the sibling connection in their oral family history.

35. Clifford E. Trafzer, *As Long as the Grass Shall Grow and Rivers Flow: A History of Native Americans* (Belmont, Calif.: Thomson Learning, 2000), 273. United States Office of Indian Affairs, *Annual Report*, 1881, viii–x. United States Office of Indian Affairs, *Annual Report*, 1883, 7.

36. E. W. Gifford, "Northeastern and Western Yavapai," 343.

37. United States Office of Indian Affairs, *Annual Report*, 1888, 8.

38. 1893 U.S. Indian Census Schedule, San Carlos Agency. United States Office of Indian Affairs, *Annual Report*, 1880, xxi; 1881, xxxiii; 1881, 8; 1883, 9; 1884, 9; 1888, 288, 372; 1893, 12, 16; 1894, 9.

39. Santa Fe Indian Institute Records, microfilm, NARA RG 75, Series 32, Roll 6. John Perkins and Maggie Hayes, "Maggie Goes Away to School for 11 Year

Exile from Family," *Arizona Republic* (Phoenix), November 23, 1959, 30:1, 3. Sally Hyer, *One House, One Voice, One Heart: Native American Education at the Santa Fe Indian School* (Santa Fe: Museum of New Mexico Press, 1990), 14.

40. John Gram, *Education at the Edge of Empire: Negotiating Pueblo Identity in New Mexico's Indian Boarding Schools* (Seattle: University of Washington Press, 2015).

41. Hyer, *One House, One Voice, One Heart,* 22.

42. Literacy and fluency in 1910 U.S. Census, Arizona Territory.

43. Perkins and Hayes, "Maggie Goes Away to School," 30:3.

44. Letter from Santa Fe Indian School superintendent C. J. Crandall to William A. Jones, Commissioner of Indian Affairs, July 1900, Santa Fe Indian Institute Records, microfilm, NARA RG 75, Series 32, Roll 6.

45. Letter from Santa Fe Indian School superintendent to Daniel M. Browning, Commissioner of Indian Affairs, April 2, 1896, Santa Fe Indian Institute Records, microfilm, NARA RG 75, Series 32, Roll 6.

46. Letter from Santa Fe Indian School superintendent to Captain Myer, U.S. Army, Acting Indian Agent, September 1897, Santa Fe Indian Institute Records, microfilm, NARA RG 75, Series 32, Roll 6.

47. Letter from Santa Fe Indian School superintendent C. J. Crandall to William A. Jones, Commissioner of Indian Affairs, July 1900, Santa Fe Indian Institute Records, microfilm, NARA RG 75, Series 32, Roll 6.

48. John Perkins and Maggie Hayes, "Maggie Is Reunited with Her Mother," *Arizona Republic* (Phoenix), November 25, 1959. Franklin Barnett, *Viola Jimulla: The Indian Chieftess* (Yuma, Ariz.: Southwest Printers, 1968), 5–6.

49. Donald R. Keller and Pat H. Stein, *Archaeological Study at Three Twentieth-Century Yavapai Wickiup Sites, Prescott, Arizona* (Flagstaff: Museum of Northern Arizona Department of Anthropology, 1985), 10.

50. Braatz, *Surviving Conquest,* 82.

51. Kitty Jo Parker Nelson, "Prescott: Sketch of a Frontier Capital, 1863–1900," *Arizoniana* 4:4 (1963), 17–38. Melissa R. Weiner, *Prescott Yesteryears: Life in Arizona's First Territorial Capital* (Prescott, Ariz.: Primrose, 1976, 1977, 1978). John S. Goff, "William T. Howell and the Howell Code of Arizona," *The American Journal of Legal History* 11:3 (July, 1967), 221–233. Barnett, *Viola Jimulla,* 5–7. Grytz, "Culture in the Making."

52. Newspaper clipping dated June 1897; "Yavapai" folder at Sharlot Hall Library and Archives.

53. *Prescott Weekly Courier* (Arizona), November 13, 1903, 4:2.

54. *Journal Miner* (Prescott, Ariz.), January 20, 1897, 3:1; February 10, 1897, 3:2; February 15, 1899, 4:1; July 5, 1899, 4:1; September 6, 1899, 2:1.

55. 1910 U.S. Census, Arizona Territory.

56. Keller and Stein, *Archaeological Study at Three Twentieth-Century Yavapai Wickiup Sites,* 12. *Journal Miner* (Prescott, Ariz.), January 20, 1897, 3:1; February 10, 1897, 3:2; February 15, 1899, 4:1; July 5, 1899, 4:1; September 6, 1899, 2:1.

57. Keller and Stein, *Archaeological Study at Three Twentieth-Century Yavapai Wickiup Sites, Prescott, Arizona,* 10.

58. Theodore Roosevelt set aside the Fort McDowell Indian Reservation for Yavapais in 1903. Later the 1934 Indian Reorganization Act recognized the status of Verde Valley Yavapais as sovereign people and the process of obtaining reservation lands began.

59. See RG 114, Yavapai County, SG3, Coroner's Inquest Records, Case Nos. 81, 130, 160, 378, 424, 510, 579, 593, 657, Arizona State Library, Archives and Public Records (ASLAPR).

60. Barnett, *Viola Jimulla*, 9.

61. Coroner's Inquest, September 2, 1913 (Records of Yavapai County, 1913), SG3 Coroner, microfilm 50.25.5, Case No. 769 (hereafter Coroner's Inquest), 35–40, 55–63. Transcripts, *Arizona v. Fernandez* (1913), submitted in appeal *Fernandez v. Arizona* (1914), 32–37.

62. Coroner's Inquest, 29–34, 44–46. Transcripts, *Arizona v. Fernandez* (1913), 32–37.

63. Transcripts, *Arizona v. Fernandez* (1913), 190–207.

64. Coroner's Inquest, 35–40.

65. Ibid., 21–25.

66. Ibid., 12–16, 47–51.

67. "Indian Wars Veterans, Prescott, Arizona, c. 1916," call number 0113p, Sharlot Hall Museum Library and Archives, Prescott, Arizona.

68. "Murder Case to Be Handled by State," *Prescott Journal Miner,* September 5, 1913, 1.

69. Deborah A. Rosen, *American Indians and State Law: Sovereignty, Race, and Citizenship, 1790–1880* (Lincoln: University of Nebraska Press, 2007). Kermit L. Hall and Peter Karsten, *The Magic Mirror: Law in American History,* 2nd ed. (New York: Oxford University Press, 2009), 142, 164–165. Daniel McCool et al., *Native Vote: American Indians, the Voting Rights Act, and the Right to Vote* (New York: Cambridge University Press, 2007), 3, 5, 8–19.

70. Major Crimes Act, 18 U.S.C. 1153 (1885).

71. Frederick E. Hoxie, *A Final Promise: The Campaign to Assimilate the Indians, 1880–1920* (Lincoln: University of Nebraska Press, 1984, 2001). David Wallace Adams, *Education for Extinction: American Indians and the Boarding School Experience, 1875–1928* (Lawrence: University of Kansas Press, 1995).

72. "Murder Case to Be Handled by State," *Prescott Journal Miner,* September 5, 1913, 1.

73. Major Crimes Act, 18 U.S.C. 1153 (1885). Sidney L. Harring, *Crow Dog's Case: American Indian Sovereignty, Tribal Law, and United States Law in the Nineteenth Century* (New York: Cambridge University Press, 1994).

74. Ray Brandes, *Frontier Military Posts of Arizona* (Globe, Ariz.: Dale Stuart King, 1960), 75–80.

75. Fayette A. McKenzie (special agent, United States Indian Census), "The Indian and Citizenship, Reprinted from *The Red Man,* Carlisle, Penn." (Washington, D.C.: Society of American Indians, 1912). Thomas J. Morgan (Commissioner of Indian Affairs), *The Present Phase of the Indian Question: Also a Memorial on the*

Extension of Law to the Indians, by the Boston Indian Citizenship Committee (Boston: Frank Wood, 1891).

76. Erin Hogan Fouberg, "Understanding Space, Understanding Citizenship," *Journal of Geography* 101 (2002), 82. Thomas Biolsi, "Imagined Geographies: Sovereignty, Indigenous Space, and American Indian Struggle," *American Ethnologist* 32:2 (2005), 239–259. Mishuana R. Goeman, "Notes Toward a Native Feminism's Spatial Practice," *Wicazo Sa Review* 24:2 (Fall 2009), 169–187. Bettina Koschade and Evelyn Peters, "Algonquin Notions of Jurisdiction: Inserting Indigenous Voices into Legal Spaces," *Geografiska Annaler*: Series B, *Human Geography* 88:3 (September 2006), 299–310. Sherene H. Razack, ed., *Race, Space, and the Law: Unmapping a White Settler Society* (Toronto: Between the Lines, 2002).

77. "The Bar of Prescott: Men Who Have Made Legal History for Arizona," *Yavapai Magazine* (June 1914), 9–10. "Juan Fernandez Tells His Story: Mexican Accused of Murdering Fellow Countryman Denies Ownership of Knife Found in Dead Man's Hand," *Prescott Journal Miner*, December 13, 1913, 6.

78. "Find Murdered Man In a Shallow Grave: Clue Given by Indians Results in Unearthing Fiendish Crime by Officers—Suspect Now in Custody," *Prescott Journal Miner*, September 3, 1913, 5.

79. Ibid., 65.

80. *Fernandez v. State of Arizona* (1914), Case No. 360, Arizona Court of Appeals, Division One, Criminal Files, Briefs and Records, ASLAPR.

81. Coroner's Inquest, 21–24.

82. "Saw Him Cover Up Grave, Squaw Swears: Prosecution Springs Surprise in Fernandez Murder Trial by Putting New Witness on Stand," *Prescott Journal Miner*, December 11, 1913, 1.

83. Featured in chapter 2, King S. Woolsey established a ranch near Prescott in 1860. He fathered and indentured two illegitimate Indian children, befriended Maricopas and Akimel O'odham (Pimas) living near the Salt River, and in campaigns in the territorial militia killed Apaches—some of them probably Yavapais—at rates that vary according to the chronicler. He impregnated the mother of his only known children when she was twelve years old, indicating his preference for young adolescent Indian girls. He impregnated her again within the first year of his marriage to a white woman, demonstrating a propensity for infidelity. When he died in 1879, Woolsey no longer lived in the Prescott vicinity, though he maintained close ties there and could have met Tcha-ah-wooeha, who would have been an adolescent in the 1870s, while visiting friends. If so, he might have called her "Mary" after his legitimate wife, Mary Taylor. What better way to hide an Indian mistress than to give her your wife's name? Since a relationship would have been illicit, it would make sense that Tcha-ah-wooeha would choose not to use the name after Woolsey's death.

84. "Saw Him Cover Up Grave," *Prescott Journal Miner*, December 11, 1913, 1.

85. Transcripts, *Arizona v. Fernandez* (1913), 369–383.

86. *Fernandez v. Arizona* (1914), 1–21.

87. Bell, "Comment: Brown v. Board of Education and the Interest-Convergence Dilemma," 518–533. *Porter v. Hall* (1928) 34 Ariz. 308, 271 Pac. 411.

88. "Who May Be a Witness in a Criminal Case," art. 10, 3rd div., sec. 14, Howell Code, 1865 Ariz. Terr. Sess. Laws, 50. "No black or mulatto, or Indian, Mongolian, or Asiatic, shall be permitted to give evidence in favor of or against any white person . . . and every person who shall have one-half of Indian blood shall be deemed an Indian."

89. "Witnesses in Criminal Actions," Arizona Penal Code 1913, secs. 1226, 1227, 1228, 235–236.

90. Transcripts, *Arizona v. Juan Fernandez*, 64, 68.

91. Keller and Stein, "Interview with Don Mitchell," *Archaeological Study at Three Twentieth-Century Yavapai Wickiup Sites*, 9–11.

92. Helen Palmer Peterson, "Landscapes of Capital: Culture in an Industrial Western Company Town: Clarkdale, Arizona, 1914–1929" (Ph.D. diss., Northern Arizona University, 2008), 27. Map of the Town of Clarkdale (James H. Howard, 1962); this map denotes the boundaries of the Indian village on the borders of Clarkdale.

93. Peterson, "Landscapes of Capital."

94. 1920 U.S. Census, Arizona; the enumerator, Warren Leroy Bell, ignored federal instructions and marked his neighbors "W" for white, "Mex" for Mexican, and "Ind" for Indian. Peterson, "Landscapes of Capital."

95. 1930 U.S. Census, Arizona.

96. Barnett, *Viola Jimulla*, 14. U.S. census schedules for Clarkdale in 1920 and 1930 include the "Indian Village" district of Native American residents living near the more elite neighborhood of "Upper Clarkdale."

97. Peterson, "Landscapes of Capital," 174.

Chapter 7. Louisa Enick, "Hemmed In on All Sides"

1. William Salter to Tulalip Indian Agency on behalf of Louisa Enick, November 30, 1920, RG 75, Records of the Bureau of Indian Affairs, Western Washington Agency, Tribal Operations Branch, General Correspondence (Old Taholah / Tulalip) ca. 1914–1951, IRA-921 folder 380, Public Domain Allotments, Skagit and Whatcom Counties (Tulalip), 1914–1937. William Salter would continue to advocate for his ailing friend, who died in 1924, leaving behind a three-year-old daughter in addition to the six children described in her letter. Salter married Louisa's youngest daughter sometime around 1935, and together they continued to write letters in regard to the family's public domain allotments.

2. Jean Bedal Fish and Edith Bedal with Astrida Onat, *Two Voices: A History of the Sauk and Suiattle People and Sauk Country Experiences* (self-published for the Memorial and Powwow Celebration of the 25th year of Federal Recognition for the Sauk-Suiattle Tribe, 2000 [2004 ed.]). Jan L. Hollenbeck, *A Cultural Resource Overview: Prehistory, Ethnography, and History, Mt. Baker–Snoqualmie National Forest* (U.S. Department of Agriculture, Forest Service, 1987).

3. Nels Bruseth, *Indian Stories and Legends of the Stillaguamish, Sauks, and Allied Tribes*, 2nd ed. (n.p., 1949 [1st ed. 1925]), 34–35. Elizabeth Poehlman, *Darrington: Mining Town, Timber Town* (Kent, Wash.: Gold Hill, 1979), 16–17. Robert H. Ruby and John A. Brown, *A Guide to the Indian Tribes of the Pacific Northwest* (Norman: University of Oklahoma Press, 1992). Robert H. Ruby and John A. Brown, *Indians of the Pacific Northwest: A History* (Norman: University of Oklahoma Press, 1981). Alexandra Harmon, ed., *The Power of Promises: Rethinking Indian Treaties in the Pacific Northwest* (Seattle: University of Washington Press, 2008).

4. The text of the treaty is available on the Washington Governor's Office of Indian Affairs website, www.goia.wa.gov/treaties/treaties/pointelliot.htm (accessed September 24, 2013). Norma A. Joseph, "Suattle Tribe of Indians vs. The United States, 1952: A Case Study Involving Tribal Land Claims, Tribal Identity, and Tribal Persistence" (M.A. thesis, University of California–Los Angeles, 1985).

5. Andrew H. Fisher, *Shadow Tribe: The Making of Columbia River Indian Identity* (Seattle: University of Washington Press, 2010). Harmon, ed., *The Power of Promises*. Frank W. Porter III, "In Search of Recognition: Federal Indian Policy and the Landless Tribes of Western Washington," *American Indian Quarterly* 14:2 (Spring 1990), 113–132. Felix S. Cohen, *Cohen's Handbook of Federal Indian Law* (Newark, N.J.: LexisNexis, 2005). David E. Wilkins and K. Tsianina Lomawaima, *Uneven Ground: American Indian Sovereignty and Federal Law* (Norman: University of Oklahoma Press, 2001). Hamar Foster, Heather Raven, and Jeremy Webber, eds., *Let Right Be Done: Aboriginal Title, the Calder Case, and the Future of Indigenous Rights* (Vancouver: University of British Columbia Press, 2007). Marcia Langton et al., eds., *Honour Among Nations? Treaties and Agreements with Indigenous People* (Victoria: Melbourne University Press, 2004). Roger L. Nichols, *Indians in the United States and Canada: A Comparative History* (Lincoln: University of Nebraska Press, 1998). Joseph, "Suattle Tribe of Indians vs. The United States." Fish, Bedal, and Onat, *Two Voices: A History of the Sauk and Suiattle People*.

6. The Donation Lands Act of 1850–1854 made 320 acres available to single men and 640 acres available to married men who settled in Oregon Territory. Between 1855 and 1862 (questionably), ceded lands remained available at subsidized rates and were then made available for a pittance once again under the 1862 Homestead Act, which granted 160 acres to applicants. Robert E. Ficken, *Washington Territory* (Pullman: Washington State University Press, 2002). Gerald W. Williams, *The U.S. Forest Service in the Pacific Northwest: A History* (Corvallis: Oregon State University Press, 2009).

7. "Gold on Skaget River," *Pioneer and Democrat* (Olympia, Wash.), July 30, 1858, 3:1. Lelah Jackson Edson, *The Fourth Corner: Highlights from the Early Northwest* (Bellingham: Whatcom Museum of History and Art, 1968).

8. Walter L. Hixson, *American Settler Colonialism: A History* (New York: Palgrave Macmillan, 2013). Margaret D. Jacobs, *White Mother to a Dark Race: Settler Colonialism, Maternalism, and the Removal of Indigenous Children in the American West and Australia, 1880–1940* (Lincoln: University of Nebraska Press, 2009). Ann

Laura Stoler, ed., *Haunted by Empire: Geographies of Intimacy in North American History* (Durham, N.C.: Duke University Press, 2006). Lorenzo Veracini, *Settler Colonialism: A Theoretical Overview* (New York: Palgrave Macmillan, 2010).

9. The Skagit are a neighboring tribe to the north of the Sauk-Suiattle. In the 1870s and 1880s, they shared many of the same challenges and leaders from both tribes often aligned against federal and state officials, such as in this case involving Linsley.

10. D. C. Linsley, "A Railroad Survey of the Sauk and Wenatchee Rivers in 1870," *Northwest Discovery: The Journal of Northwest History and Natural History* 2:4 (April 1981), 210.

11. Ibid., 220.

12. Ibid., 232. Wawetkin is perhaps one of the most well-known leaders of the Sauk-Suiattle tribe and is discussed at length in the tribal histories cited throughout this chapter.

13. United States Office of Indian Affairs, *Annual Report of the Commissioner of Indian Affairs to the Secretary of the Interior* (Washington, D.C.: Government Printing Office, 1873), 306.

14. United States Office of Indian Affairs, *Annual Report*, 1874, 337.

15. For American Indians and homesteading laws, see chapter 11 of Cohen, *Cohen's Handbook of Federal Indian Law*.

16. "Exploring the Homestead Timeline," on the Bureau of Land Management Homestead Act and General Land Office webpage, www.blm.gov. D. S. Otis, *The Dawes Act and the Allotment of Indian Lands* (Norman: University of Oklahoma Press, 1973). Kristin T. Ruppel, *Unearthing Indian Land: Living with the Legacies of Allotment* (Tucson: University of Arizona Press, 2008). Rose Stremlau, *Sustaining the Cherokee Family: Kinship and the Allotment of an Indigenous Nation* (Chapel Hill: University of North Carolina Press, 2011). Wilcomb E. Washburn, *The Assault on Indian Tribalism: The General Allotment Law (Dawes Act) of 1887* (Philadelphia: Lippincott, 1975).

17. *Vancouver Independent* (Vancouver, Wash.), December 11, 1879, 4:1.

18. Robert E. Ficken, "The Fraser River Humbug: Americans and Gold in the British Pacific Northwest," *Western Historical Quarterly* 33:3 (Autumn 2002), 297–313. Daniel P. Marshall, "No Parallel: American Miner-Soldiers at War with the Nlaka'pamux of the Canadian West," in *Parallel Destinies: Canadian-American Relations West of the Rockies*, ed. John M. Findlay and Ken S. Coates (Seattle: University of Washington Press, 2002), 31–79. Adele Perry, *On the Edge of Empire: Gender, Race, and the Making of British Columbia, 1849–1871* (Toronto: University of Toronto Press, 2001).

19. "Indian Troubles," *Puget Sound Mail* (LaConner, Wash.), October 16, 1880, 3:2.

20. "The Indian Demonstrations of Hostility to the Surveying Party, on the Skagit," *Puget Sound Weekly Argus* (Port Townsend), October 29, 1880, 1:2.

21. Ned Blackhawk, *Violence over the Land: Indians and Empires in the Early American West* (Cambridge: Harvard University Press, 2006). Albert Hurtado,

Intimate Frontiers: Sex, Gender, and Culture in Old California (Albuquerque: University of New Mexico Press, 1999). Coll Thrush, *Native Seattle: Histories from the Crossing Over Place* (Seattle: University of Washington Press, 2007).

22. "Skagit Indian Troubles," *Puget Sound Weekly Argus* (Port Townsend), November 5, 1880, 5:3. Leo Braun, "The History of the Sauk-Suiattle Tribe," reprinted in the *Concrete Herald* (Concrete, Wash.), June 21, 1951. Poehlman, *Darrington: Mining Town, Timber Town.*

23. "Col. W. J. Pollock," *Puget Sound Mail* (LaConner, Wash.), March 19, 1881, 3:1. A similar report appeared in "News Items," *Puget Sound Weekly Argus* (Port Townsend), March 11, 1881, 3:3.

24. United States Office of Indian Affairs, *Annual Report*, 1880, 165. The surname Campbell is among those included among Sauk-Suiattle allottees and on twentieth-century tribal enrollment documents, but it is unclear whether the John Campbell referred to here considered himself Skagit or Sauk-Suiattle.

25. Paige Raibmon, *Authentic Indians: Episodes of Encounter from the Late-Nineteenth-Century Northwest Coast* (Durham, N.C.: Duke University Press, 2005).

26. Braun, "History of the Sauk-Suiattle Tribe," 3. Bruseth, *Indian Stories and Legends of the Stillaguamish, Sauks, and Allied Tribes.* Poehlman, *Darrington: Mining Town, Timber Town.*

27. 1885 U.S. Indian Census Roll, Tulalip Agency.

28. Early twentieth-century accounts of Sauk-Suiattle history written by local citizens make clear that some white residents accepted the tribal claim that they had been illegally and violently removed from their Sauk Prairie home. See especially Nels Bruseth and Elizabeth Poehlman, cited above.

29. United States Office of Indian Affairs, *Annual Report*, 1884, 173–177; 1885, 184–185, 192–193.

30. C. Joseph Genetin-Pilawa, *Crooked Paths to Allotment: The Fight over Federal Indian Policy After the Civil War* (Chapel Hill: University of North Carolina Press, 2012). Frederick E. Hoxie, *A Final Promise: The Campaign to Assimilate the Indians, 1880–1920* (Lincoln: University of Nebraska Press, 2001). Otis, *The Dawes Act and the Allotment of Indian Lands.* Ruppel, *Unearthing Indian Land.* Stremlau, *Sustaining the Cherokee Family.* Washburn, *The Assault on Indian Tribalism.* Each of these are excellent histories. All emphasize the detrimental effect of allotment on reservation tribes, unlike the Sauk-Suiattle who claimed off-reservation allotments under section 4 of the Allotment Act.

31. Allotment Act quoted from Washburn, *The Assault on Indian Tribalism*, 70.

32. United States Office of Indian Affairs, *Annual Report*, 1891, 673.

33. Ibid., 1893, 24.

34. Ibid., 1891, 458; 1893, 24.

35. Ibid., 1894, 23.

36. Locating documentation for all of the Sauk-Suiattle allotments has proven painfully difficult, a problem shared by the Sauk-Suiattle allottees and federal officials who processed them as well as by historians. Of the families who filed their

applications in April 1895, some were Skagit and some were Sauk-Suiattle, though all of Arntzen's paperwork listed the allottees indiscriminately as members of the Skagit River tribe, which would prove problematic in the twentieth century. The papers gathered for this chapter can be found in the National Archives and Records Administration, Seattle, RG 49, General Land Office—Washington Tract Books, vol. 137, p. 195 for Joe Campbell; RG 49, Bureau of Land Management, Oregon State Office, Mixed Land Cases, Washington/Oregon, ca. 1919–1968, RIP 512, box 1409, Allotment File 03860 for Mary Charley; Allotment File 03861 for Old Charley; Allotment File 04368 for Josie Campbell; RIP 512, box 1410, Allotment File 04316 for Annie Charley; Allotment File 04367 for Sammie Charley; Allotment File 04369 for Ed Campbell; Allotment File 04372 for William Harrison; Allotment File 04382 for Betsy Poison; RIP 470–471, box 1295, Allotment File 04371 for Emma Harrison; Allotment File 04373 for Sally Towne. RG 75 records of the Bureau of Indian Affairs were also consulted for this chapter and are cited where directly relevant. Washington Indian agents involved themselves in the Sauk-Suiattle issue only occasionally and their records are largely silent on the public domain allotment question. That so many historians rely on RG 75 and not RG 49 records for tribal histories is likely why much of the information recounted in this chapter has not already been chronicled.

37. United States Office of Indian Affairs, *Annual Report,* 1895, 21; 1896, 27.

38. Ibid., 1895, 22, 441.

39. Ibid., 1896, 28–29.

40. Ibid., 1895, 318.

41. Cleveland established the thirteen forest reserves in 1897, but they were not designated as reserved lands until 1898.

42. Steen, *The U.S. Forest Service,* 33–34. James G. Lewis, *The Forest Service and the Greatest Good: A Centennial History* (Durham, N.C.: Forest History Society, 2005). Williams, *The U.S. Forest Service in the Pacific Northwest.*

43. Williams, *The U.S. Forest Service in the Pacific Northwest,* 44–48.

44. United States Office of Indian Affairs, *Annual Report,* 1897, 26–27.

45. Ibid., 24.

46. Ibid., 1900, 56.

47. Ibid., 1901, 59.

48. Ibid., 1903, 40–41.

49. Ibid.

50. These are allotment applications 04491, 04487, 04526, and 04563 in the National Archives and Records Administration, Seattle, RG 49, Bureau of Land Management, Oregon State Office, Mixed Land Cases, Washington/Oregon, ca. 1919–1968, RIP 513, box 1411. Records do not indicate whether sons Francis and Dick were allotted.

51. Nancy F. Cott, "Marriage and Women's Citizenship in the United States, 1830–1934," *The American Historical Review* 103:5 (December 1998), 1440–1474. Michael Grossberg, "Crossing Boundaries: Nineteenth-Century Domestic Relations Law and the Merger of Family and Legal History," *American Bar Foundation*

Research Journal 10:4 (Autumn, 1985), 799–847. Leslie J. Harris, "Law as Father: Metaphors of Family in Nineteenth-Century Law," *Communication Studies* 61:5 (2010), 526–542. Hendrik Hartog, *Man and Wife in America: A History* (Cambridge: Harvard University Press, 2000). Karen Anderson, *Changing Woman: A History of Racial Ethnic Women in Modern America* (New York: Oxford University Press, 1996), 67–91.

52. Douglas Brinkley, *The Wilderness Warrior: Theodore Roosevelt and the Crusade for America* (New York: HarperCollins, 2009). Zachary Michael Jack, *The Green Roosevelt: Theodore Roosevelt in Appreciation of Wilderness, Wildlife, and Wild Places* (Amherst, N.Y.: Cambria, 2010).

53. Lewis, *The Forest Service and the Greatest Good.* Harold K. Steen, *The Beginning of the National Forest System* (Washington, D.C.: U.S. Department of Agriculture: Forest Service, 1991). Steen, *The U.S. Forest Service: A History.* Williams, *The U.S. Forest Service in the Pacific Northwest.* Gerald W. Williams, *The Forest Service: Fighting for Public Lands* (Westport, Conn.: Greenwood, 2007).

54. United States Office of Indian Affairs, *Annual Report,* 1907, 65, 67.

55. Allotment File 04526, RG 49, Bureau of Land Management, Oregon State Office, Mixed Land Cases, Washington/Oregon, ca. 1919–1968, RIP 513, box 1411, NARA Seattle.

56. Allotment File 04491, RG 49, Bureau of Land Management, Oregon State Office, Mixed Land Cases, Washington/Oregon, ca. 1919–1968, RIP 513, box 1411, NARA Seattle.

57. There is some indication that Samuel applied for an allotment on behalf of his son Dick; NARA records in Seattle include a listing for Dick Enick, though not enough documentation exists to include that parcel in this discussion. There is no known evidence that Samuel applied for an allotment in Francis's name. RG 49, General Land Office—Washington Tract Books, vol. 138, p. 81, NARA Seattle.

58. Agnes Enick Allotment File 04487, RG 49, box 1411, NARA Seattle.

59. Williams, *The U.S. Forest Service in the Pacific Northwest,* viii, introduction by Mike Dombeck.

60. "Some Things Done at Spokane Meeting: Irrigation Work Promoted," *The Ranch: A Journal of the Land and the Home in the New West* (Seattle) (September 1, 1909), 26:17.

61. Astrida R. Blukis Onat and Jan L. Hollenbeck, *Inventory of Native American Religious Use, Practices, Localities and Resources: Study Area on the Mt. Baker–Snoqualmie National Forest Washington State* (Seattle: Institute of Cooperative Research, 1981), 213–308. Hollenbeck, *A Cultural Resource Overview,* 138–150.

62. Allotment Act revised June 25, 1910, ch. 431, sec. 31, 36, stat. 863.

63. United States Office of Indian Affairs, *Annual Report,* 1885, 192; 1900, 600.

64. "Cougar Attacks Boy, Sister Wields a Club, Animal Is Driven Off," *Tacoma Times,* Saturday, April 5, 1913, 1:1.

65. Onat and Hollenbeck, *Inventory of Native American Religious Use, Practices, Localities and Resources,* 228–230.

66. Family members shared this communal memory of Agnes Enick and her encounter with the cougar in 1913 during my visit to the Sauk-Suiattle tribe in 2013.

67. RG 49, Bureau of Land Management, Oregon State Office, Mixed Land Cases, Washington/Oregon, ca. 1919–1968, RIP 512, box 1410, 04315, NARA Seattle.

68. RG 49, Bureau of Land Management, Oregon State Office, Mixed Land Cases, Washington/Oregon, ca. 1919–1968, RIP 513, box 1411, 04491, NARA Seattle.

69. James D. Anderson, *A Woodsman Remembers: The Life and Times of James D. Anderson* (n.p., 1996), 134.

70. RG 49, General Land Office—Washington Tract Books, vol. 140, p. 81, NARA Seattle. The Washington Tract Books include an entry for an Indian Allotment made by Samuel Enic on behalf of his son Dick Enic on August 26, 1903, but there are no other records indicating the fate of Dick Enic's allotment. It may be that Dick Enic's allotment was not canceled, and passed on to his wife Agnes Jones, who married Dick in 1917, was widowed when Dick died in 1918, and then married William Martin in 1919. Dick died on October 22, 1918, according to a death certificate indexed at the Washington State Digital Archives, www.digitalarchives .wa.gov.

There has been some confusion about Agnes Jones Enick Martin and Louisa's oldest daughter Agnes Enick perhaps being the same person. I believe this is because Agnes Jones Enick married William Martin as Agnes Enick. That Agnes Enick, Dick's sister, did not marry William Martin is evidenced by Agnes Jones Enick Martin and Agnes Enick appearing separately in census records throughout the 1920s and Agnes Enick appearing in the 1925 and 1930 census as Lee Metcalf's wife, while Agnes Jones Enick Martin appears in those census files as William Martin's wife. Louisa's daughter Clara died on March 23, 1923, according to a death certificate available at the Washington State Digital Archives. Francis Enick died in June 1989.

71. Agnes Enick Allotment File 04487, RG 49, box 1411, NARA Seattle.

72. There are extensive records in the Office of Indian Affairs records held at the National Archives and Records Administration branch in Seattle that are related more generally to Sauk-Suiattle land disputes, but this chapter cites only those documents immediately tied to the Enick family.

73. Louisa Enick Allotment File 04526, RG 49, box 1411, NARA Seattle.

74. Felix S. Cohen and Nell Jessup Newton, *Cohen's Handbook of Federal Indian Law* (New Providence, N.J.: LexisNexis, 2012), 1075–1078.

75. Charles Roblin's report can be found in box 1, folder 15 of the Edwin J. Allen Papers, Center for Pacific Northwest Studies, Western Washington University. This discussion focuses specifically on Louisa, Sam, Agnes, and Mabel Enick's allotment claims, referring to others only as they support the analysis offered here. Relevant materials consulted for this chapter, but not quoted here include: RG 75, Tulalip Agency, TU05, Letters Received from the CIA, 1906–1909,

box 8a, 1892–1894, folder "Letters Received Sept.–Dec. 1893"; box 10, 1904–1905; box 11, 1905–1906; box 12, 1906–1907; box 14, 1908–1909. RG 75, Tulalip Agency, TU07, Letters Sent to the Commissioner of Indian Affairs, 1878–1915, box 25, 1885–1896. RG 75, Tulalip Agency, TU41, Correspondence Regarding Allotment Claims, 1901–1923, box 334: "Allotment Ledger 1883–1910," "Heirship Ledger 1911–1919," "Correspondence Re: Allotment Claims," NARA Seattle. These documents referred to Sauk-Suiattle land concerns, but not in direct association with Enick family members.

76. Copy of Roblin Report in box 1, folder 15 of the Edwin J. Allen Papers, Center for Pacific Northwest Studies, Western Washington University.

77. Onat and Hollenbeck, *Inventory of Native American Religious Use, Practices, Localities, and Resources,* 232.

78. Louisa Enick Allotment File 04526, RG 49, box 1411, NARA Seattle.

79. Ibid., File 04563.

80. Ibid., File 04526.

81. Ibid.

82. Ibid., File 04563.

83. U.S. Indian Census Rolls, 1885–1940; 1921, 1922, and 1923, Tulalip Indian Agency, Suiattle Indians. Box 1, folder 15 of the Edwin J. Allen Papers, Center for Pacific Northwest Studies, Western Washington University. Louisa Enick died on June 17, 1924, according to a death certificate available at the Washington State Digital Archives.

84. Leo or Levi Metcalf explains his tribal lineage in a letter of October 26, 1953, to the superintendent of the Western Washington Indian Agency, Z80 Enrollment, Indian Claims Commission, Roll 28: Sauk-Suiattle Family Trees, NARA Seattle.

85. RG 75, Tulalip Agency, TU41, Correspondence Regarding Allotment Claims, 1901–1923, box 334: "Allotment Ledger 1883–1910, Heirship Ledger 1911–1919, Correspondence Re: Allotment Claims," in folder titled "Individual Claims for Allotment," NARA Seattle.

86. Box 1, folder 15 of the Edwin J. Allen Papers, Center for Pacific Northwest Studies, Western Washington University.

87. RG 75, Records of the Bureau of Indian Affairs, Western Washington Agency, Tribal Operations Branch, General Correspondence (Old Taholah/Tulalip) ca. 1914–1951, IRA-921, folder 380, Public Domain Allotments, Skagit and Whatcom Counties (Tulalip), 1914–1937, NARA Seattle.

88. Letter from Mrs. Agnes Metcalf to Tulalip Indian School on February 13, 1932. RG 75, Records of the Bureau of Indian Affairs, Western Washington Agency, Tribal Operations Branch, General Correspondence (Old Taholah/Tulalip) ca. 1914–1951, IRA-921, folder 380, Public Domain Allotments, Skagit and Whatcom Counties (Tulalip), 1914–1937, NARA Seattle.

89. Letter from Marie Salter to Mr. Upchurch at Tulalip Indian Agency on January 18, 1937, RG 75, Records of the Bureau of Indian Affairs, Western Washington Agency, Tribal Operations Branch, General Correspondence (Old Taholah/

Tulalip) ca. 1914–1951, IRA-921, folder 380, Public Domain Allotments, Skagit and Whatcom Counties (Tulalip), 1914–1937, NARA Seattle.

90. Other Sauk-Suiattle women would continue to carry out this search for documents from federal officials in the 1940s and 1950s as the tribe collected applications for tribal enrollment, acting with the sovereignty they claimed even before the federal government acknowledged the tribe. That story is better told in Joseph, "Suattle Tribe of Indians vs. The United States" and in Fish, Bedal, and Onat, *Two Voices: A History of the Sauk and Suiattle People.*

91. Joseph, "Suattle Tribe of Indians vs. the United States."

92. Margaret Szasz, *Education and the American Indian: The Road to Self-Determination, 1928–1973,* 3rd ed. (Albuquerque: University of New Mexico Press, 1999). Vine Deloria, *The Indian Reorganization Act: Congresses and Bills* (Norman: University of Oklahoma Press, 2002). Elmer R. Rusco, *A Fateful Time: The Background and Legislative History of the Indian Reorganization Act* (Reno: University of Nevada Press, 2000).

93. Robert W. Gordon, "Critical Legal Histories" *Stanford Law Review* 36 (1984), 57–125. "Symposium on Gordon's 'Critical Legal Histories,'" *Law and Social Inquiry* 37 (Winter 2012).

94. Joy Harjo, "Returning from the Enemy," *A Map to the Next World* (New York: Norton, 2000), 69–96; excerpts from 75, 77; italics and syntax as in original.

Chapter 8. "The Acts of Forgetfulness"

1. Readers can search the Washington Territorial legal records catalogued as the Frontier Justice collection at the Washington State Digital Archives, www.digitalarchives.wa.gov.

2. K. Tsianina Lomawaima and Teresa L. McCarty, *"To Remain an Indian": Lessons in Democracy from a Century of Native American Education* (New York: Columbia University Press, 2006), 12–13.

3. Joanne Barker et al., "Open Letter from Indigenous Women Scholars Regarding Discussions of Andrea Smith," *Indian Country Today,* July 7, 2015.

Index

Page numbers in italic type refer to illustrations

31–32, 153; sexual assault of, 34–35; stereotypes of, 71–72. *See also* inheritance claims of mixed-race children
mixed-race families: abandoned by white father, 37; under Canada's Indian Act, 68–69; economic and social status of, 79; in San Juan Island, 61–64, 284n13; surname changes in, 45, 55
mixed-race marriage. *See* interracial marriage
mixed-race women: border-crossing by, 15; kinship networks of, 63–64, 74–75, 133, 146–147, 151, 152, 153, 171–172, 174–175; racial and ethnic identity of, 88, 89–92; sexual assault case, 58, 73–80; sexual stereotypes of, 75, 79
Mogollon Rim, 26, 185
Mojave Apaches, 185
monoracial marriage, state-sanctioned, 51
Morgan, Joseph H., 198, 200
Mormons, 108–109, 114–115, 294n48
Mount Baker–Snoqualmie National Forest, 8, 254, 263. *See also* Washington National Forest
Mowry, Sylvester, 101

National Archives and Records Administration (Seattle), 258
Neahr, David, 50
Nelson, Peter, 66
Nicola, Patricia Hackett, 134, 300n10, 302n28
Northern Pacific Railroad, 145, 147; land survey for, 218–219
Northwest Federation of American Indians, 133, 173
Northwest Ordinance (1787), 40

Oakes, D. W., 65
Oatman, Olive, 29
Ogo, Linda, 261, 262
Ojibwe, 230–231, 265
O'Keane, John, 223, 224
Oliver, A. J., 196, 200, 201
Onat, Astrida, 263–264
oral tradition, 1–4, 17, 82–83, 102, 181, 188–189
Oregon Territory, 60, 81
Oregon Trail, 81
Oregon Treaty (1846), 60
Organic Act (1863), 30
Osborn, W. J., 117
Ostergard, Carl, 65
O'Sullivan, P. W., 198

Pacific Northwest Quarterly, 134
Parkey, Isaac, 123
Pascoe, Peggy, 134–135
Pee Posh, 25, 36, 96, 97, 98, 101, 106
peonage, 28–29, 40
Perley (Washington), 227
Pesqueira, Ignacio, 22
Phelps Dodge Company, 210
Philbrick, C. W., 221–222
Phoenix (Arizona), 24, 36, 41, 47, 49, 53, 55
Phoenix Herald, 112
Phoenix Indian School, 209
Pierce, Charles B., 172
Pig War, 10, 60–61
Pima-Maricopa reservation, 107, 121
Pinching, Herbert, 123
Pinchot, Gifford, 232–233, 236
Pinkham, Albert, 145
Pinole Treaty (1864), 25
Plummer, Charles, 147
Point Elliott Treaty (1855), 216, 217, 222, 228, 236, 238
Polk, James K., 10, 28
Pomeroy family, 109, 110, 115, 119, 128
Porter, DeForest, 53
Port Townsend (Washington), 62, 171–172
Poston, Charles D., 26
Potter, A. F., 240
Prescott (Arizona), 24, 27, 47, 179–180, 183, 188, 191, 210; Sharlot Hall Museum Library and Archives, 258, 260, 261. See also *Arizona v. Juan Fernandez*
Prescott Courier, 126, 191
Prescott Journal Miner, 191, 196
productive and reproductive labor of Indigenous women, 4, 10, 33–35, 62–63, 92
property rights, to off-reservation lands, 8–9, 16–17
prostitution, characterizations of O'odham women and, 99, 102–104
public domain allotments for nonreservation Indians: Allotment Act provisions for, 225, 226, 238; application process in, 226–228, 318–319n36; bureaucratic incompetence in processing claims, 234–236; cancellation of Enick family claim, 240–243, *244,* 245–249, *250,* 251, *252,* 253–254; eligibility for, 230–231; Enick family petition for, 17, 212, 214, *215,* 216, 218, 232, *233,* 234–235, 236; in forest reserve land, 23–239, 228–230, 231–232, 233–236; shared, 237–238
public domain homesteads, 232

RECENT TITLES